REIMAGING AMERICA

Edited by
MARK O'BRIEN
and **CRAIG LITTLE**

Foreword by
BERNICE JOHNSON REAGON

A Voices of Dissent Project

New Society Publishers

Philadelphia, PA   Santa Cruz, CA

)

"Putting Our Heads Together" © 1989 by Hattie Gossett and Jawole Willa Jo Zollar

Inquiries regarding requests to reprint all or part of *Reimaging America: The Arts of Social Change* should be addressed to:

New Society Publishers
4527 Springfield Avenue
Philadelphia, PA 19143

ISBN 0-86571-168-2 Hardcover
ISBN 0-86571-169-0 Paperback

Printed in the United States of America on partially recycled paper by Wickersham Printing Company, Lancaster, PA.

Cover art: "Amerika XI," 1988, by Tim Rollins and Kids of Survival. Watercolor, pencil on book pages (*Amerika* by Franz Kafka) on linen.

Cover design by Barbara Hirshkowitz
Book design by Tina Birky and Barbara Hirshkowitz

To order directly from the publisher, add $1.75 to the price for the first copy, 50¢ each additional. Send check or money order to:

New Society Publishers
PO Box 582
Santa Cruz, CA 95061

New Society Publishers is a project of the New Society Educational Foundation, a nonprofit, tax-exempt, public foundation. Opinions expressed in this book do not necessarily represent positions of the New Society Educational Foundation.

Contents

III
Making the Work

IV
Audience: Exchanges in a Closed Space

V
Breaking Boundaries

Acknowledgments

We would like to thank the many people who played important roles in the shaping of *Reimaging America*. Almost all the essays and interviews included here were created explicitly for this project. This made the journey from conception to the printed page a long and fruitful one. Each and every one of our authors have shown us tremendous generosity of spirit, effort, and patience throughout. Special thanks to Bernice Johnson Reagon, whose remarks at the 1987 Voices of Dissent festival helped to crystallize our thoughts about the crucial issues facing socially conscious artists today, and who reworked and expanded her comments into a foreword for this book.

Thanks to Mat Schwarzman, project director for the 1987 Voices of Dissent festival in Philadelphia, who shares with us the credit for creating the original blueprint for this anthology. Although he moved to San Francisco in 1987, he has used his talents as a writer and editor to advise us again and again.

We are grateful for both the support and the vision of New Society Publishers, particularly to Barbara Hirshkowitz, who patiently nurtured the project and ourselves throughout. Also to Tina Birky who shared the design with Barbara and typeset the text, and to Yvonne Keller, our copyeditor.

We are very pleased that Editorial El Coqui of Chicago will be publishing a Spanish language companion volume featuring the essays of Elizabeth Catlett, Alvan Colon, Elizam Escobar, and Margaret Randall, along with an introduction by Dr. Luis Nieves Falcon. We are grateful to Alejandro Molina of Editorial El Coqui, whose efforts made this possible, and to Elizam Escobar for his work in translating the chapters.

There are others who, although their words are not necessarily included in this book, shared their ideas with us personally or in manuscript form. They contributed significantly to the understanding which we bring as editors. Thanks then to: Ann Cooper Albright; John Paul Batiste; Ria Beer, Sue Coe and Mandy Coe of Red Bird Collective; Judy Branfman and Lisa Maya Knauer of the Alliance for Cultural Democracy; Kimberly Camp; Steve Durland; Olivia Gude; Tom Kalin; Ruby Lerner; Erik MacDonald; Diane Neumaier; Sharanya Nike; Juan Sánchez; Sonia Sanchez; John Yau; and Howard Zinn. Thanks as well to Brigid Rentoul, for her legal acumen and moral support.

This book evolved out of the 1987 Voices festival and we would like to recognize the contributions of the people we worked with to create that event. Thanks to Jenny Milner, assistant project director; to the members of our advisory panel, Joan Braun, Robert Brand, Saul Broudy, Janet Kaplan, Martha Kearns, Cary Mazer, Jonathan

Stein, and Clark White; to the many Philadelphia artists and activists from our community support group; to Carole Boughter and Michael Serkess; to June Fortunato and Bryce Little of the documentation committee; and to WXPN-FM, particularly Julie Drizen and Joan Schuman, for providing audio documentation of the 1987 Voices conference.

Mat joins us in thanking Gerry Givnish and the Painted Bride Art Center staff for their support and collaboration in Voices of Dissent. A special thanks to Gil Ott, who served as project director for the second Philadelphia Voices festival, The Arts of Social Change, in October 1989. Thanks also to Johnny Irizzary and Luis Sanabria of Taller Puertorriqueño.

For their financial support of *Reimaging America,* we thank the Chace Fund and the Pennsylvania Humanities Council. We also thank the funders of Voices of Dissent: Bread and Roses Community Fund, the Funding Exchange, the National Emergency Civil Liberties Fund, the Pennsylvania Council for the Arts, the Pennsylvania Humanities Council and Craig Eisendrath, the Philadelphia Foundation, the Sun Company, and We the People 200.

The thanks above are shared by both Craig and me. A few more are mine alone. Thanks to my family, in particular to my brother, Kenneth O'Brien, who has been a source of great companionship and support for me for many years. Mat Schwarzman's counsel and friendship have been so consistent over the past few years that it is hard for me to separate my own ideas and words in this book from his. And Kit Warren has commented on each line, shared each crisis and soothed most every fear. For that and for her love, I thank her.

To all those voices we have not heard from,
the silenced and the condemned,
this book is respectfully dedicated.

Foreword
Nurturing Resistance
Bernice Johnson Reagon

There is money going overseas
To buy changes that will never come
Dollar-backed contras spill the blood of the people
In small nations we won't leave alone

There are contras in Nicaragua
U.S. trained death squads in El Salvador
I hear Jonas Savimbe holding hands with apartheid
Is being led to drink at the trough

U.S.A. sponsored violence
Creates refugees all over the world
They pour into LA, DC, and Arizona
Seeking Sanctuary from our guns

Meanwhile in the corporate board rooms
They talk about the debt as if it could be paid
But money borrowed and loaned for:
    Guns you can't eat
    And buildings you can't live
    And trinkets you can't wear
It is a debt not owed by the people

There is money going overseas. . . .
To buy changes that will never come
Dollar-backed contras spill the blood of the people
In small nations we won't leave alone

**Bernice
Johnson Reagon**

Bernice Johnson Reagon
lives in Washington, D.C.,
where she is a curator at the
Smithsonian Institution,
National Museum of Ameri-
can History, as well as
founder and leader of Sweet
Honey in the Rock, a
Washington, D.C.-based
vocal Ensemble of Black
Women singers.

("Ode to the International Debt")

"Ode to the International Debt" is one of a group of songs I wrote when I spent a year at the Institute for Policy Studies. When I was asked to present something for their annual winter festival, I asked several of the research fellows to give me some of their latest papers on the state of the world from their particular area of research and analysis. I wanted to see if I could sing progressive contemporary analysis. I did a suite of six pieces; Sweet Honey in the Rock, (the vocal group I work with) moved two of those works to performance level one year later. We continue to work on several others.

Socially conscious artists are not born. We are culturally oriented and trained. As an activist in the Civil Rights Movement I learned about the relationship between organizing for change and being a cultural artist. Most of us who became known during that time as singers or songleaders saw ourselves as organizers, specifically, SNCC (The Student Nonviolent Coordinating Committee) field secretaries. I saw again and again the connections between being an effective leader and a cultural artist. Participating in that struggle for change taught me about being challenged to trust my inner voice about how I and my people were doing in the world. The movement gave me the opportunity to use my own perception of how things were as the foundation upon which to base my actions and to make my decisions. It was here that I learned about the sweetness of struggle in my life. That, in the midst of standing against opposition, even when at great risks, there is a satisfaction of knowing on the deepest level that who you are to yourself is the same essence you offer to the world in which you move.

Culture of Struggle

I grew up in a culture of struggle where, without any specific spoken warning, I received clear messages of boundaries in all aspects of my life that were not to be crossed, rules that were not to be broken. I internalized these messages, thus setting up a control mechanism to protect myself against acting freely. I went around in life with this inner warning light or buzzer that would be triggered if I considered any action that was considered inappropriate behavior. There was a tape in my head that chanted, "If you do that you are going to be killed." This warning system worked to control my actions at home, in school, in church, and in the larger society. I am not here talking about a physical murder. I am talking about a fear of being shut out, cut off if you behaved in unacceptable ways. Within the home, the school, and the church, you had a sense that this structure of boundaries was set up by people who cared about you and wanted you to do well. They organized community structures so that all pressures would be applied to make you make the right choices. In the larger society, with its blatant racism, there were clearly marked places for you to live and function. When one considered challenging those narrow, twisted spaces, the inner buzzer system went crazy. You felt inside that you would be inviting total destruction if you considered behavior that was outside the parameters drawn by whites who controlled your community.

There was a life inside the boundaries. There were ways of being fed and centered on a worldview that made us know somewhere deep inside that life based on racism was wrong. That white people were not superior. We knew this best because we cleaned their homes, we took care of their children, we knew how they treated each other, we knew how they treated us. We knew they were not superior. Everywhere—in church, in school—we were drawn into powerful creative experiences that said that we were worthwhile, that there was a reason for us being alive, and it was not to serve white men and women. I had teachers who talked to us between the prescribed lessons to tell us in a hundred ways that things could change.

I heard old men and women sing in church, "I'm so glad trouble don't last always." I thus also internalized the perspective that we as a people were living through a time that had to change, and we had to be prepared for functioning and living productive, respectable lives.

It was the Civil Rights Movement that taught me that one did not always get killed for going up against the powers that controlled your life. The movement taught me that if you went across the line, you were offering your life, but it was not always taken. The space between being alive and becoming conscious of my own beliefs and being killed belonged to me. I could, once I put my life where my beliefs were, really stand for what I felt deeply about. It was the first time my life really made sense as an empowered person. It was the first time I felt what I said and did made a difference. I could affect the space I operated in if I offered my life to back up my actions.

The relationship between singing and that struggle was crucial for me. The training for being a singing fighter had begun with learning about the role of music in African-American culture and the role of the artist in the leadership of the community.

Growing up in a traditionally based home and community, I had seen that it was important for leaders to also be cultural artists of great power. Content went beyond text; the virtuosity of delivery of a talk, sermon, or speech included both what was said and whether the speaker could tune her or his words with feelings. Information passed within the traditional forms of the African-American culture is concrete reality. It helps if one lives "the life one sings about," but the singing itself is a concrete offering that can be and is used by those gathered within the sound of the expression. Our people respond when information is heard and felt. We are culturally socialized to test experiences by how we feel when we sit under the power of someone's voice. This is talk that goes far beyond an aural experience. Exchanges between leaders and their constituents had to be transforming experiences where a bonding was created by all gathered, a community was formed in the process of giving and receiving through talk and song.

My central training was as a singer. I learned very early that I had to affect the space I sang in. The air that people breathed carried the sound of my voice as songleader joined by their own. I am now describing a feast of song, where that which is consumed is also created by the consumers, and what you take in is more than you give out because when you put it out, it is enlarged by the sounds of others who commit themselves to participate in the creation. Creating a congregational song means creating sound images that so affect the environment that people walk into you several blocks before they get to you as a source of the sound. Black people singing together is a pulling sound; when you hear it you want to go to it and to get in it. You want to belong to that group that is being born in that singing.

Having been trained in African-American southern communities to sing, I then was charged to go to schools to learn the way of the larger society. I trained in Western-structured institutions run by my people to be a scholar and scientist in the history of this nation. It was my experience in the Civil Rights Movement coming in the middle of these two learning systems that made me reshape how I would try to operate in the world.

As a scholar at the Smithsonian Institution, I have made every effort to do work that validates the presence of my people in this world as a vital and central part of who this country is. I have produced programs that through research, analysis, and public presentations make clear that African Americans belong to a world family of culture based in Africa and that the most prolific sacred music form created in the twentieth century in the United States of America is the gospel music of the urban Black church.

"America"

I operate out of the assumption that I am the United States of America and that I am central to anything that is really happening in this country that is worthwhile. I recognize that I am a secret. I also recognize that among the people who do pay attention to the fact of my existence and the existence of my people—our history, our contributions, and our culture—we are presented as being subcultural, as if we are outside, the other—a tangent, a limb or something that if lost by the main body, life would not be threatened. The inference is that if you, the United States of America, lose us, you would still be. This is a lie, I know that without me, there would not be a United States of America to talk about. My people are central to what is the main cultural power and fabric of this society. The distortion and outright denial of that fact are central to the lie perpetuated as myth that the culture of this country is not African-American at her core.

It is the same kind of mythology that is wrapped up in the ownership of terms like "America." Most of us say the word and we only see the United States of America. We do not see the Americas and all of its peoples and their cultures and their histories. The collective psyche of this society is based on denying the existence of a society that is multi-cultural and composed of many peoples and classes, existing in a world that is very small and dominated by women, children, and peoples of color. We steal the identity of being American from millions of others throughout the hemisphere who should share that identity equally in our minds and thus in our daily practice. When we use the term America as a synonym for the United States of America, we are denying other peoples their space, reality, hope, and territory.

Re-imagining America for me is smashing the mythology, and ending the robbery that is so basic to the general collective consciousness. Re-imaging America is to embrace the reality of the human community and life on the planet and to try to understand partnering with responsibility and love for all that makes up our universe as we understand it, as well as that which is still beyond our knowing.

Culturally Grounded Internationalism

All of my work has to do with my sense of being very central and being part of a larger constituency that is the heart of what this society can be. When I think of the future, I think of myself as being a part of laying the foundation for the evolution of a society where many peoples can live and share the same world without killing, exploiting, and ruling each other. Whenever I offer an image as a singer, as a scholar, it is that vision that drives my efforts. I also make clear that in this living and sharing the world with many peoples and cultures, I will always be an African American woman, and all my offerings will come from that base. That being in the world as a daughter of daughters of daughters of African parents is not a contradiction to being able to live in a multi-cultural society.

In the context of the African American community experience, there are all of these songs that are about church or praying—information that says that Black people are very conscious of what is going on in the larger world we live in and how it impacts on us. We are not a cocoon people. Our culture is constructed with internal boundaries; there are always ways to enter and leave. In doing my work, I have continued to operate from that perspective. You don't have to move from your base in order to participate in the larger world; you don't have to obscure or go beyond your cultural soundings in order for peoples of other soundings to make use of your offerings.

The community I celebrate is that universe of progressive peoples who share with others a loose collection of values and ideals about human and environmental society. In my mind most of these people are culturally united. They do not in local communities always work together. They may not really like each other. However, they do share a vision of a less oppressive society. They dream of a less violent world; they care intensively about whether there will be a tomorrow. When I speak through my singing and my research, it is that constituency I try to nurture and validate.

> We come to you
> You in every color of the rainbow
> With your freedom and struggle stances
> In every position of the moon and sun
>
> We come to you
> Offering our songs and the sounds of our mothers' mothers
> In libation
> To everyone of us
>
> There really is a community
> We have seen and felt and been held by you these ten years
>
> There is a community we belong to without geographical boundaries
> D.C., Atlanta, Berea, Chicago, East St. Louis, L.A., Toronto, Chiba, the Bay
> area, Newark, Seattle, Chapel Hill, Boston, Frankfurt, London, Richmond,
> Little Rock, NYC, Denver, Albuquerque, Nashville, Brixton, New Orleans,

Vancouver, Portland, Berlin, Albany, Durham, Tokyo, St. Louis, Detroit,
St. Paul, Dallas, Peoria, Jamaica . . .

There really is a community
Lovers
Searchers
Movers into life
Fighters and builders
Of a place where military machines, hatred of women, abuse of children,
homophobia, societal male suicide, racial bigotry, starvation, work that kills
and cripples, social orders driven by greed, the U.S.A. invading whoever . . .
this week,
Where this dying and acting out of fear, anger, and terror
will find no feeding ground
I wanna be there.

> (written July 1983 for the tenth anniversary album release
> of Sweet Honey in the Rock, "We All . . . Everyone of Us.")

This community is everywhere . . . in order to do the nurturing, others like me
must share in the ownership of the airwaves so that the food we offer can be received
from those who would eat from our palettes. Our visions of the world, the universe, and
the future have every right to ride the waves and be accessible to all who would choose.

Community of Organizers

I sing to those who will listen. It is important to talk to the convinced. I am often
asked if when Sweet Honey sings, "Aren't you singing to yourself?" The progressive
community of this country is one of the most fragile in the world. We suffer from
illusions of being in better shape than we are because we think it follows that if we are
Americans, we must be great! We are in great need of understanding our
vulnerability, our need for validation, maintenance, nurturing, and celebration. We
need to learn how to be longtimers and not be forever limited by operating
ahistorically and responding to crisis after crisis.

I like to think of the life of a woman I call my political mother, Ella Jo Baker.
Before her death in 1986, she put in over a half century of consistent organizing, full-
time no matter what her specific job was. She understood that in being an organizer,
she had to also be a creator or trainer of organizers. I offer this life's work, which is
really more than fifty years, for as a child Ella Baker had to be sent to live with her
grandmother after her resistance to abuse by a white boy made her unsafe in her own
community. Often we get involved in a struggle for change that affects our
immediate lives, and rather than that being a beginning, after ten years or so, we
float away. Some of us say that what we do at that point is go on with our lives. We
are still decent people, but we are not able to sustain forty to fifty years as organizers.
I happen to believe, as with Ella Baker, you can fight for change anywhere and for as
long as there is the breath of life.

It is important to gather together to nurture and feed as a community committed to being a presence in a society beyond our own meager lives. When moving in new territories as an organizer I use the model I learned in the Black church and as a field secretary for SNCC. First, there is a home base; there is a place that you can go back to for shelter, rest, and re-orientation. It is from there that you move into the world offering your message and work sometimes to people who will throw rocks at you, throw you in jail, or slam doors in your face. Facing the work of this intensity, we do not have to apologize for needing to return to home base. There must be a strategy for going out, organizing, speaking, and raising issues and then coming in to yourself and your community for a check-in. It is important to have a safety zone to refuel where you can eat your dinner with others who understand and will protect your need to be vulnerable.

Multi-Issue Struggles

We live in a time when we have to be able to function across issues. Sometimes I sing before audiences that give great responses to one verse in a song because that verse calls their name; the next verse goes placidly by because they have not developed as organizers and socially conscious people to celebrate the struggle for a world where we can all exist together.

I wrote a song with my daughter, Toshi, for the film "On Becoming a Woman," produced by the National Black Women's Health Project. The film speaks to the need to fill the communication gap between mother and daughter when young Black women move into puberty and begin monthly periods. This personal issue may not seem like a political one, but I say that knowledge and the control of knowledge goes hand-in-hand with being able to control people's lives. The lives of women are shaped and placed by definitions of who we are and what we should be used for in our families and in our communities. Information about how we function as physical units is so highly charged with taboos that we only whisper about ourselves to those we trust and will not tell others that we think things that happen to us are important enough to talk about with somebody else. The song is Toshi and I talking across generations about our bodies changing and thus our position in society:

> Mama sister I wake up my body's not the same
> My feelings run deeper than they ever run before
> I am feeling so strange about changes in my life
> Can I sit awhile with you and ease my changing times
>
> Are you here by my side
> I am here, I will listen while you tell me
> About the ways of the woman rising in your life
>
> Daughter, woman I'm aware of what you're moving through
> You see I have walked the same road only yesterday
> I came to my mama as you have come to me
> I will sit awhile with you and ease your troubled times

> I am here by your side
> Are you here, will you listen while I tell you
> About the ways of the woman rising in my life

Choosing

I once wrote a song that said "You have to choose to be a sister of mine." It was my way of saying that I come into my space loaded down with the experiences and changes of my life. I have chosen a path and I am picky about my company. I want to walk with those who will claim a different world and will hold real space daily through real living. To do this we have to choose.

You have to choose and keep on choosing. Everyday we are offered opportunities to sell out ourselves and our principles. I count it as a rare blessing to have developed as a young adult around people like Ella Jo Baker and Septima Clark. With fighters like this I had examples of people who really worked for a living, paid their bills, and were always in every part of their lives taking a stand for the things they believed in. It made me have the feeling that I could live that kind of life, where my life's work was working for what I believed in for myself and my communities. You can choose to stand. You only have your life to lose, if they take it you may not even know it because you'll be dead, or if you do know it you can just begin to strategize to come back again. I urge people to take risks. I urge myself to go beyond those boundaries that say stop. In my stancing, I have never been alone.

I heard Ron Dellums say that progressives are the majority in this country, but we do not often speak as the majority. Many of us are very much taken with being a minority. Many of us who work very hard for change also participate in denying the impact of our efforts. Even as we challenge the forces that try to keep us down, we keep waiting for someone to come so we can really get started.

Well, I see you all the time, and find it unbelievable how many of us don't know we exist. Sometimes artists are the only people who can announce to you that you're okay. It is our work to show you what we see and to nurture, cradle, and change these images. At our best, we are your mirrors. We show that we really do exist and are enough for the work we have before us.

Introduction

Re-:   Again, anew; Used as an intensive.
Imaging: 1. Making or producing a likeness of. 2. Mirroring or reflecting.
           3. Symbolizing or typifying. 4. Picturing mentally, imagining.
           5. Describing so vividly as to call up a mental picture of.
America: The Western Hemisphere lands of North America, South America,
           and Central America.*

This book is one of an ongoing series of projects linked under the title *Voices of Dissent,* which provide a forum for socially conscious artists, cultural presenters, theorists and activists to share, discuss and evaluate their work. It is an attempt to refine our understanding of what motivates and sustains us as artmakers, and of how and under what conditions our art can effect social and political change. As a critical endeavor, it aspires to the activist mandate Pat Aufderheide outlines for Left cultural criticism: "to chart how culture is shaped, so that we can understand how it changes, and seize opportunities to alter it in ways that create possibilities for greater social justice."

The Arts—a term we use to incorporate a broad spectrum of creative expression, visual and verbal, written and performed, "no-tech" and mass media—are a territory where many of the cultural codes, symbols and myths we share are both created and reinforced. The images of ourselves the arts reveal serve as a filter through which society defines itself, and against which we, its individual members, measure the need for, and possibility of, action. In this sense, the work of socially conscious artists in the United States is vitally important. It assures that political, social, ethnic and cultural communities traditionally excluded from the cultural mainstream participate in that process of definition.

Indeed, the "America" of which our title speaks does not inhabit only those fixed geographical boundaries set out in dictionary definitions. It exists also, and perhaps

Mark O'Brien

Mark O'Brien was a founding member of Big Small Theater, a Philadelphia-based political theatre company, with whom he acted and wrote for five years. He was co-project director of the 1987 Voices of Dissent Festival, and consultant for the 1989 Arts of Social Change conference at the Painted Bride Art Center. He currently lives and acts in New York City.

---

* *The American Heritage Dictionary,* Second College Edition (Boston: Houghton Mifflin, 1982).

more importantly, within the realm of public consciousness. This "America" is rarely (if ever) an accurate mirror of the "America" one would find through demographic analysis, and it is never a neutral concept. Limited in scope to the United States, it reflects the values and aesthetics of a mostly white middle class and erases social, racial and class divisions with an occasional inclusory gesture towards the "other." The imagery of socially conscious artists—African American, Latino, Caucasian, Asian American, and Native American, male, female, gay and straight— negates this singular, homogenized, imperial America. At its fullest, this work dares, in the words of poet/critic John Yau, to be an art of "embodiment," one which "invents a present large enough to contain us all."

Craig Little

Craig Little is a freelance writer, editor, lighting designer and filmmaker living in Philadelphia. His first feature, *Unusual Dawn* (Cornell Films, 1987), was recently aired on public television. He is currently on the staff at the Yellow Springs Institute for Contemporary Studies and the Arts.

During the past decade there has been a growing interest within progressive circles in the United States in the potential contribution of the arts in shaping and strengthening our respective struggles for social change. In part, this is the result of looking out at the rest of the world: at the roles that visual art, theatre and song have played in movements for social change in Africa, Central and Latin America, as well as to the vibrant critical literary and film traditions in Eastern Europe. It is also a testament to the work of thousands of arts activists working in cultural fields here in the United States at the local and regional level. The ability of artists in this country to move beyond themselves and their individual projects and consider the broader implications of their work in turn owes a great deal to the efforts of organizations such as the Alliance for Cultural Democracy (ACD), Alternate ROOTS, the Black Rock Coalition, National Association of Arts Organizations (NAAO), PAD/D (Political Art Documentation/Distribution), TENAZ (Teatros Nacionales de Aztlan), Union for Democratic Communications, as well as to the documentation work of other anthologies such as Neumaier and Kahn's *Cultures in Contention,* Lucy Lippard's *Get the Message,* the Greywolf Annual, *Multi-Cultural Literacy,* and Hillary Robinson's *Visibly Female,* to name a few.

At the same time, interest in the arts as a vehicle for social commentary has been piqued within the culture at large. Previously marginalized art practices are no longer burrowing their way out into mainstream art canons, they are being pulled out—often root and branch. In commercial art galleries, theatres, museums, concert arenas, cinemas and television, previously apolitical artists are finding that when they communicate ideas about the world around them, audiences are eager to listen.

This is unquestionably a cause for celebration. It also calls for some form of evaluation. For while it is readily apparent that "content" is streaming into cultural arenas and, far from destroying the standard of the arts, is invigorating them, it is less apparent what, if any, reciprocal effects this increasingly politicized cultural activity is having in generating action in other spheres.

In large part this is due to a lack of any clear understanding of how, when, and why the arts affect people's political behavior. At the extremes, arts evangelists make wildly overblown assertions about the power of art to solve all the world's problems, while others prefer to limit artists' roles to making banners, performing at fundraisers, and warming up crowds before speeches. Somewhere in between these poles is the recognition that while art alone does not replace the need for other forms of political action, the specific images and experiences of art provide unique moments of reflection and communication that lie outside the scope of other forms of political discourse. Given the inadequacy of conventional arts criticism as a framework to evaluate politically engaged artwork, there is a very real need for what Steve Durland of *High Performance* has dubbed "ambitious artists" to develop and articulate their own criteria for judging their work and the contexts within which it is presented. Many contributors to this anthology have noted that we are often trapped by assumptions and criteria of the very culture we work to transform. This results in framing false dichotomies about what defines or drives our artistic practices. As Ricardo Levins Morales puts it: "When they accuse us of being no more than political pamphleteers we shout 'Damn right, and proud!' When they scream 'Form!' we bellow 'Content!' "

Voices of Dissent grew out of the efforts of a group of Philadelphia theatre artists to reckon with many of these issues in our own work. As part of this process, we looked to what we could learn from the experiences of other artists, past and present. Our first project was a month-long festival and three-day conference, in April 1987, which was organized as a counter-celebration of the Constitutional Bicentennial. Set against a backdrop of "official" celebrations which packaged artistic freedom in the United States as an abstract, passively inherited historical commodity, *Voices* focused on contemporary artists' work. By relating their work to various historical traditions of artistic dissent in this country, it claimed freedom of expression as an active challenge, a right which has and continues to be reestablished in each generation.

One high point of the three-day conference was the panel presentation: "The Imaging of America." The participants—singer/scholar Bernice Johnson Reagon, saxophonist/composer Fred Ho, writer/puppeteer Theodora Skipitares and sculptor Richard Posner—alternately sang, played, showed examples of their work. Responding to questions from the moderator, Janet Kaplan, they spoke about how the images they created were grounded in their understanding of what America was and could be.*

The session was exhilarating. We saw how the panelists gave form to their ideas;

---

* Bernice Johnson Reagon has revised and expanded her remarks from that panel in her foreword to *Reimaging*.

each able to tap into a specificity of life experience, clarity of purpose, control over their respective media, which enabled her or him to give substance to conceptions that were alternately critical and visionary. There was also the excitement of witnessing a gathering of individuals from a wide variety of disciplines and regions of the country—panelists and audience alike—becoming visible to each other and tentatively aware of their relationships as a group.

In the closing session of the Voices conference, historian Howard Zinn spoke about how activists and artists need to rethink the ways we conceive of and make change:

> We need to address ourselves to creating a new kind of future . . . but we must not think of heroic acts. Our tendency is, in a sense, to emulate the culture which thinks of heroes and stars. And we need to think, instead, of change as the result of an infinite number of very small acts taken by people in the faith that they will add up to something enormously important.

We have assembled this anthology by focusing on socially conscious artmaking in this spirit: as attentive to the discrete elements of our daily practices as to the grander ideals they sustain. We asked more than forty artists, writers and presenters to discuss the issues faced or relationships entered into by an artmaker in the process of creating art. We asked them to speak from their own experience, individually or in a group, about impulses and intentions behind the work, sources drawn upon and contexts within which the work takes place, creative processes developed, audiences sought and reached, and the need for constant re-examination of limits.

These dividing lines, corresponding to the book's five sections are nowhere near as clean or constant as the more conventional ones based on artistic discipline, subject matter, or ideology. But because they reflect the day-to-day choices that any artist must negotiate, we believe they hint at a way to better understand how the arts actually function. They do not offer a unified model of political art, or a hierarchy of forms of artistic engagement. We hope, instead, that they will provoke new ways of thinking about cultural practices that challenge mainstream artistic, social and political realities both from those who have not seen the arts as a forum for social activism, and, most importantly, from those who have.

As we become more visible to each other and to the mainstream, the differences as well as the shared elements of our approaches will become more explicit. This can be divisive, or it can be a strength, a tool against stagnation and rigidity. We need to recognize that all socially committed art practices and intentions are not the same, and that these differences must be respected and cherished. Inasmuch as our differences are worked through or around, or that we simply learn to build upon each others' separate efforts, these struggles will take place not on a theoretical plane, but in our everyday practices and their specific circumstances.

We offer this anthology as a step in the process not only of reimaging America, but also in rethinking our role as image makers within that process.

Mark O'Brien
February 10, 1990
Brooklyn, New York

Personal Impulses, Social Intentions

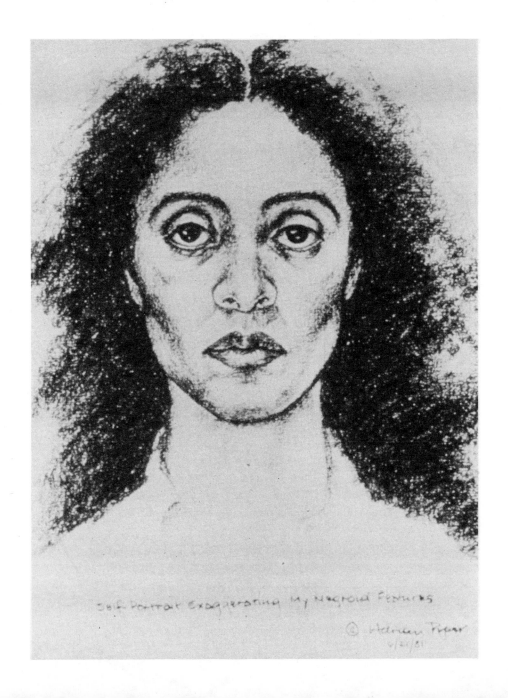

Self Portrait Exaggerating My Negroid Features

© Adrian Piper
6/21/81

Personal Impulses,
Social Intentions
Introduction

The Studio Museum of Harlem featured the work of politically conscious Black artists in an exhibit entitled "Art as a Verb."* This metaphor neatly captures the sense of art as a personal statement that carries in it the expression of an action; a step taken consciously, with a strong sense of purpose. Like the artists in the Studio Museum show, *Reimaging*'s contributors all share an understanding of their intentions as inherently social, in contrast to conventional Eurocentric views of the artist as a solitary figure removed from society, blessed by an almost divine inspiration or tortured by the lack of it. A sampling of the intentions that they ascribe to their work reveals a wide range of actions: to record, name, remind, inform, scare, caution, critique, speculate, envision, support, share, comfort, validate, vilify, purify, heal, celebrate, sing, honor, enrage, refuse, incite, shock, embarrass, embolden, subvert, activate, bridge, transform.

What does it mean to claim one of these, or any social intention for one's work? If, as Margaret Randall suggests in her interview with James Miller, the realization of the social dimensions of one's individual expression can be tremendously empowering, are there obligations this carries as well? Limitations along with expanded possibilities? How does an artist balance social intentions with other more personal impulses s/he brings to the creative process? How can recognizing these ambitions provide a basis for self-evaluation or for understanding another's work?

The opening section of *Reimaging* includes reflections on artmaking as both a personal and social act. For Edgar Heap of Birds, the social dimension of his role as a Native "maker" is a given; a duty to help "form the future," that is entrusted to him by his tribal community. For other contributors living in a diverse and changing society, social roles are less fixed. Critical and visionary functions must be reclaimed. Responding to perceived needs around them, they search, in the words of Ricardo Levins Morales, for ways of "scratching where it itches."

For each contributor the nature and implications of their artwork is intricately

---

* "Art as a Verb, the Evolving Continuum," March 12–June 18, 1989, was curated by Lowery Sims and Dr. Leslie King Hammond. A catalogue is available from Maryland Institute, College of Art (Baltimore: 1988).
Previous page: "Self-Portrait Exaggerating My Negroid Features," Adrian Piper, 1981.

bound up in a personal understanding of the nature of artistic communication. Elizam Escobar critiques what he considers to be the overly functionalist "message" orientation of North American political art. He argues instead for art practices that recognize the symbolic nature of artistic communication, and which strengthen the role of the imagination as "one of the leading political processes that pushes forward the liberation of the human spirit by rescuing and creating new territories of freedom."

Like Escobar, Margaret Randall addresses the relationship between artistic freedom and the state. She discusses how both the ideas and experiences of artistic freedom that North Americans have contrast with those of various Latin American societies. She describes a notion of "collective" freedom which, she argues, helps account for the more pluralistic and participatory cultures she has experienced in Mexico, Cuba and Nicaragua.

Working both as academic researchers among, and as advocates for various refugee communities in Philadelphia, folklorists Margaret Mills, Sally Peterson and Bill Westerman bring a different perspective than most other contributors. Keeping one eye on their roles as observers in a cross-cultural context they provide clear illustrations of the changeable social functions of art; functions which are neither fixed, nor uniformly positive. Their essays reinforce the difficulty of setting simple or broad normative interpretations on the role of cultural expression and presentation.

Mills notes that even as cultural expression documents refugee group experiences and preserves a sense of cultural identity, it also sets the terms for, and establishes channels through which, a community enters into social and economic relationships with its host culture. Thus control over cultural presentation and production are often extremely important in establishing political and economic self-sufficiency.

Westerman's treatment of oral testimony by Central American refugees as performance is striking. To some, the power of experience and emotion that such storytelling carries seems too "authentic" to be considered as performance. But recognizing testimony as a poetic art form, and considering the ways in which it is refined, both to make it more accessible and to enable the stories to be told over and over as they must be, does not belittle or deny the circumstances that led to its creation. It does, however, raise important questions about the distinctions that we make between art and "reality," fiction and nonfiction. This is an issue which we will return to repeatedly in *Reimaging,* where it is almost impossible to consider the power of many artists' work apart from the circumstances of their lives.

The Importance of Being Artist

Ricardo Levins Morales

"The question is," said Alice, "whether you *can* make words mean so many different things."

"The question is, which is to be Master," said Humpty Dumpty, smugly explaining to Alice the power of language: He or she who controls the meaning of words—and therefore people's understanding—wields the power to control far more. Human consciousness is given shape by images, rhythms, sounds, words: the tools of the artist. The significance of this fact is obscured to us artists by the elitist myths—at once disparaging and exalting—that surround art. The potential power of art as a force for change has long been known to censors and dictators. It is a potential that can be fulfilled once we rediscover and proclaim the rightful and natural place of art and artists in the life of our people.

Ricardo Levins Morales

Ricardo Levins Morales is a Jewish Puerto Rican parent, artist, and organizer. He works for the Northland Poster Collective in Minneapolis, a distributor of art of the labor, peace and justice movements, and is a coordinator of the Alliance for Cultural Democracy, a national network of cultural workers.

The Battle Over Culture

The battle over meaning is everywhere reflected in billboards, radios, newspapers, workplace rules, video stores, zoning ordinances, television, and spray-painted walls. These public spaces are the arena in which society speaks to itself. They are shaped by and in turn help to shape who we think we are. Whoever controls these spaces has tremendous power over the meaning of language—and the imagery of thought. The battle plans are hammered out in journals of the advertising industry, the inner circles of political campaigns, and CIA headquarters. They are also shaped in union halls, community theater meetings, and church social action committees.

This decade has seen the growth of networks of activists who explicitly look to culture and human consciousness as the terrain upon which struggles for social change ultimately take place. Many of those who accept that premise describe themselves as "cultural workers." Cultural workers encompass teachers, organizers, artists, publishers, distributors of cultural goods, radio producers, concert promoters, and many more. They are those whose work is intended to affect the ways in which people understand themselves and their world.

It is difficult to write about art from a radical or revolutionary perspective without railing against "them." "They" are the artworld critics; curators; record, film, and advertising executives; publishing magnates; and others who control or define the bulk of artistic production in our society.

I will indeed refer to "them" and the folly of their elitist ways. I think however that it's important to define our cultural/political work in terms of our own visions and experience, independent from the voices of art world orthodoxy. Often in our rebellion we accept the limiting definitions that are cast upon us. When they accuse us of being no more than political pamphleteers we shout "Damn right, and proud!" When they scream "Form!" we bellow "Content!"

We lose in this exchange. In accepting the artistic ghettos they fence us into we surrender vast areas of our peoples' cultural experience.

Art as the Dreamlife of a People

I learned the power of fantasy on the street. At age eleven I found myself uprooted from my highland Puerto Rican barrio, wandering an alien maze of city streets. This new landscape was controlled by the Chicago police—armed and arrogant as an army of occupation—and by the competing remnants of the disintegrating street-gang armies. All of these parties were intensely interested in young men of my age. I felt extremely vulnerable. The rules of survival itself seemed to be controlled by forces far beyond my own control.

To survive on my own terms, without being beaten up, ripped off, or recruited, seemed too tall an order—for these were the only options offered. In my mind I rehearsed a thousand variations of confrontations in empty lots and dark alleys (like most sensible young males I avoided the brightly lit avenues where the police held sway). As I played out my daydreams in real-life encounters I discovered an unexpected freedom. If I declared my own rules—"Sorry, brother, I don't have much cash now and I need it all"—they were often respected, even by those who should have been able to overrule me.

I learned that my fantasies—a realm to which I retreated for comfort in the face of my fear—had provided me with real avenues for action. They had led me to discover that the supposed rules of the game are not the real rules—once I cease to consent to them.

If, as the African revolutionary leader Amilcar Cabral described it, culture is the "collective personality of a people," then the arts are its collective dreamlife. In the absence of coercive control the arts, like dreams, are naturally drawn to the deepest hopes, fears, and truths that are suppressed in daily life. Whatever the stresses in your life you wish to avoid, you can count on encountering them in your dreams.

One of my greatest inspirations has been the Latin American New Song movement, especially its Chilean pioneers. They transformed themselves from performers of and for the student Left into the creators of an authentic voice for their people's aspirations. Moving easily between songs of love and songs of land reform, between nonsense verse and traditional lament; they dissolved, rather than accepting, the barriers that divide politics from the rest of life.

What these musicians accomplished was to master the "dream language" of their people as expressed in ancient and contemporary musical traditions. They then used it to voice the secret hopes and feelings that were not finding expression in the commercial culture monopoly, dominated by imported, "Western" music.

In a class society such as the United States the so-called national art scene represents the rather confined dreams of a small segment of the population. It's considered a sacred duty for artists to remain isolated from any broad community that might influence their art. Artwork must remain personal in the narrowest sense while fitting into the moment's specifications for saleable work. Alienation is one of the requirements. A friend told me of a midwestern painter who finally got a favorable review of her show after having worked in New York for a couple of years. The critic was elated that, in contrast to her earlier, optimistic paintings, her new work was starting to shown the "angst" (read depression) of a mature artist.

The greatest form of pressure that cuts artists off from the living currents of their communities is the designation of some subject matter as "political." As it applies to art, "political" is a clear "no trespass" sign forbidding access to whatever the ruling elite does not wish people to think about. It varies from country to country and over time. New York artist Lisa Blackshear's paintings of interracial couples would be politically explosive in South Africa, cause some discomfort in the U.S., and not raise an eyebrow in Brazil. In South Africa the book *Black Beauty* was banned for although it was a story of a horse, the linking of the two words in its title was seen as dangerously revolutionary by the censors. In General Pinochet's Chile teaching evolution is seen as subversive because it describes a world in which change is constant and inevitable. It is therefore seen as challenging the rigid stability preached by the dictatorship.

The "political" label—and the funding, performance space, display, and publishing decisions that enforce it—serves to prevent artists from fulfilling their function as conveyors and interpreters of their people's dreams.

For the majority of the potentially artistic population a form of dream suppression is practiced. Organic cultural expression is discouraged by the denial of resources and the promotion of the arts as the province of a gifted few. In the crude tracking system of the schools an artist is whoever is left when the rest are bludgeoned into silence. Those who survive this assault on their creativity may pursue it through art schools where they'll be safely taught to respect the taboos.

These systems of suppression and control are far from fully effective. At best they

work as damage control to limit the number of artists v
imaginations of those who do. But still, artists who have been s.
cultural industries—as well as those who develop outside of
system—are drawn by the gravitational pull upon the artist to explo.
communal life.

Too often activist artists ourselves accept the "no trespass" signs of the eli_ , simply choosing to set up camp on the other side of them. Thus we miss the subversive potential coming straight from the deepest springs of artistic inspiration. If we listen and convey the dreams of our people, we will ignore the signs and property lines. If we violate the warning signs, it will be while being true to our mission as artists. To grasp the full potential of cultural creation as an arena for social transformation we must go beyond seeing ourselves as simply "political artists," "oppositional art," or even "voices of dissent."

My People Are Who I Love

The great tide of cultural and political awakening that swept across the U.S. social landscape from the spring of the civil rights movement fed and was in turn nourished by a blossoming of artistic expression and exploration. Artists, caught up in the upheavals of their communities, gave direct voice to them. Their drawings, poems, songs, and jokes were a daily barometer of people's feelings and understandings. This cultural outpouring represented the efforts of the exploited and marginalized to reclaim and reassert their own unique identities. Thus Blacks, Chicanos, American Indians, gays, lesbians, Asians, and others proclaimed the power and beauty of their own cultural values in defiance of the dominant, melting-pot ideology.

The initial response to this upsurge attempted to contain it (while protecting conservative notions of "high art") by channeling it into such categories as "ethnic art." Under this system we are each the artistic spokesperson for a particular cultural population whom we represent to the world through the use of certain recognizable styles or symbols. (White male artists are exempted from these limits and are free to do whatever they want.) This schema, while seeming to finally give official recognition to cultural diversity, is ultimately reactionary. As painter Patricia Mainardi stated fifteen years ago in response to attempts to define a "feminine aesthetic" for women artists, "Women artists must be free to explore the entire range of art possibilities. We who have been labeled, stereotyped, and gerrymandered out of the very definition of art must be free to *define* art, not to pick up the crumbs from the Man's table. . . . "[1]

As a printmaker I work within a well-developed tradition in Latin American art. Silkscreen printing, my medium of choice, has reached one of its most advanced expressions in my homeland of Puerto Rico. But these choices are a product of my history, not of obligation. Certainly, it's natural that my work will reflect the rhythms, colors, and smells that have shaped me. It's understandable that I should address those who dream in the same secret codes or speak with the same gestures. But to see in our heritage a wall around our art limiting our styles, our messages, our "voice," is to be disarmed.

Like millions of my fellow humans I'm what is known as a person of mixed heritage. We are rivers that spring from multiple sources. To purists in search of "ethnic art" and "authenticity" (a much abused term), we are an invisible category. We also happen to be the majority of real-life people.

The truths that are expressed in our art will be shaped, at least indirectly, by the real-life people we know, love, and listen to—whoever they may be. The only "authenticity" worth aspiring to as an artist or as a person is to be authentically, uncompromisingly who you are.

My people will be defined for me not by racial or ethnic or national categories but by who I love. My relationship to them, not questions of style, media, or political line, will determine the usefulness of my work.

Art, like language, is a means of communication. If I wish to communicate with you—not just talk at you—I need to know something about you. For starters it helps to know what language you speak. The more intimately I know you, your language, your way of seeing, the more able I am to choose words or images that will be meaningful in your life.

Scratching Where It Itches: Learning My People's Dreamlife

Eduardo Galeano tells the story of the first contact between a band of Spanish conquistadores and a native head of state in what is now Paraguay. The Spanish priest read long passages from the Bible and then waited expectantly for a reaction. The Indio leader stood in silence for a time. "It scratches," he affirmed at last. "It scratches very well. But it scratches where there is no itch."

The key to scratching where it itches is to know where it itches. Stories are my way of learning about my people. I love stories. The prints I create are mostly other people's stories. In them I try to reflect the sometimes frightening dignity which is to me the central fact of human existence.

During the process of producing a poster I often work alone. I learn about the ways my work affects people through the stories they tell me, and those that filter back to me by indirect routes. I cherish the stories: the political exile who didn't believe that my screen print of Guatemala was created by one who had never been to her homeland; the woman who credited a woodcut of mine with providing her with the strength and clarity to leave an unsatisfying relationship; the school librarian whose interviewer hired her, he told her, because of her enthusiastic response to my poster on his office wall.

Listening to stories is my main schooling as an artist and an activist. As a teenage hitchhiker crisscrossing the continent, I listened hungrily to people who would share freely the details of their lives with a passing stranger.

Later I learned how to eavesdrop on the lives of other communities. I turned to their artistic dream life. One year I went on a binge of reading the writings of Black women. I can't remember what started me. A collection of short stories by Black women, *Black-Eyed Susans*, had just been published.[2] I devoured novels, essays, poems, hearing the rhythms, soaking up the details, the feelings. Listening to the stories. On the bus, in the laundromat, I watch faces, fascinated by the tales they tell, and those they hide. Sometimes the political struggles I've been involved with have opened doors for me into other communities, providing opportunities to learn new recipes, gestures, ways of seeing. The stuff of falling in love.

All these stories enrich my life. Ultimately it's how I live, who I make myself into, that will affect the lives of others and the direction of change in the world. The artwork I create is a series of progress reports from that process. I return my art to those who nourish me. I hope it will act as a magic mirror, reflecting back, but in new ways, their own and each other's stories; exposing the beauty and strength that is there.

My introduction to art classes, after moving to the States, was confusing for me. Here we were, learning art, an activity that for me had always meant comfort, escape. But here there were rules, "correct" ways to draw, fears of doing it wrong. I had friends who were afraid to draw. I began leaning on them to try, showing them tricks, getting them to doodle with me. Maybe it was a bit like forcing water on them to quench my own burning thirst. Scratching where I itched.

I'm still scratching in the same place. It's the place where we store the lies that hold us back; that keep us from knowing our true power and the joy it contains.

One of the challenges for the cultural worker is to identify the forms of internalized oppression that affect their people and consider the best ways to attack them. We each carry the scars of our oppression, the internalized messages of invalidation that everyone who was once a child has absorbed. It's a little different for each of us, it varies from people to people. It's different for women than for men. We have different "itches," determined by our own and our peoples' histories.

If we want our art to be a force for social change we need not only love our people and learn their dreams. We must also learn to think critically about them, as we would for a loved one to whom we wish to be a worthy ally.

Yes, to Life: Art as Craft

If the first ingredient for effective revolutionary art is love for one's people, and the second is clear thinking about one's people and their dreams, then the third is craft.

We experience the world sensually, as a place of textures, sudden smells or colors, laughter, heat. To develop our craft is a tribute to that sensual world; a proof that we care enough to pay attention to detail; a statement of faith in the sense that any labor of patience and love is.

"Recording the details of our lives is a stance against the bombs with the mass ability to kill, against too much speed and efficiency. A writer must say yes to life, to all life: the water glasses, the Kemp's half-and-half, the ketchup on the counter." So writes poet Natalie Goldberg.[3]

We develop our skills as we try to translate the nuances of shape, motion, color, and feeling that we observe around us into our paintings, songs, and pots. The time spent teaching ourselves to do this well is a gift to ourselves. It's a kind of self nurturing that is worked into our art and reflected outward. A gift to our communities.

Attention to detail, to craft. It's the life-affirming nature of artwork that while not revolutionary certainly has its part in the broad current of social transformation. The quilts, clothing, wood- and beadwork, weaving and gardening. The careful use of the world's resources combined with thinking about people's needs.

Artist, Heal Thyself

Every night, whatever the weather, I step outside and look at the sky. It helps me feel connected to a larger world beyond my city streets; to my people, scattered across a thousand lands, working, struggling, breathing under the light of this sky. Sometimes the stars seem to shine back to me with the gaze of ancient faces. People who crisscrossed these lands in times long past. People to whose survival we owe our own. The silent night sky reflected their questions and ideas about the world as tonight it does mine. This is my link of intimacy with them. Perhaps another fifteen thousand years in the future someone else will share these quiet moments and it will be my gaze they imagine in the stars.

I see myself as a representative of that future. As an organizer I've learned that without a future it's difficult to organize the present. If the sun probably won't rise tomorrow we may as well throw our beer cans on the lawn, our chemicals in the sea, our topsoil to the wind. If there's no tomorrow then living for the pleasures of the moment, getting it while we can, is a reasonable thing to do.

In my time and in my adopted, second homeland, the U.S., hopelessness reaches epidemic proportions. It is the toxic by-product of racial, sexual, class, and every other oppression. It weakens our ability to act, to see beyond the "rules of the game" to other ways of being.

In a society governed by lies, cynicism becomes the street corner philosophy. Hope and respect are scorned and hungered for. To be optimistic, in a broad, social sense, is to be regarded as some kind of nut. At the same time, to express hope in a persistent and credible way is to be sought after like a water merchant in the desert.

The fear (worse yet, the resignation!) about nuclear holocaust is one of today's most widespread and paralyzing expressions of hopelessness. It hangs before our daily lives like a misty curtain, dimming the bright colors of the world. It is the ultimate message of disempowerment: "In the face of this, you are nothing."

Artists are as infected as anyone else and their art can become a reflection of their people's nightmares. Much of the art that tries to grapple with the dangers of nuclear weapons does little to challenge the disempowerment. Anti-nuclear art is usually a desolate wall of grief and fear, inviting the viewer or listener to leave their comfortable life of distraction for one of despair. Some people continue creating scenes of destruction year after year in an apparent hope that someone will come along to reassure them that it just ain't so.

My impression is that for a brief moment twenty years ago, the mushroom cloud, doomsday art played a positive role. At a time when the reality of the arms race was hidden from the public mind these images helped to break the silence. It was a conversation starter. Since then they have tended to reinforce the passivity they were meant to challenge.

When faced with problems that seem bigger than ourselves we sometimes wait around hoping that sooner or later a grownup will come along to set things right. Our supposed grownups aren't always so helpful. "Their" experts blandly assure us that we can run along and play, everything's under control. "Our" experts are mesmerized by the deadly scenarios of destruction with which they try to frighten us into action. Your presence, reading this, is a defiance of both scripts.

So we must be our own grownups and tap our own sources of hope. As artists we must find the resources to work through our own fears if we're to help our people move through the dangers.

Every inhalation is an act of hope. Medical people say that when a person loses hope they stop breathing, they die. In every living human there remains an ember of self-love. It's the hidden story behind every headline. An ember that when kindled becomes the driving force of history.

Missing that fact means missing the whole story. Sometimes even in our moments of generosity we miss it. Antiwar art of our day often depicts third world people as mere victims: tortured, beaten down, cheated of life. European and U.S. cartoons against the war on Vietnam fit this pattern (Vietnamese art did not). This artwork is a form of protest against injustice, and as such is praiseworthy. Without the bond of love however, the acknowledgement of dignity, it remains an act of pity and can never project the power of real solidarity.

I am suggesting that art that disempowers is best kept to oneself. This is self-censorship at its best. Being honest with your loved ones does not require saying anything that pops into your head. You remain aware of whether your words will be hurtful or irresponsible. Art seen as the dreamlife of a people is a useful metaphor. But a metaphor is not the same as reality. This one breaks down because with art we have the tremendous power to choose what we say. Thus art becomes conscious dream-telling, responsible creation with the potential to affect the life of our people.

When I learned to drive I was told to steer by the farthest visible point on the road, not by what was right in front of my wheels. If you stare downward assuming you'll probably be hit by a truck before the next bend anyway, it's likelier to come true. In an uncertain landscape, our greatest safety comes from steering by the stars.

The Importance of Being Artist

The nature of art as flowing from the emotional, symbolic, "right-brain" side of experience makes it inherently subversive. The more a society has to hide, the greater control it must exercise in order to keep artists from doing what comes naturally: exposing its most private dreams to the light of the sun.

We artists have no special answers unavailable to other people. What we have is work that's intricately entangled in our people's dreams, hopes, and self-images. Like it or not we are part of society's process of dreaming, thinking, and speaking to itself, reflecting on our past, and finding new ways forward. Our greatest challenge is to accept that what we do with our work and our lives is exactly as important as we believe our people and their world to be.

Notes

1. Patricia Mainardi, "Women Artists and Women's Studies," in *Feminist Revolution,* by Redstockings (New York: Random House, 1975).
2. Mary Helen Washington, *Black-Eyed Susans* (New York: Doubleday, Anchor Press, 1975).
3. Natalie Goldberg, *Writing Down the Bones* (Boston: Shambhala, 1986).

Waking Up to Smell the Coffee

Reflections on Political Art Theory and Activism

Greg Sholette

Greg Sholette

Greg Sholette was a charter member of Political Art Documentation and Distribution (PAD/D). He helped develop the PAD/D "reading group" on theory, art, and politics which in turn created *Not For Sale,* a project against displacement in 1983-84, and PAD/D's anti-gentrification exhibitions on the Lower East Side of Manhattan. He has exhibited with Group Material and independently as a "visual-political artist" over the last nine years. His most recent exhibits of note are *Unknown Secrets—Art and the Rosenberg Era* (a traveling exhibition); *Los Angelitos: Day of the Dead II,* November, 1989, at the Alternative Museum, New York City; and *Groundwork,* a stencil-art project against the Nuclear Navy Port planned for New York City, 1989.

It is opening night at the Museum of Modern Art. A broad and well-displayed exhibit entitled *Committed to Print* is featured in the main gallery. Over 150 works with explicit political messages are grouped together under headings like *Class Struggle* and *War and Revolution.* Tonight we are toasting the "maturation" of "political art" in an institution built in large part with money amassed from the union-busting, Ludlow Massacre days of John D. Rockefeller. Throughout the intervening years the Museum of Modern Art's (MOMA's) primary function has been to establish the market value of a certain de-politicized formalism, whose patriarchal lineage reached its apex in American abstract expressionism. How is a serious political artist supposed to contend with this situation?

One of the more salient ironies we can credit Postmodernism with has been the legitimization of artists and art groups whose raison d'être had been a critical, hence peripheral, relationship to the market. Nonetheless, the art industry has managed to retain an aura of outsiderness and opposition about this work. Over the past few years, in the face of such compromised surroundings both inside and outside the art market, and ambivalent about both positions, my own framework for art and politics had become largely undone. I realize that two

25

largely unexamined premises have underwritten narratives from which to argue the political claims of my own work and that of others. The first established political merit using the often hermetic language of *theory*. The second did so by the seemingly obvious route of *activism*. Sifting between the familiar faces at the Modern, these arguments began to take the form of a schizoid tableau, as I imagined how the practitioners of these positions were adjusting themselves to this opening.

Removed from "the street" the political art activist becomes a conspirator. While going through the proper rituals of the opening, the activist's homing instincts remain directed outside the antiseptic walls of MOMA to something which is non-elitist and grassroots; something which will one day liberate political art and release it back into the fray of life. Even from such depths as the Saatchi Collection their longing reaches out like Penelope pining for the shipwrecked Ulysses. In the meantime they weave and wait for the day their miserable capitalist suitors will be dispatched by the people.

The political art theorist on the other hand is not so easily seduced by fantasies of revolt. The theorist does not even believe in the "R" word. For the theoretically-oriented political artist every context is a particular ideological arrangement which must be "deconstructed." The theorist knows that even the activist's desire for liberation can play a part in one's oppression by projecting utopian solutions that eventually reify into mental stumbling blocks. Only by accepting the path of endless intervention as its own reward can a radical politics hope to be realized. Each time the status quo is challenged within its high art fortress it is another step along that road. The theorist subscribes to a kind of "Route 66" format of cultural opposition.

"Political Art," Greg Sholette, 1988 (12" x 36" Photo-Dioramas and Relief)

The Political Art Theorist

The comparative liveliness of "political art" in an otherwise lame, post-neoexpressionist market has brought with it an infestation of theory. Theories about art's social dimensions have begun to turn up in all branches of the art industry. The theoretical artist can enumerate dozens of texts where important battles have been fought in the theater of art and ideology. Most veteran theorists haven't only demystified with the Frankfurt School, but have demythologized with Roland Barthes, *bricolaged* with Claude Levi-Strauss, deconstructed with Jacques Derrida, gone on digs with Michel Foucault, and looked for little *a*'s with Jacques Lacan. But what does it mean when an artist says his or her work is informed by theory? In the natural sciences a theory is a model of a given phenomenon which is then tested against the empirical world. This model must generate experiments which can then support it, "proving" it to be the best guess to date regarding the phenomenon in question. In the art world on the other hand, theory seems to have the opposite function: it is the proof that the "model" or art has validity. When the names of Baudrillard, Lacan, Foucault, and Derrida are invoked, all sorts of speculations are suddenly anchored. It's as if their assorted exegeses had come to signify "the empirical world" for the art world. In fact, artists really use words like "informed by," "experiment," and "theory" in a metaphorical way.[1] Yet for many, these metaphors continue to imply some sort of privileged interpretation regarding "meaning," or the underlying "textuality" of experience, this in spite of the warning by Jacques Derrida that ". . . metaphor is never innocent."

Given the metaphoric nature of art theory, it is perhaps more important to consider not the modest uses of theory,[2] but the very *mise en scène* of theory: theory as a form of socioeconomic behavior. As artists, critics, and buyers began to lift terms from fields like semiotics and psychoanalysis, a new style in the trade language of the art industry developed. Magazines like *Artforum* and *October* underwrite its value; people at openings disseminate it. In the best sense, theory can provide a healthy skepticism towards the dangers of rigid thinking. But when a display of one's theoretical knowledge is called for, this incredulity towards dogma gives way to a kind of policing of the discourse. At an opening, in an article for a professional journal, or even at a job interview, the seriousness and skill of one's theoretical interpretations are carefully noted. Unfashionable or idiosyncratic views are likely to be given demerits or censored.

What then does theory do for the artist? On a certain level talking theory is only a form of specialized social interaction. On another level, it is always about one's professional mobility. Much like the artist's stylistic trademark, speaking theory is a form of economic aggression in a limited marketplace. Once the sign of an artist's opposition to the mainstream art industry, theory now opens doors. Once a means of clarifying the role of dominant ideology, theory now obscures it.

Again a tableau comes to mind:

Imagine hundreds of graduate students, media analysts, academics, and assorted artists cloistered in universities like fifth-century abbeys. Every few days a laundry chute spills out another large pile of news clippings, advertisements, video cassettes. The monks and nuns labor over the smallest bits of cultural debris, attempting to compile a comprehensive index to the semiotics of late capitalism. But while they can never work fast enough to keep up with the flood, they remind themselves that "resistance" according to one well-known theorist-critic is "only a deconstructive strategy based on our positioning here and now as subjects within cultural significations and social disciplines."[3] Has a better means of dissipating the energy of an oppositional intelligentsia ever been devised?

The Vanguard as Redemption?

The political art theorist, much more than the activist, is likely to envision his or her work as part of, or a response to, a certain modernist tradition—usually the Russian avant-garde or dada. It is through this genealogical pedigree that the theorist attempts political redemption.

Unfortunately, due to a number of converging factors, both internal and external, the Russian avant-garde—Eubo-futurism, productivism, constructivism—was long ago robbed of its political dimensions. Fashionable references to Russian constructivism in the works of postmodernists like Ashley Bickerton, Thomas Lawson, Peter Halley, or Allan McCollum expose the extent of our loss. Radical intentions return as parodic devices deployed not for socially useful ends, but instead aimed at illustrating the collapse of the avant-garde to an audience already saturated with modernism's repetitious and lately cynical attempts at transgression.

Unlike the energetic monks and nuns of the semiotic abbey who are perpetually one step behind their task, these postmodernists resemble nineteenth century taxonomists at a garage sale carefully selecting just the right cheesy curio, bit of kitsch, cliché, souvenir, or forgery that will signify the terminal state of western culture. This necrology has been touted by the postmodernists and their artworld supporters as a tactical blow to the glass jaw of western culture: the belief in progress. Of course the real economic powers in the art industry easily turned this threat on its head. For any good dealer knows that an art-world iconoclast is not simply the toppler of current idolatry but the bearer of new, if subtler, objects of worship and investment.

This appears to resemble the tomfoolery of dada, and I would argue that it is dadaism, not the Soviet experiment with its dream of art as socially integrated and useful, that authorizes the political claims of most political art theorists. Long before poststructuralism, the sabotaging of meaning and the transgression of moral and social codes were carried out by the dadaists as they thumbed their mostly bourgeois noses at the aristocratic pretensions and militant nationalism of their own class.

However, with exceptions like Tristan Tzara or John Heartfield,[4] dada remained antisocial, even misanthropic, sarcasm.

Ever since political art theory put a premium on subverting the language of the dominant culture, exhibitions have rolled into view claiming to deconstruct everything from gender roles to the World Bank. One prominent critic-theorist claims that the work of certain feminist media artists is able to "undo and redo the meanings purveyed by mass media images."[5] All this through the deployment of art collages in a gallery! This inflated rhetoric has become standard fare for a generation of critics, theorists, and artists alike.

Today the claims of vanguardism are like faulty bank loans. No one can afford to admit that the avant-garde is bankrupt so the myth of its radicalism just keeps rolling over. Incredibly the very target of cultural vanguardism, the bourgeoisie, has turned the avant-garde into a kind of court art, thus preserving its own alleged antithesis. Having rejected "romantic" notions about the possibility of sweeping social change, the political art theorist winds up looking a lot like the postmodernist artist. Both initially reject the torch of avant-gardism, while their skepticism towards social practices actually leaves them no alternative but to accept it.

The Political Art Activist

At times the imagery produced by the activist artist resembles that of the theorist. But while activist painters may make use of modernist approaches like collage or expressionism, they always brings us around these formal embellishments to a content, which points us to something outside the the art work and its immediate context. If the theoretical art we just described employs a characteristic look, utilizing photographs and text with only an occasional, often parodic use of painting, activist art by contrast is thoroughly catholic. Murals, banners, agitprop, street art, and posters sit alongside traditional high art forms. Debates about the avant-garde or postmodernism are usually dubbed irrelevant.

If, however, we look for the moment at this production as images which eventually are circulated through galleries, "alternative" spaces, and books and magazines; their overall effect is one of delivering to an informed, usually white, urban consumer the suffering or the resistance of people who live in mostly tropical, post-colonial nations. Much like secularized icons, these images suggest that repression is a force both universal and singular. Before we look at these images we have the usual share of problems with the landlord, the boss, and finances; after viewing them we are in solidarity with peasants in Peru and refugees in Beirut. The hollow slogan of "the personal is the political" is flopped on its head, but these momentos of oppression stop short of confronting our own agendas as politically and economically secure voyeurs of the struggles of "others."

To be fair the activist artist cannot be judged on these grounds alone since the activist exists within a matrix of cultural work that might include organizing both artists and non-artists, working on neighborhood projects like community murals, introducing non-mainstream points of view into the streets or subways, and teaching about these ideas. These activities are clearly important, especially when they enrich local political causes or confront prevailing ideas of what culture is supposed to be. But political art activists underestimate the demand for "politically correct" commodities on the part of the Left itself. That this commodification in the form of graphics, posters, paintings, and photographs opens the door to co-optation, while extending the reach of the left's message, is one of the many contradictions political artists must deal with. Thus it is surprising the word *contradiction* is seldom found in the vocabulary of the political art activist. Instead we read that their practice is part of a movement towards a progressive culture, a democratic and pluralistic "people's art."

A People's Art?

People's art avoids contradiction as well as political compromise by allegedly operating outside the influence of dominant culture; that is both the high culture of museums and concert halls, as well as the "popular" culture of television and the music industry. Dominant culture is "anti-subjective, technocratic, and escapist"; it is *their* culture. People's culture by contrast is "energetic, unslick, empowering;" it is *our* culture.[6]

Since words like *culture* and *movement* imply both integration and tradition, where do we locate, and how do we relate to this other tradition? I won't argue with the assertion that western high art has offered no real opportunity for peasants, women, people of color, or the working class to represent themselves to themselves. I would go further by insisting that western art history has been possible thanks largely to the leisure time and surplus capital generated by these "others." Indeed the history of representation is virtually synonymous with the representation of a succession of ruling classes, by its male artists.

Why then hasn't the activist artist made a complete break with this history, with its vocabulary and iconography? Because much of what constitutes examples of consciously oppositional art has either appropriated, mimed, parodied, or evolved out of their contemporary counterparts in high art. Those cultural practices that remained untouched by dominant ideology; like folk dancing, quilting, or the carving of walking sticks; are also the least capable of conveying direct critical content. With the emergence of "popular" mass culture the situation becomes much more complicated. Take graffiti, once championed as both a people's art form and an expression of hostility to the status quo. Not only did graffiti artists use pop culture images including the negative representations of women, but graffiti's absorption into the art market further muddied the claimed separation between "our" culture and "theirs."

If our inventory of oppositional art actually dances in and out of dominant culture in a complicated scenario, the claims that it forms a "movement" are also open to question. Fragmented moments of opposition are just that—fragments, acting more like negations of what is called history, than the constituents of a separate tradition. By not trying to smooth out these contradictions, or compress them into a "movement" we may do more, as Walter Benjamin said, to "rub history against the grain."[7]

What is troublesome about this is that we no longer have some self-contained thing called "people's art" that can be taken off the shelf and used as a ready-made referent for our practice. This is especially disconcerting for artists first trained in the western high art tradition who want to "drop out" for political reasons. Intellectuals who seek a divorce from this history appear to stand on the same ground as certain anthropologists who long to discover the noble savage—a people uncorrupted by modern civilization. The encounter seems to have always been just missed. If not spoiled by some recent contact with western culture—a bartered tin can or pocket knife—then by the anthropologists' own methods of intervention.

So it is with our desire to speak the language of the "people." When we are not bringing with us the baggage of western high art always already part of our very terminology, the people themselves disappoint us by preferring Sylvester Stallone and Michael Jackson to Paul Robeson and Diego Rivera. I sometimes think that if a genuinely democratic and participatory culture did emerge in this country, the left would not recognize it. While the white left praises the importance of remaining *outside* the culture establishment, those who have been locked out because of color or gender would prefer to have the choice of whether to take such a heroic stand. When we go on a safari to find either lost tribes or genuine people's culture it is in part a journey into our own desire to relocate ourselves in a harmonious state of social relations; unslick, energetic, and empowering.

E Pluribus, Pluribus

Cultural democracy as a movement proposes to speak for the polyphony of voices past, present, and still to come, which reject or are rejected by dominant ideology. Since rummaging through the past cannot bring forth a unified people's art movement, the activist turns toward the future. In order to avoid becoming simply the advocates of these other cultures, and channeling public money in their direction thereby risking the same "museumification" that people's art is defined against, the activist posits pluralism as the very model of a liberated society to come. Not surprisingly this future resembles the horizon of cultural possibilities presently embraced by the activist. This brings us to the central assumption underlying the theory of the political art activist. It is only by projecting backwards from the point when a future, emancipated society turns around to reclaim our present diversity as its historical overture, that cultural democracy can assume the coherence of a movement today.

The remoteness of such a future, given the state of the American left, is just one problem. In order to proclaim ourselves to be the legacy of an unborn culture we have to believe in a historical teleology like that found in Hegel's metaphysics. On the Hegelian stage, history has no lasting contradictions, neither is any performance wasted. Its economy is such that even bit players are taken into account in the final act. It is unthinkable therefore within this metaphysics to suggest that the American left might be a historical cul de sac during a time when "history" is being made elsewhere—in Asia, eastern Europe, and in non-industrial nations.[8]

Directly Confronting Our Situation

Nevertheless if I take the same irreverent attitude towards this theory as I did with the political art theorist, then it may be that the urban intelligentsia, myself included, has no historical guarantee or special ideological inheritance due us. That we continue to speak in the name of these Others is not so much an act of empowerment as it is of power—power in having access to the dominant language and its cultural markets. For ultimately we are constructing our relationship to history as an uncertain narrative at best. When we mold the fragments of other's traditions into a "people's art," we need to assess both the risks and the benefits (who takes the risk and who gets the benefits?). We need to ask who is setting the agenda and why.

I return to the opening at the Museum of Modern Art. Despite their defensive posturing, the theorist and the activist now appear to operate within a terrain that is more similar than the polarization of their language would admit. Whatever objections the activist might raise against postmodernism, for instance, the impact of its deconstruction of ordered hierarchies and totalizing thought can be seen reflected in the activist emphasis on pluralism. Not that the activist has bought the "whole nine yards" of the poststructuralist's glorification in fragmentation; for the activist pluralism functions symbolically, resolving in some hoped-for future the contradictions of the present. Neither are dreams of a non-alienated cultural community altogether missing from the theorist. That the theorist's "redemption" often takes on the appearance of the avant-garde's "golden years" during Weimar Germany and revolutionary Russia is evidence of both the nostalgia and the hope lurking in much theoretical art and its discourse.

Contrary to our insistence on being judged by the philosophy we hold, it is in the constellation of desire, personal history, historical circumstances, contradictions, power relations, metaphysics, romanticism, nostalgia, and even career interests that the "political" fabric of our lives is constituted. "Talking theory" may be just one more form of behavior, one more conversation within this scenario, but it is a conversation even the activist cannot avoid, any more than the theorist can abandon in practice all metaphors of totality or images of liberation. Both are dependent on one discourse or another to mediate between political desires and the messy, often compromised spaces of American society.

The last ten years have found us plodding along with no overarching political movement of our own, no well-defined alternative network for our work, and a growing pressure to be part of an ever more accessible mainstream culture industry. Perhaps by directly confronting this *realpolitik,* the complex motives we operate from, and the limitations history puts upon us—all of this without denying the simple pleasures of our craft, even the humor of our predicament—we can begin to redefine the use of the word *opposition* when we put it in front of our practice.

Notes

I would like to thank Janet Koenig as well as Mark O'Brien and Craig Little for their useful comments and suggestions.

1. Some scientific theorists, such as Paul Feyerabend, argue that even the natural sciences are based on tropes and metaphor. Regardless, once theory shifts from a search for the "truth" to one of use or politics, we must ask who uses it and to what ends? This is essentially the question I have tried to put to the political art theorist.

2. Indeed this paper's line of argument is dependent on *my* readings of theory, some of which follow this text.

3. Hal Foster, in *Recodings: Art, Spectacle, Cultural Politics* (Washington, D.C.: Bay Press, 1985), 150.

4. Tzara joined the anti-fascist underground as other dadaists fled to pursue their art, while Heartfield's anti-fascist photomontages extend well beyond the dadaist penchant for the absurd.

5. Abigail Solomon Godeau, *Sexual Difference: Both Sides of the Camera,* exhibition catalog (New York: Columbia University, 1988), 4.

6. I have paraphrased Arlene Goldbard, Don Adams, and Charles Frederick from PAD/D's magazine *Upfront,* Winter 1983-84 and Fall 1985.

7. Walter Benjamin, "Theses on the Philosophy of History" in *Illuminations,* by Hannah Arendt (New York: Schocken Books, 1969), 256.

8. The dangers of this line of thinking are more apparent as the right begins to resurrect Hegel to explain the triumph of the West over socialism. See "What Is Fukuyama Saying?" *New York Times Magazine,* Oct. 22, 1989, 38.

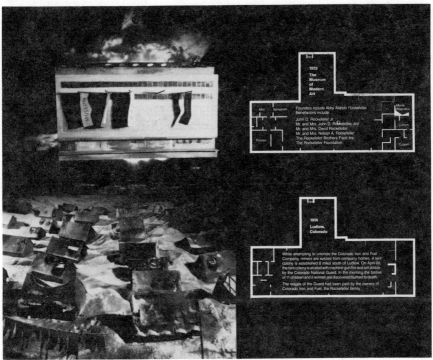

"Culture and Barbarism," Greg Sholette, 1989 (36" x 42" Photo-Diorama and Text)

The Role of
an Alternative Museum

Geno Rodriguez
Interview by Mark O'Brien

Mark: I'd like to start by talking about the role you you see the Alternative Museum playing, first within the art community, and then in the broader society.

Geno: Our role is to be a responsible and visionary organization, concerned not with what people want to get from an arts organization but with what we believe they should be getting. In terms of the general public, we feel we have, like any museum, a strong educational obligation. The role of the educator is to enlighten. The question is to enlighten in what direction? Enlighten how?

MOMA (the Museum of Modern Art), or the Met (the Metropolitan Museum of Art), or most traditional museum's idea of education is to present artifacts for the viewer to look upon, consider, and make his or her own interpretation about. My idea of education goes further. I don't believe that as an educator I can or should teach anything I don't

Geno Rodriguez

A working artist, Geno Rodriguez is co-founder and director of the Alternative Museum in New York City. Founded in 1975 to help "expand the boundaries of the American mainstream," it is the first museum of contemporary art in the U.S. founded and operated by artists. He is best known for his provocative political role in the arts community and for the sometimes-controversial exhibitions he curates.

believe in. No institution is neutral. If you are doing exhibitions which deal with socio-political issues, it is irresponsible to put up images and not take a stand about fascism and not have an opinion, or to pretend not to have an opinion, about the content of those images. So we serve as a forum for people to experience provocative or controversial ideas. To agree, and more importantly, to disagree.

At the same time, it is our obligation to nourish provocative and challenging arts ideas within the art community. We have a responsibility to challenge and provoke the artists we work with. Some of our shows have specific themes. And in these, you could almost say we commission, although there is no money transferred. We require artists who are going to participate work within the confines of a particular theme.

We use the arts and the artists in order to provide a visual dialogue. For example, in "Disinformation, The Manufacture of Consent" (1984), I assembled thirty-three artists whose work showed how the national consensus is formed by the media. Most of the artists did not have work related to this theme, so they made new pieces.

Now coordinating this kind of thematic exhibition is not simply a matter of going around to artists' studios to look at work that already exists. Most of the time we find people are not making the kind of work we feel creates a substantive dialogue. It's hard to find artists working on issues that affect people on a day-to-day level.

Mark: Why is this?

Geno: Because artists like myself are victims of their history, victims of their time. When I started art school in 1962, artists in America were involved in formalist concepts. The whole scene was art about art. And they imparted this to younger artists when they taught, and that's what those young artists taught when they, in turn, taught younger artists. And so now we have a world of art that is art about art. Artists lock themselves up in a room and they paint for themselves and their fellow artists. The general public is usually not thought about much. I know; I used to do it.

I was reading a book by a Palestinian writer and was struck by a passage about how important poetry is to the Palestinians. He says Palestinian poets don't have time to write about their poetry. The Palestinian writes about Palestine and the concept of peoplehood rather than abstraction. And in order to make this poetry effective, he writes in very simplistic, very romantic terms. He does this not because he's clichéd or corny, but because his poetry is not meant for the few. This poetry is meant for the nation of Palestine.

This is precisely the opposite of the American artist . . .

Mark: But, surely there are many artists today whose work addresses political issues.

Geno: True. But let's make a differentiation here between art which is about politics, and art which is political. These are two different things. If an artist makes a painting of a person who is beaten to death, this to me is not, in and of itself, political art. Although it can become political depending upon the context in which it is presented. In and of itself, it is art *about politics,* and usually does not inform the viewer as to the reasons for the problem depicted. It is a painting of someone who has experienced violence. What does it mean? What you need is something which talks about why the person was beaten up. Who beat him up? How could this be allowed to happen? How often does it happen? And above all, how could I, the viewer, do something to stop it? That is what a political work of art should be.

Mark: For an artwork to *be* political, is it not enough for it to present a political event, it must also provide a context within which the event can be understood, a context within which the viewer can not only observe, but take some action?

Geno: Sometimes the artist can create the context. If you took this same painting and smuggled it into South Africa, and installed it in a town hall in the middle of the night so everyone who came in the next day would see it, then the painting becomes "active." It is politicized by the context within which it is seen. Most American artists trying to make work with social/political imagery are not going anywhere with their work. They are painting situations and putting them into white-walled galleries where rich people (either rich in money or rich in education) come in, look, and say, "Oh!" "Yes!" "Wow!" But no one burns up their shares in Mobil Oil. No one gives up their money!

The tragedy is that the system has been smart enough to co-opt artists into producing art that is just *about* politics. This art is successful, is making money. Consequently, it is what younger artists emulate. After all, most artists' first concern is "making it" in the art world. It's funny, ten to fifteen years ago everybody was saying, "Art and politics don't mix, they're like oil and water!" Our response was to show they did mix. Now, politics has been aestheticized. Robert Pincus Witten, the critic, says so! . . . Art about politics is everywhere. "See," the critics say, "they do mix!" So my reaction is, Wait a minute, this shouldn't be so easy. We've gotta find a mixture which doesn't go down so easily.

I get quite offended by the "art" I see floating on electronic billboards, filled with weird cryptic sentences that could mean "Jack me off," or "Back off jack." Actually, it doesn't mean anything. What's more, it's electronically engineered and has little artistic merit. I think political work, if it is going to be called *art,* must also include some degree of aesthetics. Otherwise it's just propaganda. There has to be a balance. But this is what the system wants on the cover of *Artforum* and *Art News.* I tell you, if you took a canvas and you put a lump of shit in the middle, people will find reams and reams of profound things to write about it. And it's all the fault of the American dream. I mean the ability for anyone to say, "I am an artist." It's like a blindfold on people. If you've got the money, your kid goes through art school and comes out with a B.F.A. or an M.F.A., they go out into the world and they say, "I'm an artist." That's the dream. But it's not enough. I wish it was as hard to get an art degree as it is to get a degree to be an eye surgeon or a brain surgeon.

Mark: So should art be only the domain of the trained?

Geno: Art is the domain of those who can see where others generally cannot. It's not for every Tom, Dick and Mary. I do see a desire on the part of some artists to create work with real social and political relevance. But who is going to show it? Who is going to see it? If you are putting provocative content into a work, especially social/political content, you should be part of a dialogue with your intended viewers. But it's not in the interests of commercial galleries to present this work. Why? Because most of the people who buy art are people of economic substance. And most of the problems in the world that are not natural problems, somehow seem to be attributed to the monied class.

The nonprofits are equally full of shit. They know they need money to pay rent and salaries. And they know the people that dole out the grants—the foundations and the corporations—are not going to give money to show work that puts them down. So we have a needy nonprofit class and a fairly intelligent monied class—at least intelligent enough to know that it won't give you money so that you can bite its hand. When you do find a "political" show at most of these places, there's a sign in front of the exhibition: "The opinions of this exhibition are solely the responsibility of the artists and not the museum."

This year, a major foundation decided they were going to give some money to the Alternative Museum. One of their people came down for a site visit and said, "What we'd really like to support are your political shows." I couldn't believe it. So I outlined upcoming shows. When I got to "Foreign Affairs—Conflicts in the Global Village," he said, "What's that?" I said, "Well it's about South Africa," and he said "Oh right on!" And I said, "It's about Central America," and he said, "Terrific!" Then I said, "And it's about the occupation of the West Bank and Gaza Strip by Israel," and he said "Oh, dear, I don't think we can fund it." When I asked why not, he said "Well, because we give grants for scholarly research and study into finding ways to create peace there." I said, "Well what's that got to do with telling the truth within the art world?" The bottom line is the grant had to be changed. They decided to fund exhibitions where the principal artists were people of color. Because of this one issue—Israel—all of the other political stuff went down the drain, in their minds. Of course, we presented the exhibit anyway!

And this is where we come in. We provide a space for unpopular subject matter. There are places that might do something about South Africa. There are definitely places that would do something about Nicaragua. But no one will touch the issue of Palestine. More money from the U.S. foreign aid budget goes to Israel than to any other place in the world. Every year $3.1 billion goes to Israel. On top of that we give them grants, contracts, and other subsidies which don't have to be repaid. And yet no one knows . . . or wants to know what's really going on over there!

Mark: "Foreign Affairs" had remarkable supporting seminars, videos, and essays. Does this provide the context you were talking about earlier? Or should the artwork itself be the focal point?

Geno: The supporting material has to be there. A photograph can be taken out of context. And to understand an exhibition like "Foreign Affairs," you have to understand that ultimately we aren't talking about images. We are talking about American involvement in these three global areas. A photograph cannot show the manipulations going on behind closed doors. Essays about all of these things put the photographs into context. At the same time, the photographs put the essays into context. These essays are written by scholars in the field; historians, political scientists, art critics, artists, and museum staff.

To present these images as art, out of context, is to self-aggrandize. There are people who make art about tragic situations around the world and sell it. They make money and they become famous. I don't understand that. What do they put back into these tragic places? Donations to the ANC, FMLN, IRA, PLO?

Of course, there are limits to the changes we can make, just as there are limits to the whole concept of museums and art as vehicles for reaching the public. The reality, the bottom line, is that these white rectangles (galleries, museums, etc.) housing objects with a dollar value to them, are all, not only antiquated, but exist only as places to entertain the rich. The working classes, the laborers, the middle class do not go to museums and galleries. They wouldn't give a diddlysquat if most museums in the world closed. Art and museums are not for them. I think the Alternative Museum would like to be (and believe me we're not successful yet) a museum for all the people. And there is again where we differ from other museums. To be a museum for all the people means providing exhibitions with substance that are of interest to people beyond the art community. It means dealing with subjects of global as well as human and personal concern. That is the role of this museum.

If I had my way, I would turn the Alternative Museum into office space. All my exhibitions would be done in public spaces. All my advertising would be done in sky writing, I'd have exhibitions on billboards in the suburbs and billboards in the ghettos, high above where people could see them every single day whether they wanted to or not. Every month, I would commission different artists to make different pieces to be shown in different subway stations. That to me is where communication should be taking place—where people are trapped and have to look at it and think about it, and where people can respond.

Mark: It seems like we've come up against a contradiction between what you are and what you want to be. Clearly the Alternative Museum is not about art in public spaces. Why do you continue to work within a museum structure if it's not what you want?

Geno: The bottom line is we too can only do what we are *allowed* to do within the system, because if somebody withholds X amount of money, I can't pay the rent, and the museum is gone. You have to have money. It's like dancing . . . two steps forward, one step backward. I'm still moving forward but it's taking a long time. For every *really* strong political show I do, I have to do *two* shows that are not as strong, and which are not necessarily political. Otherwise, there would be no money. We would kill the goose that lays the eggs. There would be no alternative forum for ideas, no showcase for new visions. But we don't compromise our shows for money, we don't tone down, we just don't do as many as we would like.

For instance, I just came back from the West Bank and Jerusalem, with an idea for a new project. I want to take fourteen artists over to the West Bank, let 'em see it firsthand. Let them spend a couple of weeks experiencing what it's like to explain to Israeli authorities why you are living on the Arab side of Jerusalem, why you are not on the Jewish side of Jerusalem. Being stopped and searched by armed soldiers and civilians (settlers!). We'll make a video to document the trip—the dialogues and roundtable discussions—and come back here where everyone can exhibit. It will be called something like "Bridges Against Occupation: First Impressions," because one's first impressions . . . you know people always discount them, but they are very important. They set a rhythm for everything which follows.

I also want to ask the artists not to focus on the Israeli occupation. I'm asking them to focus on correlations. For example, one of the artists is already saying, "Well, I could do something relating the border between Mexico and the United States and the border between Israel and the occupied territory." Another one says, "Hell, I'd like to do something related to the British occupation in Northern Ireland." It will be something about Palestine and the Israeli occupation, which really puts it into a world context. And then, of course, all the catalogues will have to be comprehensive and well documented. We'll have seminars with speakers who can talk about occupation. To me, this is something—whether anybody comes, whether they agree or disagree with me—it's something important to have done.

*   *   *

Last April 27 fourteen American artists of different ethnic backgrounds went to the West Bank and Gaza. The exhibition, "Occupation and Resistance: The Intifada," will open at the Alternative Museum on March 3, 1990.

The Work of an Anarchist Theater

Judith Malina

I am sometimes asked if I believe it to be true that theater can create revolution. And I like to point out that the history of revolutionary change shows us that there has never been a social restructuring that has not been preceded by cultural upheaval.

From the historical perspective, cultural expression always sets the social agenda, creates it in fact, and the artist is privileged to decide in which direction to inspire / instruct / invigorate the stream of history.

The role of the artist in the social structure follows the need of the changing times:

> In time of social stasis: to activate
> In time of germination: to invent fertile
> new forms
> In time of revolution: to extend the possibilities of peace and liberty
> In time of violence: to make peace
> In time of despair: to give hope
> In time of silence: to sing out

At the moment of revolutionary energy, the artist's work is most gratifying, the satisfactions of being in concert with a spirit of renewal of social forms invigorates and makes for a joyous art.

But a time of germination, such as the one we live in at this writing, is even more important, because this is the moment at which the code is ingrained. Now the form of the action is determined, in which is contained, like the nucleus

Judith Malina

Born in Kiel, Germany, in 1926, Judith Malina emigrated to the U.S. as a child with her parents. In 1947 she and painter-husband Julian Beck (d. 1985) founded The Living Theatre as an alternative to the commercial theater. She has directed and/or performed in all of the more than eighty plays presented around the world by The Living Theatre, including J. Gelber's *The Connection*, K. H. Brown's *The Brig*, B. Brecht's *Antigone*, Else Lasker Schüler's *I and I*, and Living Theatre collective creations *Frankenstein*, *Paradise Now*, and *The Legacy of Cain*. In 1989 she and current husband Hanon Reznikov opened The Living Theatre on Third Street in New York, where the company continues its work today.

Thomas Walker in *VKTMS,* by
Michael McClure, 1988 (photo:
Gianfranco Mantegna)

Judith Malina as Antigone in *Antigone,* by Bertolt Brecht,
1967 (photo: Bernd Uhlig)

in the atom, the great enigma of the ends and the means. It's at this early point, at the crux of germination that the poet can turn the palindrome of *evil* into *live*.

In defining the relation of the artist to the struggle of the people, Julian Beck's *The Life of the Theatre* examines the role of the visionary as a revolutionary force. As Julian creates the work—written on the stage, or backstage, or in jail, or tripping in Volkswagen buses—he reflects on its validity:

> To make something useful. Nothing else is interesting to the audience, the great audience. To serve the audience, to instruct, to excite sensation, to initiate experience, to awaken awareness, to make the heart pound, the blood course, the tears flow, the voice shout, to circle round the altar, the muscles move in laughter, the body feel, to be released from death's ways, deterioration in comfort. To provide the useful event that can help us. Help.[1]

Is the socially conscious artist born rather than made? We egalitarian anarchists insist that we are *all* born to be socially conscious, and all born with the creative capacity of the artist, but deplete our creativity and our courage. Thus, the question really should be: if all of us are born potential artists, what makes some of us not develop to our fullest human scope? And when art has answered that question it follows that the anarchist artist will ask: "How can we create a world in which everyone achieves the full creative life?"

There is a lineage of artists and philosophers from which we all derive, some from the heritage with which we were born, as in my case the Jewish tradition; some from adoptive affinities, as for me the French Moderns or the Hellenist philosophers. And then fate or biography provides us with teachers and examples. My mother's Weimar modernism, and her abandonment of the stage for a rabbinical marriage, my father's gift of emotive rhetoric in the pulpit, my mother's recitations deriving from Alexander Moissi's fantastic dramatical style: these were my roots.

Certain teachers enter our lives a little later, as into mine came Anna Curtis Chandler, great storyteller of the Public Library and dramaturge extraordinaire of my elementary school. And Eric Gutkind of our congregation, mystical scientist-philosopher. Then came Julian Beck, who traveled through forty-two years of artistic voyaging with me, seeking to further the Beautiful Nonviolent Anarchist Revolution.

And in the cellar of the Beggar Bar, Valeska Gert, the Grotesque dancer who inspired the expressionist movement with her concept of *Unregelmassigkeit* (unevenness), taught me about the jagged edge of artistic daring.

Erwin Piscator, at the Dramatic Workshop of the New School, taught us the obligation of the actor and director to a political commitment. Paul Goodman first showed us that anarchism was art and Dorothy Day of the *Catholic Worker* showed us that anarchism was holiness.

Antonin Artaud, John Cage, Jackson MacLow and all those post-Dadaist art philosophers of the '40s and '50s were part of our work and the whole spirit of the peace movement. They inspired us and inspire us still, as when the women sit in earnest attendance at the nuclear plant sites.

As anarchists we take it upon ourselves to diminish the distinction between the personal statement and the community. As anarchist artists we need not "speak for" the community, but *be* the community.

In our work with the audience, The Living Theatre has sought for decades to create a unified field with our spectator-participants. Often we seek out those whose cultural distance from us is great—people whose language we do not speak, whose customs are new to some of us—working among the Turkish *Gastarbeiter* of Germany or the *favelados* in Brazil, or the farmers and shepherds of Sardinia.

In the community organizing campaign which was the essential part of *The Legacy of Cain* cycle of plays, The Living Theatre sought to explore the further limits of the work of the cultural worker as a community activist.

Living as an itinerant anarchist commune, we shared our means and work, and traveled far and wide to find valid fields for our theatrical and political efforts from 1963 to 1984. Originally, *The Legacy of Cain* was Sacher-Masoch's title for the master/slave model that we have inherited in all our social institutions. We went where we thought we could be most useful, and created there a concerted campaign to define the fundamental principles of anarchist pacifist revolution in terms of the environment that we entered: the gates of the Pittsburgh steel mills, the shanty towns of Brazil, the occupied factories of Italy. We brought with us an ambitious plan for combining theatrical events and direct action in order to transform the consciousness of our spectator-participants.

We lived within the community, and worked in support of those groups already working for social change. We furthered, encouraged, or helped create all kinds of communal forms: food co-ops; daycare centers; alternative schools; forms of Wobbly solidarity; and new views of tenant, school, or workplace organization along more collective principles. Many of these alternative structures still flourish.

And all the while, in the streets, we presented plays that spoke to the community, and we presented plays created collectively with our neighbors, and we participated in local activities that concerned their lives. And insofar as we shared their lives, we shared ours also.

In 1989 the Living Theatre is beginning this process anew in its space on New York's Lower East Side, where poets and outcasts meet among the urban ruins.

The artist creates a map. It is our obligation to make this map useful to the spectators, to find a way to seduce, delight, and inspire the community to sustain the visions and actions that we enact. In this way we are both dependent on and responsible to the community.

The art-making process must therefore parallel and reflect accurately the purposes expressed. If we propose freedom, we need to create our works in a libertarian manner. If we speak of non-hierarchical solutions and inventive leaps, we must make them in the process as well as in the resultant art work.

The Living Theatre has always had as a goal, in both subject matter and work process, the obliteration of the separateness of our lives. We aim for the unification of our artistic lives with our domestic lives, our economic lives, our sexual lives, our political goals, and our quotidian conduct.

Julian Beck used to quote the rabbis: "Our struggle is our glory," he said—and so too our struggle is our art. We have worked hard to develop various forms of non-fictional acting. So that for example, in *Mysteries and Smaller Pieces*, or in *Paradise Now*, we were able to play only ourselves, creating a theater experience in which the audience too could play itself—each one bringing the drama of her own person to the work.

We must seek out the audience, we must educate the audience, we must be instructed by our audience, and we must find ways to merit their attention. If they don't come, it's our task to figure out what will attract and inspire them, not knowing yet how to speak truth to power. This is the subject of our study and experiment. The language in which we speak must be the language of the audience and at one and the same time the highest poetry. We must above all have a point of view, a clear vision that paves the way between the utopian future and the present situation with practical solutions.

The fundamental principles are never invalid. For whatever the present situation poses, in struggle and in glory; the way of peace and human respect known as equality—that is, the principles of anarchism and pacifism—seem to hold true. Anything and everything is better done peacefully and freely. Therefore our images, our symbols, and our language; while we bend them to suit each time and space; are always basic. Whether we discuss AIDS, homelessness, peacemaking, or ecological sanity, the humanization of the consciousness of performer and audience is the equivalent of what the anarchists call "The Triumph of the Idea," i.e., the idea that society has no need of coercive forms of organization.

And so the revolutionary theater artist searches to find new ways to involve the audience in the action, to deepen the personal, the intimate contact between the actor and the spectator, to create a unified artistic field in which the spectators become performers is the paradigm of that peaceful society in which all of us want to live, but which we are trained to disbelieve and to distrust. The work of the artist is to create the possibility of trust.

Notes

1. Julian Beck, *The Life of the Theatre* (New York: Limelight Editions, 1986), 9.

Creative Expression and the Refugee Experience

Margaret Mills, Sally Peterson, and William Westerman

Creative Expression and the Refugee Experience

Margaret Mills

The main problem for folklorists who do refugee studies is the comparative lack of attention paid by aid-givers to the areas of cultural expression and artistic performance. This inattention persists partially because those concerned with the practicalities of refugee service provision tend to frame the refugee as a victim; relatively helpless and therefore both deserving and in need of aid. They tend to assume the disarray of refugee culture, rather than to emphasize or facilitate the development of channels for creative refugee self-expression. Given that their primary responsibility is essential services, it is not surprising that policy makers would tend to see refugees as passive victims. As in other entitlement or dependency programs, however, this implies that those recipients who manifest autonomy or critical views of the service systems with which they interact are too much in control of their own lives to be "real" refugees.

Policy studies predominate in refugee scholarship. This work, by sociologists and demographers, is generally quantitative and aimed at high-level abstractions concerning human population movements. The very impersonality of this scholarship of human suffering reminds us that the choice of any mode of documentation, even prior to its analysis, is a political act, both in roots and consequences. The intense personal experiences and intellectual and ethical stands of refugees, which they often articulate in powerful words and cultural performances, are systematically filtered out of most

Margaret Mills

Margaret Mills was born and educated in the U.S. Her significant field research has been in Iran, Afghanistan, Pakistan and Denver, Colorado, in archaeology, folklore, urban policy/ ethnography of the AFDC system, refugee studies, and education development. Mills is associate professor in the Folklore and Folklife Department at the University of Pennsylvania. She is presently completing a book, *"Sit Down with People of Wisdom . . . ": Rhetorics and Politics in Afghan Traditional Storytelling,* forthcoming from the University of Pennsylvania Press.

policy-oriented literature. The politics of our scholarship censors and mutes these voices in favor of interpretive authority granted to the outside scholar, though refugee voices remain powerfully, often frustratingly audible to front-line refugee service providers. Acknowledging that we all have political agendas, we must then examine where our goals and motives run parallel to those of our research subjects, and where they do not.

Folklorists have tended rather readily to claim the role of cultural advocates for the people they document. Antiquarian scholars earlier celebrated the cultural equivalent of the endangered species, often with rather rosy constructions of the groups' preindustrial past. In recent decades, Third World development and liberation movements challenge any nostalgia based approach to folklore scholarship. We are compelled to address social and technical innovation and voluntary and involuntary social change, as fields for personal and societal self-determination; often at the expense of the "tradition," that has been the folklorist's standard object of study.

For folklorists, the advocacy issue with regard to refugees is manifested in the question of the ascribed cultural disarray of refugees and the framing of refugees as helpless clients. While the research climate of the 1970s described refugees as reactive to outside stimuli,[1] more recent formulations are beginning to portray refugees as decision-makers with some control over their own fate.[2]

Not only folklorists or others who document culture, but also community workers of all kinds who organize and facilitate cultural performances, have a role to play in making refugee voices audible to both policy makers and to the general public. If successful, this audibility means political empowerment and autonomy (not just service provision) for the oppressed groups. Those who become refugees rapidly become aware of the importance of persuasive and moving "performances" of their stories. One striking effect of the refugee experience is this commodification of the refugee's story. A story of flight that conforms to the service providers' definition of "proper" refugee status is exchanged for such things as goods, services, and visas to desirable countries of secondary refuge. If a story does not conform to the aid-giver's definition of refugee status the storyteller is denied that status. For example, persons who left Haiti because they could not feed themselves or their dependents, who attempt to enter the U.S. are considered "economic refugees" ineligible for asylum.

Refugees' own voices, largely censored out of policy literature, may thus be forced into highly edited forms in their face-to-face interactions with institutions. Yet accurate and psychosocially effective representation of refugees' needs must be tied to their own modes of expression. We must assume that even those suffering from acute displacement are making sense of that experience, are sorting it out for their own survival. They refer it to their prior meaning systems even while those meaning systems may in turn be under pressure of revision. They reorganize themselves socially with reference to the experience of flight—not just after the fact in the relative calm of refuge, but progressively, in the process of flight from the earliest detection of peril onward. They also express these emerging meanings to those whose evaluations of their behavior matter to them, both inside and outside the group(s) with whom they identify. In the progression from opposition to home conditions, to flight, to refuge, to resettlement, perhaps to repatriation, refugees' identification of self with group is challenged. Regional, ethnic, and sectarian distinctions which were determinative of association patterns at "home" are often blurred or invisible (or just of marginal importance) to hosts and care providers, so the refugee must reframe his or her own identity variously for different audiences—the newly constituted "refugee community," the service providers, and the indigenous host community.

"Reasons," like "meanings," are highly socially contexted constructions, subject to interpersonal negotiation. Thus what shall count as "rational" decision-making is a highly cultural affair. Ascribing rational choice and some degree of self-determination to refugees can have negative results. It empowers them yet in the same motion can end up blaming them. While refugee empowerment (conceptual or practical) can function as a form of advocacy for the group, it thereby threatens in both deep and superficial ways the bureaucratic structure of service provision and its basic rationales. If refugees are seen as having chosen flight, and furthermore as capable of strategically effective self-representation, not just inarticulate grieving, there is a potential implication that not to flee was a viable option, whereas desperation, the lack of choice, is the common currency, the index of authenticity, of refugee experience. The refugee may be caught in a double bind: denied power of choice or self-expression, or else denied authenticity and aid.

So folklore documentation which emphasizes the persuasiveness and cultural power of refugees' self-expression has deeply ambiguous political implications. At best it lays the groundwork for refugees to mount their own cultural performances and be heard directly. But refugee advocates quickly discover that different groups' cultural repertoires include expressive behavior which is either better or less suited to the hosts' ideology, more or less able to annex the pattern of cultural codes available in the host country. Hence some groups appear more articulate, more adept than others at self-presentation, with all that that implies in legitimization and acceptance in the new environment.

Food for instance is a very accessible code, in the United States, for expressing positively construed "foreignness," at least up to a point. (Cantonese acceptance of dog and cat as foodstuffs remains beyond U.S. appreciation and fuels negative stereotypes of Asians in general.) Folk festivals invariably include ethnic food booths that draw crowds of enthusiastic eaters to presentations of ethnic cuisine which are usually several removes from their original styles of preparation and presentation. They nonetheless invite the eater to "share" a foreign culture in a non-threatening way. Sampling the food of an alien group entails at least tentative trust and acceptance of their aesthetic values, and of *their* willingness to offer us hospitality and nurturance. Shared food is thus the socially incorporative substance par excellence. Yet it also marks off social boundaries. Refugees may have their own constraints which restrict their participation in American "equal opportunity eating,"[3] and tensions often develop when the children of refugee families express preferences for American common diet rather than the home cuisine.

Some channels of expression actively used within the culture of origin are nonetheless ambivalently regarded by refugees themselves. For instance, music is powerfully expressive for Afghans, but musicians are not highly respected, and song is not acceptable to those in mourning, which may include virtually everyone in a refugee camp or neighborhood. The performance of sung political poetry, important in the early years of the anti-communist resistance, has subsequently been discouraged by religious authorities in the refugee camps, for these and other reasons.[4] Some key themes of such Afghan poetry, *jihad* (holy war) and martyrdom, are furthermore ideologically uncongenial to non-Muslim hosts and service providers, making the music problematic for performance either within the group or in self-presentation to outsiders.

Some channels may be less threatening to the host country: women's domestic crafts may be easier to use for interethnic communication, as the Hmong have done; than would men's competitive sports, which the Hmong also enjoy within their communities. Some channels provide for an expression that endures beyond the performance, which the receiver keeps and can return to as an ideological icon, for instance, the Hmong story cloth on an American living room wall, or a videotape of a music or poetry performance, a festival or ceremony. Some events are very powerful intracommunity markers, but do not "go public" very well: e.g. life-cycle rituals (birthdays, christenings, weddings, funerals) as opposed to New Year ceremonies or other calendrical ceremonies, which as general celebrations can more easily be shared with outsiders. Yet calendrical festivals often are used intracommunally to reinforce personal bonds (e.g. the Hmong courtship activities which are central to the New Year festival), a function which undergoes an emotional reframing if the calendrical event is opened to large numbers of outsiders.

Also central to the public/private dichotomy is refugee use and adaptation of living and working space, public and private:[5] An influx of refugees into a low-income neighborhood may threaten the local social order, but appropriately reframed public cultural performances by the refugees can aid their assimilation into the local social structure and its round of ceremonies (through Fourth of July and other civic parades and fairs). A refugee community may well create *itself* around a project such as launching a cultural center, the dedication of a place of worship, or often the creation of a burial society and the acquisition of cemetery land for the group. Obviously, a community center lends itself to outreach beyond the community while a burial society, equally important to the psychological well-being of the group, does not readily "go public." Those interested in facilitating refugees' self-representation and empowerment within the host community may devise ways that one type of project can support the other: staged events for the general community may raise funds for projects mainly for the internal use of the group.

Such projects require expertise in approaching civic bureaucracies and fundraising groups, and a familiarity with the forms of American public performance, so that refugee cultural expression can be successfully reframed for American performance contexts. Those outsiders with expertise in public programming, whether festival, theater, or exhibition forms, have a role to play in helping refugee groups to approach civic organizations, design cultural displays and write grants in order to mount effective, publicly accessible statements of refugee culture and experience. Programmers need to dedicate some of their own energy to research the communities they represent.

The design and facilitation of effective programming must take into account the class or social position of the refugee prior to flight, to understand the range of cultural expressions in use in refuge, and the ways those expressions might be "packaged" for a wider audience. Most refugees who reach the U.S. legally are middle class or above, and somewhat urbanized, because the U.S., like most countries of secondary refuge, has selective policies for legal admission of refugees transferred from within their initial havens, and travel costs are an additional filter. Most refugees who make it to the U.S. were relatively empowered where they came from, and at least superficially share some values of the dominant U.S. culture. The peasant farmers, traditional craftspeople, and semiskilled laborers who are in exile tend to remain in regions adjacent to those they fled. Thus the segment of refugee culture represented by ethnic groups in secondary countries of refuge is not necessarily representative of the general cultural profile of the country of origin. The preindustrial arts and crafts and indigenous folk music and other performance traditions which make good folk festival fare may be far from the experiences of many urban middle-class refugees, while the urban culture of the middle class may lack, for performance purposes, a distinctive ethnic flavor.

Authenticity and nostalgia become complex issues in ethnic programming.[6] Underlying them is the still deeper and more essential issue of aestheticization: public programs generally win friends for ethnic groups by aestheticized celebration of selected elements of the culture in question, but the essential refugee experience is hardly celebratory. Successful representation must celebrate the vitality and expressive power of the refugee culture, but simultaneously recognize the problem of cultural loss and displacement, the need for witnessing and for redress.

One basic issue that resists aestheticization is that of the ideology of flight in the refugee's culture of origin. For Afghan Muslim refugees, *hijra,* flight to avoid religious persecution, is a meritorious act modeled on the Prophet Mohammed's retreat from Mecca to Medina. These ideological resources help to combat feelings of ambivalence or guilt over abandoning the home community.[7] Such ideological positions often intensify in the face of host country prejudice or indifference; for example, the return to observant Islam by Muslims in non-Muslim countries of refuge, or the engagement of American churches in the Sanctuary movement, which builds on liberation theology in the face of U.S. government policy regarding Central American refugees.

The lack of attention to refugee cultural expressions in previous research on refugee decisionmaking and social organization demonstrates the need for cultural documentation in service to advocacy, even while revealing the problematics of our position as outsiders to the cultures for whom we would wish to act as advocates. Nevertheless, self-presentation is an acute need in refugee communities, for both personal and institutional purposes. Folklore research has a role to play in refining and rendering more effective the translation process through which refugee cultural expressions can be brought to a wide audience, and empower refugees, practically and psychologically.

Notes

We would like to express special gratitude to the refugees, exiles, and displaced people—Afghan, Hmong, Salvadoran, and Guatemalan, who have so generously trusted us with their stories, songs, embroideries, and other forms of personal artistic expression. Special thanks to Pang Xiong, Mao Moua, Xee Yang and PaVue Thao and to numerous Salvadorans and Guatemalans in the U.S. whose real names we cannot publish (and often do not even know) at this time, for their contributions to this article.

Thanks as well to Itzek Gottesman and Mark O'Brien for encouraging us to participate in the Voices of Dissent conference.

1. E.g. Egon F. Kunz, "The Refugee in Flight: Kinetic Models and Forms of Displacement," *International Migration Review* 7(2) 125-146, 1972.
2. Cf. Dorsh Marie DeVoe, "Framing Refugees as Clients," *International Migration Review* 15(1): 88-94, 1981; Heribert Adam, "Rational Choice in Ethnic Mobilization: A Critique," *International Migration Review* 18:377-381, 1984 and Michael Hechter and Debra Friedman, "Does Rational Choice Theory Suffice? Response to Adam," *International Migration Review* 18: 381-388, 1984.
3. Roger D. Abrahams, "Equal Opportunity Eating: A Structural Excursus on Things of the Mouth," in *Ethnic and Regional Foodways in the United States,* ed. L.K. Brown and K. Mussell (Knoxville: University of Tennessee Press, 1984), 19-36.
4. David Edwards, "Poetics of Order in the Afghan Resistance," paper delivered at the annual meeting of the American Anthropological Association, Chicago, Illinois, November 1987.
5. Christine A. Cartwright, "Indian Sikh Homes Out of North American Houses: Mental Culture in Material Translation," *New York Folklore* 7(1-2): 97-111, 1981; Shalom Staub, "The Near East Restaurant: A Study of the Spatial Manifestation of the Folklore of Ethnicity," *New York Folklore* 7(1-2): 113-127, 1981; Paul D. Starr, "Troubled Waters: Vietnamese Fisherfolk on America's Gulf Coast," *International Migration Review* 15(1): 226-238, 1981.
6. Cf. Shalom Staub, "Folklore and Authenticity: A Myopic Marriage in Public Sector Programs," and David Whisnant, "Public Sector Folklore as Intervention: Lessons from the Past," in Burt Feintuch, ed., *Conservation of Culture: Folklorists and the Public Sector* (Lexington, KY: University Press of Kentucky, 1988), pp. 166-181, 233-250 respectively; and Richard Handler and Jocelyn Linnekin, "Tradition, Genuine and Spurious," *Journal of American Folklore* 97:273-290, 1984.
7. Cf. Liucija Baškauskas, "The Lithuanian Refugee Experience and Grief," *International Migration Review* 15(1):276-291, 1981.

Hmong "Flower Cloth" and the Marketing of Refugee Art

Sally Peterson

Many years ago my father, my mother, they do very tiny stitching
  —more detail.
Today we change some because we need for sale.
  Just sell, just make money,
but you still keep your colors.
And you still keep the design.[1]

Sally Peterson

Sally Peterson is a Ph.D. candidate in folklore at the University of Pennsylvania. She has written several articles on *paj ntaub*, the traditional needlework and batik arts of Hmong women.

With these words, Pang Xiong describes a common refugee experience: the metamorphosis of a traditional art into a tourist commodity. Translated literally as "flower cloth," the art of *paj ntaub* (pronounced "pa ndau") encompasses the embroidery, appliqué, and batik work practiced by generations of Hmong women in the highland regions of Laos, Thailand, North Vietnam, and China. For centuries, *paj ntaub* needlework has decorated the festive and quotidian dress of both men and women; its ancient designs have served as distinctive markers of Hmong ethnicity. Traditional exchanges of *paj ntaub* enact the continuity of family, of community, of what it means to be Hmong.

Throughout the Second Indochinese War (1954–1975), a large proportion of Lao Hmong fought alongside the Royal Lao forces against the communist nationalists. The establishment of the Republic of Democratic Peoples of Laos in 1975 forced more than a hundred thousand Hmong to flee across the Mekong River to refugee camps in Thailand. Over eighty thousand subsequently resettled in the United States, while others began new lives in France, West Germany, Australia and Canada. In order to help support their families, Hmong women in Thai refugee camps and in resettlement countries have instituted a new kind of *paj ntaub* exchange: investing their time, traditional designs, and creativity into needlework creations for sale to consumers in the Western world.

Hmong women explain that the phenomenon of marketed *paj ntaub* did not begin with the advent of refugee status, nor is it limited to Lao Hmong. But the flight from persecution in Laos to sanctuary in Thai refugee camps stranded the Lao Hmong with few economic options—and so women began producing marketable *paj ntaub* at an unprecedented rate. Relief workers from various international aid agencies willingly served as brokers in the development of marketing networks. Many advised the Hmong to adapt their color schemes and item inventories to appeal to European and American consumers.

Traditional *paj ntaub* design obeys mathematical principles of bilateral and quadrilateral symmetry; complex patterns are systematic, repeatable, and predictable. Straightforward operations allow needleworkers to expand traditionally diminutive pieces into larger and larger squares, forming panels for purses, pillows, wall hangings, tablecloths, and bedspreads. Following suggestions from relief workers, camp residents further extended the application of traditional designs to such familiar Western accessories as eyeglass cases, change purses, pincushions, coasters, Christmas ornaments, and other inexpensive items. Designs once identified with specific regions or Hmong subgroups became standardized and simplified for presentation to the world outside. This broadening of women's repertoires, while allowing for increased means of expressing Hmong identity in general, blurs the reliability of needlework as an indication of specific Hmong group membership.

The confluence of traditional skills, exposure to Western tastes and marketing practices, and the relentless need for supplementary income endemic to refugee camp life also produced an innovative form of embroidered art known as story cloths. Differing radically from their traditional geometric counterparts, Hmong story cloths present pictorial scenes: particularly popular are panoramas of daily life, illustrated legends, tableaus of the Lao mountain environment and graphic accounts of historical events. Many story cloths provide English captions to the embroidered scenes; since most artists do not speak English, they rely on Hmong interpreters to supply them with translations.

The commodification of *paj ntaub* represents the sole means of survival for thousands of refugees; its production is organized, competitive, and at times the focus of political tensions, both between rival refugee factions and between the Hmong and their Thai administrators. The latter have claimed that the income resulting from the sale of *paj ntaub* has discouraged refugees from seeking resettlement.

Women who have resettled in the United States continue to sew and sell *paj ntaub*. Many sell only occasionally, through church- or community-sponsored craft fairs, bazaars and flea markets. Several of the larger Hmong communities sell through American-sponsored retail outlets devoted to Hmong art. Although most of these shops follow a cooperative model, they vary in the amount of control exerted by the resettled refugees. Many of the craft businesses, funded by nonprofit agencies, are mandated to "preserve culture"; the sponsors expect all pieces to be handstitched by the women from whom they purchase and will not knowingly accept needlework shipped from refugee camps. This places the Hmong in an intolerable position; they must choose to either lie to their American patrons or disappoint relatives in the camps. Generally, loyalty to the family prevails. The stress resulting from this conflict induces many women to withdraw from the cooperatives.

A few women manage to sell *paj ntaub* independently, and rely entirely upon the resulting income. These women tend to travel the craft fair circuit in their region, and maintain a large inventory of *paj ntaub* items. Frequently they accept pieces on commission from Hmong women in their community and from Thai refugee camps; they may at times have on hand the work of over thirty women. Usually these craftswomen have had previous exposure to marketing tactics in Laos, and rely on their experience and business acumen to gauge which items will be popular with their customers. They relay this information to their suppliers, thus retaining a tight control over their stock. Several such entrepreneurs return to the refugee camps each year to personally replenish their inventories. Their mobility and frequent interactions with the larger American public does not follow traditional Hmong precepts of the roles of women as wives and mothers. Yet the women are seldom viewed as individual operators; in the eyes of the community, they represent their family and their clan.

Increasingly, *paj ntaub* makers have sought for means to control both the creative and management ends of their enterprise. In the refugee camps, visiting ethnic art exporters offer an alternative to the volunteer agency (VOLAG) organizations, with their externally-imposed, fixed prices and quality controls. In the United States, some cooperative ventures sponsored by outsiders dissolve due to their failure to respond to the consensus of participating Hmong members concerning operating procedures, or because of an inability both to meet overhead costs and to pay decent wages. Splinter groups develop their own cooperatives, or management of the original group reverts completely to Hmong control.

Paradoxically, story cloths, the form which blossomed as a result of extra-cultural influences, offer Hmong artists the most individual, creative control. While onlookers may suggest topics, concedes one artist, "[H]ow can they know what is Hmong culture?" Which events, which stories, which details of daily life to portray are decisions that rest with the Hmong artists. Much story cloth production does reflect the vagaries of ever-changing public taste. Certain design types will be popular for a while, then give way to a new style. Yet recent trends indicate that the messages in the cloths speak more to the artists' interests and concerns than they did formerly, and that less effort is made to provide observers with cultural interpretations. A recent cloth, for example, illustrates the visit of a ritual shaman to a farmer's home to perform a healing ceremony, but unlike earlier cloths, no English subtitles explain the esoteric meaning.

Story cloths that chronicle recent history serve both to inform a foreign public of the Hmong experience, and to provide personal expression for deeply held emotions of loss, anger, and grief. The bombing of villages, the murder of women and children, the battle deaths of soldiers, and the perilous crossing of the Mekong River present mute, embroidered testimonies that tempt the world's compassion as well as its pocketbooks.

Story cloth popularity has offered the Hmong a means to convey political messages to their own communities. Drawing upon the artistry and needlework skills available in a refugee camp, a campaigner for the United Lao National Liberation Front (ULNLF) ordered hundreds of cloths displaying symbols of Lao nationality. The cloths were sold exclusively to Hmong, and the money raised was contributed to the ULNLF cause. These story cloths now hang in Hmong homes in cities throughout the United States.

Story cloth stitched in Thailand circa 1987. This scene depicts a Hmong army encampment in the Laotian mountains; village life continues in the shadow of war. Collection of Pang Xiong Sirirathasuk. Photo by Sally Peterson.

Pang Xiong Sirirathasuk selling *paj ntaub* at a craft fair in Philadelphia, 1987. Photo by Sally Peterson.

Hmong *paj ntaub* exhibits characteristics that perhaps define the genre of refugee art. The refugees draw upon traditional expressive culture to produce a commodity that both provides a rapid economic return and continually reminds the world of a politically desperate situation. Initially dependent upon the aid of cultural outsiders, the dispossessed eventually repossess this cultural resource, taking steps to control both management and creative expression. At the same time, new forms develop (such as story cloths), accomplishing economic and communicative goals, while capturing the attention and imagination of the refugees themselves—as consumers.

Framing *paj ntaub* as "refugee art," however, presents some interesting questions regarding the future of the needlework as an economic commodity. Although some 40,000 Hmong continue to reside in refugee camps, many in the United States have shed their refugee status and entered the mainstream as fully employed, taxpaying Hmong American citizens. Some have achieved their goals with the help of *paj ntaub* sales. Although the delicate designs of *paj ntaub* and the nostalgic images of story cloths represent their past, they are not accurate reflections of contemporary Hmong American life. Issues of cultural preservation, though occasionally symbolized by *paj ntaub,* are more directly concerned with the theoretical and practical problems of education, English language acquisition, job training, community development and unity, welfare dependency, and the roles of women.

Paj ntaub has not disappeared from the contemporary Hmong American scene. Older women who can afford *not* to make *paj ntaub* for sale continue to sew traditional pieces for younger relatives' New Year celebrations, for babies entering the world, and for elders leaving it. The increasingly affluent younger generation, often now unskilled in the art of *paj ntaub,* can afford to buy exquisite pieces from their elders or from those in refugee camps. The future of *paj ntaub* is uncertain, and certainly unpredictable. Folklorists versed in the dynamics of tradition and change would suggest that Hmong flower cloth will outlive its status as refugee art, and remain an important marker of ethnic identity, despite changes in form, style, and function.

Notes

1. Interview with Mrs. Pang Xiong Sirirathasuk; Philadelphia, PA, April 19, 1985. I would like to thank Pang Xiong, Mao Moua, Xee Yang, and PaVue Thao for their contributions to this article.

Sources

Crystal, Eric. "Buffalo Heads and Sacred Threads: Hmong Culture of the South-east Asian Highlands," in *Textiles as Texts: Art of Hmong Women from Laos,* Amy Catlin, ed. Los Angeles: The Woman's Building, 1987.

Dewhurst, C. Kurt, Yvonne Lockwood, and Marsha MacDowell, "Michigan Hmong Textiles," in *Michigan Hmong Textiles,* ed. C. Kurt Dewhurst and Marsha MacDowell (East Lansing, MI: The Museum Michigan State University, Folk Culture Series 3:2, 1983), 15–25.

Donnelly, Nancy D. "Factors Contributing to a Split within Clientelistic Needlework Cooperative Engaged in Refuge Resettlement," in *The Hmong in Transition,* Glenn L. Hendricks, Bruce T. Downing, and Amos S. Deinard, eds. (New York: Center for Migration Studies of New York, Inc. and the Southeast Asian Refugee Studies of the University of Minnesota, 1986), 159-173.

Peterson, Sally. "Translating Experience and the Reading of Story Cloth," *Journal of American Folklore* 101, 6–22, 1988.

Smalley, William A. "Stages of Hmong Cultural Adaptation," Hendricks, *The Hmong in Transition,* 7-22.

Refugee Testimony from El Salvador and Guatemala

William Westerman

I want to tell you that what you are hearing is not
just [me].
It is the cry of those who suffer tortures in the
prisons.
It is the cry of our peasant brothers and sisters who
flee from the bombardments.
It is the cry of the children who weep for a crust of
bread.
It is the cry of a suffering people who ask for
your help,
and your support,
and understanding.
And we are clear
that the peace of our people is in your hands.
—Roberto Sánchez
personal testimony, October 8, 1986

> ## William Westerman
>
> William Westerman is a doctoral candidate in Folklore and Folklife at the University of Pennsylvania. He is currently writing a dissertation on the folklore of the Sanctuary movement and the Underground Railroad. He served as co-chair of Central America Refugee Action in Philadelphia from 1986 to 1988.

Sometimes refugees come to a new country because they have had to flee quickly, under the pressure of events; and sometimes they come more slowly, after careful planning and deliberation. They come without possessions, but they do not travel light. Inside themselves they carry the weight of memories. Every person brings a lifetime of experiences within a culture and a historical situation that shapes and colors the way each person communicates in a new situation. For each life story that includes safe arrival in a new land, there are the stories as well of those who didn't survive, and who live on only in memory, in story, and in inspiration. As it is said in Latin America, these are the ones who are *"presente!"*, alive, present in spirit.

Since 1979, the U.S. has seen an influx of refugees from El Salvador and Guatemala, nearly a million by some estimates. These refugees have fled civil war, military and paramilitary death squads, and U.S.-sponsored bombings and counterinsurgency campaigns. These have left over 70,000 civilians dead in El Salvador, and between 20,000 and 100,000 dead or disappeared in Guatemala.[1] So great is the repression and terror that no one is unaffected, and each refugee arrives in this country with stories to tell. Stories of family and friends found dead in the street or in a ditch. Stories of torture or detention. Stories of loved ones forever disappeared.

Few arrive with legal residence papers or any documentation. Those who are arrested by the Immigration and Naturalization Service (INS) or who apply for political asylum face a difficult battle to stay in this country. Fewer than three percent of Salvadorans and one percent of Guatemalans receive political asylum, and though there have been bills proposed in Congress to permit Salvadorans to remain in this country, after ten years most remain unwelcome. Denied legal representation or coerced into submission, many refugees have been silently deported back to El Salvador and Guatemala.[2] This legal situation circumscribes the openness with which they can practice their culture let alone find jobs, housing, education, and medical care.

Salvadorans and Guatemalans in the U.S. have tried to maintain their culture in a considerable variety of ways. Certain art forms have survived better than others, in part because certain arts continue to serve community needs and require only available materials. Cooking, for example, as well as music and carpentry, remain traditional activities in Central American communities in the U.S., since many basic ingredients and tools—corn, beans, and rice, as well as guitars and lumber—are readily available. Other traditional arts and occupations have become dormant in the new culture, such as basket-weaving (since certain fibers cannot be found here) and hat-making (peasant hats have little functional use in North American cities). Those arts that have survived are rarely shared outside their own community. But folklorists are well aware that one of the arts we all carry with us is the ability to tell stories, specifically stories of personal experiences that have befallen us.

Many Salvadorans and Guatemalans (speaking of them together here, though their circumstances are often different) do not tell their stories. They remain quiet either out of fear or out of pain, as if not telling were a way of not remembering. Some, after having been arrested for arriving *sin papeles* (without papers) speak only to church workers or lawyers. In private, some will tell friends—North and Central American alike—about the disappearance of their sister or the death squad that showed up at their door. Others need say nothing at all, but offer their testimony through the scars borne on their bodies and minds.

But a select few have decided to go public, bearing witness to the suffering of their people. The select few are often those who faced persecution in their home country— religious workers, students, union workers, and human rights workers. The audiences they find here are composed of the same types of people. Speakers often have some formal educational background and some sense of mission. In telling their stories, the Central Americans often eschew political analysis or numbing statistics in favor of the personal experiences that have led to their exile.[3]

The telling of these "testimonies" has been a major means of education and intercultural exchange between Central and North Americans. Many of the people involved with the Sanctuary movement, a loosely organized group of over 400 congregations offering shelter and support to Central American refugees, and with other Central America solidarity groups, clergy and lay alike, attribute their own involvement to hearing a Central American speak. The direct contact between refugee and U.S. citizen has had a profound effect in hundreds, if not thousands, of cases. "Storytelling is the heart of the Sanctuary movement. That's why [the movement] exists," as one U.S. church member said.

What emerges from listening to the stories of Central Americans is solidarity. Through face-to-face interaction the problem becomes human. Testimony introduces an individual—a real, concrete, living, breathing human being. As television brought the war in Southeast Asia into our living rooms, it is now the refugees themselves who bring the Central American conflict home (significantly, though, to fewer people).

As more refugees came and interest spread, the giving of testimony spread too, and the practice reached a peak in 1986. But times changed; refugees who arrived at the beginning of the decade have become adjusted to some extent to new communities and new lifestyles. Their experiences in their homelands have receded further into memory, and they have developed other methods of working with North Americans on social justice issues. Giving public testimony is no longer as widespread as it was, though new repression may well lead to more refugees and more testimony.

Refugee testimony is a political statement of one's humanity and of one's survival in a violent, repressive society. But it is also an artistic voice and as such is a way of taking control of one's situation. These people do not passively accept their fate, but instead go out to the public in order to create better conditions for the people of their country. They become not victims of history, but producers of it. The tools they use are stories, testimonies, and sometimes songs, or even paintings and embroideries; all records of their life histories. Life story narration is both a political act and a verbal performance, a poetic art form. The scripting of history itself becomes not just a collection of acts and deeds, but a collective process of creation.

Testimony is also a form of religious commitment. Many of the Central Americans who speak here have been influenced by the practice of liberation theology—the grassroots movement among the churches in Latin America that demands an end to the sinful oppression, violence, and poverty that characterize most of Latin America. This religion inspires not only belief but action, action dedicated to constructing the Kingdom of God on earth. Just as the poetry of personal storytelling is not merely words, so those who practice liberation theology follow the Biblical mandates to feed the hungry, clothe the naked, set free the oppressed, break every yoke, and—not least—welcome the stranger, the refugee.

Their testimonies then are acts of art, acts of faith, and acts of defiance, of dissent, of liberation, of therapy even, and of love. They are a way of staying alive and staying human. In the words of the great Guatemalan poet Otto René Castillo, himself an exile until he returned home to Guatemala only to be captured and burned alive by the army in 1967. He writes:[4]

> In exile you can lose
> your heart, but if you don't,
> never
> will they be able to murder its tenderness
> or the vital strength of its storms.

Notes

1. Recommended sources of documentation include Amnesty International and Americas Watch reports, as well as reports of the Catholic Church. See also bulletins from the nongovernmental Human Rights Commission of El Salvador and organizations of mothers and family members of murdered people and political prisoners such as COMADRES in El Salvador and the Mutual Support Group (GAM) in Guatemala. Good background sources include Renato Camarada, *Forced to Move* (San Francisco: Solidarity Publications, 1985); Charles Clements, *Witness to War* (New York: Bantam, 1984); Phil Wheaton and Luisa Frank, *Indian Guatemala: Path to Liberation* (Washington: EPICA Task Force, 1984); and Michael McClintock's two-volume work, *The American Connection: State Terror and Popular Resistance in El Salvador and Guatemala* (London: Zed, 1985).

2. See the recent U.S. District Court decision in *Orantes-Hernandez v. Meese.* "The official U.S. policy has been to stop at nothing to deny Salvadorans their rights to due process and safe haven."—National Immigration Project of the National Lawyers Guild, *"Orantes* Victory," *Central American Refugee Defense Fund Newsletter* (March 1988): 1-3.

3. Published examples of Central American testimony and refugee testimony can be found in a variety of publications, including Scott Wright, ed., *Testimony: The Massacres of Cabañas and Chalatenango, El Salvador, 1984, Bombings and Bacterial Warfare, 1985* (San Antonio, TX: CRISPAZ, 1985); Martha Gellhorn, "Testimonial" (*Granta* 11:141-154, 1984); and Rigoberta Menchú, *I. . . Rigoberta Menchú,* ed. by Elisabeth Burgos-Debray, trans. by Ann Wright (London: Verso, 1984).

4. Otto René Castillo, "Exile," in *Let's Go! Vamonos Patria a Caminar.* Trans. by Margaret Randall (London: Cape Goliard Press, 1971). Translation here my own.

Strategic Compromises
AIDS and Alternative Video Practices
John Greyson

AIDS is a war. Perhaps it didn't have to be—we'll never know. AIDS is a plague of government indifference, medical negligence and right-wing opportunism. AIDS is an epidemic of sexual intolerance. Like most wars, AIDS has been turned into megabucks by the multinational media industry, who exploit paranoia and ignorance with every new cover story and "in-depth report." Like most wars, AIDS was made into a war by those who consider that whole (disenfranchised) sectors of the population are expendable. Like most wars, these same opportunists shed public tears for the tens of thousands of those dead (whose dignity they irrevocably deny). Like most wars, these same opportunists ignore the needs of the hundreds of thousands who are fighting to stay alive.

These are unsubtle words, because AIDS is a war, not only of politics and medicine, but also of representations. While the mass media's response to the health crisis has been anything but uniform, the results have nevertheless (in spite of "good intentions") been lethal. In stark contrast, a subculture of alternate media is fighting back. From the front lines of the battlefield, artists, community activists, and cable producers have launched a counteroffensive against such deadly discourses.

These "unsubtle words" are excerpted from the program notes I wrote for a six-night exhibition of AIDS tapes[1] by independent producers and artists, that was presented in Toronto in October, 1988.[2] These words express polemically and schematically an opposition common to left cultural criticism, an opposition that (ex)poses the "lies" of the commercial mass media against the "truth" of oppositional media practices.[3] They claim that alternate media can be used by "the people" to transform society. As media critic Hans Magnus Enzensberger says, "The open secret of the electronic media, the decisive political factor . . . is their mobilizing power."[4] These words serve to place the groundswell of independent videotapes addressing AIDS shown in the exhibition within a

John Greyson

John Greyson is a Toronto-based video artist whose eighteen tapes and films include *Moscow Does Not Believe in Queers*, *The AIDS Epidemic*, and *Urinal*. He currently teaches video at California Institute of the Arts, and is working on a feature film called *Zero Patience*, a murder-mystery musical about Patient Zero and the "source" of AIDS.

rich history of social change media and the "committed documentary,"[5] one that dates back to the Bolshevik revolution, one that has born witness to the many other wars for social justice.

Polemically insisting on the vitality of these tapes as effective weapons for social change, such simplifications are perhaps defensible in activist terms. However, such optimistic expressions end up erasing the complexities and contradictions of how such tapes are produced and experienced, creating the illusion of a unified, uncomplicated field of alternate media. But when each tape is examined in depth (interrogating the varied representational practices used, the funding sources that shaped its script, the type of community it came out of and/or is intended for, etc.), it becomes clear that easy generalizations about the praxis of such AIDS tapes (and indeed, of any social change media) are elusive, to say the least.

Media producers are dangerously closer to the belly of their particular beast (the film industry) than other visual artists. Caught between two mythologies (that of the artist, whose individual "vision" is supposed remain pure, unfettered by responsibility to audience, and that of the commercial film/TV producer, whose hierarchical yet collaborative industrial production mode constantly compromises vision in favor of reaching the audience) they must care about both vision and audience. They therefore learn the necessity of strategic compromises.

Over the past year, I've previewed 150 AIDS tapes (for the exhibition and also for a sixty-minute compilation of clips from AIDS tapes for Deep Dish TV, an alternate satellite network).[6] They included the following:

1. Cable access talk shows addressing such topics as discrimination experienced by PLWAs (persons living with AIDS) and lesbian efforts against AIDS

2. Documents of performances and plays addressing AIDS

3. Documentary (memorial) portraits of PLWAs, most of whom had died by the time the tapes were completed

4. Experimental works by artists deconstructing mass media hysteria, lies and omissions

5. Educational tapes on transmission of and protection against the HIV virus, designed for specific community audiences (women, Blacks, Latinos, youth, prisoners), often commissioned by AIDS groups

6. Documentaries portraying the vast range of AIDS service organizations and support groups that have sprung up around the country

7. Safer-sex tapes, that adapt the conventions of porn to teach their bi (bisexual), straight, and gay audiences the eroticization of safer sex

8. Activist tapes, which document the demonstrations and protests of an increasingly militant AIDS activist movement

9. A growing handful of tapes for PLWAs, outlining issues of alternate treatments for HIV infection and AIDS-related diseases

Such categories are immediately suspect. For instance, which of these tapes would not be "educational," given that they all seek to comment on some aspect of the AIDS crisis? What definition of "activist" are we using—are "activist" tapes defined solely by the inclusion of street demo footage? What constitutes enough formal innovation to qualify for the moniker "experimental?"

Certainly useful to programmers organizing screenings, these expedient categories nevertheless do little to elaborate the complexity of the work they seek to contain. Generalizations about how these tapes differ from mass media offerings similarly collapse when put to the test. For instance, it's often claimed that independent tapes address issues that the mainstream media has generally ignored or misrepresented. However, any survey of network television AIDS coverage in the past year (dramas, sitcom episodes, documentaries, news updates) must conclude that the dominant media shift and shimmy much faster than any media critique can allow. Compare the appalling morbid sentimentality of the made-for-TV melodrama *An Early Frost* (1986), chronicling the return-of-the-dying-yuppie-fag-prodigal-son-to-the-bosom-of-his-impossibly-middle-class-family with the (relatively) more sophisticated recent offering *The Ryan White Story* (1986), based on America's favorite PWA, the working-class kid from Kokomo who successfully fought to attend school and is cheating the AIDS-is-always-fatal prophecy five years after his diagnosis. (All right, the show was appalling in its own right—but its representational practices reflected a very different agenda than its predecessor, with its story focused on the struggle of a PLWA to combat discrimination and live a full self-determined life.)

News coverage similarly has been transformed in some instances, primarily through the efforts of the AIDS activist movement, who have created *new* news through demonstrations, successfully zapped mass media offenders for journalistic AIDS crimes such as irresponsible reporting, and also worked to educate reporters and editors about issues that have been ignored or suppressed.

One material reason that the mass media have been somewhat responsive, and that some AIDS representations have not remained as hysterical and fear-mongering as they once were, is that some of their producers have *personally* been affected by the epidemic, much more so that their counterparts workings on issues like the homeless or Nicaragua. After all, a *New York Times* reporter rarely hangs out with a Sandinista or a street person, but they may well have a friend of a friend who has AIDS.

However relatively horrendous mainstream media representations continue to be, they are always moving, attempting to keep pace with the shifts (both reactionary and progressive) in dominant and oppositional discourses of AIDS, be they scientific, bureaucratic, governmental, or grassroots. Any theory of the mass media that sees such AIDS representations as monolithic misses the daily contradictions and slippages.

However, it's not overstating the case to note that the dominant representational clichés the networks and studios cling to for dear life (the suffocating conventions of dramas and sitcoms, documentaries and news updates) severely contain, indeed cripple, the sort of messages that are allowed to be broadcast. Information *must* be linear. Narratives *must* have closure. Authority *must* be constituted by an "expert." Television always speaks about AIDS from its mythical "outside" position of objectivity—even its so-called sensitive dramas about gay PWAs somehow always manage to erase any sense of being *inside* a community. It's perhaps here that the greatest claims can be made for an "us" versus "them" position, if one maintains that what most characterizes independent media production is their confident insiders vernacular, and the formal challenges that such a perspective suggests.

However, the range of the independent tapes previewed includes many that embrace conventional representational practices. Some cling to tried-and-true methods of documentary authority. Others prioritize "education" of a target group with inevitable simplifications and distortions. Some embrace formal tropes that are embarrassingly clichéd (didactic, too sentimental, you name it). These users of mainstream conventions are sometimes motivated by a desire to be politically effective, to communicate to as broad an audience as possible through the reassuring use of familiar constructions. In other cases, the producers thoughtlessly reproduce these conventions because they have no gripe with the mainstream and its messages—their independence is more determined for them by the lack of a CBS freelance contract.

Similarly, many of the tapes were made in collaboration with AIDS service organizations, reflecting to a greater or lesser degree the politics of the sponsor. What does this do to notions of "independence?" Artists choosing work this way have done so for diverse reasons—sometimes as a political choice, deciding to be answerable to/ engaged with their community; and sometimes as a "straight" commission that pays the rent. How do such material conditions impact on questions of autonomy, of intentionality?

Contemporary media critics, especially those engaged in the post-structuralist/ feminist/semiotic/psychoanalytic debates concerning theories of representation, have rightly insisted that all film/video constructions are texts that speak on several simultaneous levels. Regardless of the producer's stated intentions, these texts are dependent more on the codes and conventions (the signifying practices) they utilize and the social context determining their reception by an audience. For instance, a producer may set out to make an AIDS education tape that speaks sympathetically to gay teenagers in their own language. However, the conventions she or he may adopt may reproduce typical pedagogical authority (lecturing) which the target teens would probably reject. Similarly, any typical classroom situation has so much homophobia built into it that a closeted gay teenager might end up feeling vulnerable and threatened by such a screening, and be forced to reject it publicly through peer pressure.

As a result, intentionality is commonly a discredited concept in media criticism, yet for any video artist making social change media (and certainly for the majority of these AIDS producers), it is a central issue. Tape after tape exhibits the active desire to communicate its particular urgent message. These dozens of dozens of producers continue to negotiate (sometimes consciously, sometimes unconsciously) a host of contradictory agendas. Form, for instance: Deconstructive strategies may capture the terrifying ambience of the AIDS culture we live in better than traditional realist practices, but will they alienate/mystify the intended audience? Politics: An activist script may be appropriate, but will the local AIDS committee (for whom the tape is intended) feel threatened by such rhetoric and not use it? Focus: Connecting various issues (like AIDS homophobia, AIDS sexism, and AIDS racism) may seem vital, yet will it make the tape too broad, too general, so it ends up simply being a token (Trotskyist) shopping list of progressive issues? Funding: Will the state arts council support a didactic documentary? Will the Red Cross support an esoteric arts tape? Guilt: Should I continue to produce experimental works that win awards on the arts circuit but never reach the AIDS community, or should I be responsible and throw all my efforts into a collective, community cable access AIDS show? And so on . . . . This continual jousting with that many-headed hydra called "effectiveness" is paramount in this AIDS war. How do we communicate our (very varied) agendas without being marginalized, and on whose terms? How do our efforts intervene and interrupt dominant discourses? How do we prevent our tapes from being neutralized and recontained within a complacent status quo?

Compromise is a term that the left righteously (indeed religiously) rejects. Yet the strategic compromises outlined above (always difficult, never completely satisfactory) are exactly the ones that makes these AIDS tapes so vital, so exciting. In order to pursue this theme, I've constructed the following "case studies" which schematically juxtapose pairs of tapes that superficially share similar subjects. In some cases, I have talked with the producers at length; in others, I'm making assumptions based on brief conversations and the tapes themselves. In all cases, due to lack of space, I've simplified and generalized some aspects of the productions.

'Til Death Do Us Part and *Another Man*

In a culture where school prayer is more acceptable than sex education, it's not surprising that the plenitude of AIDS tapes for youth are having a hard time finding an audience.[7] That is, there's megabucks in the AIDS education market—every school board wants an AIDS tape. They just want it to say what *they* believe about AIDS. It's also not surprising that the tapes have been organized around one agenda: prevention. Prevention, of course, is the cornerstone of the Reagan/Bush administration's recent and begrudging response to AIDS, which has criminally ignored every other aspect of the health crisis. In other words, it is assumed that today's youth have no interest in how teenagers cope with *having* AIDS, no interest in the politics of medicine, no interest in the interconnections between health care and poverty. . . . The political and social are erased, leaving only the personal: how to protect yourself. It should go without saying that this is vital information that every youth must get (and is still not getting). It should also go without saying that "prevention" agendas run the gamut from naive appeals for celibacy, to murderously inaccurate endorsements of monogamy, to nonjudgmental advice on condoms and cleaning your needles. An excellent critique of several of these tapes appeared in *AIDS: Cultural Analysis, Cultural Activism* (issue 43 of the theoretical journal *October*), which has become a veritable "red book" for activists working on issues of AIDS and representation.[8]

While most of these tapes talk down to kids in a traditional pedagogical fashion, *'Til Death Do Us Part* attempts to subvert this condescension by turning over the means of production to youth themselves. Or at least, halfway. This twenty-minute film is adapted from the Washington-based Black Youth Theatre Ensemble's collectively-produced play about AIDS. A freewheeling mix of rap, skits, gospel, and dramatic scenarios sketch out the social impact of AIDS, as written and performed by a talented group of teenagers. On paper it sounds terrific. The fact that it's also one of the only productions to target Black audiences makes it even more promising, given the fact that twenty-five percent of all PLWAs in the U.S. are Black and Latino.

The rap songs are vibrant: "This is Alvin on the mike, when I talk I talk it right. . . . So take my advice and have safe sex, don't share needles—yeah, I think that's best." Their take-offs on TV ads, satirizing the commodification of sex (edible underwear, toothpaste for added sex appeal) are humorous. An all-too-familiar implicit message begins to assert itself, however. The (bad) sexual marketplace has perverted the (good) institution of sexual love within marriage—and when you succumb to its sinful pleasures, the result is AIDS. In a similar conflation, a mimed needle-sharing scene (again, premised on selfish pleasure) results in retribution. Thus, sex and drugs *cause* AIDS. The last half revolves around an embarrassingly clichéd representation of Death, voraciously seducing and claiming the entire cast, including a gratuitous baby doll wrapped in a blanket. Despite the rap songs' realistic advice, the overall message is distinctly Catholic: sin will condemn you to the everlasting fires of hell.

I showed the tape to several members of the Toronto-based Black CAP (Coalition for AIDS Prevention), who reluctantly admitted they couldn't use it in their outreach to the Black community. Beyond the offensive moralism and scare tactics, it never *once* mentions gay men or youth.

It's unclear how "excerpted" the film is from the original production, and who made the editorial choices—filmmaker Ginny Durrin or the Theatre Ensemble (who have the script credit). I suspect that what happened is an all-too-common problem: that in putting the piece together, dominant political agendas (from facilitators, TV, educators, "authorities") were internalized and reproduced by the Ensemble. Many media projects, attempting to empower the disenfranchised by giving them the means of production, have run into the same problems—those "enfranchised" end up denying their own experiences, their own authority, and say instead what they think people (usually the facilitators) want them to say. And they are certainly sincere, to the point of not recognizing their complicity in this hegemonic process.

At the same time, such an analysis runs the risk of extreme condescension, suggesting that the theatre group capitulated completely to the demands of dominant ideologies. Looking at it another way, the tape is a good example of compromised strategies going way too far. Perhaps the ensemble were consciously calculating what they thought they could get away with, not only with their authorities, but also with their peers. "Queer" content or realistic drug scenarios might jeopardize both their funding and their image. As a result, *'Til Death Do Us Part* (despite its moments of street smarts) comes off like a wannabe *Cosby* episode.[9] Politics are erased, poverty and AIDS are ignored, and ultimately the Bush/Reagan agenda is validated by the very people (Black youth) that could arguably suffer the most from the administration's murderous policies.

Stills from *Another Man*, by Youth Against Monsterz (courtesy V tape)

In stark contrast *Another Man* is a lively safe-sex music video that in five short minutes takes aim at the politics of AIDS and scores a bull's eye. Like *'Til Death Do Us Part,* it was collectively written by a group of "youth." However in this case there was no "adult" supervision, and they directed, produced, and edited it themselves (okay, some of them were in their twenties). Variously called the Mr. Tim Collective or the Anarchist Queer Collective, an ad hoc group of straight/bi/gay punks-about-town, they recruited friends at a local Toronto art college and co-op post production facility to help out with the technical aspects, and produced it on a three-figure budget. Scenes of straight and gay interracial couples under the bed covers are superimposed with the directives: "Use a condom" and "Use your imagination." Two punks make out in a bus shelter, framed by one of the forbidding just-say-no-type city-sponsored AIDS info posters. Jerry Falwell is shown spewing forth some sort of homophobic gibberish; his image is frozen and a superimposed condom is pulled over his head. A woman talks about how Canadian customs routinely censors lists of safer-sex practices featured in American gay magazines. The song which unites these disparate elements is upbeat, celebratory, and decidedly defiant.

Used in a classroom setting, this tape could instigate far-reaching discussions about safer-sex practices, homophobia, and youth sexuality. Two predictable blockades will prevent this in all but the most exemplary circumstances. School boards have never been remotely interested in independent art tapes, especially those that use the word "fuck" (once) and that adopt a freely associative, nonprescriptive (and therefore threatening) form. Secondly, even if *Another Man* ever finds its way into a classroom, all sorts of students, socialized by a homophobic and conformist culture, could easily turn against such queer anarchy, especially if the teacher was unsympathetic to the tape and the issues raised. By remaining true to its origins, the tape will be kept out of the schoolyard, where it is needed most. However, it is enjoying an active distribution life on the art circuit and through various AIDS distribution projects.

Chuck Solomon: Coming of Age and Danny

> The mass media has allowed PLWA's (with few exceptions) several severely proscribed roles, as Simon Watney has noted: the self-hating "queer" dying pitifully in a hospital bed, abandoned by the world; the dangerous "carrier" whose "irresponsibility" is hysterically condemned; and the "innocent victim" (usually a child or woman) who was "infected" by a transfusion or "carrier."[10]

Alternate portrait tapes of PWAs constitute a significant political statement unto themselves, endowing their subjects with a dignity that the mainstream (with a few exceptions) has summarily denied them. Moreover, because these tributes are often requiems, they perform a vital pedagogical function, implicitly teaching audiences a language for processing loss that our death-phobic culture has denied most of us. Diametrically opposed to the broadcast obituaries for deceased celebrities which coldly isolate the individual according to outstanding achievements, these portraits capture the subtler details that matter most to friends, families, and lovers.

Chuck Solomon: Coming of Age is perhaps typical of this genre of tapes, produced mostly within the gay community. Initially conceived simply as a document of Chuck's fortieth birthday party by independent producers Wendy Dallas and Marc Huestis, the tape cuts back and forth between the cabaret performances and moving interviews with the performers—Chuck's collaborators and friends. The founder of. Theatre Rhinoceros, San Francisco's premiere gay theater company, Solomon himself speaks with vitality of his life and work, and the difficulty of coping with the AIDS-related deaths of both his lover and brother. The huge outpouring of love and affection from the 350 assembled is extremely moving, as is Solomon's invitation to them all to attend his fiftieth birthday party. He died nine months later.

Executed from within the close personal networks of Solomon's life, this is more an intimate home-movie tribute than an "objective" (and therefore distanced) portrait. While this captures the inside of a community beautifully, it also means there are no warts showing. Bitterness, fear, and anger are all absent, despite the fact that he was one of San Francisco's more outspoken activists. Capturing his warmth, wit, and dignity, the tape memorializes the legacy he left to the city's theater community. It's impossible not to be moved by this unabashedly sentimental tribute, even though it tends to elevate him to the status of gay sainthood.

I can't quibble with the urgent collective need we all have to "honor" our dead, especially in a culture that can't deal with death. However, is it perhaps unfair that Solomon should be singled out for such a tribute when so many of the other 60,000-plus AIDS-related deaths passed unheralded? Doesn't this tribute have a responsibility to condemn the government and medical establishment for allowing Solomon and the others to die from their homophobic neglect? Obviously no one tape can bear the burden of everything that needs to be said, and these are questions that the culture, as much as the tape, must answer. By insisting on its roots as a home movie, a celebration of this alternate family supporting one another, the tape is somewhat vindicated in its tight focus and sincerity, and has found an appreciative audience throughout the gay community. [11] It has also enjoyed success in Europe, where it has been broadcast on British and Spanish TV, but so far PBS has refused to air it. Huestis thinks the problem is that it's "too gay." That PBS feels threatened by this incredibly sweet and innocent portrait of Solomon is shocking, but no surprise when you consider their appalling track record on both AIDS and gay issues. [12]

A far more demanding experimental tape, *Danny,* has so far remained marginalized on the video art circuit. Structured as an impressionistic requiem, it reconstructs a sketchy portrait of an unapologetically flagrant disco queen through layers of slides, landscapes and processed imagery. Originally Danny and producer Stashu Kybartas had planned to collaborate on a tape about his experiences with Kaposi's sarcoma, a disfiguring cancer that sometimes accompanies AIDS. However, he became sick, and moved back to his parents' home in Ohio, where he died. The tape pieces back together the fragments of what they did shoot (mostly slides), organized by Kybartas's voice-over, which speaks directly to the dead Danny.

Of all the portrait tapes I've seen, this is one of the only ones that refuses to make a narrative out of the subject's life. It refuses to justify choices, to explain Danny's lifestyle, to make effects have causes. No attempt is made by either man to sum up, to make sense of, to "understand" AIDS or death. Instead, glimpses of a "gay" lifestyle that is now almost taboo in terms of representation are offered, with a refusal of anything approaching moralism.

Danny at one point catalogues a typical weekend in his heyday: the beach, the discos, the packaging of his crotch in button-fly jeans for a night out, the drugs, the sex, the cruising. Tinged with nostalgia, this brief reminiscence subverts the traditional judgment of such "hedonism." His lifestyle, far from being the "cause" of his illness, was simply a fact, the way he and so many others lived and continue to live. A recurring disco punctuation: "I'm standing on the outside of the inside where I want to be." Stashu recounts the time they were in the studio together, taking slides of Danny's lesions, and they touched—something happened—again, with the subtlest of gestures and the most specific of stories, desire is reintroduced, into a story where traditionally it is assumed that automatic celibacy accompanies the HIV sero-positive test result.

These fragments never editorialize, either in sentimental or political terms, and it is this refusal that has prompted some unease among some straight *and* gay viewers. They would seem to prefer a more streamlined narrative, where the "dirty" ambivalences of the gay ghetto were sanitarily summed up by a safe, prescriptive conclusion. If Solomon becomes a saint, Danny remains a Judas, betraying the "respectable" gay community (wherever that is) with his kiss.

Coming of Age chose to compromise the complexity of Solomon's life, in part because it was made as a collaboration with him—not only as a celebration of his achievements and his community, but also as a way he could make a record of his thanks. *Danny* started as a collaboration between subject and producer, and became Kybartas' complicated response to the untimely death of his friend, thereby compromising its potential for a broad, popular audience. Both choices grew out of the specific lives (and deaths) of their title subjects, demonstrating a formal, political, and personal responsiveness that the mainstream media (with its unshakeable conventions) finds impossible. Both *Danny* and *Coming of Age,* as disparate as they are, speak from direct gay experience, without apology and without generalization. It is in their specific words, of sorrow, confusion, and tribute, that we begin to find our own.

Testing the Limits and *Fighting for Our Lives*

Collectively produced and released in 1987, *Testing the Limits* signaled a definitive turning point in representations of AIDS resistance. Born out of the crucible of the early ACT UP meetings (AIDS Coalition To Unleash Power, a group dedicated to fight for the social, medical and political rights of PLWAs), the tape is a freewheeling collage capturing various battlefields in the AIDS war. In its fast-packed twenty-eight minutes, it explicitly attempts a rewriting of AIDS agendas, insisting on an analysis that refuses to patiently explain or pacify. Having no time for polite requests, it passionately demands.

The speaking subjects are often on the street, in the middle of demonstrations, shouting to be heard above the chants. A rapid-fire progression of AIDS activist issues is sketched out: testing; quarantine; educating drug users to clean their works; the politics of safer sex education for target audiences; condemnations of the U.S. health care system; demands for the immediate release of promising treatments and drugs for PLWAs; and denunciations of how racism, sexism, homophobia and poverty have shaped official responses to the AIDS crisis.

Several formal strategies make *Testing the Limits* distinct from solidarity tapes of other struggles. For starters, the tape's purposefully rough look and rapid-fire pace make for a breathless viewing experience, much faster than most activist documentaries. Secondly, the collective foregrounds their active participation in the movement, both through their intimate camera angles and their rapport with their subjects. One quibble: there is an unfortunate reliance throughout on *New York Times* headlines to "prove" or "illustrate" verbal points made, despite the fact that the tape explicitly condemns mainstream coverage of the epidemic. This contradiction is never adequately addressed.

What's not apparent on the first viewing is the careful and calculated progression of issues, leading viewers through a complicated analytic framework that insists on connections but doesn't foreclose them. The tape is disturbing because it refuses to "explain" anything thoroughly, at least by the conventions of broadcast TV. Instead, its rapid succession of issues and agendas, speakers and crowds, delivers an effective and incendiary message: "Where are you in this war?" By refusing to contain any one issue through closure, *Testing the Limits* forces viewers to position themselves, picturing themselves finally (however uncomfortably) in the midst of this groundswell.

Still from *Testing the Limits*

Fighting for Our Lives, by Ellen Seidler and Patrick Dunah, operates from the opposite end of the formal spectrum. Adopting the tried-and-true conventions of broadcast documentaries, it sets out to capture the range of San Francisco's response to the AIDS crisis. Linda Hunt (of *The Year of Living Dangerously* fame) serves as interpretive BBC-type narrator, conferring a disquieting respectability on the subject. In fact, the documentary's tone is at distinct odds with its content. It talks frankly from within the gay community about political tensions between AIDS service groups, the vital role of lesbians in AIDS work, and the racism that has characterized funding and hindered the vital outreach that needs to be done in the city's Black and Latino communities. While this narrative acknowledges some contradictions, it also—by its very form—must erase or streamline others.

For instance, there is an interview with Randy Shilts, the conservative and controversial gay author of the bestselling *And the Band Played On,* an extremely egotistical and partisan version of the epidemic's history that equally blames the government, the medical establishment, *and* the gay movement for the health crisis. Shilts is allowed to speak "objectively" about the closure of the gay baths, despite his hysterical anti-sex views on the subject. [13]

We are presented with the "story" of San Francisco's response to the AIDS crisis. We are introduced to some of the issues and efforts, which are then recontained and summed up in a neat package at the "story's" conclusion. Linda Hunt assures us that they are fighting for their lives, and the *they* is very important. An inevitable result of such representational practices, it means *we* are never implicated, never involved, except as voyeurs.

This very palatable form allowed it to be broadcast as part of a series of AIDS tapes on KCET (the Los Angeles PBS affiliate) while *Testing the Limits* was rejected, despite intensive lobbying efforts on the part of the programmer. Now (and I'm not necessarily playing devil's advocate): Does this make *Fighting for Our Lives* more subversive (and hence more effective) than the latter, since its reassuring form probably encouraged straight suburban viewers to watch it, and therefore see the gay community portrayed (however voyeuristically) with some degree of subtlety and dynamism? *Testing the Limits* would no doubt alienate those same viewers—its passionate militancy would be all too easily dismissed, and switched off. Indeed, depressingly large sectors of the gay community would probably respond in the same way. The thousands of white, middle-class gay men who have achieved some measure of comfort and security would no doubt feel even more threatened than their straight counterparts by the tape's images of a multiracial grassroots movement that has taken to the streets, because the tape implicates them directly. In contrast, Linda Hunt implicitly reassures her viewers that sit-ins are only one option in a menu of choices, that all efforts are equally important. Her reassuring mediation (compromising important political issues in the process) has perhaps spurred many apolitical gays and straights to get involved in a nonradical AIDS service organization—and who's going to say that's a bad thing?

An opposite argument can also be made. *Testing the Limits* should be broadcast all over the country, precisely because it will upset and not pacify. It has in fact since been broadcast on WNET, the PBS affiliate in New York. AIDS is *very* upsetting and *very* present—arguably (polemically), any documentary that isn't as upsetting as the crisis is shouldn't be broadcast. Secondly, there is a large audience desperate for these very taboo images of activism—gays and straights of all ages and races who would be immensely empowered and politicized by such incendiary representations. Conservative gay men *should* feel threatened, and *should* be shaken out of their complacency. Thirdly, broadcast distribution is hardly the ultimate outlet. Community screenings around the country may not deliver the same numbers, but their social status as communal events makes for another vital sort of "effectiveness." At a recent Toronto AIDS forum, organized by AIDS Action Now, *Testing the Limits* began the evening, followed by speakers on a variety of subjects. In the ensuing public discussion, audience members repeatedly referred to the tape: "I really agree with what that woman said about dental dams . . . " It became clear that for much of the audience, the tape constituted the same direct authority as the live speakers, addressing issues that would otherwise not have been raised.

Effectiveness and Strategic Compromise

This recurring question of effectiveness is obviously and most importantly contextual, dependent not just on audiences and their politics, but also on their response to media form. For instance, youth may intuitively respond more positively to the anarchic sensibility of *Another Man,* than the conventional histrionics of *'Til Death Do Us Part.* However, conditioned to validate didactic object lessons in what to think (especially around issues of gender roles and sexual preference), they might (at least, in front of their peers) claim to prefer the conservative politics of the latter. Gay audiences addicted to *Dynasty* are no doubt more comfortable with the sentimental narrative of *Coming of Age* than the disjunctive subtexts of *Danny.* AIDS organizers, even those involved in the issues that ACT UP champions, have at times complained that *Testing the Limits* is too fragmented, too inconclusive, that it doesn't tell a story, and have programmed something more conventional (like *Fighting for Our Lives*) instead.

Each of the above choices, opting for the reassuring tape over the demanding one, presumes that audiences prefer to be passively entertained instead of challenged. This condescending truism is rampant in production and distribution circles (partly because of conservatism, partly because it contains a grain of truth), and AIDS artists who want to reach audiences take it very seriously. Two contradictory polemics express the poles of this debate: "AIDS is a war, there's no time for artsy debates about formal issues. We have to make clear, effective propaganda that reaches as many people as possible!" versus "AIDS is a war, not just of medicine and politics but of representations—we must reject dominant media discourses and forms in favor of a radical new vocabulary that deconstructs their agendas and reconstructs ours!"

Most artists, consciously or unconsciously, negotiate their way between these two positions, attempting to meet audiences halfway. Each of the six tapes in these "case studies" made a series of strategic compromises, negotiating the difficult terrain of "effectiveness" in six different ways, each according to their particular context. *Danny* and *Chuck Solomon: Coming of Age* prioritized the very personal voices of their subjects over other concerns, and ended up making works that speak to audiences who never knew the title characters. *Another Man* and *Testing the Limits* used inventive versions of seductive media tactics to "sell" their radical political agendas, and succeeded in reinventing how we imagine representations of safer sex and activism respectively. *'Til Death Do Us Part* and *Fighting for Our Lives* prioritized conventional moralism and conventional documentary values respectively in an effort to reach larger audiences, and ended up selling out their subjects—which in turn accounts for their relative distribution success.

The desperate need for alternate AIDS media images remains as pressing today as it was in 1981. Whole subjects and issues have still not been addressed. At the same time, the rich and energetic video subculture has laid a firm foundation for (hopefully) hundreds of new tapes. Each of these artists will in turn have to negotiate their own set of strategic compromises, each interrogating their own aesthetic and political responses to this question of "effectiveness." Our critical response must be even more tough *and* flexible, responding in detail to the particular context that each tape comes from, refusing the temptation of any single programmatic prescription. Like current wisdom concerning treatments for HIV infection and the opportunistic diseases that can accompany AIDS, we must recognize that this representational war will only be won when we select and combine, appropriate to each case and context, a variety of "cures."

Notes

1. For a complete list of alternate tapes and films on AIDS, contact: The Media Network, 121 Fulton St., New York, NY 10038 (212-619-3455).

2. Throughout this essay I will sometimes use "tapes" and "video" as a short form for speaking about both video and film—a bit of revenge against decades of thoughtless critics who say "film" when they mean both video and film. This "festival" of twenty-five tapes was presented at A Space, 183 Bathurst St., Toronto, Canada M5T 2R7 (416-363-3227). A modest program is available.

3. For an excellent critique of representations of AIDS in the mass media, see: Simon Watney, *Policing Desire: Pornography, AIDS and the Media* (Minneapolis: University of Minnesota Press, 1987).

4. Hans Magnus Enzensberger, "Constituents of a Theory of the Media," *Video Culture* (Rochester: Visual Studies Workshop, 1986), 97.

5. Phrase coined by Tom Waugh. See Tom Waugh, ed., *Show Us Life* (Metuchen: Scarecrow Press, 1984), xiv.

6. This 60-minute compilation, *Angry Initiatives, Defiant Strategies*, was one of sixteen weekly specials satellite delivered to over 300 cable access stations around the U.S. in the spring of 1988. Other subjects included Central America, Latino images, and disarmament. For more information: Deep Dish TV, 339 Lafayette St., New York, NY 10012 (212-420-9045).

7. AIDS education tapes for youth audiences include: *AIDS in Your School, The AIDS Movie, AIDS-Wise, No Lies, AIDS: Answers for Young People, AIDS: Can I Get It?, AIDS: Changing the Rule, AIDS: Everything You and Your Family Need to Know, AIDS: Questions and Answers, AIDS: The Classroom Conflict, AIDS: The Facts of Life, All of Us and AIDS, Condom Education in Grad Schools, Sex, Drugs & AIDS. . . .* The list goes on and on.

8. See especially: Martha Gever, "Pictures of Sickness: Stuart Marshall's *Bright Eyes,*" and Douglas Crimp, "How to Have Promiscuity in an Epidemic," in *AIDS: Cultural Analysis, Cultural Activism, October,* issue 43 (Cambridge: MIT Press, 1987), 109, 237.

9. *The HIV Anti-Body Test for the Black Community,* designed as an educational tape for anonymous HIV test sites in San Francisco's Black community, similarly uses a dramatic form, but its content is completely nonjudgmental about both sex and drugs. The information is clear and engaging, especially when it stresses the politics of testing—unfortunately, it too assumes a straight audience, and never once mentions gay sex.

10. Simon Watney, "Common Knowledge," *Art and Crisis: AIDS and the Gay Politic, High Performance,* issue 36 (Los Angeles: 1986), 44.

11. Huestis and Dallas organized a forty-two-city tour of the film and four others in the summer of 1988, accompanying the already legendary Names Project, a quilt commemorating those who have died.

12. Gever, "Pictures of Sickness," 111-12.

13. For a summation of Shilts's conservative, anti-sex views, see Crimp, "Promiscuity in an Epidemic," *October,* 238-246.

The Artist as Maker

Native Makers Alliance

Hachivi Edgar Heap of Birds
Joe Dale Tate Nevaquaya
Patricia Mousetail Russell
Richard Ray Whitman

The Native Maker believes in the optimistic circle of life. To offer, share, contribute, teach and create—these actions serve to foster constructive change and renewal for the earth.

Makers thrive throughout native cultures all over the world. Expressing one's self against all odds and forms of repression, Makers shall forever find it a necessity to accept the challenge to comment and create.

To form the future is the duty we entrust to these artists/tribal citizens. This future is built upon the quest for economic fairness, ethnic understanding, and respect for personal individuality.

Hachivi Edgar Heap of Birds

Hachivi returned to the Cheyenne and Arapaho reservation area in 1980 after studies at the Royal College of Art, London, Tyler School of Art, Philadelphia, and University of Kansas. Headsman of the Tsistsistas (Cheyenne) Elk Warrior society, and a follower of both the Keeper of the Sacred Arrows and the Tsistsistas Sun Dance Priests, Hachivi is a caretaker of the tribal ceremonial ways.

Hachivi is associate professor of painting at University of Oklahoma. His drawings, paintings, video and public messages have been exhibited at Orchard Gallery, Northern Ireland; Documenta 8, West Germany; Museum of Modern Art, NYC; Exit Art, NYC; and Walker Art Center, Minneapolis, MN.

UTERINE HATS

DEATH FROM THE TOP

American Policy

On the dawn of November 29, 1864 after the Tsistsistas (Cheyenne) had relocated along Sand Creek, with government permission to supposedly safe lands, a brutal attack was executed against our peaceful village. Every single Native in the camp was murdered or captured by the United States armed forces.

Many Tsistsistas men, women and children were slaughtered while running from their lodges and as they attempted to escape up the creek bed. Without weapons, many of the Cheyenne who had survived up to this point were cornered by the soldiers up against the earth wall of the creek. They hurriedly dug holes in the mud and sand in order to hide from the lethal rifle shots. Finally these remaining men, women, and children were murdered in their holes.

After the killing was complete, America's monstrous soldiers found sport in cutting open the bodies of the dead Tsistsistas women. These soldiers feverishly sought to destroy the Native womb. They were intent upon ripping away the uterus of the Cheyenne, taking away the once loving home of our future infants. After seizing the wombs from the silent bodies, the soldiers paraded each uterus upon a stick and then fashioned the female organs into ornaments for their hats.

In retrospect these ghastly actions are not simple American history nor outcomes of the "Indian Wars." They have become the foundation for the economic devastation of Native people and for the modern creation of Colorado, Kansas, and Oklahoma.

After the Sand Creek and the Washita massacres and the burning of these villages,

RELOCATE YOUR
DESTROY SPORT

American Policy

the Tsistsistas tribe to this day struggles to recover and participate in non-Indian America. The current Native struggles are ones of economies and lands. The atrocities that were committed by the white government and the economic unfairness that persists form a racist attitude. This attitude mandates that *what has befallen the Native America of today is not and need not be the best of situations.* While in contrast, white America certainly claims the best of life for themselves. It is theirs for the enjoyment, and they alone occupy the "top." Furthermore a sharing of white people's accumulated or stolen privileges with Native Americans is not forthcoming.

Sharing what the earth gives and what one has created is a firm unspoken *Native Policy* throughout these tribal lands. To secure privilege, to hoard, and not to share the means to develop a comfortable livelihood with Native Americans and other people of color in this nation is truly an *American Policy.*

Native expressions in the arts today can no longer remain only cultural window dressing for America. Native artists must cease to entertain the white notion of the romantic and mythical Indian. Today as Native artists we must seriously commit an element of our movement to strongly challenge the grave social imbalance of *American Policy.*

Edgar Heap of Birds
Headsman of the Elk Warrior Society
Cheyenne Arapaho Nation

T'soyanaha / Richard Ray (Whitman)

T'soyanaha/Richard Ray (Whitman) is of the Yuchi tribe, which is enrolled as part of the Creek Nation, but is also of Pawnee descent. He is from Gypsy, Oklahoma, and studied at the Institute of American Indian Arts (Santa Fe), the Oklahoma School of Photography, and the California Institute of the Arts. In addition to his photography he frequently works in multi-media, painting, and as an actor. His exhibitions include the C.E.P.A. Gallery/SUNY Buffalo; Light Work/ Community Dark Room, Syracuse; American Indian Community House Gallery, New York; several university galleries in Oklahoma and several exhibits at the Individual Artists of Oklahoma.

Statement

Richard Ray Whitman

At times Native artists have been too accommodating or conciliatory, and have turned their backs on commenting about our present-day sociopolitical economic realities. Too often our outrage against the true Native reality is numbed by the potential success of art marketing strategies. Some Native artists have decided to select only a small piece of Native existence to make art about, having decided that to challenge the dominant white culture is not the "Indian way."

A lot of times I hear them say, "It is not the Indian way to involve yourself in a form of protest, to show these kinds of political realities of today." So I talked to some of my elders, and they say quite the contrary. It *is* the Indian way to be involved in defining who we are in the universe, to be concerned about our identity, and how we go into the future.

Pawn shop calling for your turquoise . . .

Pawn shop calling for your turquoise . . .
Plasma center calling in the name of humanity
Supplement your income, bonus veins . . .
     Come dance on concrete and be happy . . .
The little boy said there was "A World for Indians"
but it was cancelled . . .

Richard Ray Whitman

I am 1,000 and 1 scratches

I am 1,000 and 1 scratches
on everyone's favorite '49 album

I am the mad-sniffer of instant reality
Bagging is my game. . . . gold my color

I am the No. 1 campus runner
My sister is the sweetheart Ball Queen
And my brother is a wino

I am all these . . . always changing
from nothing to someone . . .

Richard Ray Whitman

"Hey Chief. . . . "

Being ourselves mercilessly
while depredations against our own
blood and flesh go on endlessly. . . .

Drinking ourselves sober
until we could only feel pain. . . .

We survive on any terms
but we live. . . . we live. . . .

Not as
privileged subjects of an anthropologist
but as children of the sun. . . .

Richard Ray Whitman

Joe Dale Tate Nevaquaya

Joe Dale Tate Nevaquaya is Yuchi and Comanche from Gypsy, Oklahoma. He studied at the Institute of American Indian Arts in Santa Fe and the University of Albuquerque. His visual work has been exhibited in *We The People* and at the Independent Artists of Oklahoma, Five Civilized Tribes Museum and the I.A.I.A. Spring Arts Festival. His poems have been anthologized in *The Clouds Threw This Light: Contemporary Native American Poetry, Thirty-Seven Oklahoma Poets,* and *What About War?* His work has also been published in *Contact II, Blue Smoke, We The People,* and *Awekekon.*

DE DEZHEHEN

DE DEZHEHEN
YAH SEKAWNH

DE AAHH
DE AAHH CHAH
DE KENH WONH
DE KENH WOHN

GHE DE BAH
DONH BAH FAH

AGAHEH NENHZEH
AGAHEH NENHZEH

No Interpretation / No Translation: Dreaming of My Grandmother's Thumbmark

Joe Dale Tate Nevaquaya

There are no true English translations and interpretations of the names and places that we are as Yuchi people. My grandmother's name is and was Ah-lau-Quan, for which there is no translation in the English tongue. I was raised an artist/poet by my elderly grandmother, a full-blood Yuchi, who did not speak, read, or write in the English language. She did not attend a formal educational institution but she not only managed to get by in her life, she thrived. Her contacts of a business nature were concluded with the act of pressing her thumbmark to whatever transaction she had. I feel there was more power in her thumb than in history and all its arsenal of oppression. We live through our expressions, not the English version of our words and deeds. Ours cannot be interpreted or translated.

Detail from woman's dress

The Medicine Wheel

Patricia Mousetail Russell

Cheyenne women own the right to make the Medicine Wheel design. Our prophet gave it to the women. The woman is the one who communicates with these spirits through carrying out certain ceremonies. Through these ceremonies, a woman earns the right to bead this design on the Sacred Tipi. Then she shares the design with the men, who can wear it on their blankets. She has the right to give the design to her husband, her son, her grandson, or her brother. The man only possesses it after she has made it and gives it to him—first, he must tell a war story at the Sacred Tipi.

Patricia Mousetail Russell

Patricia Mousetail Russell is a self-taught artist dedicated to preserving a unique art form and the folklore of her Cheyenne heritage. A native Oklahoman, she is the daughter of a Cheyenne tribal chief. Her work has toured as part of "Lost and Found Traditions," an exhibit of the Native American Federation of Arts, as well as with the "Makers" exhibit. She conducts workshops through the State Arts Council of Oklahoma Artist-in-Residence program.

Detail from child's cradle board

The Flag—and Where I Come From

My grandmother told me where our family comes from—from Chief Black Kettle's village which was massacred on the Washita River in November 1868. My grandmother's family, members of the Hair Rope band, camped with Black Kettle before General Custer's cavalry attacked. The night before, the coyotes came close to the camp and cried. At that time we still had some men who could understand what they were saying. They said for everyone to pack up and go because the soldiers were coming and everyone in the camp would be gone before the sun came up. Tough Feathers and his wife Menoweo were in the camp. Menoweo was a sister—perhaps a first-cousin white man's way—to Black Kettle.

Black Kettle had been given an American flag to show he had made peace. He refused to leave because he believed the flag would be respected. Some others decided to stay, including those too old to get away. Menoweo refused to leave her brother. She said if Black Kettle was going to be killed, she wanted to die there with him. Her husband said he wouldn't leave her and would die there, too. They decided to send away their two sons, Tough Feathers, who was nine, and Magpie, who was eight. They packed food for the boys and sent them away with ten horses. The boys were crying and didn't want to leave. But their parents told them that they had to go and carry on their blood. They said never to come back to this place, no matter what happened, but to go on. Then they whipped their horses to make them run away.

The two brothers traveled several days, often crying, before they found their relations north of there.

Tough Feathers was my grandmother's father. He became our tribe's Arrow Keeper, which is our highest priest. When the government built the first Indian houses, he still lived outside his house in the tipi. My grandmother told me to respect the flag because it belongs to the Cheyennes now. The white soldiers ran over their flag when they killed Black Kettle and our other people. They dragged it on the ground. Our people were the ones who held up the flag and respected it, so now it belongs to us.

Art of Liberation:
A Vision of Freedom

Elizam Escobar

The *political* is found in the least likely of places, covered by multiple layers of ideological counterfeiting and acculturation. Our daily lives, our dreams, love, death, and even our bodies are all spheres of "invisible" yet intense political and human dramas that take place behind the "visible" political struggle. This inner struggle is, above all, more painful and more real. For it is from *inside* that we must decide our real needs, both material and spiritual. Art of liberation springs from this perspective, recognizing the power of the imagination's struggle. Throughout history, the imagination's struggle against prohibitions based on fear and ignorance has been one of the leading political processes that pushes forward the liberation of the human spirit by rescuing and creating new territories of freedom.

Elizam Escobar

Elizam Escobar is a painter, poet, writer, and a political activist in the movement for an independent and socialist Puerto Rico. Sentenced to sixty-eight years for his participation in the clandestine armed struggle for the national liberation of Puerto Rico, he has been in prison since 1980.

I have been active in the struggle for Puerto Rican national liberation since the '60s. From the socialist-Marxist perspective, I have simultaneously engaged in political-direct[1] as well as art/cultural work in support of this struggle, but not always with the same intensity or understanding.

In my "first period" I separated "personal" work—my paintings—from more "public" works—political illustrations, propaganda, caricatures, etc. Both activities were done under the dictates of my ideological assumptions. Nevertheless, there were always elements that would completely or relatively escape the dictates of my "ideology." Thematic elements drawn from my particular experiences exposed me to conflicts between what was supposed to be and what actually was, creating tensions that were contained by oneiric images (political monsters, doubts repressed by ideology, etc.). Formal elements, devalued by socialist realism and other "realist" aesthetics also escaped.

The "second period" began when I moved from Puerto Rico to New York, and was defined by an almost total exclusion of painting due to the demands of my job (schoolteacher), my political-direct work, and my mixed feelings about art. I was under the influence of a politics of "art is useless unless it is for direct propaganda purposes." My work was limited almost exclusively to political caricatures for the party publications. (Not a bad thing.)

In my "third period," I made an almost about-face toward "personal" painting, but this time working as a "professional" artist for different cultural institutions, where I combined teaching art with learning other art techniques. At that point, I was seriously dealing with the fundamental question of the relative autonomy and the specificity of the theory and praxis of art (i.e., that art has its own "rules" within a space that is its own but always in relation to all other levels or spheres of "reality," so to speak), not out of an academic or abstract drive but as a result of an accumulation of experiences. Both my political and artistic commitment were more intense than ever.

In 1980, I was arrested, together with ten other Puerto Rican *independentistas*, and accused of seditious conspiracy and participation in the Puerto Rican armed clandestine movement for national liberation. Since then I have been in prison. Here, my "fourth period" is taking place, and it is from the perspective of these experiences that I consider the visionary role of the artist.

"Odiseo Paranoico," Elizam Escobar, 1988 (48" x 72" acrylic on canvas)

The Structures of Simulation

We live in societies divided into social classes, where there is no true consensus, only the fictitious and spurious consensus determined by the ruling classes. Electoral processes are national epics manipulated in the name of the people to legitimize social control and coercion. To resolve these contradictions we must assume the class struggle in all its diverse forms and confront the questions of Power. Only then will the immense majority of excluded, oppressed, and exploited obtain the real power.

But we cannot wait for the day when the majority will rule in order to bring forward the structures needed for building a free, just, egalitarian, and non-classist society. We must build within the ruins and the hostilities of present conditions by creating transitional alternatives now. We must build socioeconomic, political, and cultural structures that are controlled by those struggling for change and the communities they serve. These structures, "schools" for discussing all these problems, will put into practice the notion that only by confronting the reality of subjection can we begin to be free and to create an art of liberation that frees people from the illusions perpetrated by dominant culture.

The contemporary State creates structures of simulation. These are indispensable both to cover the real nature of the system and to show tolerance and acceptance for dissidents. Furthermore, they not only create their own structures, but they obligate us to create our own.

For example, the ruling classes create the simulation of cultural democracy (the illusion of real political power, equal opportunity and the freedom of difference in order to make others believe that they have a real participation in the cultural space) through the mass culture and the media. They need "false enemies" to wage relatively inoffensive and limited "cultural wars" that end up strengthening the social body's health.[2] One example is what happened to the spontaneous street graffiti expression: from symbolic exchange it became another commodity with status exchange value. In Puerto Rico under colonialism, popular art is institutionalized and becomes a folkloric domestication of the people's unconscious. Some of the Left's culture of resistance has been depoliticized by obligating artists to make false choices between a sort of one-dimensional domesticated "nationalist art" and mass culture. This way, artists either turn their "criticism" against an abstract enemy or they wear themselves out by contributing an "original" aesthetic to the status quo (but always in the name of "Puerto Ricanness") because they fear the worst evil, that of U.S. statehood—to the benefit of the colonial bourgeois lackeys. Part of the Puerto Rican independence movement reproduces itself as a simulation model through this "cultural nationalism." At the same time, artists are domesticated by continuous government subsidies, status, fame, wealth, and by aspiring to national titles, while those who persist to the contrary, whose politics are to unveil the whole system of simulation are censored even by some orthodox Left publications who want to reduce the debates to their own political good, that is, they won't allow dissent within the dissent.

Paradoxically, art (as the power of imagination), the only "true" simulation, is the one that can lead us to the *understanding* (not necessarily to the resolution) of that other "false" simulation.

"El heresiarca" ("The Heresiarch"), Elizam Escobar, 1988 (48" x 72" acrylic on canvas)

The Culture of Fear

But in order to liberate art from the nets of political power, we, the artists, must first liberate ourselves from the nets of the *culture of fear,* and the inferiority/superiority complex we have in our dealings at the political-direct level. If art is to become a force for social change it must take its strength from the *politics of art*, art's own way of affecting both the world and the political-direct. It must take strength from that specific manner in which our praxis expresses the aspirations of the people, the political collective unconscious, the contradictions, etc., through a symbolic language. But the *politics of art* will happen only if the power of the imagination is able to create a symbolic relationship between those who participate, the artwork, and the concrete world; and then always understanding the work of art's sovereignty (or relative autonomy) in relation to concrete reality.

What is important is not the didactic pretensions that we possess the solutions, but the idiosyncratic ways in which works of art can bring out the real aspects of the human condition in particular and specific contexts or experiences. Art is, from this perspective, an encounter where we have the possibility for a symbolic, political, and real exchange.

Since our forms are also used to deliberately appeal to people for political-direct goals, it is logical that at some point these strategies become dominant and in conflict with the internal problems (the how) of art. If we can understand how the political affects and shapes everything else, and the difference between the specific practices of art and the practices of the political-direct, then the artist would be clearer on how to decide his/her strategies, sources, themes, aesthetics, etc. When it comes to the theory and praxis of art, the *political* is beyond any "political (direct) issues."

Most U.S. "Political Art," as I have come to understand it, wants to present political-direct issues through images, in a clear and communicative form, irrespective of the medium, the style, or the aesthetic selection. It presupposes that one can predict the kind of political effect a work of art is going to have. Thus the important thing is the message. This emphasis on the message is akin to Marshall McLuhan's naive optimism "the medium is the message," and finds its extreme in the inversion of McLuhan's dictum: "The message is the message." Both are founded in the arbitrariness of the sign, which artificially separates and reunites everything in terms of a signifier (in this case, the medium) and a signified (here, the message). The political and the symbolic are de-politicized by the imposition of a code that comes directly from ideology since as Jean Baudrillard argues, "every attempt to surpass the political economy of the sign that takes its support from one of its constituent elements is condemned to reproduce its arbitrary character."[3]

In this way the participants are excluded from creating meanings other than those already transmitted by the message since once the signal is sent either you accept it or reject it. There is no need to search for more. In this respect the *art of the message* shares common ground with the *formal theory of communication*[4] which goes like this: transmitter (encoder)—message—receiver (decoder). One speaks, the other doesn't. The message is assumed to contain information that is legible and univocal, based on a pre-established and rationalized code composed of signs. Two terms are artificially reunited by an objectified content called message. The formula has a formal coherence that assures it as the only *possible* schema for communication, since a code names everything in terms of itself and anything else that is not "designed" or "adapted" to the agency of the code cannot be utilized since it won't work in this schema. The problem then is that this structure denies the ambivalence of exchange; the reciprocity or antagonism between two distinct interlocutors. As soon as ambivalence shows up the structure collapses, since there is no code for ambivalence, and without code no more encoder, no more decoder.

I am not saying that U.S. "Political Art" is equal to this over-obsession with "communication," but that it is constricted to the code if its intentions are mainly to present a message. Thus, anything that is not in the sign form is ambivalent and it is from ambivalence (i.e. the impossibility of distinguishing respective separated terms and to positivize them as such)[5] that any symbolic exchange (allusions through images, discourse, objects, etc.) can emerge. On the other hand, this impasse is, of course, disturbing, since we cannot absolutely do away with the signific code.

The ironic dilemma is that we have to make use of this code though we realize that it reduces and abstracts the irreducible experience of that which we call "liberation" (or "freedom," "desires," "needs," etc.). It is the all-too-familiar situation where words (like "liberation," "political," "freedom of expression") take command over the real concrete experience and are used to legitimize and justify a practice or a state of things. There is a brutal difference between "freedom" as exchange-sign-value or slogan of ideologies and abstractions, and the real freedom of experience—one that is as necessary as it is terrible. Even under extreme repression, individual freedom is unavoidable as we must keep on exercising our decisions and responsibilities. Here again art comes to the rescue, because it has the inventive power and wit to deride, deceive, and betray censorship as well as self-censorship.

But how one is going to affect others is another matter, since it is almost impossible to know how an artwork will be taken. The effect is always diverse, contingent, and unpredictable. Whether this ambivalence is richer than a clear-cut message is for others to decide. But the important thing is that an artist must reestablish an element of confidence through his/her intentions of being as honest as possible and as consistent in his/her views as convictions allow. In this sense a "solitary voice" is as strong as a collective one.

Works of art are provocations, but in order for an artist to be provocative she/he first has to have true vocation, that is, true dedication to her/his art and to those who have been reduced to invisibility. It is from there that art cannot only obtain relevancy but also can transcend its immediate references.

The political aspect of art thus is to confront all of reality, without ideological permissions and through its own means. In order to discover our real needs we must be incredulous about what we are told and why we believe it. We must re-find the internal relationship between human desires and aspirations and human necessity, but in a new way. We must put into question any philosophical system or form of knowledge that claims to be the only and absolute truth. To that Marxist thought of freedom ("freedom is the knowledge (or recognition) of necessity") I add a concept of art: *art is the necessity of freedom.*

Art, Prison, and Liberation

Twenty-five centuries ago, when Socrates was incarcerated, he wrote his first and only poems. Ever after, the experience has been repeated. In prison, many non-artists, men and women of action and thought who never saw art or poetry as important or "useful," have engaged in some sort of creative expression. Art has come through prison. But also through art, prison has come to the outside; many poets, writers, and painters have had some essential experiences in prisons or other places of internment, and many others have become writers or artists in prison. Certainly, art usually comes to the rescue of those who have to confront these conditions at one point in their lives, people who otherwise may never have done much or anything for the defense or estimation of art. Art demands certain introspection, solitude, and abandonment; and certain confrontation with the self and death; that is, themes that are usually repugnant to "revolutionaries" and "practical" people unless it has to do with heroism or the glorification of a personality. Therefore, it is no surprise that adversity and forced solitude are able to liberate that "obscure" region of the imagination.

In prison life, there is—consciously or not—a constant and extreme interaction between the pleasure principle and the reality principle (for example, the realization that in politics as in love one must learn how to wait), much sublimination/desublimination, daydreaming, hope/cynicism, disillusionment, anger, unreality, skepticism, repression, censorship, and hypocrisy. All this shapes one's life and art. We are penetrated as much by the means of communication as people on the outside; sometimes more, because of our encloistering and lack of direct outside contact. This combination of suppression and diversion keeps prisoners as apathetic consumers and participants in a vicious circle. The human condition, in a state of extreme control and intensity, distorted to the most complete absurdity: either life is only a simulacrum (the art of the living death) or only through simulation are you able to survive.

There are exceptions, but the final balance is dehumanization, a waste of human lives. Cheap slave labor, and the continuation of criminal activity through other means and under different circumstances, are what characterize the "rehabilitation shop" of a society that is itself in need of radical transformation. The decadence of this society is displayed in its prisons through a spectacle of extreme collective madness. To "liberate" this experience through art is a responsibility to others.

Prison has reconfirmed to me the great importance of art in our lives because the deep reflection and the intense involvement that art requires help us to better understand the real necessities and the true meanings of freedom, for the individual as well as the collective. And to fight for that truth, to defend that truth, art also becomes a weapon. A weapon not only because one can create meaning for one's own existence or inspire others to continue the struggle. But simply because one can understand better the intrinsic relationship between the visions coming through the praxis of art and those unveiled aspects of the too-much-rationalized and arbitrary aspects of our ideologies, as well as our daily mechanical rituals and common nonsense. My own experience of repression expressed through art can relate to other general human experiences of repression and exclusion better than, let's say, if I start to think through my "ideological eyes." Art must spring from real life.

If art becomes theoretical discourse, *that* is also a necessary weapon. To theorize art directly from the praxis of art is a necessity in opposition to those who would like to keep art as inoffensive "aesthetics" or as mere echoes of the political-direct. And since some people would like to reduce art to a slogan of metaphysical proportions, one must always make the distinction between the art of propaganda, publicity, or design; and art as an act of liberation. The fundamental distinction is that an art of liberation can neither be a model nor a specific aesthetic or style. It is a concept and an attitude with no specific formulations, only that it must be open to any strategy that can help liberate art (and through art, people) from the dictatorship of the logic, politics, and metaphysics of the sign.

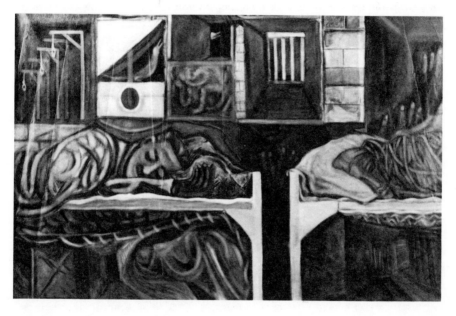

"La tortura del sueño" ("The Torture of the Dream"), Elizam Escobar, 1988 (48"x 72" acrylic on canvas)

Art of Liberation

To me, art is the best argument for talking about freedom and about necessity when one does not separate the body from the spirit. In my experience I have learned more about politics through art than through politics. And by *art* here I mean all the arts and their discourses—and all the ways in which the symbolic and the power of the imagination influence the political-direct and help us to better understand social reality.

I do not express this with blind enthusiasm. I have come to suspect all those who depend on and are moved only by enthusiasm. So when I say that I believe in the fundamental role of art in life—to provoke, to provide a critical outlook, a paradoxical reassurance of our common humanity—I am not implying that this is a universal, shared judgment. Nor am I saying that art should conquer the world. It is enough for me to be conquered by art and to be able to let it go wherever it must go. So my bet on art is my bet on life. It is my bet on the possibility of linkage between the political struggle and the struggle for survival in a hostile environment. I am not referring merely to prison per se, but to all those environments created by the prison of social systems, in the name of the people and freedom, as well as by the prison of "communication." Political awareness makes us confront all that reality. It makes us both assault the status quo and critically inspect ourselves.

Art is an extension of life, and if you have artists whose politics are insubornable, committed, and uncompromised, then they become as strengthening and inspiring to others, artists and non-artists, as art is to life.

Notes

1. The *political* is ubiquitous in today's world, but its more pure form is when you engage *directly* in the struggles for change and power. Tactics and strategies involve who does or does not exert power, who has the right to decide for society: to lead, prescribe, normatize, control, and manage the social reality. So for the purpose of making a differentiation between this more specific aspect, I would call this one the political-direct.
2. See Roger Bartra, *Las redes imaginarias del poder político* (México, D.F.: Ediciones Era, 1981).
3. Jean Baudrillard, *For a Critique of the Political Economy the Sign* (St. Louis, MO: Telos Press, 1981), 160.
4. Based on Roman Jakobsen and criticized by Baudrillard.
5. Example: "The Sun: The vacation sun no longer retains anything of the collective symbolic function it had among the Aztecs, the Egyptians, etc. It no longer has that ambivalence of a natural force—life and death, beneficent and murderous—which it had in primitive cults or still has in peasant labor. The vacation sun is a completely positive sign, the absolute source of happiness and euphoria, and as such it is significantly opposed to non-sun (rain, cold, bad weather)." Baudrillard, 98.

Art and Prison: Elizam Escobar

For much of the past ten years Elizam Escobar has painted and written from behind prison walls, serving a sixty-eight-year sentence for seditious conspiracy and related activity. On April 4, 1980, he was captured, together with other Puerto Rican men and women fighting for the liberation of Puerto Rico. The government accused them of belonging to the FALN, the Puerto Rican Armed Forces for National Liberation. They immediately declared that they were combatants in an anti-colonial war against the United States government which illegally occupies their homeland. As they viewed U.S. colonial authority over Puerto Rico illegal, they believed it their right to combat that illegal authority by any means necessary, including armed struggle.

Their views consequently led them to claim the status of prisoners of war, rejecting the authority of the U.S. courts over them. Thus, when the government (state of Illinois and federal) indicted them and put them on trial as though they were criminals, Elizam and his comrades refused to participate in the trials, which they saw as criminalizing their legitimate political struggle for self-determination—every nation's right under international law.

The government, of course, conducted the trials in their absence. Creating a hysterical anti-terrorist atmosphere, the government obtained guilty verdicts in spite of the paucity of evidence against most of those charged.

The hysteria carried over to the prisons, which now hold fourteen Puerto Rican prisoners of war, all of whom are classified as maximum custody prisoners, in spite of their exemplary conduct in the face of ten years of harassment, assault, isolation, and castigation.

When he was moved to the federal prison system, Escobar painted prolifically at Federal Correctional Institution (FCI) Oxford, Wisconsin. Artists and supporters in nearby Chicago organized a national tour of his work, "Art as an Act of Liberation," and published an accompanying catalogue. The show opened in Chicago in November of 1986, and within one week the Bureau of Prisons packed Escobar off to FCI El Reno, Oklahoma, where he was unable to paint for a full year. "We determined that El Reno was better able to provide the type of security and supervision necessary while still providing programs and services," said one BOP administrator, in spite of the fact that El Reno had no room for Escobar or his belongings, no art program, nowhere to store art supplies, and no place to paint.

He was able to resume painting in December of 1987 only because of a vigorous campaign waged by the art community and the independence movement. Escobar continues to paint and to write poetry, theoretical essays, and articles through which he seeks to promote a debate on the role of art and politics. He is currently held at FCI El Reno, No. 88969-024, Colorado Unit No. 2, Post Office Box 1500, El Reno, Oklahoma 73036.

—Jan Susler

The Writer and Artistic Freedom

Margaret Randall
Interview by James A. Miller

Miller: From 1961 to 1984 you lived in various societies undergoing revolutionary transformation: Mexico, Cuba, Nicaragua. Tell us something about the nature of artistic freedom as you experienced it in these societies.

Randall: In 1961 I was a young, struggling writer living in New York City, a woman, a single mother. I didn't have a college degree. I worked at odd jobs—I worked in the garment district, I worked as a model, as a waitress, a secretary—to support myself and my son. My basic drive in life was to write; I knew I wanted to be a writer and all of my energies went into that. I had begun to read my poetry in New York at the Deux Maggots and some of the cafés, and to publish in the incipient little magazines of that era. I had just broken into that world—not the big-time publishing world, but the world of writers who talked to one another. Most of us were out of the beat tradition or the Black Mountain tradition.

When I went to Mexico, I discovered a whole wealth of writing; young literature in a language I already knew, that I had been completely unaware of. I fell in with the young poets in Mexico City, some of whom were from the States, some from

Margaret Randall

Margaret Randall is a writer, photographer, teacher, and political activist whose most recent books are *Memory Says Yes, This is About Incest, Albuquerque: Coming Back to the USA,* and *The Shape of Red: Insider/Outsider Reflections* (with Ruth Hubbard). She is currently working on her first novel.

James A. Miller

James Miller is asssociate professor of English and director of the American Studies Program at Trinity College, Hartford, Connecticut. His articles and reviews have appeared in *The Nation, Zeta, The Year Left* and *Callaloo.*

Mexico, Peru, Columbia, Nicaragua. As we began to read one another, our big concern was that we knew nothing about each other's work, each other's thematic concerns, stylistic concerns, or craft concerns. We didn't even know who our mentors were. They had never read William Carlos Williams or Ezra Pound, we had never read Cesar Vallejo or Pablo Neruda. And so a couple of us created a magazine called *El Corno Emplumado* (*The Plumed Horn*), committed to building a bridge between both cultures. Struggling with that magazine for eight years opened up a whole world to me.

One of my first discoveries in that world had a great deal to do with artistic freedom. Those of us north of the border, of the Rio Grande, in North America (which we, of course, called America) had been born and bred to believe that poetry, art in general, was somehow beyond any kind of political or social concern. It's not that I'm saying that as North Americans we don't have that heritage, but those of my class and/or ethnicity in my generation were not aware of it. We were ivory-tower artists. In Mexico, these young poets, all of them, the best of them, were vitally concerned with what was happening in their countries, and their work reflected that. There was also no sense that one had to write about those things only. One could write about love, death, fear, land, nature, or revolutionary struggle; and it was all perfectly acceptable grist for the creative mill.

The second thing that really hit me was the role that poetry and art in general played among ordinary people throughout Latin America—which it simply did not play in the United States. In the United States, to be a poet was something your parents sort of wished you hadn't chosen—unless you had "made it" and your books were bringing in thousands of dollars. It was something so marginal, so unessential to what one was taught to conceive of as one's life; it was irresponsible. It could be your hobby, but it certainly couldn't be your central concern. In Latin America, to be a poet or any kind of artist is considered a worthy and revered profession. The label *poeta* (poet) is a title of respect. In Nicaragua, Ernesto Cardenal is a Catholic priest and so might be called "Father," he's a minister of state, so one might call him "Secretary Cardenal" as we would say "Secretary Schultz," but he's also a poet, so he's called "Poet Cardenal." That's the title he prefers, that's the title people give him. The artist is seen as useful to society, his or her product a necessary object or event.

Latin American countries which consider themselves democracies, and especially the Latin American countries that have revolutionary systems, are very supportive of the arts. Both Cuba and Nicaragua spend much more, proportionately, of their national budgets on art and culture than is true of the United States. Both countries have ministries of culture*—something the United States has not thought it necessary to establish in a more than two-hundred-year history. Again, it's the value placed on artistic production. In Nicaragua, the brigades of writers and dancers and musicians and artists and theater people who systematically go to the war zones are as important as the fuel lines and the food lines and the ammunition lines. It is

---

*This interview took place before Nicaragua, faced with the ongoing devastation of the contra war, reduced the functions of its Ministry of Culture, moving it from the level of Ministry to that of institute.

considered absolutely essential that people's spiritual needs be met, and art is very much considered a spiritual need. As a result, the Ministry of Education, the Presidency—a number of different entities and institutions within these governments—spend a large percentage of their budgets supporting artistic endeavors: publications, grants for individual artists, collective aid to artists, unions that see to the needs of artists: health needs, work needs, exhibiting or publication needs. This is also true in Mexico, and it's part of the tradition in countries like Columbia, Peru, Venezuela, and Argentina.

Both Cuba and Nicaragua have shown an extraordinary respect for the multiplicity of their ethnicities, racial origins, folk cultures, and creativity of all kinds. Compare Cuba's support of its Afro-Cuban music and dance, or Nicaragua's attention to the culture of its Atlantic Coast—both Black and Miskito—with the support Native American or African American culture has received here, at least until jazz and other examples became an exportable commodity worldwide.

Moreover, cultural policies in both Cuba and Nicaragua are made by cultural workers—those men and women who paint, write, dance, act, sing, sculpt, etc. Not by a few artists who have become famous but by vast assemblies of artists of all ages and experience. This can only happen when there is a ministry of culture or some other agency capable of being in touch with the country's artists, bringing them together, and effectively engaging them in discussion. I was fortunate to live in Cuba and Nicaragua during years when all sorts of cultural policies were being discussed and made—everything from the basic copyright laws, crediting, and payment for works rendered, to the need for freer criticism. I would love to see an official government agency in the United States bring hundreds of thousands of artists together to discuss such matters, and then approve policy that makes the fruit of such discussions law.

Miller: The term *artistic freedom* is often invoked in this country as an unquestioned right, as basic as the rights of life, liberty, and the pursuit of happiness. This usage carries with it distinct political overtones as well, implying certain guarantees for artists in this country which are not necessarily available to artists in other parts of the world.

Randall: Every society defines its freedoms and regulates them in some way. More sophisticated societies, industrially advanced societies, define or manage the relationships between peoples, the state and freedoms in a much more sophisticated way. So in a place like the United States, people are told that we have all the freedoms. We're told this in such a deeply ingrained and early starting way that we believe it; and in such a sophisticated way that we don't question it—until such time as, in each of our lives, we come up against the ways in which some of those freedoms may be denied us.

Conversely, in countries where we have been taught that there is no artistic freedom or freedom of expression (which, of course, for us, are the socialist countries) the fact that their freedoms are conceived in a different way—less as individual freedoms, more as collective freedoms pertaining to an entire society—gives us the message that there are no freedoms. Yet it's simply a different way of looking at what freedom is.

Miller: What does this idea of "collective" freedoms mean concretely?

Randall: When I say "collective freedoms," I am speaking of all kinds of freedoms: the freedom to grow up healthy, to study, to be employed, to enjoy the benefits of culture and relaxation, the freedom from worry about one's children, their futures, the freedom to acquaint oneself with what's happening in the world, the freedom to create.

We artists in the United States are free to exercise our craft, no one tells us what to write. We have the freedom to express ourselves, but we might be too homeless or hungry or poor or tired to think about it: unable to give it our best creative energies. Basic social welfare guarantees are the basis for any individual or group artistic expression, because it's inconceivable that one write or paint or make music or theater or whatever if meeting one's basic needs take up such a percentage of one's energies that the mere possibility of artistic creativity is obliterated in the effort. In the socialist countries these freedoms—the freedom to grow up, to enjoy the best possible health, to study and work, to have a roof over one's head and food on the table—are taken seriously for all people.

Collectively conceived freedoms in places like Cuba and Nicaragua mean, moreover, the freedom to read and write. Both nations launched comprehensive literacy campaigns as among the first all-out efforts of a new revolutionary government in power. In the case of Cuba, illiteracy was reduced from more than half the adult population to about twelve percent, and has been lowered much more through follow-up programs in succeeding years. In Nicaragua an even higher rate of illiteracy had to be dealt with. It was in the seventies overall, and in many rural areas more than ninety percent of the adults could neither read nor write. The literacy crusade brought the rate down to about twenty-three percent.

This has made freedom for artistic creation a much more tangible possibility for a much greater number of people. There may not be as many places to publish as in the U.S.; there is not as much money to spend on a vast array of broadcasting possibilities, publishing possibilities, and so forth; there are not as many grants. But it's a different setup and different needs are recognized and addressed.

In addition, both of these countries, countries infinitely poorer than the United States and with histories of imperialist and oligarchic exploitation that translate into generations of real economic and cultural debt, have political systems which are much more *participatory* than our own. In Cuba every important new law is set out in draft form for the entire population to discuss, criticize, and amend. These discussions take place in neighborhoods, schools and universities, military units, and workplaces. Tens of thousands of suggested changes are tabulated, considered, and in many cases incorporated into the final wording of the law before it is voted on in a democratically elected body.

This provides a freedom to know about and effect changes in the laws that govern one's life. That's important. It gives people a real sense of connection with the forces that control their lives, and that cannot be overemphasized in avoiding apathy, the "who cares?" attitude so evident, for example, here in the United States, especially during periods of political campaigning. In Cuba I remember so many neighborhood or regional gatherings, at which ordinary people had and took the opportunity of questioning candidates or elected leaders. Their questions were direct, and discussions were aimed at the communal and hands-on solving of problems. In Nicaragua the "Face the People" evenings are legion by this time—many foreigners have witnessed these open-ended gatherings, at a school, in a neighborhood, on a collective farm, or at a workplace, where people confront their leaders about problems and demand realistic responses.

Miller: Tell me more about artistic freedom as a relative condition. Do you mean relative in relationship to the stages of development or to the political circumstances of various societies in the world. . . ?

Randall: Both. There is a relationship between artistic and other freedoms and the degree of security a state possesses. Sometimes individual freedom may affect the very existence of a state. And every state protects itself. Every society protects itself, we don't even have to talk about states; we can go way back to so-called primitive societies. They develop a series of customs, regulations, or laws regarding what is permissible and what is not in order to insure the perpetuation of that society.

Miller: You almost seem to be suggesting that artists have more "freedom" in societies where they are virtually irrelevant or, at least, not central to the. . .

Randall: In some ways, but, there again it's relative. In this country, if we are not well looked-upon by the institutions of society, we don't get the grant money, we can't publish. Publishing in this country is very political, and in dozens of ways: political if you're on the left, political if you're a woman, political if you're Black, if you belong to one of the so-called minorities.

Miller: But if the poet is held in such high esteem in societies like Nicaragua, does the corollary not also exist? That is, that the relationship between artists and the state is likely to be much more highly charged?

Randall: Absolutely. It's much more highly charged and much more subject to the laws that we spoke about earlier regarding how freedom of expression is handled vis-à-vis a particular state.

I think that to understand what's happened in countries like Cuba and to understand the enormous degree of artistic freedom in a country like Cuba—and I do believe there is an astounding degree of artistic freedom—you have to understand what is meant by the phrase, "Within the revolution everything, outside the revolution nothing," that Castro used in his 1962 "Words to the Intellectuals" speech. This was immediately taken up by the propaganda machine in the United States and parts of Western Europe as denoting a total control of creative expression in Cuba. But in Cuba it wasn't interpreted like that at all. It never meant that unless you parroted the revolution, as the Communist Party of Cuba articulated it, you were out. It did, however, assert that a basic right of the Cuban revolution was to defend itself against the obstacles which the U.S. and other Western powers were contriving against it. Everyone in the society was expected to do their share to maintain the revolution, and artists and writers were not exempt.

There have certainly been times in the thirty-year history of the Cuban revolution at which official censorship, or a kind of self-censorship that some Cuban writers have felt in order to fit in with the state vision of what is appreciated or nourished in that society, has prevented them from being critical. But the nature of the revolutionary process has made it possible to address and deal with those issues. I think that censorship of any kind is dangerous, and I think that self-censorship is probably the most dangerous of all. The Cubans have never really attempted to impose—either in form or in content, subject matter—limits of any kind on their artists. The old sort of socialist realism—although there are some people in Cuba who practice it—has never been fashionable or encouraged above any other artistic style.

A young Cuban poet named Victor Rodriguez told me,

> You know, it seems to me that to you people, revolutionary poetry has to have a raised fist, it has to have a red sun coming up in the East, it has to have a tractor. I don't need to write about those things; I may, but I probably won't. My poetry is revolutionary because I was born and bred in the revolution, and so my vision is the vision of a more humane world, of a world with greater vision, of a world where certain values—of fellowship, of human generosity, of internationalism—are givens. That's my vision. I can write about any of the things that you write about, but my vision is a different vision and that's what makes me a revolutionary poet. It's not whether I write about a tractor, or a rose. I can write about an ivory tower, but I'm going to see it differently than you.

Miller: Bringing these ideas back to the United States arena, could you comment on how these ideas relate to your experiences since returning home early in 1984.

Randall: As you know, I face a deportation order, the refusal of the U.S. Immigration and Naturalization Service (INS) to grant me residency because of the nature of some of my books. The INS has invoked the ideological exclusion clause of the 1952 McCarran-Walter Act—an act passed over President Truman's veto, at the height of the McCarthy period. Yet thirtysome-odd years later it still governs immigration here.

I could say a lot about this case—I have, and undoubtedly will say a great deal

more before it's over*—but since we're talking about artistic freedom, I'd like to highlight the line of questioning used by government lawyers at my hearing in March of 1986. On the witness stand and under oath, these were some of the questions I was asked:

"Is it true that you once wrote a poem to Ché Guevara?" "Is it true that one issue of the literary magazine you edited in the sixties in Mexico City was dedicated to Huey Newton?" "In that magazine did you also run an ad for a bookstore selling Marxist literature?" "In a 1971 poem about the Attica prison uprising, did you call the prisoners your 'brothers' and the police 'pigs'?" "Have you ever written a poem praising free enterprise?"

The implications of each of these inquiries should be clear. Responding to one of the questions from the prosecution—I can no longer remember which one—I explained that my use of a particular word or phrase had been a metaphor. "What's a metaphor?" the attorney asked.

As a result of my own experience with U.S. immigration policy, I have learned that artistic freedom in this country also passes through some pretty crude and amazing bottlenecks. Early on in my petition for residency I was called into an immigration and naturalization office and subjected to a taped interview in which a number of my books were opened across a tabletop and certain passages highlighted in yellow magic-marker. I was asked "to explain" those passages. Some were critical of U.S. policy in Vietnam; others quoted women I'd interviewed-Cuban women, Nicaraguan women—speaking about their own experiences. Still others were not even written by me, but about me by someone else, most notably in an introduction to one of my early books of poetry.

My writing was eventually charged—by these "literary critics" from INS—with "advocating the doctrines of world communism." And how do they define what constitutes "advocating the doctrines of world communism?" In my case, they claim that criticizing U.S. policy in Vietnam, or pointing out that Cuban women are better off under the present revolutionary government than under the Batista dictatorship, constitute such advocacy. I would point out that such statements— reflecting the views of hundreds of thousands of U.S. citizens who are not communists—can hardly be so defined. I would also point out that advocating the doctrines of world communism, in a country whose communist party is legal, is a right protected by the Constitution.

What can we say about artistic freedom in a country that sets its immigration

---

* The Board of Immigration Appeals (BIA) finally handed down a 3–2 decision in July, 1989, to the effect that Margaret Randall had not in fact lost her U.S. citizenship, thus avoiding the First Amendment issue. In August, 1989, INS desisted in its attempt to deport Randall, and the case was over. Support for changing the unconstitutional clauses of McCarran-Walter is still needed, of course.

officials up as literary critics, or retains laws that not only affect someone like myself, but have kept out such artistic giants as Pablo Neruda, Gabriel García Márquez, Graham Green, Carlos Fuentes, Dario Fo, and Farley Mowat? The first two have won Nobel prizes for literature, yet they were deemed too "subversive" for the American public.

Since I've been back, something else that's caught my attention is the way in which officialdom—particularly during the eight years of Reagan—has subverted our language itself, so that the public usage of words that once had one acceptation has now become quite other, in some cases the opposite of the original.

Take the word *life*. Those who deny women's right to reproductive choice call themselves "right-to-life." They place the arguable life of the unborn above the lives of adult women. Typically, they are the same people who vehemently and scornfully disregard the lives of South Africans, Nicaraguans, or people of color anywhere. Yet few challenge their perversion of the word *life*.

In current U.S. foreign policy, the words covert and overt have been switched, often subtly, and no one seems to notice. In hindsight, intervention in the internal affairs of Chile (including activities supporting the murder of a democratically elected president) is seen as "wrong." On the other hand, our CIA sending ten million dollars to affect the outcome of an election in Panama is simply announced on the evening news. The way language and values have been subverted in this country has made that something about which we can now be quite open and matter-of-fact.

Take the word *revolution* itself: it once had a very solemn and sacred meaning, in our history as well as that of others. Today its most frequent popular usage is in the context of "a revolutionary new deodorant or motor oil." The distortion of language promotes a distortion of assumptions, ideas, reality itself. It is the tactic by which increasing poverty may be termed economic growth, and even some of those most intimately affected may accept and use the terminology.

A barrage of subliminal attack, as well as the obvious mockery of meaning; a language of racism, classism, sexism, heterosexism, ageism, able-bodyism and the rest; tends to rob us of the freedom to be who we truly are. And this is a devastating attack on our freedom to create. Surely artistic freedom begins with the freedom to claim and experience our identity.

Thinking about the Rosenbergs

I can't think about the Rosenbergs without wanting to cry.

I don't have any idea where I was on June 19, 1953. I was a junior in high school. Around that time I went to the senior prom at Medford High in

Boston, because my boyfriend was graduating. There was a beach party afterwards and I didn't fit in.

I didn't know where I was on June 19, 1953, and I didn't know where I was for another fifteen years or so, until the late '60s, when I was finally radicalized by events and found out that I lived in America, spelled with a K.

But I do have my McCarthy era memories. There was a lot of talk at the family dinner table about McCarthy, about Communists, especially when we visited with my aunt and uncle who were more radical than my liberal parents. I'd heard my parents talk about how some of their best friends, people I knew, were commies in the '30s when they lived in New York. So I said one day, "Hey Daddy! I'm going to tell everybody at school you're a commie!"

My gentle father, then a dean at a southern university and in the process of integrating the medical school, my gentle sentimental father, who had never hurt me, suddenly reached out and grabbed my arm. He held it so tight it was really painful. "Don't you *ever* do that," he said (he *hissed,* as they say in novels). I felt his fear passing into me like an electric shock. It was a shock. I was shocked. I remembered it for years.

I remembered it when men on the roofs of government buildings took pictures of us in marches against the Vietnam war. I remembered it when the FBI raided an Artworkers Coalition meeting and when they arrested artists for the "People's Flag Show." I remembered it when the FBI called me about an action in the early days of the women's movement. I remembered it when Hilton Kramer wrote in *The New Criterion* that I *had* been a promising writer until I "fell victim to the radical whirlwind." I remembered it when I sent for my NY State Red Squad file and they told me they couldn't give it to me because it would expose an informer. I remembered it when Jeremiah Denton started his House Un-American Activities Committee-like anti-terrorist committee under Ronald Reagan. I remembered it when Margia Kramer started working on the Jean Seberg/Black Panther files. I remembered it when the telephone man came to fix my unbroken phone just before I went to Cuba for the second time and it turned out others on the trip had also had unexpected visits from the phone company.

I remembered it in Colorado when a friend called me and I never heard the ring but she could hear the conversation in my living room, though I hadn't picked up the phone. I remembered it when the Center for Constitutional Rights began monitoring harassment in the Central America movement and exposed government spying on the Committee in Solidarity with the People of El Salvador, which I work with. I remembered it when Political Art Documentation Distribution (PADD) had its grant vetoed by the Reagan-appointed National Endowment for the Arts director. I remembered it when I got obscene phone calls from someone purporting to be my boyfriend—my Black boyfriend—before I went to Nicaragua the first time, and I remembered it on my return, when he picked me up at the airport in a borrowed car and the car's owner, whom I didn't know, began to get obscene phone calls about me. I remembered it when I and the thousands of artists across the country participating in Artists Call Against U.S. Intervention in Central America were called "dupes" by fellow art critics. I remembered it when an artist and co-worker from El Salvador called to warn me they were harassing his friends, and I asked my teenaged son to get rid of his tiny marijuana plant.

I remember it now as George Bush campaigns against a "card carrying" member of the American Civil Liberties Union and dredges up familiar red-baiting techniques. But I don't remember where I was on June 19th, 1953, when the Rosenbergs were murdered. I can't think about the Rosenbergs without wanting to cry, and without remembering my father's terror.

—Lucy R. Lippard

From a presentation at Hillwood Art Gallery, Long Island University, September, 1988. Held in conjunction with a traveling exhibit, "Unknown Secrets: Art and the Rosenberg Era."

"The Rosenbergs: Framed Conspiracy," Juan Sánchez, 1987 (46" x 68" oil and mixed media on canvas)

Culture and Community, Sources and Settings

Culture and Community, Sources and Settings
Introduction

At first glance the teacher appears aloof, frozen at attention as he stands in front of his students. Flag, teacher, globe, alphabet flashcards above the blackboard, even the uniformly laid out desks and the repeated pattern of the tiles take their place in a familiar chain of educational authority. A closer look reveals two questions printed on the blackboard—*WHAT IS CULTURE?* and *WHO ARE YOUR ANCESTORS?*—which suggest a different logic at play in the scene, and sets the eye roving for new details. Around the picture frame, ancient Yoruban and Egyptian symbols float amidst continents and countries—Africa, South America, Caribbean islands—freed from their assigned places on the globe by children who proudly claim not just their heritage, but their own places in the African diaspora. The flag, the globe, the patterns of the desk and floor recede, giving way to a new visual rhythm punctuated by the patterns in the children's hair and the self-portraits that face them. Now the teacher stands as sentinel, guide, in this rite of self knowledge.

"If You Don't Know Where You Come From, How Do You Know Where You Are Going?" is one of a vivid series of paintings that comprise Willie Birch's "Personal View of Urban America." The classroom scene echoes Birch's own commitment to develop empowering culturally based educational programs for his mostly third world public school students. On another level, it reflects the choice that Birch and other contributors in this section have made to making art rooted in the experiences and serving the needs of their communities.

In an era of tremendous geographic mobility, when barely half the people in the United States live out their lives in the same immediate geographic area they are born into, the notion of community is both seductive and ephemeral. The search for legitimate, nurturing social environments has led many artists and others to an understanding of community beyond strict geographic lines—to community defined by shared workplace, economic class experiences, political or religious beliefs, racial, ethnic or cultural backgrounds.

Common to these perspectives is an awareness of the continuous process of change and transformation in communities. Within this context, as Fred Ho notes, the artist must be willing to be "an archivist, archaeologist, oral historian, social historian, and social worker all rolled into one." Similarly, Jawole Zollar talks with her friend and occasional collaborator, Hattie Gossett, about how her work draws on a wide variety of culturally based sources, ranging from everyday life experiences in New York to African American spiritual and storytelling traditions, to the poetry and prose of other women artists of color.

In common usage *community art* has become a designation for arts programs funded by the state and/or private corporations that are essentially a form of social service, or cultural workfare. In spite of nominal commitments to increasing funds for community-based art programs, funding priorities remain skewed in favor of established, professional *high art* or *performance culture* organizations. Under these conditions, many arts activists whose goal is supporting the political and cultural empowerment of the communities in which they work, find themselves, as Tim Drescher discusses, in the ironic position of being funded to do community maintenance work: keeping people happy and/or occupied, who might otherwise be making trouble for the state.

This notion of *community art* also reinforces narrow ideas of community as an aesthetic category. Too often, both proponents and critics of community-based art projects assume that *authentic* community art must look and sound a certain way: unslick, unsophisticated, limited to simple rhythms, primary colors and, as Richard Cruz of Kids of Survival puts it, ten-cent words instead of ten-dollar ones. Amalia Mesa-Bains and others underline the degree to which engaged community art practices change to meet the community's changing needs. Speaking of the evolution of San Francisco's Galeria de la Raza as a community art space over the past two decades, she writes, "Blends of new folk art forms, and mixed media have expanded the artistic scope while blurring the distinctions of categories from fine to folk."

Taken as a whole, the contributors to this section clearly undermine the viability of *community* as a definable or fixed aesthetic category. Rather than safeguarding community art as a repository for passing cultural forms, they shift our focus to artistic practices based on ideas of actively shared commitment and exchange.

The Art of Community

A Dialogue

Tim Rollins, 33
and Kids of Survival (KOS)
Richard Cruz, 18; George Garces, 16;
Nelson Montes, 16; Carlos Rivera, 17;
Annette Rosado, 16; Nelson Savinon, 17

Tim Rollins

Tim Rollins is project director of the Art & Knowledge Workshop, Inc. in the South Bronx. He is best known for his collaborative work with Kids of Survival (KOS), a group of fifteen South Bronx youth.

February 1, 1989, The Art & Knowledge Workshop, Longwood Ave., South Bronx, New York. Photo by Christine Thomson.

Tim: Before we begin our discussion, I should tell you that this will be printed in a collection of writings edited by the people from a project called Voices of Dissent.

Carlos: What's that—dissent?

Tim: That's when you disagree with something, when you differ and argue against an authority. This authority can be a person, or a government, or a tradition. I also think that sometimes we can't just dissent against what *is*—things in the world today that we disagree with; we need to dissent against old ideas of what *should be* that don't seem to be working. So, instead of just writing about how we've integrated our art with our community here in the South Bronx, I thought we'd talk about these issues, demonstrating to the readers how we do what we do instead of simply describing it.

First of all, when many people think of community and art, they immediately think of art made by local people being shown in the lobby of a bank, a school festival, or maybe something more ambitious, like a mural in or on the side of a neighborhood building. Things like that. I've hoped that our project here over the years could explore this relationship between art and community, pointing to new ways of working.

But before all this, a question: Do you think our community has any genuine interest in art? Is art important?

Richard: I think the majority of the people living here don't really care.

George: I think that people are so preoccupied with their own lives and problems that they have little interest in the art around them. They kind of just pass by and don't appreciate the public art things because they see them every day.

Richard: It's mostly the moms that take the time to look. They're more concerned with how the neighborhood looks and can relate to the art in the community.

Nelson S: They don't notice the art around here.

Annette: They just think it's pretty.

Tim: Hmmmm. My experience has been the opposite. Just because people don't make this big *deal* about art, doesn't mean it's not important. It's kind of nice to just have it be a regular part of everyday life. One reason I like working in this area of the South Bronx is that the ability to make visual art, visual culture, is very respected—a lot more than from where I came in rural Maine. (Nelson's brother Carlos enters the room.)

Carlos: Tim, can I talk to my brother for a minute? (Nelson and Carlos talk while the rest of the group waits.)

Nelson S: Tim, can my brother hang out here for a little while? This posse [a local gang] is after him.

Tim: Yeah, sure. You had better lock the door, though. Do you think gangs are interested in the visual arts? (Laughter.)

Nelson S: They love tattoos.

Tim: When I was working as a teacher at I.S. No.52, it seemed that any kid who could draw or paint well could have serious respect.

Richard: Yeah, that's true. Once the word gets out that you're good in art, people are always coming up to you, asking "Draw this for me?"

Nelson S: I *hate* it when people ask me to draw stuff for them, like I have to prove something. I bet that's why a lot of artists keep to themselves.

Tim: That's one theory. You say that the visual arts aren't so important here, but then compare, say, our area with your average Manhattan neighborhood, where there is very little visual public art except for advertising. Here in the Longwood District, you can see four or five major public artworks in a fifteen-minute walk. My question is: Why here?

George: Maybe people on the outside, hearing the South Bronx is bad, send the art up here because they think we need it—that it will make our community better.

Richard: Look at what art is in the community and stays up and what art gets wrecked. It's interesting. I guess it depends.

Tim: I remember a summer youth project that did those paintings that were up on the Prospect Avenue subway station. They got hurt immediately. Why?

Richard: Probably because they were so easy to get at!

Tim: Do you think it had anything to do with their quality? They were pretty poor works.

Richard: It depends. Yeah, the paintings were bad, but even if they were good, I think people would have tried to destroy them. They were made by neighborhood kids and they were destroyed by neighborhood kids.

George: Lots of people want to get attention by destroying works of art.

Tim: Still, it speaks for the importance given to visual art. Why bother if art makes no impact?

Richard: Our art isn't art for the community, like we're supposed to be the interior decorators for the block. Our art is made with the community. Everybody's up here in the studio, coming in and out, asking questions, things like that. What do you think, Carlos? You're being too quiet.

Carlos: I think people are into art, because it's a good way to express yourself in the community. A lot of people have got a lot of problems here, and they don't feel like telling their problems to nobody, so art helps. Sometimes art is the only way to live, to get stuff out. Maybe if people have to walk past a piece of art everyday, they get tired of it and it disappears to them.

Annette: You want to know the truth? I don't think the community cares about the art itself so much. You know why? Because people here like to *gossip* a lot! They don't care about the art—they care about who *did* the art, where they came from, what they are like, all that. They get interested only when someone is around to talk to them.

Carlos: Sometimes I think people get mad when they see a work of art go up, not because it's bad, but just the opposite. The art looks real good, but *they* didn't do it, *they* didn't have no part of it. So they just want to mess it up. They're jealous. This isn't the majority, now. Most people respect art, even if they don't understand it all.

Annette: People who respect art are people who like to see things change—and not everybody can deal with change.

Nelson S: Yeah. New things freak people out.

George: Art has power, and many people would like to have that power, but they don't have the skill or time or education or discipline to get it together, so they can turn into the enemies of art.

Tim: This is beginning to sound like the plot to *Star Wars!*

Carlos: There are people who wreck stuff to impress people. If you can ruin something, then you're a big man. I'm not concentrating on the negative. I'm telling the truth.

Tim: Hey, art has always been a victim and a survivor at the same time. So, when some works of art go up in a community, you feel that often people feel left out?

Richard: Yeah, like an alien landed.

Tim: But all artworks like this have to be approved at a community board meeting.

Richard: Can anybody go?

Tim: Sure! Don't you know that? The problem is, to be honest, most community members don't. And guess who are the first to scream after these sort of decisions are made? Participation takes time and energy.

Carlos: . . . and effort. Those people who wreck stuff—destruction is their art.

Tim: There's an old saying: "It takes a skilled carpenter to build a barn. Any fool can tear one apart."

George: Sometimes I think you know when something is important when it makes you want to laugh at it—not because it's funny, but you want to put it down because you don't really understand it. Like, remember when we first heard Schubert's *Winterreise* and we were laughing and mocking it? When I think back, I think we laughed because that kind of music—classical music—kind of challenged our pride.

Tim: Do you think that "fine art" challenges the pride of the community sometimes?

Carlos: Yup!

George: Definitely.

Carlos: Some people look at the art and get furious because they don't understand it.

Annette: People aren't stupid. They know artists make history.

Carlos: Everybody wants to make history and not be shut out in the cold.

Annette: A community without art is boring.

Tim: And an art without community is boring.

Carlos: Yeah, but a lot of murals and stuff are so corny! It's like the artist thinks people are dumb and can only understand simple things.

Nelson M: If you showed people on the street two drawings, and one was realistic and the other was something else, they'd prefer the realistic one, the one easiest to understand.

Richard: Most people think art is something nice to look at instead of being something to look at *and think* about.

Tim: Let's say a *lot* of people were organized in the community. And they all decided to work on this mural, but somehow, instead of being realistic, the mural was becoming this wild thing that no one had ever thought of or seen before. Do you think the community would like this work when it was finished?

Richard: Sure! Everyone would brag about it! And when relatives came over to visit, everyone could explain the meaning to them. They become teachers. Art can be or look like anything. There just has to be an understanding about the work between everybody.

George: A real public art would be an art that involves as many people as possible.

Carlos: This kind of project nobody would touch, because it would belong to everyone. If someone touched the painting, it would be like touching the furniture in their house.

Annette: I like the art that's here in the neighborhood, but I don't like it. Some of the murals look nice, with nice colors. And at least it doesn't show people taking drugs or skeletons or big hypodermic needles and stuff like that. I'm sick of that kind of art. You can see that on your block *for real* everyday! You don't need to see it all big on some wall in your face!

Tim: I think Orozco said that the last thing workers want to see on their walls when they come home is a picture of people working.

Nelson M: The art around here is boring.

Tim: Maybe *you* bore the art!

Nelson M: What I mean is that some of the paintings don't represent the people living here.

Tim: That's interesting, because a community is not just a place. A community is a group of people living and working in a particular place. A community is how the people living here relate—there is the invisible part of community which may be the most important—the responsibility we have to each other connects the lives of the people here.

George: I never thought about it that way.

Tim: And that is what everyone should say when they see a work of art.

Richard: A lot of the art around here looks like art for children—simple forms, bright colors. It's not talking those ten dollar words. It's talking those ten cent words.

Tim: Why are all the art programs around for kids and not adults?

Nelson S: So what? People just don't want to come. They just want to watch TV— you know—be couch potatoes.

Tim: Here we are talking about The Community without asking this: Do you think community as we've talked about it exists anymore, or is it some old idea we won't let go of, you know, like The People, The Masses, The Working Class, The Rich?

George: Well, I don't see a lot of people supporting each other and working together.

Nelson S: Maybe people are scared to relate. You know, you just go out to buy what you need and then go back home. Maybe you have friends that you talk to on the phone, or you go hang out on the corner.

Tim: Do you think this is just a problem in communities that don't have a lot of money?

George: Nah. Compare here to Manhattan! It's worse there! Everyone seems like they have their little group of friends, their jobs. They don't hang out. They rent videos.

Richard: People connect here in the South Bronx because there isn't much else to do!

George: Well, everybody likes to gossip, and that's a way of communicating. If you look at it a certain way, it shows that at least people care about each other here, even if we all have to survive on our own.

Richard: I know people care about the workshop. They know we bring something positive to the community.

Tim: Do you think if we just packed up and moved the whole operation down to Soho . . . ?

Nelson M: We should!

Tim: You're just saying that because you and your brother are being chased right now!

Richard: We would be missed, even if only by all the parents and teachers and kids who know we are here.

Tim: Sometimes I'm asked why we don't work out of a storefront on street-level, you know, "face-to-face" with the the community.

Carlos: There's a big difference between who is hanging out on the street and the community.

Richard: If we were in a storefront—it would be like a store with everybody coming in all the time, hanging out, asking for money, not letting us do the work. We would be even more vulnerable to the negative people around.

Annette: That's right.

Carlos: We can do more for this community by being kind of secret and closed than if we were open to everybody.

Annette: And things have changed here. I'm not just talking about the crack stuff. Guys act really different now. I mean, there's no respect for girls anymore. It used to be that if a guy liked you, he would come and visit your parents and—

Richard: Oh, come on! Those were the old days!

Annette: Don't give me that!

George: What does this have to do with what we're talking about?

Annette: It's like your community is one way one day, and then you wake up and it's some different kind of place!

Tim: What sort of art do you think the community wants?

George: Something positive. When you make art that has negative images, it's like always seeing the bad things just keeps the bad things happening officially here in the South Bronx. You see so many negative images about this community on TV and in the news. You know, you just start playing the role. If everybody thinks that the South Bronx is bad, and if you live in the South Bronx, then you'll start acting bad.

Richard: That's not true! Just because I'm from the Bronx doesn't mean I'm bad!

George: I didn't say that! But you *act* like you're bad!

Richard: I know—but that doesn't have anything to do with me coming from the Bronx!

Tim: Oh yeah? Then why do all these young men from the Bronx walk like they have a twenty-five-pound bowling ball between their legs? (Laughter.)

Richard: Maybe it's because of the stuff white people say about us. Anyway, not *everyone* walks around the Bronx like they've got a bowling ball between their legs!

George: We're not talking about everybody—we're talking about you!

Richard: So what?! I walk that way because my father walks that way!

George: He must be from the Bronx!

Richard: He is!

Nelson M: It runs in the family! (Laughter.)

Annette: Have you ever seen the way a gang walks through the block?

Tim: Looks like they got their hips broken at some point.

Carlos: They just want respect.

Nelson S: I think if you believe art should show what's going on in the world, and if what's going on is bad, then you have to be honest and represent some of the negative things in public art. That could wake people up and help change things.

Richard: It's a start.

George: But you have to show images of hope. Things maybe begin to change when people feel like they have the power to change things, instead of everybody staying, hiding at home worrying and complaining and watching TV. Art is better than TV because it stays still. Art is more there forever.

Carlos: TV is all about entertainment.

Tim: Do you think that art can be entertaining?

Carlos: Hell, yeah! It's the best!

Richard: Hell, no!

Tim: Just because you're an art freak, Carlito, you can't expect everyone—

Carlos: Well then people had better start getting their butts into museums!

Tim: I think the community should never be talked down to. Pretty colors and safe, familiar imagery just don't make it. The artist has a responsibility to the community, but the neighborhood also has a responsibility to cooperate with the artist's ideas.

Richard: When you get down to it, art is just for the people who like art.

Tim: Ah, so art is like . . . bowling? Stamp collecting . . .

Carlos: Art is for everybody. Well, it should be for everybody, but the way it seems now, Richie is right. Art is for art freaks.

Richard: It's the same old thing. People want to be entertained by something. With art, you have to be able to entertain yourself with your ideas about your work.

Nelson M: It's hard. Museums are boring.

Tim: There is some art that *is* boring. And if you're not used to them and don't understand what's in them, museums can be boring, you're right. But still . . .

George: But look at how the schools teach about art!

Richard: Yeah. We're taught that art is just fun—like a free period.

Annette: They think art is a break from "real" work . . .

George: The schools don't think art is as important as English, or math . . . and they don't think it's difficult! If schools considered art to be important and taught the kids about the history of art and how to do art like they teach us how to do math from kindergarten on, then art would be as important in life as being good in math and English is.

Carlos: The people who grew up with loving art are lucky.

Tim: We're lucky because in the seven years we've been working together, we've made this great thing from nothing by ourselves. But you kids should realize how unusual this is. I know we've worked our butts off and we deserve it, but having this intense involvement with fine art is a privilege.

Nelson S: But you can't hand people knowledge about anything like it was food stamps.

Tim: It's easy for you to say, but you forget the time when you didn't even realize you might be interested in art in a serious way.

Nelson S: Knowledge is like anything else. If someone *gives* it to you, you don't really appreciate it. But if you earn it—fight for it—then it means a lot to you.

Annette: I think that even though we don't have a piece outside of the community yet, we are the best known artists around here not because we have paintings all over the place, but because of what we *do*. We *are* the art. We are a different kind of art. We're a team. We're a good example for people to learn from. We got it. We got the dream. We got everything. And now what we want is history. And I guess that's what every community wants—a place in history. Community art is to say: "Look! We were here! We exist! Remember us!"

Tim: You know, there's this romantic idea that making art in the community is this transcendent, uplifting experience. Well, lots of times it isn't. To be honest, it can be a real pain in the ass. You have to deal with sponsors and committees and self-appointed representatives of the community more than with the actual people living here. And often these representatives and their bureaucracy are seriously out of touch with the sensibility of their constituents.

George: Too often the community and their representatives are only interested in artists when they want something done cheap for them—like when they want signs or banners for block parties and stuff. All of a sudden, they're interested in art.

Tim: You're right. The role of the artist isn't to decorate the surroundings. I think the artist should be allowed to work *with* the community as an equal partner. And artists have to be smart enough to build in structures for social participation *as part* of their artwork. The artist can show the community what skills it already possesses to create its own culture, while the community can direct the artist towards the ideas, forms and contents that really matter to the people. It takes both a good artist and a good community to understand this.

"The Scarlet Letter I," Kids of Survival, 1987/88 (108" x 140" acrylic, watercolor and bistre on book pages on linen)

Tim Rollins and KOS

A former teacher in South Bronx public schools, Tim Rollins has evolved his work teaching reading through art to educationally disadvantaged high school students into an extraordinary synthesis/dialogue/confrontation/hybrid between literature and art, "high culture" and street knowledge, the collective and the individual, and the student and the professional. Working first with the standard school literature such as *The Red Badge of Courage* and *The Scarlet Letter,* Rollins encouraged his students to translate the themes of these texts (such as courage and cowardice or social stigma) through their own related experiences into visual images. What would their personal red badge or scarlet letter refer to and how might it look? Finding a unifying visual principle—a single color, one dominant shape—with which to organize and coalesce the disparate images that emerged, Rollins and his students superimposed the resulting images onto a rectangular grid made up of individual pages from the book being studied.

Over pages from Ray Bradbury's futuristic novel, *Fahrenheit 451,* for example, they impressed ashes from burnt books, making direct reference to the literary holocaust described in the novel. At the same time the ashes evoke associations with physical holocaust: the burning of houses, of streets, of virtual neighborhoods that has become synonymous with areas of the South Bronx. Onto pages from Daniel Defoe's *Journal of the Plague Year,* the word "Abracadabra," written in blood, was inscribed in a triangle. While referring to the medical magic that proved incapable of containing the plague in Defoe's time; it is resonant with the inability of science to eradicate our contemporary plagues, especially AIDS, which is spreading in high drug-use areas like the South Bronx with particular intensity.

The works produced by Rollins and KOS are often not overtly political in terms of obviously radical imagery. The symbolism of the various "scarlet letters," for example, is often too personal to be universally understandable. Rather it is their making of the art that is radical, that serves to overcome the silencing and numbing of illiteracy and cultural invisibility.

—Janet Kaplan

Janet Kaplan is associate professor of art history and Chair of the Liberal Arts Department at Moore College of Art and Design in Philadelphia. She teaches and writes about twentieth-century art, women's issues, and the arts and social activism.

Our Cultures Speak for Themselves

Rudy Martin

The New York City American Indian community is a microcosm of the national American Indian community in the sense that we have over fifty-seven tribal nations represented here. The American Indian Community House addresses the cultural and social needs of this community. We try to do so with the understanding and sensitivity necessary when servicing such a cross section of cultural differences: different languages, ideologies, and social issues.

As the director of Public Relations and Information for the American Indian Community House, not only must I keep these various differences in mind when working for my community, I must also act as a liaison to the non-Indian and to the rest of "Indian Country." It is our responsibility to educate and inform as best we can. Within this context it is permitted for me to express my feelings as long as I make it clear that I do so with respect for their many individual priorities. I *present* but don't *speak for* my community.

Most non-Indian people, generally, are totally unaware of the multicultural diversity among the roughly 280 tribal nations in the United States. So it is ambitious, at best, to assume that any one person can "speak for" all of us. However, any time a Native American expresses him or herself publicly they are deemed to be doing just that.

While still maintaining some "attachment" to their heritage, contemporary American Indian artists are expected to make political statements. Their personal reflections are immediately seen as representative of a general "American Indian point

Rudy Martin

Rudy Martin is director of public relations for the American Indian Community House in New York City. Affiliated with the New York Martin Luther King Commission on Nonviolence, he is a member of the Ethnic Equal Opportunity Committee of the Screen Actors Guild, the New York City American Indian Heritage Committee, and the New York State American Indian Advisory Council Committee. He works extensively with the media to try to correct misconceptions, break down stereotypes, and present a true picture of American Indian people to the public.

of view." But in reality their statements are judged by non-Indians in accordance with the stereotypes, images, and misconceptions that non-Indians have of Indians. If an artist does not fit into the preconceived notions of the patron, the artist is viewed as "less than authentic" or "less than traditional." If the artist's work expressed personal anarchic or colorful representations of Native imagery, then the expectations are fulfilled and the viewer is secure in maintaining his or her ignorance. An Indian artist has the difficult choice of either promoting themselves as an individual or as an American Indian. Often the economics of the times influence that decision.

These economic pressures have in many cases forced some Native Americans to become "progressives"—i.e., believers in American progress—which has allowed the very core of their beings to be compromised. For example, strip mining is an affront to the spiritual foundation of Native peoples, yet some Native American people; because of the influence from government schools, television, books, drugs, or economic need; have been convinced that strip mining is important to the Manifest Destiny of America. So, they think they should be in favor of strip mining. Some are even active in their spiritual ceremonies, which are basically a reaffirmation of their relationship to the environment. They justify their "progressive" feelings by saying that "it is for the good of the tribe or nation." They have been fooled into thinking that the survival of our cultures depends on economic stability. Native American people today embody what happens when societies who believe in individual expression are severely limited in practicing this and are forced to "adopt" lifestyles alien to them. The traditions and cultural attitudes are intertwined in many cases with non-Indian values. Still, these "progressive" feelings are by no means the norm. Traditional Natives exist who still maintain their identities in their pure forms with lifestyles that reflect this daily.

The Iroquois people, for example, traditionally take many days of careful deliberation before they even select a spokesperson. That spokesperson then can address only one issue for one day. Someone who has the temerity to try and speak for all Native American people without being designated to do so, does a disservice to the listeners as well as the people he or she allegedly speaks for.

The American Indian communities of North America communicate with each other now more than ever. We have many issues in common; lost identities, re-establishment of traditional values, plastic shamans, environmental degradations, and sovereignty and treaty right infringements. Major battles are being waged in courts, schools, and in the media around these problems. They bond us together spiritually and morally. We support each other as best we can. We advise on and publicize one another's concerns, but we each address them individually, with respect for our particular priorities.

All in all it is hard to be an American Indian, especially if it is recognized what being American Indian means. It requires courage, commitment and dedication to adhere to this heritage that, nevertheless, survives against all odds. Like the environment they stand for, American Indian cultures have been beset and invaded by unnatural forces, forces determined to pollute their very being. When American Indian and non-Indian people respect who we are, as a people, we will have taken the first step towards real community. A community that shares the love of Mother Earth and truly respects the individual's right to self expression; that, as a goal which we can *all* work for, speaks for itself.

The Real Next Wave

Multicultural Artists and Empowerment as Sources for New American Art

Fred Wei-han Ho

How alternative are the "alternatives"? A casual survey of the "experimental" or "new" performance scene in the U.S. confirms that what has come to be called New American Art (or "new forms" or "new wave" as some funders and presenters label today's experimental performance work) is neither really new nor that American, but a continuation of Eurocentrism and white chauvinism. The democratization of American culture remains a major challenge.

In the yuppie-appealing new performance market, entertainment, titillation and the thrill of the exotic predominate over social criticism or revolutionary visions. The occasional "blending" of Third World rhythms, dance and visuals, when done without regard to cultural context and intent, is nothing more than exoticism—the spicing up of an otherwise tired Euro-American scene. This is the white bawana syndrome in which liberal, well-meaning white composers have the resources to hire Third World musicians in "fusion" works of grand scale. Totally apolitical and without regard to social and cultural context, these works continue imperialistic cultural expropriation. (If only Paul Simon would understand why *Graceland* drew such heat for its obliviousness to apartheid.)

A large part of the problem is that virtually all of the "new wave" presenters and booking consortiums are led by whites. Communities of color (African American, Asian American, Latino and Native American) lack sufficient economic resources

Fred Wei-han Ho

Fred Wei-han Ho (formerly Houn) is a Chinese American composer/arranger, baritone saxophonist, writer, and multimedia artist based in San Francisco and New York City. He leads the Afro-Asian Music Ensemble, whose latest recording, *We Refuse to be Used and Abused,* is on Soul Note Records, and the Asian American Art Ensemble, whose latest recording, *A Song for Manong: The Soundtrack to Part 3 of Bamboo that Snaps Back,* is on AsianImprov Records.

and institutional development to have their own producing networks. Therefore what is promoted and presented proceeds from the experience and sensibilities of a virtually all-white circle, with little possibility for artists of color to find significant alternative support. Those token few artists of color who are presented are politically nonconfrontational, carefully avoiding issues of racism and the struggles of their communities; and are not deeply rooted in their respective cultural traditions. Here, as in the mainstream, the most assimilated are the most acceptable.

Our struggle as artists of color is for legitimacy, respect, and fair compensation—fundamentally a political struggle for the expansion of democracy and for full equality. We must not be defensive about our identity. I am an Asian American artist, not an artist who simply happens to be Asian American. I am proud of my people's heritage and draw from the heritage and experiences of Asians in America as my own organic cultural inspiration. Too often, in reactive fear of being "ghettoized," we opt for "colorblind" rationalizations (e.g., "I'm an artist" or "My work is universal"). This defensiveness arises from the stigma of inferiority that white supremacist society has foisted on our cultures. Of course we are artists! Pride in our heritage and identity doesn't imply inferiority on any level nor that our work is less "universal." Our art must confront the ubiquitous realities of racism and national oppression and not cop out in "art for art's sake" apologias.

In the struggle to discard the biases contained in our training and socialization processes, artists of color must, as Amilcar Cabral put it, "return to the source." This is the task and responsibility of embracing the lives, thoughts, and feelings of our communities in order to deeply understand our experience. For me, as an American-born Chinese of white suburban middle-class background, it is an ongoing process of coming to know the Chinese American community in a comprehensive and intuitive way.

In taking up this task, the artist of color is often necessarily an archivist, archaeologist, oral historian, sociologist, and social worker all rolled into one. Layers of distortion, misinformation, neglect, and omission need excavation. For example, when preparing to do a multimedia work on Filipino Americans, I realized that much of what even Filipinos regard as their folk songs are products of their colonization by the Spanish and not necessarily true folk culture. The really indigenous music that survives today is *kulintang* music of the southern Philippines. Yet many Filipinos, influenced by a colonial mentality, consider this music to be "primitive" and "dirty."

The folk and traditional cultural forms of our heritages as peoples of color provide a rich wellspring of community memory and oral traditions, of songs, dances, rituals, symbols and crafts. As an Asian American artist, I feel that the great bulk of the early history of the immigrant laborers remains largely untreated in artistic works. The experimental possibilities, utilizing traditional forms and historical subjects, are boundless.

Upon doing work in the largely immigrant community of Boston's Chinatown, I came to recognize the importance of language and the folk culture of China as important formal considerations. Artistic form and approach must always be in the context of the social and cultural experiences of the people which one's art addresses and for whom one's art is made.

Use of tradition doesn't have to mean deference to political or artistic conservatism. I have also found, in doing benefits with my jazz ensembles for a Chinese immigrant audience, an enthusiastic response to innovative, experimental, and radical artistic forms. When we combined indigenous *kulintang* music with avant-garde jazz—a radical combination never before done in the U.S.—traditional Filipino community audiences were ecstatic. The new and experimental will pose a challenge to the status quo whether it be in culture or community politics. And the most dangerous and powerful work is connected to the breadth of cultural sources, yet dares to transform the entire culture.

The cultural work of the progressive or revolutionary-minded artist of color seeks to change reality, to offer insight, and to inspire a vision, spirit and possibility for change—to liberate. This liberation results not from abstract calls or propositions, but from gathered experience and collective reflection rendered in a dramatic manner through our art. The score for an experimental opera of mine, "A Chinaman's Chance," synthesizes elements of Chinese opera with jazz, while the libretto presents the collective, heightened, "bitter strength" voice of the coolie laborers in militant attack on the white bourgeoisie (railroad barons) and the labor aristocracy (anti-Chinese labor demagogues) as well as Chinese foremen and profiteers who sold out.

Often, the artist of color is told that "crossing over" to a "general audience" is the mark of artistic achievement and success (often remarked as "artistic maturity" and "appeal"). The cultural chauvinism in this notion is clear. There is nothing wrong with performing and presenting one's work to one's own community—being presented by outside groups is not necessarily an indication of higher artistry.

Local, state and national arts funding and presenting organizations must be made to adopt cultural affirmative action not only in proclamations, but in funding allocations, panel review processes, and administrative management. We must make them commit to a systematic and active fostering of the cultural life and artistic growth of the communities of color in America. Sharp criticism and demands for democracy and equality must be made to any purported "American" art activity that in fact is Eurocentric and white chauvinist, as cultural pluralism is the genuine American way.

I use the term "multiculturalism" to mean "cultural affirmative action"—the necessity to support and develop the arts and culture of African Americans, Latinos, Asian/Pacific Islanders, and Native Americans. The political empowerment of Third World communities and the building of a strong community base to support our cultural work is key to the demand that mainstream institutions practice multiculturalism. Artists of color must build unity with political activists and other sectors of our communities that work to develop and control our own institutions and the political, economic, social, and cultural life of our peoples. The electoral political campaigns must include a cultural agenda, and business sectors of our communities should become a network that supports our social and cultural development.

In the Bay Area, for example, Asian American progressive musicians formed AsianImprov Records (AIR), a music/recording company to promote and distribute the cutting edge of our music. One goal is to develop a consumer market among Asian Americans for their own music. But AIR is more than simply a music and business partnership. A political body, the artists/organizers work with the Asian American movement to promote the growth of progressive culture, and to organize vehicles for distributing and promoting progressive Asian American music.

AIR also seeks to enter the general contemporary and modernist American music scene, but on its own terms. By developing close working relationships with progressive and supportive music critics, presenters and other musical organizations, AIR is contributing to the effort for a real alternative, multicultural and experimental American music movement, one that does not necessitate one culture crossing over to be acceptable to another.

A profoundly new American culture is emerging. The struggle of artists of color to assert their work is part of a redefining of what is American. The implications are revolutionary.

From "A Song for Manong: Part 3 of Bamboo that Snaps Back," a tribute to the Filipino American immigrants. Fred Ho (saxophonist) with members of San Francisco's Kulintang Arts. Photo by Kingmond Young.

Putting Our Heads Together

Jawole Willa Jo Zollar
Interview by Hattie Gossett

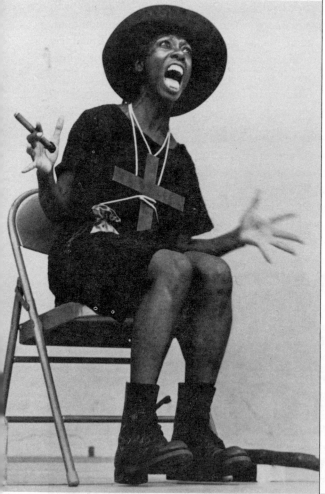

Jawole Willa Jo Zollar in her "LifeDance I ... The Magician (the Return of She)". Photo by Hakim Mutlaq.

Jawole Willa Jo Zollar

Jawole cut her teeth on scat singing and honky-tonks resplendent with hip-swiveling, shoulder-shaking, fast-talking, exotic dancers "who were not the least bit vulgar." Her mother was a cabaret singer in the blues tradition. She brought her dance education to New York City in 1980 and founded Urban Bush Women in 1984. The company synthesizes the spiritual influence of her upbringing with the technical demands of her formal dance training. In uniting concern for the history and actuality of African Americans with her interest in cross disciplinary theatrical forms, Jawole has received international recognition for her unique talent in improvisational dance performance.

Hattie: My name is Hattie Gossett. I am a writer, and I am interviewing my friend Jawole Willa Jo Zollar in her apartment on a high floor in a tenant-controlled, beautifully maintained walk-up building in the Bronx. It's a gray, rainy, muggy day. The humidity is one hundred percent, the temperature is 55, even though it's only the middle of February. The interview takes place in Jawole's small, rose-colored bed-sitting room, furnished with wicker, cotton-print and satin-covered pillows, hardwood, books, a sprinkling of shells, crystals, and other found objects.

Jawole, please describe your early Kansas City performance experiences, the types of shows, choreography styles, venues, audiences?

Jawole: My sister and I started at the Joseph Stevenson School of Dance when we were about six and seven. Stevenson was a significant influence in Kansas City. He had studied with Katherine Dunham,[1] been a ballroom dancer and a tap dancer, and was interested in synthesizing all these elements. We studied tap, Afro-Cuban, and flash dancing, a style people nowadays would associate with the Nicholas Brothers. It's more acrobatic than tap. Mr. Stevenson was the only one in Kansas City offering these kinds of training.

> ## Hattie Gossett
>
> Hattie Gossett, author of *Presenting ... Sister No-Blues* (Firebrand Books, 1988) and former magazine editor, has taught college-level journalism and Black women's literature. Her writings have been performed by jazz, reggae, theater, and dance artists. Hattie's work as a spoken-word artist takes her to festivals, conferences, bars, jails, shelters, theaters, and street corners around the country. She frequently works as a researcher and dramaturge with Urban Bush Women.

After my sister and I had been at his school for a while, we became part of his revue which performed for cabaret shows. A social club would have a party, rent out a cabaret hall, and hire Mr. Stevenson to bring his revue as the entertainment. People always got dressed up. These were definitely big social events. The type of show we did depended on the sponsoring organization—whether it was The Links[2] or Sam and Dave's 19th Street Social Club or the postal workers union or a debutante ball. Most shows included a comic emcee, a flash act or a tap dance act, an exotic dancer or a stripper, and a James Brown-type act as the feature. We were in the children's act doing Afro-Cuban dance. There was always a live band. In those days everybody partied to live bands. We had to go to the band just before the show and tell them what songs to play, what tempos we wanted, where we wanted the breaks.

Hattie: Because there was no six weeks of rehearsal with the band.

Jawole: Right. It was a different type of thing. We had a set act, we knew all the standards, so it was easy because the bands at that time were used to working with dancers. In our yearly recitals we would do a whole choreographed, costumed show featuring various kinds of dancing. One of the Afro-Cuban dances we did in clubs was from a larger show called *The Sacrifice,* involving African drums and an elaborate painted backdrop of a volcano. As kids we weren't too concerned about what any of this meant. We learned the routines and did them. It was only years later that I realized the meaning of these dances. Our costumes were real clothes—we never used leotards or other standard dance wear. Though we studied it, ballet was never really a big part of the curriculum. The emphasis was more on capturing the street band dance feeling and Afro-Cuban dancing. Tap definitely was a big part of it. Since I was never any good at tap, I didn't pursue it.

Hattie: And was this before integration, before Black people were legally allowed to rent facilities in white hotels?

Jawole: Right. However, we didn't have any sense of that. We thought Kansas City was all Black because we grew up in all Black surroundings and it felt natural to us. We had no sense of restriction. In hindsight I understand people didn't go downtown to the white hotels until the '60s, which is when I left Mr. Stevenson to go to college.

Hattie: Could you say something about your sources of inspiration—writing, music, other?

Jawole: That's a very interesting question because depending on the day it's asked, the answer varies. Since we've been talking about some of my early experiences, I recognize—not for the first time—that early training, the classes, doing the recitals, shows, has been a constant source of inspiration. Mr. Stevenson repeatedly emphasized how dance comes from the inside out; you don't take something and put it on from the outside. So styles are very important. One reason I've been so attracted and inspired by Black music and writing, particularly the work of Black women writers, is because the sense of style is so distinctive. Musically, you recognize the style of each musician. You hear Coltrane and know that's Coltrane, you know that's Ornette Coleman. I think this knowledge inspired me on a greater level to really deal with style. Specific writers have inspired works. Jamaica Kincaid's novel *At the Bottom of the River* inspired an early work for the company called *River Songs.* Reading her book made me think about everything that could happen at a river; if you grew up in a river society, for instance. *Anarchy, Wild Women and Dinah* was inspired by many, many literary sources, including Ntozake Shange's *Colored Girls* to Toni Morrison's character Sula. More recently *Shelter,* one of the sections of *Heat,* contains one of your poems. *Heat* was inspired by many writers, particularly Thought Music, the writing/performance trio of Jessica Hagedorn, Robbie McCauley, and Laurie Carlos,[3] all of whom not only collaborated on the writing of the piece, but performed in it as well, plus Laurie was the director. So I think words have always inspired me though in college I was discouraged from dancing to words.

Hattie: Yeah, I wanted to ask you about that. It seems kind of unusual to me to hear a dancer say she's inspired by words.

Jawole: Oh, I don't know about other dancers but the thing I like about words is this: If I'm trying to find an idea, if I go out and look at other choreographic work then I'm left strongly with the image of that work. If I read something, my imagination is more open and more fertile. Because if a book or a piece of writing is on it for me, especially fiction, it becomes so vivid I can see those characters, I can see the scene—like a movie playing in my mind. The words act as a stimulant to my imagination in a way choreographic works don't. Also when you're reading you can stop and space out on an idea. You can stop and . . .

Hattie: Fast forward?

Jawole: . . . into stream of consciousness. When you're watching something you can do that, which I do, but then I realize oh, I've missed something going on in the production and I have to keep tuning myself back.

Hattie: Plus you can read any time you want.

Jawole: I don't have to go somewhere, get dressed up, get on the train.

Hattie: Will you say something about your experience as part of more than one creative community? For instance, you are part of what in New York is called the downtown community. And at the same time you are part of uptown[4] performing communities in Harlem and the Bronx and of a national touring community which takes you to women's festivals, to Appalachia, to African American festivals, and to postmodern dance venues in the U.S. and abroad. I see you as a solo artist, and Urban Bush Women* (UBW) as a company, as a part of these different communities which aren't necessarily in opposition to each other.

Jawole: I've always been involved in different communities. In college I was a member of the Black Players Guild, and I worked with a political organization, all while working in the dance department. I found something interesting in all of these places. I guess one of the reasons I don't always think I'm a part of the downtown community is I dislike the term. For most people downtown means mostly white, and I think there's a lot of truth to that. I think the more interesting question is why am I included in the downtown community?

Hattie: That's another way of looking at it. Why didn't the powers that be just let you languish in Harlem or the Bronx?

Jawole: Why Urban Bush Women? Who knows? When we started as a company the scenario I had written in my head was: we would have a premiere concert, we

---

*Because she has worked in close collaboration with them, Jowale acknowledges her gratitude to the members of Urban Bush Women, whose continued creative initiative helps bring forth the work. Past members are: Anita Gonzales, Carla McSarlane, Janice Reed, Carol Webster, and Robin Wilson. Current members are: Grisha Coleman, Theresa Tousar, Christina Jones, Christine King, Viola Scheely, and Marlies Yearby.

Urban Bush Women and Jessica Hagedorn, Robbie McCauley, and Laurie Carlos, Thought Music, in "Heat." Projections design by Leni Schwendinger. Photo by Johan Elbers.

would have thirty, forty people a night, we would struggle for five to seven years, maybe get a *New York Times* review, then maybe start to get some recognition. And I was prepared to go that road. When a different scenario developed, I couldn't have been more surprised. So who knows?

Hattie: What about your experiences in Harlem, the Bronx, or other communities?

Jawole: When I first moved to New York I lived in Harlem and studied at Dianne McIntyre's Sounds in Motion on 125th Street.[5] Harlem was pretty much my world. And I loved it. I saw creativity there—a vibrance missing from other parts of the city. Through all the madness of city living I saw people's desire to make work, make art—like the guy who paints murals on the metal security gates that protect stores at night. His work really impressed me because here you have block after block of these ugly security gates and he made art out of them.

It was an inspiring time for me. Dianne McIntyre was very encouraging. She gave me studio space, she produced studio concerts for developing choreographers. I met most of the UBW company at Sounds in Motion. I met a lot of musicians, theater people, visual artists. It was a hub of the arts—the Studio Museum in Harlem[6] was nearby and Roger Furman's New Heritage Theater[7] was in the same building as Sounds in Motion.

Hattie: What about performing in communities like Harlem and the Bronx? What is it like in terms of audiences, facilities, support? Is there interest in your work?

Jawole: That question is always complex. The presenter has so much to do with it. If a presenter hasn't done marketing homework, you may end up with a very small audience. On the other hand, if a presenter does marketing homework, you'll likely end up with a good audience. There's definitely an interest in our work. At the same time there's an economic problem in this country, so when you're talking about any people of color, their institutions are probably in financial distress, the resources are more limited. Sometimes I also think presenters are simply worn out from a lot of years of running the organization and getting it to survive with proportionately less support. Urban Bush Women did a 1988 Bronx season. We put a lot of energy into marketing and getting people out. I feel real good about the results. We were very successful in getting a different type of audience than downtown. What I learned from our Bronx season is the need for context. When you perform for people for whom theater-going is not a part of their regular experience, if you want to reach them, if you want to have a real dialogue, and you want them to feel that dialogue during the performance, then it's important to provide context.

Hattie: Now, you said something a minute ago about the difference between audiences in Harlem and Bronx and downtown. Could you elaborate?

Jawole: A friend of mine, actor John O'Neal, tells the audience, "This isn't television, you can talk back to me." Black audiences for the most part understand and will talk back and respond. They understand live theater means interacting with performers. For my work that response is crucial.

Hattie: Do you feel sustained in your creative vision by the response from this audience?

Jawole: Performing is giving out energy and when you're giving it out if you don't feel it coming back you're worn out after a performance. It's different from being tired after performing. When an audience has been there with you and given you that energy back, you're sustained. Afterwards you may feel tired, but not wiped out. When you have to go out there night after night it's important. Other sustaining forces are money earned through my work which enables me to live without having an outside job, and the support of other artists. The thing I love about New York is the supportive artist community.

Hattie: You have created two characters—I don't know if they are representative of your work, but I like them. And I've noticed a lot of other people do, too. The two I have in mind are Aunt Dinah from *Anarchy, Wild Women and Dinah,* and another character I call Rev. JZ. Will you say something about who these women are and where they came from?

Jawole: Aunt Dinah came out of conversations among the company trying to remember a childhood game about Aunt Dinah. One of the members of the company said, "Oh, I remember it." Somebody else said, "But I played a different Dinah game." And then somebody else said, "I know a different Dinah story." Then someone brought in a Dinah song her mother had taught her. It turned out that there's a body of work around this person Dinah. Who was she? So I started doing research to determine if she is a fully documented character like High John The Conqueror about whom there is a written, documented body of work. There was hardly anything documented about Dinah. Her material is mostly scattered in people's memories of songs and games. So we kept investigating and finding more stories about our undocumented worker Dinah. Some of the material, like the songs by Bessie Jones you brought to us, originated in South Carolina and Georgia.

Why wasn't she documented? There is an almost exclusively male focus in written materials on Black folk heroes. A lot of the songs and stories we found had to do with Dinah as a strong, independent woman. She did what she wanted to do. She didn't take abuse off of a guy. During slavery she was independent and strong and was probably one of those slaves who just kept on running and kept on running. You couldn't keep her. That's where we got the "anarchy" part of the title. She did not follow the conventions of society. I think about all the Aunt Dinahs I have known— from lesbians who decided to raise children to my mother who made her own path. Some women want to make their own way. They are struggling against their oppression as women. Then you introduced me to the concept of the wild woman from the song "Wild Women Don't Get the Blues" by Ida Cox and I knew Dinah definitely was a wild woman. That's how the work became *Anarchy, Wild Women and Dinah*. Edwina Lee Tyler[8] and Tiyé Giraud[9] collaborated on the piece and performed in it. From the beginning, Edwina provided strong clues about the personification of Dinah, and she won a Bessie for the music she composed for the piece. Tiyé expanded the company's musical horizons with the songs and games she contributed and her vocal coaching and scoring.

As the story grew we all started discovering things. The "Girlfriends" section of the piece came about when we discovered how Dinah supported other women. She had a community of women around her that was strong. (Singing) "I'm going away, to see Aunt Dinah." A lot of songs had to do with going away. After collecting all this material and working with it, we wanted to be like Dinah, walk like Dinah. She was our role model. Everyone in the company started bringing out the Dinah in herself. This was a really strong process, a major growth period for the company. The idea of being strong, independent, saying who you are, assertive—in fact, we have come to that on the stage.

Rev. JZ, on the other hand, whose real name is The Magician, comes from *Life Dances,* a series which will eventually include twenty-two solo works examining the Tarot, Christian mysticism, and aspects of various African religions. So far I have done four in collaboration with Edwina Lee Tyler and Tiyé Giraud. There's a part of them in me, but only a part. Rev. JZ evolved from the Tarot card picturing The Magician. In developing these characters I tried to connect Christian and African religious symbols, and how I interpret them. The characters are also based on very personal kinds of experiences which are hard to talk about.

Hattie: Rev. JZ / The Magician seems so striking and profound to me because we see her as she progresses through a whole line of change. When we first see her she is in black combat boots, an old lady's black dress and hat, with a big cross around her neck, waving a Bible, and she's drinking out of a wine bottle and preaching. At the end, we see her in a much different state of dress and behavior. How does she grow or progress from her initial manifestation to her final one and what does it mean? Is she just an old crazy drunk lady? Or is there some other meaning?

Jawole: Well, there is meaning. It has to do with transformation. All the *Life Dance* characters have to do with unlayering of the self. Whatever people are on the outside—bag person or account executive—they have layers underneath. If you peel away those layers what do you get? The *Life Dance* characters all have memories they don't understand. Maybe The Magician is drinking because she has a memory that drinking and preaching go together. Well, in certain African rituals, that's true. But her memory is displaced and out of context so she's stuck.

I see people in the street who we would term crazy and wonder what has gotten ahold of them. What are they trying to remember? There's a guy I see on 125th Street who wears all these buttons and signs and I ask myself what is he trying to remember? In other societies people like this are nurtured so they can peel all that away. Our society casts them off. The guy carries so much, everything he has put on his body has a meaning. I don't think it's an arbitrary thing. There's a reason. But it's out of kilter because we live in a society that's out of kilter. That's what interests me about the characters I develop.

Notes

1. Katherine Dunham is an African American anthropologist, choreographer, dance educator, and performer who has made major though frequently overlooked contributions to American dance theater. Her Dunham Technique enables Western-trained dancers to learn the intricacies of West African and Caribbean dance. During the '30s, '40s, and '50s, when she was based in New York City, her school was a crucial training institution, her choreography was featured in major Hollywood films and Broadway shows, and her company toured to major dance and theater venues all over the world. Her school is presently located in East St. Louis, MO. The Alley Company in 1988 did a season devoted to the recreation of some of her outstanding works.
2. The Links is a nationwide African American social-educational organization whose members are usually doctors, lawyers, teachers, and other professionals.
3. Born and raised in the Philippines, Jessica Hagedorn is a writer, performer, director, and teacher now living in New York City who enjoys working often with Jawole Zollar. Her multimedia performance pieces include *Mango Tango, Peachfish, The Art of War, Tenement Lover.* Pantheon Books will publish her first novel, *Dog Eaters,* in 1990; other books include *Dangerous Music* and *Pet Food and Tropical Apparitions.*

Robbie McCauley wrote *My Father and The Wars* and *Indian Blood,* parts of a multimedia serial work with music by Ed Montgomery, which she performed in New York at Franklin Furnace, St. Mark's Danspace, and The Kitchen, and on tour throughout the eastern states with her company. Robbie has collaborated with choreographer Fred Holland in *Delicate Prey* and *What I Like About Us.* She is also a vocal coach and acting teacher. Excerpts from *My Father and The Wars* have appeared in *Catalyst* magazine.

Laurie Carlos, who has worked in theater since she was fifteen, won an Obie as an original cast member of *For*

Colored Girls and a Bessie for her work with Urban Bush Women. New York State Council on the Arts (NYSCA) commissioned her to write *White Chocolate* for a 1990 BACA-Downtown production; she also won a New York Foundation of the Arts (NYFA) theater fellowship. Laurie wrote and directed *Non-Sectarian Conversations with the Dead, Organdy Falsetto, Where's Armenia?* and *Monkey Dances.* Carlos works with Butch Morris, Don Meissner, Hattie Gosset, Ntozake Shange, Thulani Davis, Bill T. Jones, Indigo Project CCNY, City Kids, and Vivian Selbo. She is the performance art curator for the 1990 Atlanta Black Arts Festival.

4. Uptown here means communities north of 96th Street, the class-color line running east to west across Manhattan. People who live below 96th Street in the power areas of Manhattan have another usage: they refer to the commercial theater district around West 42nd Street and the Carnegie Hall-Lincoln Center area from 57th to 72nd Streets as uptown. This interpretation really isn't logical since it assumes all life ends at 96th Street and ignores the rich cultures which thrive above that class-color line. For these people, downtown means below 14th Street—Soho, the West Village, the East Village.

5. Dianne McIntyre is a major African American choreographer, performer, and dance educator whose studio-school and company, in existence since the 1960s, both bear the name Sounds in Motion. She has formulated a movement style incorporating elements of modern dance with traditional African and African American dance, and exerted enormous influence on the modern dance world.

6. The Studio Museum in Harlem, founded during the 1960s, is devoted to preserving and exhibiting African American and African visual arts. Presently it is located on 125th Street slightly west of the location mentioned in the interview.

7. The New Heritage Theater was founded in the 1960s by director, writer, and actor Roger Furman, who was artistic director until his death in the mid-80s. Furman established a tradition of presenting new works, adaptations, and readings as well as training in theater arts. The theater is now housed in the City College of New York (CCNY) complex.

8. Edwina Lee Tyler, percussionist, composer, choreographer, dancer, vocalist, has toured Europe, the U.S., and Africa as a solo artist and with her ensemble, A Piece of the World. Edwina has performed with the Capoieras of Bahia, the Eva Jessey Choir, the Marie Brookes Children's Theater, and Dance Theater of Harlem, where she also served as Director of Percussion Studies. She composed the music for Ayoke Chenzira's film *They Dance to Her Drum,* about legendary African American choreographer/dancer Syvilla Fort, and is to be the subject of Edwin Kim Kimber's video documentary *To Be a Massai.* Her first recording, *Drum Drama,* is available through Ladyslipper Distributors.

9. Tiyé Giraud, vocalist, composer, actress, storyteller, vocal coach, began her musical career at age four on the stage of the Apollo Theater in Harlem. Proficient on a number of instruments, she has recorded with Pete Seeger, appeared in off-Broadway plays and at clubs and colleges as a solo artist and with bands. As a shekere teacher and folklorist, she has traveled the world giving lecture-demonstrations which explore the interrelationship between the blues and other forms of African-based music. The musical director of UBW, she also performs with Ladygourde Sangoma, of which she is a founding member, and was formerly the lead singer with Women of the Calabash.

Knowing Our History, Teaching Our Culture

Willie Birch

There is little difference in the way I create and the way I teach art. I see no separation between my dual roles of artist and teacher—the two complement each other. I have been teaching art for eighteen years—the past seven have been in special art programs for mostly "Third World" public school students. The satisfaction I gain seeing a group of students grow in self awareness during the course of my workshops is the same satisfaction and fulfillment I feel in completing a sculpture or series of paintings. As both an artist and a teacher—as an artist/teacher—I look for ways to inform my diverse audiences about issues that concern me.

My educational experiences during the '50s and '60s played an important part in shaping this philosophy. As a child growing up in a segregated South, my teachers were all African Americans. I had the good fortune to receive a public school education from teachers who seemed to genuinely care about the future of their students. This care motivated me to learn. I showed promise in drawing and painting, and one of my art teachers took a special interest in me. She created an after-school art program, for me and a few other classmates, and by the age of fourteen I was convinced that I would become an artist. What being an artist meant to me would take shape over the next few years.

In high school, I studied history with a teacher named Mr. Higgenbotham. One day he closed his classroom door. He told us that he was about to teach us information about ourselves that was considered illegal by the school system, and that if the "powers that be" were to find out, he would lose his job. What Mr. Higgenbotham taught us was then called "Negro History." What he instilled in us was a desire to understand and learn the truth about ourselves as African peoples, even though it might have jeopardized his future.

> ## Willie Birch
>
> As a visual artist, Willie Birch's work evokes the inherent beauty and dignity of people who suffer from premeditated as well as unintentional neglect in our urban society. As an artist/teacher, he tries to convey to his students the idea that art can be a means of empowerment, serving as an inspiration to question the world we live in, and to decide what role to play in creating the future.

Later, as a young college art student during the '60s, I first experienced the work of a socially conscious visual artist named Faith Ringgold. A professor who had attended an African American art conference brought back slides of her works along with those of other African American artists. Although I was impressed by many of the works, Ms. Ringgold's paintings moved me profoundly. They were extremely direct and violent, honest in their depictions of what I and many of my fellow brothers and sisters were experiencing. One piece, which depicted Black and white figures attacking each other in a racial confrontation, haunted me, stirring images I wanted to forget. I had never before been confronted with such vital work—work that evoked my personal experiences in America. I was inspired to create a series of works addressing such issues as discrimination, the Vietnam War, and the impact of Martin Luther King's death.

The Power of Art

My work is rooted in the notion that art can provoke social change. I do not believe that my art—or any art—can eliminate racism, apartheid, drugs, sexism, AIDS, or nuclear war. But when experienced, art can raise the people's consciousness, which is the first step in achieving social change. Throughout the world, artists are using their individual and collective talents to keep social issues before the public, forcing people to question their respective roles and responsibilities in shaping our future.

As an artist, I do not live in a vacuum. I am constantly absorbing the life of my community, recording it in my public and personal works. My wood carved sculptures take many months to create and are the product of intense periods of reflection. They are memorials or monuments to this community in its broadest sense. Abstract in form, they draw on the collective memories, aesthetics and spiritual ideals of the African diaspora. My paintings come much more quickly, and the ideas they contain tend to be more spontaneous impressions of my immediate community. In these, I am sometimes compelled to create works that do not exclusively represent the positive aspects of that community. Some of these images are not the ones many Americans expect to see, especially as "Art." But a major function of my art is to serve as a historical record of my times. I want to force the viewer to see not only "America the Beautiful," but to confront situations and events that bring into question our human values—the America that flashes across our television screens in times of crisis. I want the viewer to reflect upon those images only seen in passing as we drive through a "ghetto" area, the forgotten America that suffers from premeditated as well as unintentional neglect—the "other" America that I live in.

For the past four years, I have been working on a series of paintings entitled "A Personal View of Urban America." These works are direct, narrative, and functional. Influenced by folk art, children's art, kitsch, and the mass media, they mix words with imagery to provide a greater clarity for the viewer. Within the paintings, words may appear as graffiti, on billboards, or on protest banners. Most recently, I have incorporated text and imagery into the frame itself, making the title an integral part of the work.

"Drug Bust on South Third," Willie Birch, 1987 (42" x 54", gouache on paper).

Teaching Our Culture

In my particular situation as artist/teacher, I feel a special responsibility to consciously help shape the visions of present and future generations by empowering my students. As an artist, I learned years ago the importance of defining one's own history. As an artist/teacher, I find it important to teach students about their own cultural background. These children will one day assume the responsibilities of maintaining and passing on their heritage to succeeding generations. Unfortunately, I feel it is not in the interest of many people in the dominant culture to teach people of color about the contributions of their ancestors to the culture of the United States and the world. Because many children of color have little knowledge of themselves, and cannot read or write, I develop art workshops that attempt to address these needs. When students learn the power of art to communicate ideas and to influence the development of observation, they also learn to make independent choices, sometimes on a different basis from what the standard school programs teach.

Workshops

My workshops are usually from ten to twenty-two weeks long. This gives me the opportunity to create a series of projects. In planning my workshops, I always set goals: a positive self-image, the importance of understanding the world, how art can be used as a means of empowerment, an increase in reading and writing skills, and the development of good work habits. I teach students of all ages, though I prefer to interact with elementary school students, finding that the younger the students, the more open they are to questioning points of view that have been presented as truths, and thus the more they are able to take in the work that comes out of the program. Because young students have a need to personalize their art, my first two projects usually address those individualized needs, keeping in mind that future projects will address the needs of the group, the community, and the world.

Most educators believe that about ninety percent of our learning is acquired visually, so I always start my workshops with a slide presentation that includes artworks from different countries. I have visited many of the places shown in the slides and am able to bring a firsthand knowledge in my presentation to the students. By showing slides of different cultures and their art—including Egyptian, American Indian, Mexican, and Puerto Rican—I expose students to the similarities and differences of cultures and art throughout the world, as well as the diversity found in this country. I emphasize the fact that the United States is made up of many cultures and that this society has borrowed or taken from other cultures without acknowledging the contributions of those peoples. An example I use is Hatshepsut's obelisk in Egypt. When that slide is shown, most of the students usually see it as the Washington Monument. This opens an opportunity for dialogue about the nature of Western culture. By juxtaposing the art and cultures of the United States with that of older cultures outside of the "contemporary Western world," the students can begin to perceive contradictions inherent in what they have been taught. I hope to raise the level of consciousness and set in motion questions about how they see themselves and their ancestors in the development of world culture.

Because a number of students I teach read below their grade level, I have created a bookmaking project. My goal for this project is to foster a love of books and what they can teach, and to instill in the students a conscious responsibility to pass on and share their experiences and knowledge with each other. Together, we read stories that have morals: the myth of Icarus, Aesop's fables, and American Indian creation stories. I then ask students to create two identical, hand-colored books, telling a tale with a moral drawn from their own experiences. I have found that even when these stories tell of unpleasant family or community experiences, they usually demonstrate that the lessons students need to learn can be found at home, in the instructions of family members or the advice of friends. At the end of the project, each student will keep one book, while the other will be contributed to the classroom or school library to serve future generations of students. The most rewarding thing about this project is that the students usually donate their better book to the library.

In a third project, students are asked to create a poster, choosing a theme they feel best expresses a social concern. Students are encouraged to list their concerns on the blackboard: racism, gun control, drug abuse, child abuse, animal abuse, babies having babies, nuclear war, etc. By seeing other classmates' concerns listed, students see other themes that they may or may not have considered. Using words and images, students are asked to illustrate the issue they feel strongest about, and, when complete, to write a paper explaining why they chose their particular subject. When the project is completed, influential community members are asked to help in displaying the posters and writings in neighborhood churches, groceries, banks, and offices. Because many people in the community know the students, the students receive firsthand responses to their work. This project becomes an important demonstration of the power of their art to communicate.

Our final project is always a public work—either a sculpture or a mural—that incorporates elements from each of the earlier projects. A recent workshop at P.S. 384, the Frances E. Carter Elementary School in Brooklyn, was organized around the theme "shelter." All of the projects dealt with how the students see themselves in relation to their immediate environment (home, school, family, and neighborhood). The final project, a sculpture for the school courtyard, bore images from the earlier stages.

In that instance, I had the opportunity to expand the workshop into a two-year program with a fellow artist/teacher, Kryssi Staikidis. The second-year projects were expanded to reach the community at large, with the public work project taking the form of three outdoor murals. The three classroom teachers involved in the program, Kryssi and I, sat down and decided that the three themes we would address in the murals would be the elderly, daycare, and fires in the neighborhood. We chose these three themes because they were issues that were already being discussed by the teachers and students in their classrooms.

After deciding which class would execute which mural, Kryssi and I met with individual classes to plan their execution. We set up appointments to visit the neighborhood daycare centers, senior citizen center, and firehouse, so that each class could see and talk to knowledgeable individuals about issues raised in their particular mural. When the classes returned to the workshop room, the students worked first individually, then as groups, organized according to the aesthetic similarities in the drawings. In selecting the three works that would become murals, Kryssi and I decided that the best way to guarantee the fairness of the final selections was to have the participating classes judge each others' work, with the understanding that we had the final decision.

When complete, the murals belong to the community. If an artwork is meaningful, it will survive because the community will accept and protect it. This is the community's way of choosing the art that speaks for it. To this day, no graffiti has appeared on these three murals.

There are workshops that do not reach their fullest potential. In my experience, when this happens it is almost always because teachers and administrators are intimidated by such programs and undermine their effectiveness and impact. Although I see my workshop as a program that is designed to complement the classroom curricula, I find that some teachers and administrators feel threatened by my vision of an empowering artmaking process. They prefer to view the workshop as a "regular" art program where art is "just" fun and games. This attitude affects the students, who usually do not work up to their potential.

I am often asked if the product is more important than the process. My answer is I do not believe it is a question of either/or, but rather a question of whether or not the objectives and goals of the workshop are met. I am told by supportive teachers, administrators, and concerned community individuals that my workshops make a difference, especially in fostering a positive self-image and developing good work ethics.

Assessing the Impact

I would say that as an artist/teacher, my impact on my community is long-range. Artists like myself whose work is labeled Black and social/political do not exist in the mainstream media. Because of the limited exposure my individual work receives I have reservations about stating how much immediate impact that work has. I know that historically art of this nature is usually recognized long after the fact. I feel comfortable with this reality.

"Shelter," 6th grade class at PS 384, Brooklyn, 1985 (approx. 12' high, oil on wood).

But as a teacher, I feel certain that I can help and have helped young students create a positive self-image. The young students we educate are our future, and if given the proper information and nurturing, will make decisions that have a positive impact on their community. By creating and teaching from the perspective of our cultural backgrounds, I know that I am bringing about and shaping another reality. And as an African American artist and a male, I also present students with an image that contradicts the negative, stereotypical ones that often appear in the mass media. I see no difference; both making and teaching art are instruments in my ongoing struggle for self-determination, self-definition, and empowerment for myself and my community.

Galeria de la Raza
A Study in Cultural Transformation
Amalia Mesa-Bains

Cultural work has been a significant part of the empowerment process in communities of color. Cultural presentation has served to signify the shared experience of the community and to resist the oppression of the larger society, and art has held up a mirror to that larger society that both indicts and defies. Within this tradition of cultural resistance, community art spaces have provided a context for social change.

Founded in 1970, San Francisco's Galeria de la Raza (Gallery of the People) is one of the many *centros* born out of the Chicano movement, a period of intense cultural reclamation in the 1960s and 1970s.[1] A key aspect of the aesthetics of *"el movimiento"* was the emphasis on everyday lived reality. Motivated by a sense of collectivity and the community's need for educational and political survival, emerging *centros* sought to provide an art that would inform and a presentation strategy that was anti-elitist and publicly accessible.

Over the years, under the leadership of René Yañez and Ralph Maradiaga, the Galeria was actively involved in the cultural life of the Mission district's Chicano/Latino community; organizing collective poster brigades, neighborhood mural projects, street spectacles, and cultural heritage celebrations. The Galeria billboard provides information for the neighborhood, while Galeria-sponsored traditional celebrations such as Día de

Amalia Mesa-Bains

Amalia Mesa-Bains is both an artist and art critic. She holds a Ph.D in psychology with emphasis on culture and identity. She curated the traveling exhibition, *Ceremony of Memory,* sponsored by the Center for Contemporary Art of Santa Fe, which presented contemporary altar and shrine work by Latino, Chicano, and Caribbean artists. A nationally known lecturer in the area of Latino art, Mesa-Bains is on the board of directors of Galeria de la Raza in San Francisco, CA. Her own installation work is touring internationally in the French exhibition, *Le Demon des Anges: Chicano Art from Los Angeles.* She has recently been appointed a commissioner of art for the city of San Francisco.

los Muertos, 16th of September, Cinco de Mayo, and the Navideña Bazaar have become annual community events. This kind of community-rooted cultural ceremony, which brings members together in shared aesthetic expression, gives authenticity to the Galeria's mission.

But any institution's attempt to provide an organic response to its community must include openness to change. The Galeria has always seen its community as reaching beyond the local Chicano/Latino population to encompass the greater Chicano/Latino population of the Southwest, Bay Area art activists, tourists, and others. Because we have relied on definitions from the national and international cultural communities, the growing cohesiveness of the national Chicano imperative has joined our concerns with other Latino and multicultural audiences.

Increasingly, demographic shifts and cultural transformations are redefining the Galeria's community and the community's needs. The community has grown to include a mix of scholars, artists, political activists, and cultural leaders from diverse places: California, Texas, New Mexico, Arizona, Seattle, Chicago, New York, Mexico, Latin America, and Europe. Increased immigration, inter-American telecommunications, and cultural transmigration have been major influences in redefining the range of cultural services we provide for the community as well as modes of presentation. Blends of new performance, folk art forms, and mixed media have expanded the artistic scope while blurring the distinctions of categories from fine to folk. Galeria presentations by former directors Ralph Maradiaga and René Yañez have ranged from an exhibit of traditional New Mexican "Santo" wood carvings, to "Stages," a multimedia performance art collaboration including multicultural artists such as Gronk/ASCO.

Throughout this transformation the Galeria has looked to scholars as well as artists as a source in providing direction. The results of the Chicano struggle for higher education have provided a visible scholarship that examines questions of cultural identity and change, and the work of scholars like Tomas Ybarra-Frausto has influenced the content of exhibitions and activities at the Galeria. The responsibility for authentic cultural presentation has grown to include publications and round tables that expand the aesthetic field. Galeria artists' monographs have provided new writers a context for Chicano and Latino art; they are also a response to the misinterpretation of Latino art within mainstream institutions.

In the larger area of the Americas the concerns of Central American solidarity and Latin American expression have also affected both the form and content of work presented at Galeria de la Raza. During periods of media disinformation that affected communities in the Bay Area, exhibits that focus on presenting cultural information take on great importance. The Border Workshop exhibition, a multimedia performance critique aimed at the realization of this north-south relationship, epitomizes the expanded notion of audience and authenticity. Artists such as Gomez Peña, Emily Hicks, and David Avalos used theater and installation to look at the exploitation of the undocumented, the immigration journey of newcomers, and media misrepresentation of these situations. In a time when new immigration policies have increased the tension for our communities these exhibits are very important.

A long-standing concern with farmworkers' rights has recently been reasserted with new and intensified focus. Ester Hernandez's exhibit, "The Defiant Eye," provided the aesthetic aperture for both the artist's personal farmworker history and the national concern with toxic pesticides. An exhibit of artwork by imprisoned Puerto Rican freedom fighters touchingly presented the art of the incarcerated. Perhaps one of the most powerful examples of the art of social commentary was Yolanda M. Lopez's "Cactus Hearts, Barbed Wire Dreams," a provocative multimedia installation which exposed the everyday commercial stereotypes of Mexicanas.

"Cactus Hearts, Barbed Wire Dreams," Yolanda M. Lopez (multi-media installation).

Under the leadership of current directors, Enrique Chagoya and Humberto Cintron, the relationship with Mexican and Latin American cultural communities in these countries has intensified to include collaborations and exchanges. The transmigration phenomenon has introduced influences in both directions. Latino and Mexicano immigration into San Francisco has reaffirmed indigenous aesthetic influences in traditional folkcrafts, community ethics, and family practices. But ironic reversals have also occurred, such as the celebration of Día de los Muertos at the Galeria (which uses an urban pageantry and folk expressiveness), which has now become an example to Mexico, with its declining tradition of Muertos celebrations.

Demands for cultural identity and economic rights have changed in the urban arena. As neighborhoods shift and change, alternative spaces are placed in new positions of leadership. Studio 24, the Galeria's store, imports and sells Mexican and Latin American folk and popular arts and crafts, books, and Chicano artists' products. The support for Chicano artists who develop new product lines such as contemporary jewelry and T-shirts is part of the Galeria's program of economic empowerment for the community. As both a commercial venture and through demonstrations and exhibitions, the store serves as a cultural bridge for newcomers, as well as an inspiration to contemporary artists in the community. The folk ethos— the cultural world view, spirituality, and sustaining beliefs of the people—has been strengthened by the presentation of family folk artists. The formal residencies of established folkartisans like the Linares of Mexico have been essential to the development of the contemporary idiom.

In the ongoing exchange with self and other, the artist finds new language. In an extended fashion the community institution must also find its language in the dialogue with its audience. Through the lived experience of their artists, the collaboration with neighborhood groups, their pursuit of critical scholarship, and experimentation with presentation strategies, the community cultural *centros* aim at an authentic service. For almost twenty years the Galeria has evolved a contemporary idiom in which memory, popular barrio syntax, ceremonial satire, personal family narrative, social activism, bilingual performance, feminist imagery, new media, and Latin American literature, theater, and spirituality have blended and fused, in a profusion of forms and meanings.

This kind of spontaneous discourse can only occur when institutional life is open to change. For the Galeria de la Raza this has meant affiliation with diverse elements such as African Caribbean expression, anti-apartheid movements, and Pan-Asian sensibilities. The relationship between Latino and Black communities has been a long-standing one. In particular, both communities have struggled to provide service, guide artists, and resist appropriation by the mainstream. The strong Caribbean connection offers the Latino and Black communities a connection because of its African presence and the Galeria looks to play a part in this continued connection. Addressing the expanding and changing communities of color in an ongoing struggle for cultural and economic empowerment is the challenge that must be met by urban *centros*. Galeria de la Raza aims to maintain its cultural core and invigorate new expression and new presentation within this transforming social context.

Notes

1. The leadership that founded the Galeria was made up of a collective of artists including Rupert Garcia, Peter Rodriguez, Francisco Complis, Ralph Maradiaga, René Yañez, and others, which resulted in the co-directorship for over fifteen years of René Yañez and Ralph Maradiaga.

Enemies Within and Without
Pressures to Depoliticize Community Murals
Tim Drescher

A beautiful image in a neighborhood, union hall, church, school or YWCA may in itself be a positive addition to a community. And it is hard to think of a working method—from artists' groups working *with* community groups all the way to a commissioned "public" artist working alone *for* the community—that could not produce an eminently satisfactory mural by any purely aesthetic standard. But beauty is only one measure of the potential of a working, creative relationship *between* artists and community members, and the most effective murals are those where the image is but the acrylic symbol of the process that created it—a political process that continues after the painting is completed.

The guiding question in a community process is not "What would you like to see?" but "What is important to the community?" By retaining this focus in our planning, muralists can realize the full potential of community murals, thus giving new and exciting expression to the ideas of others not skilled in visual communication.[1]

When a mural project integrates process and product, then not only does the finished image help people understand something, but the process helps them to grasp their own potential for doing something about it. As someone involved with community murals for almost two decades, I can see that the successful integration of process and image is as difficult as it is because of very real obstacles. If a community mural project is to withstand challenges to its integrity, including external and

Tim Drescher

Tim Drescher has documented, photographed, written, and lectured about the worldwide community mural movement, as well as worked on mural projects, for nearly two decades. He currently lives in Berkeley, CA, and teaches in the Department of Interdisciplinary Humanities at San Francisco State University. He edited *Community Murals Magazine* from 1976 to 1987.

internal forces acting to depoliticize its imagery, then artists and community members must consciously develop their relationship from the start, with full awareness of both the possibilities and potential difficulties within this arrangement.

Let's look at five forces that can weaken the politics of images and processes of making community murals: 1) censorship; 2) bureaucratic pressures for "compliance"; 3) the need to develop designs before official project approval (and funding) is given; 4) long-term effects of relying on vocabulary amenable to the state in order to receive financial support; and 5) the urge to "broaden one's audience."

Censorship

Both conservative and liberal politicians recognize the potential power of true community artmaking and so attempt to control it. They worry when they see residents of a housing project organizing to demand their rights. And when they see community arts contributing to organizing, they may move to stop them. Outright censorship is rare, but is effectively accomplished through other means. The standard method is to object not to a design's politics, but to its aesthetics, its failure to meet "acceptable quality standards."

If such censorship is masked, how can we do anything about it? One answer is to be so aesthetically strong in their terms that they won't be able to lodge an objection to quality. But since aesthetics is rarely the issue, this is likely to be a Sisyphean task. As Los Angeles muralist Yrena Cervantez recently pointed out with reference to the city's arts bureaucracy, "You must be inoffensive to everyone," as if this were possible and not just a code for "You must not try to depict anything different than what the authorities will allow." A more effective method is to come into a review meeting with overwhelming community support, saying that "the people who are going to live with this project support *this* design completely," thus shifting the burden of compliance to the review board. Its members will find it much more difficult to object to a design backed up by three or four hundred signatures than to a design and an artist. If we can succeed in changing the criteria, quibbles with aesthetics will become insignificant.

What about self-censorship? Muralists at the 1978 National Muralists' Convention in Chicago were asked, "Who here does *not* pre-censor their work?" Only one hand was raised (by a muralist who was painting U.S. flags). Dozens of muralists admitted that they knew which images the various official bodies would frown on so they kept them out of their designs rather than face denial of a project or the enormous burdens of fighting against political censorship. The problem is very real. Artists may legitimately decide that "the political goals of this project will be met most effectively if we 'weaken' the imagery in order to get on with the process of producing the mural." But we should also consider whether greater political effectiveness could not be achieved by fighting to retain the community's preferred image rather than actually painting the mural.

Pressures for Bureaucratic Compliance

A second way in which politics are diffused is through pressures for bureaucratic compliance: the meetings and paperwork required in any project with government or foundation funding. These seem innocuous, but have potential for lessening the will to political struggle.

The demand for attendance and records from funding agencies may not necessarily be malign (although I have witnessed instances where officials were perturbed that an artist being paid through the Comprehensive Employment Training Act (CETA)* was not at the wall painting every day from nine to five!). Indeed, we should keep clear records for our own purposes. Sometimes the requirements are actually helpful because they provide a format for those of us whose creative inclinations do not flow towards careful record keeping. But they also encourage arts groups to duplicate those modes of organization in their processes, internal and external, which build *their* ideology into *our processes*. The problem is that in a project of any magnitude, bureaucratic/administrative requirements are quantitatively significant and demand much energy and time, reducing that available for the project itself. However, if you want to keep your funding, you must butter up the officials responsible, or at least comply with their rules. One begins to worry about satisfying regulations and not alienating officials instead of getting on with the job at hand of utilizing a community arts project as one element in a larger scheme of political organizing.

How to avoid this? It is a difficult situation, and made more so by our tendency to believe that we must do everything ourselves (because we have always *had* to do everything ourselves). Here the benefits of working with a group become obvious. Such tasks can be spread out among the members, or rotated regularly. This may mean that members will spend periods of time administering rather than painting, and thus it is important to remember that *everyone* who contributes to the project deserves notice. The important thing is who helps produce, not merely who paints.

A perhaps somewhat idealistic suggestion is that everyone in the core group receive the same amount of money. This organizational scheme works against any tendency towards hierarchic organization, and builds an amazingly close working group that has potential for keeping together over a long period of time. It also has the advantage of structurally encouraging members to watch out for each other, to help each other avoid burn out, to keep the whole group's efforts in reasonable balance. If someone has been doing what they feel to be enough work, and no one else is willing to take on even an important project, then it should not be done, and the group should recast its projections about the scope of its efforts to fit the available

---

*CETA was a federally funded, locally administered program in the mid to late '70s.

energy of its members. Realization of this also helps prevent discrimination against members who have special needs such as families or outside jobs. With intelligent planning and foresight (there are veterans around who can think these things through), energies best directed at political efforts need not be redirected to fulfill deadening bureaucratic requirements.[2]

Getting Design Approval Before the Project Is Funded

A third way in which politics gets weakened in community mural projects is through the requirement that a design be developed before approval is given and before money is granted to fund the project. When an agency grants money on Friday, it wants to see paint on the wall on Monday. Under these conditions, artists must either develop their base of community support and participation in the project on their own—something not economically feasible for most community artists—or do the design alone. Either way, this burden of the bureaucratic process tends to move the community out of the design process.

Community participation from the outset is crucial, and muralists need financial support from the beginning, not merely for the tip of the iceberg—painting the image on the wall. Given their priorities, funding agencies are understandably reluctant to buy a pig in a poke. But when a team of artists has a track record that demonstrates their ability to carry out a community-based project from beginning to end, an agency shouldn't be bothered by not seeing a sketch.

Although few precedents exist, I am convinced the answer lies in organization over the long term. For instance, Oakland Wallspeak, of which I am a member, began with a quite modest initial project to establish our credibility to funders. We viewed it as a pilot for a larger multiple mural project to be painted a couple of years later. The pilot project gave us time to learn how to work together as a group and to learn how the bureaucracy functioned. It *also* established a precedent for being funded before designs were developed. This early funding gave the community (in this case a housing project) an opportunity to participate throughout.

Long-term Effects of Reliance on Vocabulary Amenable to the State

Owen Kelly's *Community, Art and the State: Storming the Citadels* describes a fourth source of danger. Kelly's opening chapter, "A partial history of community arts," is enormously valuable for its delineation of the consequences of relying on the state for financial support.[3] He notes that groups seeking funding have "learned to stress certain parts of their work and gloss over others." The parts "glossed over," of course, are where the expected political impact resides. Later, younger, second-generation artists form new groups not with the "actual aims of the existing groups" (the parts "glossed over"), but with "their ostensible aims as processed for their annual reports and grant applications." These "laundered aims" coincide, of course, with the aims of the funding agencies and distance new generations from the original group's intentions.

Kelly concludes that instead of empowering communities to understand and begin to move against some of the horrors caused by the state's skewed priorities, artists hereby become tools of "one branch of the state sent in to clear up the mess left by another branch of the state."[4] This makes us welfare workers rather than political organizers. Unless this sort of simultaneous existence is openly recognized (in process and imagery), long-term effects may remain hidden to both muralists and community members, who "are just happy to be doing some art."[5]

The Dangers of the Urge to "Broaden the Audience"

For working-class oriented community artists, the final way in which politics are diluted is perhaps the most insidious of all. But it favors more of what many artists want, what they have been trained to want their whole lives as artists: acclaim, respect, future commissions, peer appreciation, and publicity. It is called different things, but boils down to an urge to "broaden the audience."[6] This usually means changing the content to reach a more diverse audience, meaning more middle class and rarely more non-Left working-class people. It means abandoning those with a greater stake in making a revolution (or making a strong stand on an issue) in favor of those with less of a stake.

To enlarge your audience without broadening it, to reach more people who share a concern for the issues you raise, you must stay where you are longer, maybe years. This may mean helping folks move refrigerators into their apartments as well as "doing art," but that *is* a way communities grow. We cannot expect people, even in the community in which we live, to respect us only if they do our thing (create art) or if we do not do their thing (apply for governmental help, slog through bureaucracies, and all that).

These dangers to political effectiveness in community-based mural projects are naturally not mutually exclusive and should be watched for to allow as politically effective a mural as possible. But if the *only* thing we do is paint murals, we miss important political opportunities. We must work in conjunction with others on many levels in a many faceted community. In the end, murals or other community arts are best seen as part of a larger plan of community organizing and not something in themselves.

Notes

1. This community involvement raises the infamous question of trade-off between aesthetic strength and participation by non-artists. The impact/unity/cohesiveness of the design suffers in proportion to the inclusiveness of the project only if we fail to recognize our proper task. See "Must Aesthetic Impact Suffer?" *Community Murals* 12(1) (Spring 1987):2. In developing the content, political artists must "play the edge"

between "going too far" politically and following the "lowest common denominator." Note also the difference between weakening an image's impact by inclusive participation of community members, which is one thing, and weakening the politics of the image, which is quite another. If the process weakens the politics, then the points of commonality must be reassessed. If we do our jobs correctly, everyone participates, but not everyone necessarily participates the same at every stage of the project. The artists exercise more control over the design, perhaps the community more so over the content (after all, they have to live with it).

2. It may be that the group feels the artists be paid at a special rate because their work on a mural must be done intensively over a relatively brief period, and the same may apply to someone with special skills such as a fundraiser. It is crucial to spell all this out before the money is at hand, so each member knows the agreement.

3. Owen Kelly, *Community, Art and the State: Storming the Citadels* (London: Comedia Press, 1984). The book goes on to provide "a political framework for community arts" and ends with "a programme for community arts." Kelly is referring to the arts establishment in Great Britain but the situation is analogous to the grant system in the U.S., p. 23.

4. Kelly, p. 30.

5. Artists may be hypocritical too when we organize mural projects and practice our own art because these pursuits give us control over our lives and the chance to work collectively, but then we tame the work to comply with a power structure and its bureaucratic representatives, thus relinquishing everything *but* our leadership role.

6. I am indebted to Malaquias Montoya for articulating this notion.

Chicago Public Art Group

"I Welcome Myself to a New Place" (detail), the Roseland-Pullman Mural Project by Olivia Gude, Marcus Jefferson, and Jon Pounds with residents of Roseland and Pullman, 1988. Photo by GudePounds.

Making the Work

Making the Work
Introduction

The Japanese word *do,* means way, or sometimes art. It is the *do* in *aikido,* the way of harmony that leads to defeating an attacker. It is also the *do* in *chado,* the way of tea or the tea ceremony. In both cases, the emphasis is on the route, the method, the process within the practice that makes up the art. The motions of aikido look awkward and strange in a still photograph, but flow effortlessly when performed by a master. And the tea ceremony cannot be reduced to the beauty of the objects and building where it takes place, one must also step into the process of the ceremony to understand its aesthetics.

What is often neglected is that all art has inherent in it an aesthetic of practice. Choices about how one works include, but are not limited to, technical and stylistic decisions. They also encompass the circumstances of making and witnessing: methods of taking life experiences and transforming them into artistic expression; choices regarding medium, and recognizing what unnoticed implications each mode of presentation inherits; ways of working with others; learning how to incorporate critical self-evaluation and the critiques of others into artmaking; and how the artmaking process itself reflects a commitment to democratic, culturally pluralistic social action. Each of these considerations carries weighty burdens of negotiation and compromise—a vast array of choices about process too often considered secondary when considering the product. Because each choice is ultimately reflected in the finished performance or object, understanding the politics behind these decisions, and locating those options with more progressive implications can lead to a more satisfying artistic process, and thus better art.

Previous page: Los Angeles Poverty Department (left to right) Elia Arce, D.J. Smith, Pat Perkins, Jenny Bass, John Malpede, Carl Bunker, Gino Denabile, Kevin Williams, Carl Grave, Ed Rodriguez, Debbie Winski, Jazzmin. Photo by Daniel J. Martinez.

Chicago Public Art Group

Over 100 adults and children work at building a 50'-long redwood train in the historic Pullman neighborhood of Chicago. Photos by Jno Cook.

Creating
Good Bone Culture
Eric Avery

I don't consider myself a "political artist." I make prints. My friend Sue Coe calls them "saint's relics." I think she means bones left when the flesh is gone. Bones are a model of how I think about prints.

The Print or Bone
(The Undoing of the World of Things)

Bones: mineral supports for a lifetime, built out of what goes into the mouth to be stored (the undertaker's business) when the flesh is gone. For me as a printmaker, the graveyard bone places are called *print collections*. The keepers who hoard and periodically show the bones are called curators. It is a dead-end game, and if it weren't for the money one can get for selling these relics to the keepers, there would be little point in moving them around.

Now what does interest me (I'm also an M.D.) are the conditions that lead to good bone culture, and that means the life that's lived. The prints follow the life. It's not vice versa. If you can look in front of you and see your life, and look behind you and see your stack of bones, you've the best condition for good bone culture. If you look in front of you and see your art, I'd suggest you put your heart in a cast, sue your teachers for malpractice, and then pack up and move to Africa.

Why Africa? Better to first ask where is Africa? Where is not referring to place. Where is, instead, a configuration, a context where life itself becomes so complicated and new, where deeply held beliefs that provide

Eric Avery

Eric Avery is a printmaker and a medical doctor living in San Ygnacio, a small border town in South Texas. During the Vietnam War he attended medical school in Galveston, Texas. In 1980 he worked as a medical doctor on the ship *Seasweep* in northern Indonesia with Vietnamese refugees, and then as medical director in the Las Dhure Refugee Camp in northern Somalia, with refugees from Ethiopia. In 1984 he helped form the Amnesty International USA (AI) group No. 306 in Laredo, Texas and now volunteers as AI's Southern Region Refugee Coordinator. His prints have appeared in exhibitions in numerous galleries and museums across the country.

structure and meaning to life all become dysfunctional. There we become more conscious of race and class; and our own culture becomes distant and foreign. This overwhelming experience undoes the world of things and leads to the construction of a world of values. For me ten years ago Africa was the Las Dhure Refugee Camp in Somalia. Today it is South Texas, where I live two blocks from our southern border, the Rio Grande. Once there, our own consciousness, our belief system, out of which we create and sustain our world, is incredibly difficult to find, to see, to know. In order to continue to live once you've been to this Africa, new meaning must be constructed. Things seen, felt, and experienced, once familiar, become new again. Another set of beliefs emerges, and the self becomes functional again. It is in this reworking as artists, in our new birth of life and understanding, that our art-making can become like life itself. Get there and then work here.

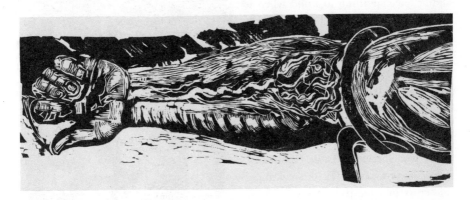

"Blood Test," Eric Avery, woodcut. Photo by Roger Haile.

The Flesh
(The Construction of a World of Values)

Working in Somalia had a huge effect on me personally and professionally. I was in charge of a medical team trying to feed thousands of starving children. Many died. Part of my job at its worst was to go through the feeding centers trying to keep the Western-trained nurses from spending all their time on the children who would eventually die. Instead, time was better spent working with children who at least had a chance if they could eat something. So food was the medicine we used.

A large shipment of canned chickens arrived from Holland. We distributed the cans to our twenty-one feeding centers, and a great meal was prepared and served. But the mothers took the hungry children out of the centers. We went to an elder to ask what was happening. He explained that food in cans was believed to be pork, and that these people didn't eat pork. We responded that this wasn't pork, it was chicken. He said that it didn't matter because these people also didn't eat birds.

Now here's the strange part of this story. If you find this Somali behavior queer, you probably eat chicken, pork, and the flesh of a whole range of other dead animals. And call it a "normal American diet." But when your world has been undone, and mine was in Somalia, you have to rethink what is "normal," challenge the "ordinary," and understand what is usual for other people.

I still haven't recovered from that refugee camp experience. I made some artwork there in the giant camp, but never worked with the image of the starving or dying child.

The art creates its own time frame. In 1987, seven years after working in Somalia, I cut my first starving child print. I saw a wooden washbowl in a shop in Nuevo Laredo, Mexico. I didn't have anything in mind when I bought the bowl, but I did like the shape. I don't know how I got the idea for doing the image I did, except that as I later looked at the bowl, the ribs of the washing bowl looked like the ribs of the starving children I'd worked with years earlier. So I drew my image into the bowl, then cut out the image, inked the surface and put handmade paper into the bowl. It's like making a pie crust in a pie pan. When it dries twenty-four hours later, the child comes out as the print.

When I got ready to title the piece, AIDS of course had become our plague (as if the starvation of hundreds of thousands wasn't). And I thought of Africa. When I was there, surely AIDS was present. But our damned medical profession has such a small presence in the underdeveloped world that we didn't yet know that this disease existed. Well, I think of all the concern for people with AIDS. And I'm one of the concerned people. But I also can't understand why starvation, which can be treated with food, always seems to take the back seat to other problems which might be more fashionable, especially when they seem so much closer to home. Why is it that starvation of children, when we are so comfortable, is not our problem? So I decided to title the piece "Starving African Child with AIDS."

Since 1981, I've lived in South Texas, two blocks from the Rio Grande, in a small Hispanic community called San Ygnacio. Only about ten Anglos live here, three of us artists.

What I've tried to do with my new pieces is to concentrate life. To increase the pressure to the eyes (gates to the soul), to put life itself in my small prints, cast in paper. Not to put dissent in. As I continue to make my prints, my life and experience enter my work. Hopefully you can see and feel this when you look at them. But what is concentrated in my work is my life, *not* my dissent.

I am not particularly interested in dissent. Except . . . when the oppressors block the ascent. Ascent on all fronts, not just with artwork. In 1984 I helped start an Amnesty International group in Laredo, Texas. There are three Immigration and Naturalization Service detention facilities in Laredo and now a total of 850 detention beds. The largest one—run by a public corporation, the Corrections Corporation of America—houses about 220 refugees, most from the war in Central America. There are currently no free legal services available. Bonds are very high, $7,500 per refugee, so a Guatemalan mother with two children can get bonded out if they have $22,500. So this privately owned detention center for profit, that detains until deportation hundreds of refugees from Central America, not only blocks the ascent of the detainees, but also our whole community's. With festering wounds in the body of the community, we can and do feel ill all the time. Ill, the body, the spirit does not soar.

Art can. Does, as life itself continues. I just wish I could spend more time in my garden. I know my work, prints, would be about the plants and not the slaughter of children.

When I was working at the Las Dhure Refugee Camp, surrounded by dying children, adolescents, and adults, trying to work with a medical team from many countries, overwhelmed by problems that called for truly creative solutions, I wished that some of my artist friends were working beside me. I felt if I could ever have the world make sense, that it would be artists who I would want to stand beside me on the barricades and in the feeding centers for the starving and dying. Creativity can find its way out when there is not even any paper or paint. Art speaks for the spirit. Art does not die. It cries and weeps as it is held in the child's lap. If I could, I'd send every young artist to an Africa. To a place of overwhelming presence that forces re-examination of the very foundation of being.

AIDS is Africa for many people. AIDS is changing the very foundation of concepts of mortality. It is further fundamentally changing the practice of medicine, of relations between people. As I live through this time of AIDS, my prints follow. Wood is a fabulous medium if you've some aggressive or frightening fear that needs expression. I made a lot of woodcuts in Somalia. And the woodchips are flying in South Texas.

Every artist needs a shot at transformation. Get it while you are young. Go to your Africa.

From *AIDS Suite,* woodcuts by Eric Avery, photos by Roger Haile.

"Summer Boogie Woogie"

"Healing Before Art"

The Bottom Line:
Where Art Meets Life

Goat Island and Los Angeles Poverty Department Making Performance Art Out of Individual and Group Struggles

Linda Frye Burnham

Contemporary art history took a sharp turn in the 1970s when "performance art" emerged to push the art experience out of the gallery and into the chambers of so-called "real life." Artists, particularly in California, began designating portions of their everyday lives as artworks: actions such as eating, sleeping, meditating and simply opening one's house to outsiders were conceptually framed as art experiences.

This impulse emerged naturally enough a dozen years earlier when painters and sculptors began creating assemblages and happenings. The artwork was translated from object to event when Time was added to its dimensions. During the Time set aside for the happening, the participants passed through real moments in each other's lives together—not theatrical time but real time. The event itself was pointed up as a life experience.

The political dimensions of this movement coincided with some of those of conceptual art: for many artists, this work was a rebellion against the dynamics of the New York art marketplace where art had become a commodity to be traded upon. Its

Linda Frye Burnham

Linda Frye Burnham is the founder of, former editor of, and a current columnist for *High Performance* magazine. She is a contributing editor for *The Drama Review,* a former staff writer for *ArtForum,* and a regular contributor to the *L.A. Weekly* and a number of arts magazines. Manager of the new 18th Street Arts Complex in Santa Monica, CA, Burnham has co-founded, with Tim Miller, a new performance space in the complex, called Highways, focusing on intercultural collaboration.

aesthetic and spiritual essences were being subsumed in capitalism. The presentation of performance art and the designation of oneself as a performance artist was, at that time, virtually a political act.

Those engaged in "art/life" performance existed at the barrier-smashing extremes of the performance movement. Carrying art out of the galleries and museums and into the streets, they made an art that couldn't be captured by anyone: it couldn't be bought by collectors, reviewed by critics, toured by arts administrators. In the case of the most extremely conceptual artists, the work couldn't even be photographed or witnessed by an audience. (California artist Chris Burden announced that he had created an artwork by disappearing from his usual stomping grounds for a period of time.)

As the '80s rolled around and another generation of artists emerged, those who called themselves performance artists were less concerned with boundaries—that question had been dealt with by their predecessors. For them, art could happen anywhere, any time, and be made of anything, even rumors. What the '80s contributed to the pot of art theory was an idea that was literally the reverse of the art/ life idea. For this generation life *is* art; an artwork cannot be made that is separate from life.

More precisely, vanguard artists and their public now recognize that the strict limitation of an artwork to two dimensions, canvas, paint, and frame is only an illusion, a fantasy, a lie. Context, frame of reference, gender, cultural differences, and political realities have been revealed as part of every artwork, just as they are *part of* every commercial image, every educational strategy and every human decision. To have experienced the avant-garde of the '80s is to have it drummed into one's head that art can no longer be ghettoized. Real life is leaking through the walls of every museum, every vault, every undiscovered cave with paintings on the walls. The circumstances of the making and the witnessing of every artwork are part of its reality.

In the larger sense, these realizations are part of an awakening in consciousness happening all over the world. As the globe shrinks, we all become more sensitive to the intimate relationship between all living things, more sensitive to our part in each others' lives, and for many this is an awakening (or re-awakening) of something that might be called a political conscience. For some artists, this means recognizing and taking responsibility for the world in which they move. It means revealing the political in the personal.

Attracted to the groundbreaking work done by visual artists in performance, artists from other art disciplines like dance, theater and music flooded into the "new performance" field as much performance-art related work has come to be called. Many began attempting to create interdisciplinary models of this newly expanded consciousness, but added to those concerns a focus on performance itself, examining in their works the character and the impact of "the mediated experience." Working close to the commercial forms of live art, they strive to wrench live performance away from entertainment and conventional theater.

For examples of work being done in this spirit, I would like to examine the activities of two contemporary performance ensembles with different approaches to the use of real life material in artmaking: Goat Island, a group of politically concerned professional artists working primarily inside an artworld context, and the Los Angeles Poverty Department, a performance troupe made up of artists and homeless people without performance experience working in art spaces as well as shelters and outdoor sites in the "skid row" downtown sections of America's cities.

Goat Island is dedicated to finding new forms for live performance before an audience to align personal material with political realities. Director Lin Hixson's eclectic approach to performance reflects a wide range of concerns, as does her double degree in dance and political science from the University of Oregon, and master's degree in performance from Otis Art Institute in Los Angeles. Her performance work is quintessentially postmodern, mixing techniques and appropriating signs and text from everyday life, news media, and entertainment to paint an ironic picture of the way we live now.

From her earliest efforts with the L.A. performance group Hangers (1979-81), Hixson has worked collaboratively with visual artists, dancers, actors, musicians, filmmakers, and others, including even motorcyclists (*Sinatra Meets Max*) and cheerleaders (*Hey John, Did You Take the El Camino Far?*). Her performances are populated with the images of cultural figures who, though we may have never met them, have influenced our lives—like Elvis Presley, Frank Sinatra, or Mad Max. Her characteristic choice of unusual locations for her performances—a floodlit park, an industrial loading dock, a train station—asks questions about where the created image ends and the functions of daily life begin, about the illusions that permeate our lives, particularly those that arise from our immersion in movies and television.

For all these works, she began with real events of her life or those of her collaborators, blending them with the events of their time to create an art/life reality within which they were inextricably mixed. An example is *Hey John,* a "bad" musical that entangled the musical comedy *Bye Bye Birdie* (which already layers the "life" of its main character with events in the real-life army experience of Elvis Presley) and Hixson's own marriage to a Vietnam war vet, revealing that our feelings about the things we actually live through are layered over and between what we have learned in art and pop culture experiences (in this case, the movies).

In 1986 Hixson's work took an important new direction. She moved to Chicago to work with three young performers, Matthew Goulish (now Hixson's husband) and the McCain brothers, Tim and Greg, forming the collaborative group Goat Island, for which Hixson serves as director. Their first work, *Soldier, Child, Tortured Man,* grew out of a rigorous, year-long regimen of writing, researching and physical workouts.

The piece takes place in a gymnasium with the audience seated in a single row on all four sides. The three performers dash onto the court in sports jerseys and literally run themselves ragged in drills reminiscent of military exercises and sports workouts, sparsely sprinkled with text and music. The experience—essentially an examination of the nature of oppression—is a physical one, nearly as exhausting to watch as it is to perform.

"Soldier, Child, Tortured Man," by Goat Island, at Performance Space in New York City, 1988. Photo by Dona Ann McAdams.

Like her role model, Elizabeth LeCompte of the Wooster Group, Hixson began the piece by searching for universal truth in personal material dredged up via an exercise. She asked each man to take a personal event and distill it down to specifics—the day, the time, the place—a factual report. They then researched a historical event that happened at approximately the same time, and, finally, created installations in their apartments that melded the personal and the historical events. (The installations were open to the public, but not publicized.)

Greg McCain chose a time when he had pneumonia as a child and correlated it with the Chicago Seven trial, happening at the same time. He appeared in his apartment lying in his bed with the veins in his feet painted blue. Behind the bed was a window and in the window was the image of a man tied to a chair, a reference to the courtroom binding and gagging of defendant Bobby Seale. Thus the adult McCain discovered that the isolated innocent child was bound to the defiant black man miles away.

Coincidentally, the other men came up with similar images of oppression from the past, and these images were the roots of the finished performance. The four began to work those images physically, without a direction. Hixson asked Tim to break down his installation into a series of movements, which eventually became a nearly military warm-up drill, then the backbone of the piece itself. They added postures of torture victims, observed from photographs, and the facial expressions of fighters. Texts and speeches from the installations suggested the three male characters that finally manifested themselves: the soldier oppressor, the child witness, and the torture victim.

What emerges is a picture of the forces that come to bear on those who are bound together in an oppressive system. (For those familiar with the artists' personal lives, El Salvador comes to mind, since all four members of Goat Island work often with CISPES—Committee in Solidarity with the People of El Salvador). While the piece does not refer to a specific political situation, it frames an oppressive mindset from different points of view: the oppressor who maintains the system, the victim who suffers it, and the child who is its witness.

Hixson's method thus massages specific detail to achieve an abstract aesthetic, challenging in its very form. The piece circled the Reagan administration and its strongman satellites, pointing a finger at the atmosphere surrounding them rather than the individual culprits. The suggestion is that until we alter the dominant worldview of force as a necessary social component, the villains, the victims, and the witnesses will continue to appear and the story will never change.

For John Malpede and his collaborators, Los Angeles Poverty Department, the content of their everyday lives on L.A.'s Skid Row is far more literally available in their performances. LAPD is a performance group that grew out of a workshop for the homeless directed by Malpede, a performance artist who was a California artist-in-residence at the Inner City Law Center on Skid Row.

What makes this group different from other contemporary theaters that incorporate non-artist populations is the method of John Malpede. He brings to this work a patchwork of experience that includes a degree in philosophy, a lot of street performance including a stint with Bread and Puppet Theater, and some radical late '70s performance art with Bill Gordh. Malpede and Gordh created Dead Dog and Lonely Horse, a man/dog and man/horse who appeared in unusual sites like a laundry, a hotel lobby, and a detective office, improvising an ongoing performance relationship for audiences that were at times uninformed about what they were seeing.

Malpede's concern for the homeless began at street level when he visited Los Angeles during the Olympics and watched street people and welfare advocates reacting to downtown "sweeps" by the police department to clean up the city while so many tourists were in town. He created a homeless character for a performance in New York, delivering a diatribe through a giant megaphone on a beach, aimed at the highrises of Lower Manhattan. Desiring more meaningful contact with the homeless themselves, he returned to L.A. and began developing the project that resulted in a successful touring company of artists and street people who make performances about the events of their own chaotic lives and those around them existing in poverty and homelessness. Malpede's method is to stretch theatrical convention around the very unconventional reality of these American lives, to try to create forms that can make manifest a rambling story by a street rapper or a diatribe about the indignities of living in single-room occupancy hotels on the most dangerous street in downtown L.A.

What began with a group of the curious who responded to Malpede's flyers handed out on the sidewalk is now an intimate conglomeration of inner-city denizens—artists, drifters, singers, actors, writers, lovers, and fighters well acquainted with life on the street. Over the last three years, the group has presented close to 100 performances on vacant lots, in artists' lofts, galleries and small theaters like the Boyd Street operated till recently by Pipeline, Inc., on Skid Row. The major productions have included: *South of the Clouds,* a group of autobiographical monologues built around an acting exercise about actions that make you feel good; and *No Stone for Studs Schwartz,* a group of improvisations on a complicated story by Jim Beame about life on the road.

A third piece, *LAPD Inspects America,* is designed to examine the condition of homelessness in America. The piece developed as a week (or longer) residency in which LAPD invades a city and collects information about homelessness there by meeting street people in the places where they gather. Talent shows and workshops are staged in parks, shelters and social service agencies, and from these local performers are recruited to take part in the feature performance of *LAPD Inspects America* in a local art space or theater. The piece is an ever-changing saga that follows LAPD's experiences in this whole process. The project began early in 1988 with a

One Reason I Love Washing Clothes

from *South of the Clouds* and
LAPD Inspects America: San Francisco

Boy I love washing clothes. One reason I love washing clothes is because of the bubbles that squish in my fingers. It feels so good. And another thing I like about washing clothes is the smell. The smell of the Tide and the Downy Fabric Softener. Mmmm! They smell so good! And another reason I like to wash clothes is the feeling of wringing out the clothes. I just squeeze and wring. It gives me the feeling of revenge against my father. He was an alcoholic and he used to beat my mother. And I hated him for that. He called her retarded. I don't think that's very funny! So I just squeeze his neck. I would just wring his neck.

Down by the Delaware River, there were wildflowers and there

Robert Clough of the Los Angeles Poverty Department. Photo by Gail Gerretsen.

would be people walking. And there would be people jogging and I would take my wash. And the wildflowers smell so good. And I'm there with my Tide and my Downy. And the water is warm and sudsy. And it smells so good. And I pick up a rock to wash with. And I beat, beat, beat the clothes. I pick up a rock and I beat, beat, beat him with a rock, like he used to beat my ma.

And down by the Delaware River I would lay all my clean wash all over the wildflowers to dry. And then I would fold the clothes and take them home. I would fold them smooth. And they smell so good. And that's why I'll wash clothes for the rest of my life.

—**Robert Clough, Los Angeles Poverty Department**

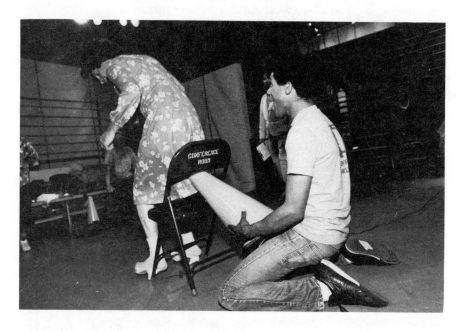

John Malpede and Kevin Williams in *LAPD Inspects America,* San Francisco Art Institute, 1988. Photo by Lukas Felzmann.

month-long residency at the San Francisco Art Institute, then traveled to Sushi in San Diego and Museo del Barrio in New York City. The New York audience saw a version that incorporated material about both the San Francisco and San Diego experiences, including jail scenes, racist episodes at the Art Institute, drug habits in the San Francisco's Tenderloin district, and a hilarious monologue about alleged discrimination against heterosexual females in San Diego women's shelters.

Their fourth piece is *Jupiter 35,* by Sunshine Mills, about the six-story fall that smashed every bone in Mills's body and changed the shape of his face. The piece explores a life-altering brush with death and Mills's realization of his need for the friendship he has discovered in the group. Mills is on stage for the entire production, performing in a hospital bed and a wheelchair.

Since the inception of LAPD in 1985, perhaps seventy people have moved through the group, with about ten to twenty now attending twice-weekly workshops. Some have remained with the group since its beginning, a fairly astonishing fact, given the transience of Skid Row. The racial mix is about fifty percent black, thirty-five percent white, and fifteen percent Latino. Some have stage or art school experience, most have none. About half are on government benefits of some kind. About seventy-five percent fall into the loose category of "street people" in that they are sleeping on the street or in cars, living daily on Skid Row, chronically unemployed or unemployable due to physical, mental or emotional disabilities.

Performers are always paid, whether it's an "artist's fee" written into a grant proposal or simply a share of the ticket sales. This rarely amounts to more than beer money. In the last year, some of the money earned in performance has been donated by the group to a housing fund to help provide individual members with the crippling security deposits required to rent decent housing. Some have taken up the demanding task of living together.

While I was the group's administrator (paper-pusher) from 1986 through 1988, I observed two important changes, in addition to the empowerment that comes with good artmaking. The experience of traveling and working together has contributed to an unmistakable deep commitment of the members to the work and to each other. This closeness and dedication, abrasive though it can be, has produced some remarkable performance work and some instances of true exhilaration. Both the San Francisco and San Diego performances inspired observers to drop what they were doing and move to L.A. to join the group, including people with good jobs and students in art school.

The other important change came with a sudden, strong influx of women into the group within the last year. The aggression and violent conflict in the work gave way somewhat to more emotional interaction, introspection and verbalization on stage about feelings, especially feelings about making performance together.

When talking about approaching a project as maverick as LAPD, John Malpede says, "It's all in how you hold it," and he holds it as lightly as possible, providing minimal direction and tolerating a lot of errant behavior. His personal involvement in the project is extensive, considering the hours he puts in. A full-time employee of Inner City Law Center, he spends at least forty hours a week on Skid Row watchdogging the welfare system in offices, courtrooms, and the streets. Then he puts in another twenty plus hours a week with LAPD, often socializing and sometimes living with the members. He is with "the homeless" most of his waking hours.

As much as it interests him to serve as facilitator for the group, bringing a performance experience to many who have never had it before, Malpede is also determined to manifest the character of the community. That is, he is wholeheartedly involved in trying to make visible an important segment of our population that we shut out of our sight and minds. What mainstream America doesn't know about life on the street and life on the road is a lot. A close look through the LAPD lens reveals an underground of elemental interaction among people who are facing a reality that most of us have managed to banish from our lives. Strength and indignity, joy and pain come in strong doses on Skid Row and LAPD's full-force rendition is a testament to the amount of power and control Malpede cedes to his performers. Almost the opposite of a bleeding-heart liberal approach to depicting life among the unfortunates, LAPD work is street life itself. "You want the cosmetic version," asks *LAPD Inspects America,* "or you want the real deal?"

Conceptually, for LAPD there's little difference between the art and the Life. Just like on Skid Row, whatever the plot, whatever the rules, whatever the cast, it is always changing. Because it's important to watch your back and be ready for anything, the group's technique emphasizes flexibility: keep 'em guessing. For example, to compensate for the fact that not everybody shows up for every performance, most actors in the cast know every part and play them interchangeably. Any performance night you might find, say, a very short female with a Central American accent playing a very tall black man with a flashy wardrobe.

While there have been dozens of rave reviews and grants for LAPD, there have also been bad reviews, brushes with the law, serious illnesses, loss of faith, betrayals, false accusations, and long periods of confusion and desperation. As I write this Sunshine Mills is still undergoing surgery connected with his six-story fall, another member is grieving over the loss of her three children to foster homes, another is mourning the death of her two sisters in a plane crash, another is facing a series of painful operations, and others struggle with recovery from various addictions. Most of what is difficult about life on the edge has to do with the politics around poverty and mental illness in America, and dealing with those issues on an emotional, personal basis certainly isn't easy.

But what probably keeps most hanging on is the excitement of change, of transformation. There's no question LAPD offers its members something essential. The basic issue of street life may not, after all, be hunger, but freedom. And that's a basic issue of art life too. Because Malpede has the nerve to leave the door always open, LAPD offers an experience of real artistic freedom, especially sweet when so far freedom's been just another word for nothing left to lose.

Finally, in artists like Malpede and Hixson, the bottom line where art and politics meet is in the individual human soul, where daily an ever-changing reality battles with love, instinct, need, memory, and ideology. Great art is surely that which holds humanity up to the light in a way not done before, in a way to jar the soul. The more we know, the more complex that vision becomes, and it is increasingly apparent to me that great art may be the most difficult task we can attempt.

Far from Finished
Deconstructing the Documentary
Jill Godmilow
Interview by Brooke Jacobson

The following is drawn from an interview conducted by Brooke Jacobson at the University of Southern California (USC) in August of 1987. It is an attempt to open up the reasoning behind Godmilow's conviction that the documentary must be deconstructed, and an attempt to understand the implications behind the resistance within the documentary community to opening up the text.

Deconstruction is the use of any number of textural strategies which, in the case of documentary film, could 1) disrupt the "naturalness" and "neutrality" of the cinema verite footage employed, 2) expose how certain ideological meanings are constructed by the hierarchical use of visual and verbal film information, 3) acknowledge that the text of the film, and all films, has been "written" and contains certain assumptions about both the subject of the film and the film's audience.

Brooke: Is documentary still a viable form?

Jill: Serious documentary work, even in its most traditional forms, is devalued in our culture. You can't give them away to PBS and the shrunken educational market has been taken over by producers like Time-Life, Inc., who make slick, classroom-length materials that teachers who have no knowledge of how to use film are perfectly happy to rent and exploit as a substitute for

Jill Godmilow

Jill Godmilow has been an independent filmmaker for twenty years. While working primarily with documentary film forms, she has also produced experimental videos and narrative features. In addition to *Far From Poland,* her films include *Antonia: A Portrait of The Woman,* and the theatrical feature, *Waiting for the Moon.* She is a professor at Temple University in Philadelphia.

Brooke Jacobson

Brooke Jacobson has taught Critical Studies in Film and Television at Evergreen State College and at Portland State University. She teaches Film Aesthetics and Gender Studies at Lewis and Clark College in Oregon, and also is developing a series of Public Access programs on images of aging.

teaching. Also, there's been a diminution of government art funding and a growing conservatism of funding policy. At the same time American universities are graduating ten thousand students a year with degrees in cinema. The competition is enormous. It's always been arduous to produce documentaries, but now it's approaching the impossible.

So if you make a deconstructed (read "difficult") documentary, you're likely to have an audience of about six people. Sadly, the production of such undervalued films barely makes sense anymore. It's an insane, intense activity, requiring years of high-energy, nonstop, seven-day weeks. I've never felt comfortable spending a lot of money and time making something that almost no one sees. I don't like the economics of it and I don't like the politics of it. Even worse—the people who *do* go to documentary films and who watch them on television are those most interested in receiving from these films a picture of the world that is culturally fulfilling, which makes them feel, ideologically, most at home with themselves and which treats them "with respect." If you create a documentary with an open text, there's little chance of anyone feeling "fulfilled" in this way.

Postcard invitation to crew party, illustration by Mark Magill

Brooke: Deconstruction is a heavily laden critical term. Do you find misconceptions about what it means?

Jill: It would be nice if there were another word. . . . It sounds so negative. But beyond that, there is deep emotional resistance to it, even to learning what it means. People in critical studies, even classroom situations, struggle against it because there is so much pleasure and security in the way traditional documentary addresses us.

Brooke: The moral issues seem to be most disconcerting in this issue of deconstruction. If we can't look to documentary to reaffirm a moral universe and know who we are, where do we look? Won't the world fall apart?

Jill: That's an excellent description of what we come to documentaries for. We come to documentaries to have it confirmed that there is order in the universe and structure in our relationship to it that is meaningful, moral, and natural. If documentary film won't confirm that, then what is knowable? Then who am I? How am I supposed to relate? Why should I do anything? What can I use as guidelines? Can it be that everything I've believed in, all the meanings I've accepted about right/wrong, good/ bad have to be re-examined and revised? Can it be that everything is a construction of culture? The horrible answer is yes.

Culture is essentially a way of organizing chaos into meaningful and satisfying structures. It staves off the anxiety of wondering what we're here for and, simultaneously, the knowledge that we're not going to be here forever. That's *why* it is produced. Culture helps us feel like we're part of something larger than ourselves. It gives identity. It organizes our lives—gets us up in the morning and off to work. If any cultural product that describes the world (and for most people, documentary film describes the world most accurately) refuses a coherent, morally satisfying description, it is violently resisted. It is denigrated, dishonored, and rejected.

But documentary is suffocating for other, internal reasons. It's a form that hasn't been rethought since Grierson. The main bulk of those produced—with a few exceptions—mimic the form of his *Housing Problems* (1935, United Kingdom). In all this time, documentary has had very little new life breathed into it. Periodically, there *have* been amazing films that proposed new techniques and opened up the language—by Bunuel, Brakage, Ruiz, Resnais, Marker, Rouch and others—but none have had lasting effect on the bulk of documentary production.

Another problem is that the press doesn't know how to respond to or write about documentaries. They have no critical concept of documentary film language. They write about documentaries as if they *are* the reality they represent. Even the notion that there is an author (who has fashioned the film text out of bits and pieces of photographed reality) is absent from their writing. They either like the reality that's presented in the film (because they agree with the film's sentiments), or they dislike it (because it fails to either convince or move them). It's rare to see good critical writing in which documentary issues are taken up. Think about how few books there are on documentary that are even readable.

There was a recent moment when I thought things might perk up. When Nestor Almendros's film, *Improper Conduct,* was first released, it got wide attention and was taken very seriously by the commercial daily press. Why was that? Because it was the first time that the political Right found in an independent documentary ideas and mythological constructions that they were interested in promoting.

Brooke: Explain.

Jill: *Improper Conduct* constructs its ideological meaning by alternating excruciatingly titillating firsthand accounts by Cuban American male homosexuals of their repression by Fidel Castro's government (shot in sensuous and colorful close-ups) with archival, black-and-white wide shots of Fidel's thumping speechifying to crowds of millions. It's a simple technique that reduces the meaning of the Cuban revolution to a single icon (massive, gray, didactic, oppressive) and pits that image against intimacy, the freedom of the individual and his libido. In the film, the "real" stories of witnesses ("evidence") stand for history, much the way the "evidence" of welfare mothers in a hypothetical liberal documentary stands for economic analysis, especially when pitted against cynical exteriors of government institutions. In neither film is there intelligent analysis—of why the reactionary political forces within Fidel's government were so threatened by the sexual "other" that homosexuals had to be rounded up and re-educated—or why it is an economic necessity for the U.S. to maintain a permanent, humiliated underclass. Both films plead for our sympathy through false identification with "victims" in order to persuade us of our own humanity and to exempt us from participation in oppression.

When *Improper Conduct* opened in New York, I thought, "This is going to shake the whole thing up because now the Right has discovered and exploited the exact same illusionist techniques that the liberal Left has been using in documentary for a long time. Now there's going to be a battle within the filmmaking community over the documentary—hopefully, a theoretical one—about photographic realism and representation in general."

It didn't happen. Instead, there was a long published argument in the pages of *American Film* over the film's actual assertion that Fidel's Cuba had violently persecuted thousands of homosexual men. There probably *was* persecution and certainly it is legitimate to document it on film, but what Almendros's critics failed to examine and protest was the film's invisible central construction: that because Cuba can be said to have persecuted homosexuals, therefore the entire Cuban revolution had failed. The combatants argued long and hard over the facts, but not over the form, so the important critical debate never took place. That was the last moment I was hopeful.

Brooke: How did you come to realize that documentary needed to be deconstructed?

In his early cubist period, Picasso was painting a portrait of a woman. One day, when the work was almost finished, the woman's husband dropped by the studio to drive her home. Picasso showed him the portrait and asked him what he thought. The husband admired the painting but remarked that it did not look anything like his wife. "And what does your wife look like?" Picasso asked. The husband reached into his pocket, took out his wallet and handed a snapshot of his wife to Picasso. Picasso examined the picture for a long time, then handed it back to the husband and said, "I didn't realize she was so small."

FAR FROM POLAND

Promotional postcard for the film, designed by Mark Magill and Jill Godmilow

Jill: I came into filmmaking quite ignorant of film history and theoretical ideas. I learned the way most people who make films learn (this may be different in some film schools today), by unconsciously absorbing and duplicating techniques and structures that were around, without thinking about what any of it meant. Yet there must have been some level of unconscious discomfort.

It wasn't until I was faced with an impossible theoretical situation, in *Far from Poland,* that I began to actually think about this documentary practice that I'd been using for fifteen years. What was my contract with it, and what was the contract between my audience and my text? Suddenly the whole practice fell apart for me and I, sort of naively, began to re-invent the deconstruction wheel. I didn't know the academic literature on the subject and I didn't have a name for what I was doing. Whatever language I can use about it now is self-taught and acquired since *Far from Poland.*

There I was in 1980 with the money, the passionate desire, the righteousness, and in fact a pretty good knowledge of my subject; everything necessary to go to Poland to make a documentary film about the Solidarity movement. But it was not to be. The Polish government was clamping down on all foreign journalists and I couldn't get a visa to enter the country. The situation demanded that I either abandon the documentary (because I could not secure the *cinéma vérité* footage that would have validated it) or rethink documentary from ground zero. I started, from scratch, to make a nonfiction film about the Polish situation without a single foot of *vérité* footage.

It was a painful and arduous process. First, I was shocked to discover how dependent I'd been on "what is possible in film." Ever since the early '50s, with the development of lightweight cameras and mobile sound recording equipment, which allows us to go everywhere and shoot anything, we've gone about shooting unthinkingly, just gathering pictures and sounds and then trying to figure out what meaning they could have. Traditionally, whole hunks of ideas are excluded from documentaries because, for whatever reason, the appropriate footage cannot be found, or filmed. But when you stop shooting and ask instead: "What is it that I understand, and what do I want to say, and how do I want to say it," you simply can't

Production still from "Far from Poland," miner's sequence, photo by David Dekok

Production still from "Far from Poland," miner's sequence, photo by David Dekok

do that. As soon as I was in the realm of ideas, having to deal with what I *thought* of Solidarity, rather than what I *could film* of it, it was a new ball game.

Later, I became aware of the taxonomic nature of editing: you come home with your cans or tapes and you study what you've got and you shuffle it around to see what it could be made to say. Then you throw out everything that might overcomplicate that primary statement, stripping out everything that would contradict your central message or attitude, unless you can "control" that contradiction and use it to suggest that the film is objective because it insists on how complex the issues really are. In that process you unconsciously write a text that you have no idea you are writing—a text that is couched in rhetoric, ideology and myth.

In the editing room, when you work your footage over for months, what you're looking for is form and structure that's *satisfying.* Satisfaction becomes the primary objective. You end up making something that satisfies as *film experience,* and the film begins to approach certain cultural norms and expectations—in terms of length, interest, rhythm, moral dilemma, characterizations of good and bad, etc. In the end, that film expresses the status quo. It can't have any provocations, or any unanswered questions, or impossibilities. It can't dream. It can't provoke imagination. Worst of all, it condescends. Its job is to describe, to explain, and to convince. To my mind, this results in a useless, destructive product—a product that basically represents the world as if the way it is, is the only way it could be. In coded language, it suggests why this has to be and explains rationally how it came to be that way. "Yes, it's a complex, unjust, and dangerous world, but that's the way it is."

Brooke: How did you originally conceive of *Far from Poland?*

Jill: I had plans full of traditional documentary strategies. I would have tried to film situations where there was stress and drama. I would have shown what it was like to *be* a member of Solidarity—which suggests, structurally, to the audience member that he/she *could* be a member of Solidarity—at a certain level in a certain town, and in this way, to construct a picture of "what the Solidarity movement was really like." I would have made it as exciting to be in Poland as I possibly could, because I would have needed to make an *exciting* film.

I'd have eliminated all the meetings that were utterly boring. That was one of Solidarity's biggest problems. The Poles had very little experience with democratic process and suddenly, overnight, they agreed that all decisions would be made by groups, democratically, and not by autocratic leaders or central committees. One of the great jokes of the Solidarity movement was that no one could have a meeting that was shorter than ten hours. In the film I didn't get to make, I could have either condensed those meetings, so that we watched decisions getting made in two-minute sequences, or I could have exploited the fact that Solidarity was having trouble acting because of this new and wonderful problem of making democratic decisions. I could have "proved" that this movement was so committed to democratic process that it "screwed itself" by never acting quickly enough to respond to the incredible and persistent harassment of the government.

Because I couldn't go to Poland and "shoot" the Solidarity movement and then

Contact prints from film frames, "Far from Poland"

fashion that footage into a unified vision, into one interpretation or meaning, I had to figure out for myself what meaning it did have. And as soon as I tried to do that, I found that there were many meanings and all of them existed at the same time—depending on where you were, whether you were inside or outside of the movement; whether you were a Pole finding it difficult to get enough to eat; or an active Solidarity member, propelled by the movement into a self-activating human being; or someone sitting 3,000 miles away, looking at it as a historian, as a filmmaker, as a leftist, or as Ronald Reagan did—for its propagandistic, Cold War possibilities. It became clear to me that it was inadequate, if not destructive, to make *one* version of the Solidarity movement on film—particularly using the codes of documentary filmmaking that suggest that *this* version is *reality*.

Brooke: What is the responsibility of the artist, if not to make meaning out of the material they find?

Jill: I think that it's to reformulate language—not just verbal language but visual language as well. To poke holes in the existing language, to make spaces, so that there is a possibility for imagination and action to work through it.

Brooke: Is this a purely formal or theoretical task, or are there real political goals that can be realized at the same time? Can you have both?

Jill: You cannot use the film language of CBS News to say anything about famine in Biafra except "isn't it horrible," which is saying next to nothing. To say something intelligent about famine in film language, you must both deconstruct CBS's language (which dominates our vision) and simultaneously frame the issues within that deconstruction. There's a force that's always active in national culture, that tends to lock in language—to make fixed meanings, to limit the possibilities of thinking and acting by limiting our relationship to one another, to language and to society. Its basic action is to define, smooth out, and lock in the boundaries of experience.

I think the artist should be pushing those boundaries back out again. Now a "successful" culture, like the American culture, will try to encompass that pushing and shoving within the culture—to say, "America is this big [Jill spreads her arms wide]: it can contain postmodernist art, it can contain anti-art, neo-geo, minimalism, punk, porno, etc." Then the job of the artist is to come up with something that can't be contained, something that both formally punctures that existing language on the subject and then, through that hole, pours new information, provocation, and radical juxtapositions to provoke not the sympathy, but the imagination of the viewer.

Brecht made the point that in good art, there should always be a visible distance between what is and what might be. When you watch a documentary that uses traditional forms there is little possibility for real transaction between the audience and the text, because these structures reproduce the universe as it is known to us. The documentary reproduces not only our relationship to film, but to all the material presented in the film. It addresses us in a way that makes us feel comfortable with the relationships that we already have to the material and to the experience of watching documentary.

It is very, very difficult to respond creatively when your culture is reflecting back to you only one set of possible relationships, only one meaning, only one image of an appropriate relationship to the world, or to money, or to people with a different color skin. The possibility for imagination is denied. You can't imagine or formulate another way of addressing a Black maid, or your grandfather, or the guy who sells you gasoline. You are unable to respond creatively to other people in other cultures or to learn anything from them about our own. You are limited to the relationship that's been described by the culture.

Good art has to be very strong to change anything, to present something new. The tendency is always to refine what's already around and to reproduce it—which says, this is what architecture is or what film is, this is what it can do and this is what we want out of it, this is why we go. It's up to the artist to puncture that definition, to say, "Wait a minute, what about this—what happens when I put those two shots together? Do they speak to each other or not?" And always it's the new art, the new ideas, that seem quite wrong, quite foreign at first. When they appear, the culture reacts like an amoeba reacting to a foreign body and tries to either throw it out or swallow it whole and pretend it was never there. The strength and originality of the idea will determine whether it can persist inside the organism or not.

It's this artistic goal that deconstruction tries to fulfill, at a very basic level—to understand how meaning is made and how things are described and how our relationships are determined by culture. Deconstruction has a job similar to cubism's at the turn of the century, when it said, "Wait a minute, this is a picture too. It doesn't look like what you call a picture, but this is a picture too." It's another way of defining what can be called what.

I've always felt that film language is about fifty years or more behind other artistic languages. It's the most regressive art form we have—always lagging behind, taking the tiniest little chances. People got into twelve-tone music in the last century. The equivalent in film art is marginalized into tiny galleries and exhibition sites today. I think the strength of the marginalizing force is related to how powerful film is in shaping our image of the world and of ourselves. That's why there's so much resistance both from the mainstream culture makers and the audience. It's very powerful. That's why film language moves so slowly, it's so heavy and you have to punch really hard at it to make those holes or spaces for new propositions.

Brooke: Of course film economics have always been used to rationalize this slowness.

Jill: Yes, the economic issue is there, but I don't think it's the main force. It's that film provides such a powerful description of who we are, and how we live, and the state wants to control that description.

The Politics of Method
Stephanie Skura

Dance is political not only because of its subject matter but because of the way dances are made, how they are structured, and what they show about people relating to each other. It is important to me as a director to develop in the artistic process and to show in performance the *psychic boldness* of each dancer. I want to show people who are independent, strong, self-revealed and autonomous yet deeply connected to and aware of each other. We want to have enlightened relationships—between director and dancers, and among the dancers.

> **Stephanie Skura**
>
> Choreographer and director, Stephanie Skura is artistic director of Stephanie Skura & Company. Her work emphasizes individualistic movement and the totality of each performer. Recent works include *Artbusiness, Cranky Destroyers, The Fantasy World of Bernard Herrmann,* and *Big Waves.*

With dance, my basic desire has been that it be more like life: multilayered, complex, sometimes interrupted, frequently ambiguous, filled with feeling, filled with thought, awkward at times, occasionally confused and even hesitant, showing attempts and failures as well as accomplishments. Traditionally in the West, dances have been made (and still are, for the most part) by choreographers who physicalize their inner life through movement, teach these "steps" to dancers, and then arrange them in geometric patterns which are constantly changing. The movements come out of the choreographer's consciousness. The structural concepts are taken from an eighteenth-century, Western, Age-of Reason ideal of order and harmony. Even at best, when the movements have meaning, the effect has much to do with the patterns displayed by the bodies onstage, and to this extent, the work is similar both to lace and to military marching displays—reassuring in its neat ordering of elements.

In the past twenty years, there have been changes in the dance world, diverse activities which nevertheless have some things in common: Attempts to find ways to express the inner life of each dancer and not just of the choreographer; attempts to find ways to structure dancing in other than geometric patterns; attempts to reintegrate dance with daily and social life; bringing dance into the streets and public places; getting together and improvising with friends as an alternative to taking class or rehearsing; performing improvisation on stage; and engaging in collaborative processes that call upon the creativity as well as the skill and intelligence of each dancer.

Stephanie Skura & Company performing *Travelog,* 1986. Photo by Johan Elbers.

All these activities reinforce psychic boldness. And they attempt to rectify a situation that happens in dance possibly because of the nature of classroom training: The dancer becomes more and more divorced from the artist, and the process of the average dancer becomes less and less artistic and more and more craftsmanlike. Choreographers as diverse as Yvonne Rainer, Steve Paxton (in his development of the form known as "contact improvisation," which has changed the look of dance during the past twenty years), Merce Cunningham, Lisa Nelson, Ishmael Houston-Jones, Yvonne Meier, Jennifer Monson, and many others have all been involved in this revolution. I see my place in all this as one who is discovering ways to choreograph—to set dances with specific, repeatable movements and structures—which give each dancer as creative and expressive a role as possible. But the work is still directed by one person—me. And I am not performing improvisations. But I am also not teaching steps.

Since I started working, I have been searching for ways to make dances that express the power and totality of individuals and the sublime chaos of the universe. Dances that show, and involve in their creation, relationships between people that are more profound than imitation and the following of the boss's orders. I have always been more interested in watching the choreographer in a dance company than in watching the dancers. Watching a choreographer dancing is watching someone moving in sync with her or himself, whereas watching the dancers is a little like watching a dubbed movie. Something doesn't quite sync up, externally and internally. This is so even though the dancers are usually better technicians. In my work, I want each dancer dancing to be as magical and captivating as a choreographer dancing movements that come from a lifetime of expression-through-movement, and the refining of that art.

I have also been working on making dance structures that relate to the specific nature of the movement itself, rather than to idealized notions about structuring technique. Instead of making perfect geometric shapes onstage, the dancers arrange themselves more the way people really do arrange themselves in life. We might learn the exact spatial patterns from a videotaped improvisation. Or we might put two or more solos together, coordinating spacing, rhythm, focus and timing in intricate and exact ways. We may be responding to the lines of force which other dancers are creating in space. And we are always incorporating accidents that happen in process back into the set choreography. I also frequently use "cinematic" structuring techniques: cuts, dissolves, having things go in and out of focus by letting other events pass in front and grab the attention. The effects of these techniques are actually more realistic than the kind of simplistic clarity we are more accustomed to seeing onstage, because they operate in ways that are more like what our eyes really do when they see things.

Dance is a physicalization of ideas, emotions and spirit. Although our work is physical, our processes grow out of a need to reintegrate our bodies with our mental, emotional and spiritual selves. Performance has been a way of expressing ideas, values, emotions and unnameable things in a more complete way than is acceptable in everyday life. We work with purely physical elements, but we devise physical elements which closely correspond to states of being.

I am gradually becoming more aware of the political implications of the artistic process, and this has reinforced my commitment to working the way I do. Although my process arose from an aesthetic need to see interesting work, I began to realize that what made interesting work interesting was all the underlying values that go into making and performing the work. The overt "content" of a work of art is not really the content—is not what affects an audience. The audience is responding to the how—the direct presence of the performance, its energy, its "feel." Especially with dance, as opposed to theater, a story is being told as soon as one or more persons move their bodies with respect to one another or their environment. Dance is such a metaphor that it has meaning—just as music has meaning—without overtly telling a story. Theater, because it is so involved with words, has, I believe, a different relationship to story. But even in theater that relies heavily on words for communication, there are many elements at work affecting the audience, other than the meaning of the words and the implications of the story. In a simple worst-case scenario: A performance has a "liberal" political message but is put together in a "conservative" way, e.g. everyone stands in a line and says the same thing at the same time with no indication of the wildness, eccentricity and magic of each individual. So really the message is nothing. The performance cancels itself out. Its message is "Don't exploit individuals," but the director exploits performers in making the work and manipulates humans into acting like puppets and being scenery. And that is what the audience will somehow sense, even though they may know nothing about performing, theater, or dance.

Even if a performance has no overt and specific "content," but shows people behaving as full beings, and shows a world which is dense with nuance and possibility and depth, with varying possibilities for interpretation; then to me the performance is political. Its very existence weighs positively on the cosmic scale. And—the audience has an experience that energizes and excites them about their own creativity and the possibilities in their own lives. This is a performance that effects change—not because of its "message," but because of its "feel." It affects the thoughts, feelings and lives of all those present.

Audiences participate in performances by perceiving them, and perceiving is an active sport. How to watch or experience a performance is something that can vary wildly from person to person. Anyone in the business of making performances can either cultivate the art of perceiving or not. I believe that a performance maker will do best by never underestimating the intelligence of the audience, always assuming that everyone out there is alive and intelligent, open-minded and creative, excited about life and aware of its depth and mystery. If the performance is open-ended enough in its possibilities for interpretation, each perceiver can creatively free associate, interpret, be stimulated, imagine, or otherwise individually respond while simultaneously experiencing some common thrust of meaning with the rest of the audience.

Rather than making work that blasts the audience with a theme that is impossible to misunderstand, I prefer to give them something that has the multifacetedness and elusiveness of real life, and to invite them to use a little perceptual muscle in watching it. Several events may be going on simultaneously, related but not in an obvious way. The audience can't possibly see it all at once. Themes may be intertwined, rather than directly connected. What each one experiences is based on individual reactions and choices.

What I love as an audience member is to be at a performance of any kind that is in touch with the flow of ideas. The ideas are free and flowing. In the process of making the piece, the performers and director free associated on a given structure within a shared context; natural responses that happened during the rehearsal process were incorporated into the score; ideas were continually added. So the performance becomes more like a meditation than an exposition, rich with facets and byways that have evolved organically over time. It is like a dream with its own rules of logic, inexplicable but inexorable. Watching this kind of work, I feel in touch myself with that fertile place. I feel possibilities rather than impossibilities. I have this response to the theater work of the Wooster Group, which has so much depth and multi-dimensionality that it tends to sharpen rather than flatten the perceptual powers of its audiences.

In order to get to this kind of depth, the creative process must involve a great deal of free association on everyone's part. As the conceiver/director, I usually start out with some movement ideas that I have been playing with lately and that seem to be fertile with potential, and that also seem to be metaphors for other non-movement themes or states of mind. Lately for example, I have started to work with sudden twitch-like movements the body does as it passes from waking to sleeping, while in that in-between state of freewheeling, indescribable flow of ideas, images and feelings. It can also be called "movement with no preparation." (Joan Skinner, creator of Skinner Releasing Technique, who has simultaneously been working with the same idea, speaks of "instant allowance, without going into some gear.")

I bring these movement ideas into the studio, and see what happens when the dancers I am working with take off with them. At all points, I try to remain open to any interesting byway they may pursue. I also communicate to them, as fully as I am able, the intertwining, interrelated themes I am working with. These may spark ideas as well. At every point in the rehearsal process, I incorporate whatever of value comes up out of spontaneous association with the given "pond" of our context. The relationships between elements may not make sense in an obvious way, but they are real relationships. The result is a work that makes sense the way a dream makes sense—imbued with texture, or feeling, and seeming to have its own necessary and inscrutable rules of logic.

One of the basic modes that our company uses to make movement is a technique I call "truncated initiation." This is improvising in which, rather than trying to follow through on the movement impulse, the job is to *not* follow through, but tune back into the body and go on to another impulse, then another, then another. Any kind of movement can follow any kind of movement—modern, classical, pedestrian, gestural, isolated, whole-body. One movement can comment on another. Any movement is okay; we don't censor any movement impulses. It's okay even to do all the things you usually do in improvisation that you are sick of doing. Somehow, by getting interrupted, they change. This is a physical analogue to "stream of consciousness" in thinking and writing. The dancer is *not* thinking, but watching her or him move is like reading somebody's thoughts; it is kinetic thinking. It is akin to meditation—very aware but non-focused, non-goal-oriented. Many different layers come up, resulting in a non-linear structure in the movement itself. Although this can seem like nonsequitur, I call it a different kind of continuity.

There are several interesting aspects to this movement mode. It is very much like meditation, and nothing like concentration. Because it frees you from having to follow through on the consequences of your actions, it opens up possibilities that might otherwise remain submerged. If the body's physical impulses were akin to channels being received by a TV tuner, it would mean that you constantly switch channels, and somehow this opens new frequencies: you can tune into channels that are deeper down, or more remote from your everyday viewing habits. The very transition from one channel to another creates interesting transitional movements of seemingly unconnectable activities, which result in a true-yet-unfamiliar state-of-body.

This is when people start seeming inexorably themselves, with a power and conviction and totality of concentration that goes miles beyond "showing what you can do." I have used this technique in teaching all levels of students—from people with no dance experience to professional dancers, and with very few exceptions the technique is amazingly easy to do. When I first describe it, they think, "Oh no, I don't think I can do it—it sounds too complicated." But as soon as I say "Go," magic happens. Everyone is themselves, expressing their inner lives through movement, not thinking, not planning, not judging, just being; acting purely on physical impulse, but each movement filled with inner life and meaning.

I am quite sure that this way of moving changes brain waves. It is a whole way of being, and very different from the preferred everyday way of being in our society. It involves an acute sharpening of the senses, an acute awareness of other people and the environment, an acceptance of yourself and whatever you happen to be doing at the moment, and a total lack of concern for results. It requires a certain comfort with not knowing what you are doing or what is going to happen next. And the irony is—it looks virtuosic!

In much of *Cranky Destroyers*, we used a movement image that I borrowed from one of Joan Skinner's releasing classes—"limbs of fury." I interpret "fury" the old way, as fire, passion, power. We imagined we were standing on top of a mountain, with a vast sky all around us, and energy passing through our limbs like volts of electricity. The movement would just send energy out into space, like vectors of force, of varying qualities and directions. People became like gods and goddesses creating the world, or prophets and prophetesses speaking in unknown tongues.

The choice of Beethoven's Fifth Symphony started out as a year-long joke. The whole previous year, while on tour, we joked about dancing to Beethoven. Our movement style is considered so eccentric, and our soundtracks usually so unconventional, that we could easily get hilarious about "the Beethoven piece." After a year of this, I figured we should really do it because it was already a reality for us. The juxtaposition of highly contemporary, and by most standards outlandish movement with a more than well-known classical music score was more than just achieving humor through incongruity.

Beethoven, in his time, went against all traditional notions of structure. He was accused by critics of his day of being very inventive but having no sense of structure. His symphonies were said to meander, need editing, and be twice as long as necessary. So I felt that we had a lot in common. Also, the Fifth Symphony seemed to me to be very idealistic in tone. It seems to say that human society is composed of great individuals moving forward together. It thinks highly of essential human nature. And so do I.

Stephanie Skura & Company performing *Cranky Destroyers,* 1987. Photo by Tom Brazil.

Collective Work
Eva Sperling Cockcroft

Remember those math problems from eighth grade? If you have a wall 15 feet high and 40 feet long and it takes one person 8 hours to paint an area 8 feet square, how many people would you need if you had to finish the wall in three days? It's an obvious fact of collective work that six people working together can do a job in more or less a quarter of the time that one person can, depending on how skilled the workers, how well they work together, and how much time they spend goofing off. And when collective work is successful, the conception will be broader than any single individual's contribution and the process will provide an emotionally fulfilling experience that yields a new sense of camaraderie among the participants.

People setting out to do collective work need to consider a number of factors, including the goals of the project, make-up of the group, and form of organization. In this essay, I will draw on

> ### Eva Sperling Cockcroft
>
> Eva Cockcroft is an activist-artist and co-founder of Artmakers, Inc., a nonprofit public artists group which has created several political murals in New York. Her murals include "Homage to Revolutionary Health Workers," in Leon, Nicaragua (1981), and "Homage to Seurat: La Grande Jatte in Harlem," in New York (1986). She is also an author of *Toward A Peoples Art: The Contemporary Mural Movement* (1977) and many articles about art and society.

experiences from various projects, such as mural-making in a community setting, publically sponsored subway art, guerilla stencil actions, and billboard alteration, to examine how to deal with these factors in different situations.

How Community Murals Happen

For a traditional community mural, the necessary money to pay an artist and assistant is routinely raised by art and community organizations from state, city, and foundation sources. Funding a political mural is much more difficult. As a result the people-power multiplier effect plays a particularly important role in political mural projects. A low budget for a thirty- by forty-foot outdoor mural would be about $7,000 ($3,000 for paint, scaffolding, and insurance; and $4,000 to keep an artist and assistant alive for two months of more than full-time work). On the other hand, ten artists could do the job in two weeks. While almost no one can afford to donate two months of full-time work to a project, most people can manage to find two weeks for something they really want to do. Also, with the energy generated by ten workers, it's easier to organize donations and benefit parties.

This people-power factor was the only way that Artmakers, Inc., a small nonprofit public arts group, could in 1985 undertake a project like "La Lucha Continua/The Struggle Continues," a political art park consisting of twenty-four murals on four buildings in New York's Lower East Side. It also allowed a group of ten artists from Artmakers to paint a fifteen- by forty-foot collective anti-crack mural in Harlem over Labor Day weekend the following year.

"La Lucha" and "Push Crack Back" were both artist- rather than community-initiated projects, yet in both cases there was involvement by and consultation with the local community. For the "La Lucha" murals, our local cosponsor was Charas, a housing organization and cultural center situated on the same block as the mural site. We set up a design committee composed of representatives from Charas, Artmakers, local residents, and community leaders to select and approve all the designs. "Push Crack Back" evolved differently. While working on a mural in a community garden commissioned by West Harlem Group Assistance (WHGA, a housing rehabilitation and management organization), I was struck by the open sale of crack and other drugs in the neighborhood. I presented the idea of an anti-crack mural to WHGA and to the other artists associated with Artmakers. Both groups were enthusiastic. WHGA provided a nearby abandoned building as the site. Artmakers donated their work on the mural as a gift to the community. We were able to use leftover paint and to borrow scaffolding from my commissioned mural, thereby eliminating the need to fundraise.

The design meeting for the "Push Crack Back" mural is an example of the kind of multiple input that a good brainstorming session can achieve. Although bringing rough sketches to a preliminary meeting is useful, finished ones are counterproductive. People tend to become attached to ideas in direct proportion to the amount of time they put into them. Everyone should bring an idea, ideally, but not a complete program. If the group's structure includes a leader or director, that person in particular should try to arrive at the first meeting with as few preconceived design ideas as possible.

Eight people came together over spaghetti and wine to discuss the project and come up with an image. Our first task was to clarify goals. One aim was to reach teenagers—the main market for crack. That led to the idea of a graffiti-covered subway train filled with weird druggies and pushers. Not only did the train image leave room for invention by the participating artists, but it also enabled us to involve local teenagers by letting them paint the graffiti tags that would decorate the train. This provided an incentive for them to protect rather than deface the mural.

Our other aim was to mobilize and encourage the adult community in their efforts to fight the crack invasion. During this period local pastors were organizing residents in rallies demanding police action to close the crack houses. To illustrate this movement within the community, we included portraits of representative community members. Out of these images grow big hands that push the train back. When the hands were being painted on the wall, one of the artists, Cliff Joseph, suggested including people within the hands as well. This turned out to be one of the aesthetically strongest elements in the finished mural.

"Push Crack Back" mural at Amsterdam Avenue and Hamilton Place, New York City, by Eva Cockcroft, Joe Stephenson, Eric Stephenson, Keith Christensen, Cliff Joseph, Camille Perrottet, Sarah Kleeman, friends and neighborhood residents. Photo by Eva Cockcroft.

Most of the debate that evening focused on whether or not to include a portrait of Malcolm X along with a quotation from his speech, "The Bullet or the Ballot": "We have to get together and remove the vices of alcoholism, drug addiction and other evils that are destroying the moral fiber of our community." Some people felt that Malcolm was no longer relevant to young blacks, while others thought his portrait was essential to really involve the local community. After much discussion we decided to include the portrait. We were surprised to discover the intensity of support for Malcolm expressed by passersby during the painting process. A number of people stopped to tell us anecdotes about Malcolm when he lived in the neighborhood. A signpainter who lived nearby volunteered to paint the quotation. In fact, it is the portrait of Malcolm that has given the piece almost iconic status in the neighborhood.

How Collective Is Collective?

The first collective group that I started, the People's Painters, involved a heavy dose of early 1970s feminist idealism. We began as three women, initially excluding men because we did not want our relationships with each other to be distorted by relationships to males. Not only were we going to eliminate ego, elitism, and hierarchy from our mutual work, but everyone was going to be completely equal. On our first project, a mural for the Livingston College Women's Center in New Brunswick, New Jersey, we adopted a common style and consciously worked over each other's images so that no area would "belong" to any one person. Even though we tried to hide it, people still got involved with the images on which they worked. The common style, however, worked quite well to minimize differences and provide unity. It is a device I still use frequently.

Total equality turned out to be an artificial and wasteful concept as initially applied because it did not allow for different skills and talents. Some people are better at figures, others at composition, and others at conception. To ignore these special talents is a false equality. A collective should be like a jazz group, not a chain gang; a place where everyone can contribute with their own instrument to play the same music. Over the next two years, People's Painters integrated men into the group and became more open to exploiting the individual talents of its members as our work grew in both complexity and strength. [1]

A good collective project needs a compositional device within which the special skills of its members can be highlighted without the unity of the piece being destroyed. This device can be a structural one such as a tree, with different scenes in the space between branches; or a style restriction. Recently, I worked with four other artists on a collective mural for the Broadway Lafayette subway station on the theme of "The Changing Face of Soho." Of the five artists in the group, three work figuratively and two decoratively. The design structure of three diamond shapes in the foreground and the adoption of a style limited to flat color and outline provided both harmony and room for everyone's skills. Within each diamond were figures representing the neighborhoods around the subway station; Soho, Lower Broadway, and Little Italy. One of the decorative artists filled the background with architectural and street patterns. The other provided the nonrepresentational color scheme with red, orange, green, and purple people with contrasting outlines. The aesthetic challenge for the artists was to produce a highly professional and sophisticated rendering within these strict limitations.

The members of the subway mural group were all exhibiting, professional artists, basically equal in skill and ego strength. This made collaboration easier. In some groups, however, the skill levels, ages, and experience of the members differ greatly. To pretend a false equality can lead to bad decisions, shoddy work, interminable meetings, and internal dissension. If a figure is incompetently drawn or if the coloring or style of one part clashes with the whole, somebody needs to raise the question frankly without fear of hurt feelings and emotional scenes. Otherwise, these problems fester and destroy the group. The least skilled and experienced members of the group are often the most insecure and the least able to accept criticism, which compounds the difficulty.

One solution to these problems is to have a recognized leader or director, part of whose job is to ensure the quality and stylistic harmony of the piece. The director can raise such questions for discussion in a way that makes the criticism less personal and therefore easier to accept. It also eliminates much power jockeying within the group and is far more time-efficient for large and diverse groups.

The site of "La Lucha Continua" project, Avenue C at 9th Street, New York City. Photo by Eva Cockcroft.

For several reasons, we chose the director model, with myself as director, for the large central mural of the "La Lucha" project. Only three others in the group had previous experience with large murals and this was a complex, forty-foot-high project that would take two months to complete. Most of the more experienced artists, moreover, were also doing separate, smaller, "individual" murals for the park. My role, therefore, was to provide the necessary consistency and coordination.

Practical reasons dictated that everything be blocked in to a certain schedule, but wherever possible the person who designed the image painted it or at least "finished" it.

The design itself was very much a collective effort. Once we developed the general concept, different members of the group sketched their various images. The left side of the mural represented the destructive reality of gentrification. Keith Christensen here designed a homeless family and a nightmare landlord scene, Judith Quinn a policeman in the doorway, and Marguerite Bunyon a child on a balcony and an evicted mother and child. On the right side, which shows actual self-help projects in the community, Rikki Asher designed the market scene, Etienne Li the community center and sweat equity workers, Therese Bimka the brick pattern structure, and Joe Stephenson the solar energy section and the big hands. The crystal ball, which reflects present activism and the future as children playing, was my contribution. To create the blueprint, each artist drew their section to scale and these were traced where they belonged. As director, I inked the tracing, making changes as necessary to make it all fit correctly and, together with Keith Christensen, did the color version of the design. The individual murals by Karin Batten, Keith, and Camille Perrottet are located beneath the collective mural. Rikki Asher and Etienne Li also did individual murals in other parts of La Lucha park.

"La Lucha Continua," completed mural at Avenue C at 9th Street, New York City, 1985. Photo by Camille Perrottet.

The form of organization that utilizes a director was necessary for this project, but is often useful even for less complex projects with less variation in skill levels. In a collective group that works together over a period of time, different members can take the "directorial" responsibility for different projects, sharing the authority and the extra work.

Core Groups and Brigades

Not all collective art projects require extensive planning and organization. Stencils and billboard alterations need little more than a few art supplies, a free evening, a few like-minded friends, and a spirit of adventure. Because of their temporary nature, they are also more appropriate for campaigns around specific issues targeted toward a particular event or mobilization. Unlike community murals, which try to provide images that express a particular community consensus, stencil projects and billboard alterations are provocative acts that may anger a large sector of the local audience. They are, legally, a form of vandalism and participants are subject to arrest. On stencil projects, we have more or less resolved this moral problem of defacing private property by avoiding residences and freshly painted walls. Occasionally, we have even been invited to graffiti the front of someone's building. With billboards the moral problem is simpler since we consider the advertisements already an invasion of public space.

My first stencil project, the Artists for Nuclear Disarmament Stencil Mural Brigade, was also the most ambitious. The concept was to create clandestine stencil murals as part of the publicity campaign for the 1982 anti-nuclear march in New York. These murals were to be composed of alternating two-by-two-foot positive and negative images. The positive and negative were each an individual stencil that could be repeated in varying sequences to "muralize" a wall or sidewalk. At the first session, the core group (Camille Perrottet, Jon Friedman, and myself) made a list of images we wanted to use—Reagan, the bomb, mothers and children, doves, etc. None of us had ever cut a stencil before, so we developed a technique together. We learned to use a shopping bag to carry the cans of spray paint and a portfolio for the stencils so that when we were not actually spraying, we were not targets for the police.

The stencil-making evolved into a one-night-a-week open workshop. People would come around eight, design and cut a stencil, and then around eleven, we would go out to put them up. We discovered that the optimum number for stenciling was five people, with one person acting as lookout and two groups of two holding and spraying.

It was the core group who designed most of the best images and held the project together. Like graffitists, we had a logo and certain other especially effective images that came to identify the project. These we duplicated and gave to whoever wanted to put them up. As propaganda, the project became effective only when the images proliferated and seemed to appear mysteriously around the city. Ironically, this project, which had so little to do with art and so much with propaganda, was the most recognized by the art world. It was represented in exhibitions at commercial galleries and even in the Museum of Modern Art.

Billboard alterations are a similar type of project, though better suited to cities more automobile-oriented than New York. For this work, a group of three to five people is best. Access to a pickup truck in which to carry ladders and paint helps. Dubbed the Venice Billboard Correction Committee by the local press, the group with which I worked when living in Los Angeles had a core group of three. One of them, Matt Wuerker, is a political cartoonist, and the other an academic. Usually we went out with at least two or three additional people. It seems almost everyone, even the most responsible law-abiding types, want to try billboarding at least once. This again can be a casual evening activity. First we needed to find a suitable billboard or two; this meant fairly low, relatively small, easily accessible, not too well lit at night, and having an image that lent itself to alteration.

In our billboards we generally used a combination of paste-ons and painted changes. For altering the text, both foreground and background colors should be pre-mixed. Everything can usually be prepared the same evening, between dinner and midnight. If everyone is clear on exactly what their particular task is, no billboard should take more than about twenty minutes.

The wittiest altered billboards need to carry both the new and the old message simultaneously, so the conceptual part is very important. Aside from good people, nothing helps insure a creative, brainstorming design session like a big pot of pasta

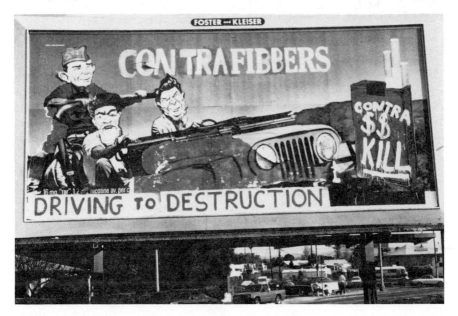

South Venice Billboard Correction Committee, Venice, CA, 1987. Photo by Eva Cockcroft.

and a large bottle of wine. This helps warm up people's ideas. Also, subliminally, well-created spaghetti (with the strands separate yet blended by a harmonious sauce) is the perfect analogy for a well-functioning collective group.

Collective Connections

Every successful group project involves compromise. The result may never be completely satisfying to any one individual participant; there's always a part you would have done better or differently. In compensation, the finished piece is richer than an individual conception because of the different perspectives and input—the whole is always greater than the sum of its parts. In that sense, every collective is a learning experience.

Making the work fun and encouraging participation and relaxation is integral to the work. Even when the artwork turns out satisfactorily, quarreling about it in the process may have left a bad taste behind and ruined the experience.

Artists tend to be solitary, often lonely people and newcomers to a community may find it difficult to meet other artists. An added social benefit is meeting like-minded colleagues with whom to discuss your personal work and develop friendships. Above all, the feelings of comradeship, shared experience, and friendship that develop through working together can be tremendously rewarding.

Notes

1. For a complete history of People's Painters see Eva Cockcroft, John Weber and Jim Cockcroft, *Toward a Peoples Art: The Contemporary Mural Movement* (New York: E.P. Dutton, 1977).

The Thing About Criticism

John O'Neal

It seems that criticism has been reduced to the status of sub-set in the process of selling the arts. This is not a good thing, because critical evaluation is an essential part of the process of making and improving art. The current situation diminishes the aesthetic functions of criticism, and contributes to the invisibility of politics in the process altogether. The problem can only be solved if critic, artist, and audience aim at the same purpose in a process that is comprised of political, aesthetic, as well as economic aspects.

Celebrated for its capacity to influence public opinion, television provides the best example of the problem. The tail wags the dog when techniques designed to advance sales are regarded as the basis for qualitative standards for the medium. Measurable impact on sales is considered as proof of the means. The aesthetic values implied are no more acceptable than the moral vacuum it conceals.

John O'Neal

John O'Neal is an award-winning playwright, actor, director, and teacher. He was a co-founder of the Free Southern Theater and he is artistic director of Junebug Productions, a performing art organization based in New Orleans, which carries a variety of performing arts programs. For information contact: Junebug Productions, Western and Southern Arts Associates, P.O. Box 50120, Austin, TX 78763.

The political and aesthetic aspects of culture are made entirely subservient to the requirement to sell.

I visualize the relationship of these elements as three overlapping circles: one red, one blue, and one yellow. Red represents content; blue represents the technique, craft, and skill employed; and yellow represents the activity of the public in relation to the work. Where all three circles overlap is a brown triangle. The task of the critic is to help all parties concerned to find and work the "sweet brown spot." Critics who aren't concerned about the whole process won't be much help.

A unity of purpose is assumed between press and public—that the press works in the public interest—but when the press is limited by no more than the requirement to sell, the contract is violated. The presumption of a unity of purpose is then converted from an ideal upon which ethical standards can be built into a ruse to conceal the self-serving purposes of the publishers. This promotes bad art as well as bad criticism.

The giant merchant slug, "Jabba the Hutt," from Star Wars is an apt metaphor. Regardless of how he got there, the decadent demon does nothing but make demands of those who seek his favors and grows fatter from endless consumption of tendered booty. Like the courtesans and courtiers who become the victims as often as they become the instruments of the demon's boundless need for more, the media becomes part of the problem. The work of thoughtful and sincere critics is often savaged by the competitive demands of the insatiable market monster and the limitations of time and space.

Like most people, I never noticed the problem until it began to interfere with things I was trying to do. In 1962 a group of us who were involved in the civil rights movement decided that a "Free Southern Theater" (FST) was needed. True to form, regional critics ignored our work. Anti-Black discrimination was expected, but when critics did finally start to write about our work, it became clear that we had underestimated the magnitude of the problem.

We lived and worked with courageous people who were risking their livelihoods and their lives to forge better living conditions; less for themselves than for succeeding generations. We thought it legitimate to use our work as artists to encourage and support those efforts. We sought to produce plays which celebrate the joys and accomplishments of those who have struggled against racist oppression. We sought to expose those things which threaten to retard or hold back that continuing struggle.

Regardless of their own personal beliefs, the critics worked for some of the key supporters of the oppressive system that we sought to eradicate. The best of them would argue with unconvincing passion that literary convention is more important than real people are; that form takes priority over substance. Unless needed to justify exploitation and oppression, the differences between "us" and "them" were ignored. It was arrogantly presumed that the standards and values of the oppressors applied without qualification to the artistic product of the oppressed, without considering that opposing experiences produce opposing ideas.

For a long time this problem of criticism remained invisible because it seemed to have no consequence for us. So long as our audiences came from among the common working people who made up the rank and file of the movement, it didn't make much difference what the critics wrote. Our audiences were far more concerned about the quality of their relationship to the local organization that had presented us.

Gradually, though, it became clear that FST had more than one important audience. Our primary audience was working-class, southern Black people and others who shared their struggles. Their lives and culture provided the content, context, and purposes for the work that we sought to do. A second audience was comprised of persons who seldom attended performances but whose judgments controlled the network of philanthropic and government agencies that control access to public subsidies. The critics who seemed not to understand or care about the people and the ideas that were central to our work had considerable impact on these policy makers.

The critic's job is to help audiences get a better understanding of the arts and to help artists do a better job of communicating with the audience. To be effective in this role depends on the recognition of common interests between audience, artist, *and* critic, and some understanding of how the particular type of art in question may be useful.

It should be like a relationship between lovers. There's no way for healthy, mature adults to avoid conflict. Conflict is integral to life itself. But if a relationship is to endure and prosper, there must be a way to resolve conflict on a "win/win" basis. If one partner wins and one loses, it's only a matter of time before both turn up as losers. Only if all parties to the relationship are trying to reach the same "super objective" can the conflict be resolved on a "win/win" basis.

The aesthetic or creative impulse is the impulse to make "it" better, when "it" is the consciousness of one's dynamic relationship to others. This impulse is an essential part of all living things, from the most lowly subatomic particle to the seething enormity of the growing, changing, universe itself. When the creative impulse fades, the destructive impulse comes to dominate and life soon gives way to death. It's axiomatic: if you don't make it better, you die.

Imagine this guy sitting around the cave nursing the wounds he got trying to kill the buffalo that his family is almost through eating. While he's thinking about it he scratches a picture of the buffalo on the wall. He studies that sketch and reruns the fight in his mind. Finally, he figures out a better way to do it next time. Sure enough, he soon becomes the best hunter in that end of the valley. He uses the picture to teach his family how to hunt. The night before every hunt they gather in front of the picture and practice their buffalo-hunting moves. After each hunt he returns to the cave and makes more drawings. Soon his wife is a good hunter and his children become even better hunters.

After a while the word gets around that this guy has these magic pictures in his cave, and that after a hunt he comes back and tells everything that happened using the pictures. Before his neighbors go out hunting, they too make a plan and they practice on the pictures. The man finally becomes too old to hunt, but when others return to tell the stories of their hunting, he leads the discussion of what they could have done better. A few millennia pass. The cave with its pictures and stories pass from one generation to the next; and there you have the birth of religious ritual, visual art, storytelling, theater, sculpture, dance, and criticism; all arising from the desire to do a better job of hunting for food. Criticism and art arise *at the same time,* from the same needs to improve the quality of the community.

In any given era there are probably many persons who make artifacts with as much or more dexterity as those we remember as great artists. That which stands out as great art is that which illuminates our own lives by giving us the clearest, strongest insight into the historical and social circumstances that prevailed at the time the art was created. This capacity to illuminate is mainly the product of the relationship between the content of the work of art and the life experiences of the persons who make up the audience for that work.

The distinctive thing about great art is the perception of the time and circumstance observed by the artists and their ability to give affective form to that vision. The pattern is complete when form serves content, which in turn reflects the needs and interests of an audience whose concerns are complemented by the concerns of the artists involved. When a work of art holds the attention of an audience, that work has probably helped illuminate something that feels important the audience's efforts to make their own lives better. The social, historical, and political circumstances are not secondary infringements on the artistic process but are absolutely essential and integral parts of the process.

In the modern period it has become quite fashionable to think of art almost entirely as the product of individualized expression. Modern artists and critics aren't alone in adopting this perspective. This viewpoint could not have survived if the audience which sustains such art and opinion did not have a complementary view.

Clearly our individuality is of crucial importance. How else could we be who we are? No motion of any type can occur except in the action of individuals. But there are two crucial points to be made: First, problems that are social or historical in nature do not yield to individualistic psychological solutions. Second, problems that are social and historical in nature invariably give rise to psychological problems while the converse is seldom true. Major problems develop when work that is grounded in an idea of community is assessed by critics who proceed from the more narrow view of art based *primarily* on psychological or individual factors. Many audiences respond enthusiastically to community-based artwork, but there aren't many critics who recognize or share the ideal. I guess that those of us who care about the matter have to accept the job of trying to do something about it.

It is increasingly evident that we live in a society dominated by greed. In practical fact, the only restriction to the profit motive is not even whether you get caught doing something wrong, but how much you have the nerve to get caught doing. With sufficient bravado you can be a hero even if you don't get away with it. Mere shades of difference distinguish Donald Trump, Ivan Boesky, Edwin Meese, and Oliver North. Law enforcement officials who don't actually become criminals too are compelled to overlook the wrongs of their comrades and to make do with the harassment of petty thugs and hoodlums who have little standing in the vast criminal oligarchies that easily replace their fallen foot soldiers.

Teeming pools of poverty provide ever greater numbers of people who are willing to take big risks for what seem to be big gains against the apparent certainty of depravity and deprivation in the ghettos. Finding no shortage of role models to support the view that everything runs by the law of the jungle anyway, "Only the strong survive!" becomes the watchword of the ill-thought race to cash in on the American dream.

In my old neighborhood—a traditional, long-standing Black working-class district—I know a young man who does a lot of the robbing and stealing. I don't enjoy a special relationship with him, it's simply common knowledge in the neighborhood, just like it's common knowledge who has what kind of drugs to sell or who collects dues for the local mafia chieftain.

What must one do to be effective for an audience comprised of that young man and his peers? Should we try to convince him to go back to school to prepare himself for a job that might pay three to five dollars per hour? Facing the certainties of unyielding poverty on one side and the *possibility* of big bucks on the other, what would you do?

"The worst thing that could happen, bro, is that some dude might blow me away and I would go out in a blaze of glory. Hell. I might even be a little jive-time hero around here." For some, the prospect of a quick, dramatic death seems preferable to the agonizingly slow withdrawal from life that poverty often makes inevitable. Once pathological behavior is endorsed as an acceptable norm, it's a small step to the point where some start to enjoy the process of killing and dying.

The twin demons of institutionalized racism and poverty are two of the major problems to be conquered if the promise of American democracy is to be redeemed. Neither artist nor critic is exempt from the problems facing our communities.

Rather, we have a special responsibility to help make it better. In order for the critic to be helpful to artists who share these concerns, he or she would have to start with similar concerns. This would enable him or her to show us what's wrong with our assessment of the situation, or show us how to improve the quality of art based on these concerns.

*   *   *

I envision a picture of old people in a small-town, clapboard church gathering to sing at a funeral about unbroken circles and better homes waiting . . . in the sky, Lord, bye and bye.

*   *   *

I have a friend named John Scott. He's more like a brother than a friend. John's an outstanding sculptor and visual artist. He tells me this story about a sailor who was laying in his bunk one day aboard ship when one of his shipmates rushed in with the message that the ship had hit an iceberg and was sinking. "I don't give a damn!" he says, "Let it sink. It ain't mine!"

*   *   *

The problems that give rise to struggles for social, political, and economic change are reflected in the cultural sphere as well. When conditions of oppression and exploitation exist, culture and ideas become important parts of the process. It is essential to develop a view that helps us to understand why so many critics have such sharply different ideas about what's important and why criticism has recently been of such little help in the effort to help make it better.

The thing about criticism is that it's just like everything else—if we want the job done right, we must help to develop the standards and the people with the skills to do the kind of criticism we believe to be valuable. We need critics who recognize themselves as members of the audience that the work seeks to serve. And whether we, as artists or as critics, identify with ethnic, cultural, religious, geographic, or other communities, we need to have a sense of how our discrete communities ultimately stand as interdependent parts of the global community of humankind and of all living things. Knowing our history, place, and culture as well as understanding how the prevailing economic, political, and social forces work are all important elements in the process of creating quality art and quality criticism.

We will not find ready-made critics waiting to take up this work just as we don't find bunches of artists or community organizers waiting in line just to get their marching papers. We have to do our own work but we must also help create the circumstances and conditions in which those who are committed to developing the strengths of our communities can become the critics that we need.

Notes

1. For information on Junebug Productions contact: Junebug Productions, Western and Southern Arts Associates, P.O. Box 50120, Austin, TX 78763.

Losing Faith
(or Gaining Perspective)
Rebecca Rice

Rebecca Rice

Black, woman, mother, writer, theatre artist, and educator, the focus of Rebecca Rice's work is to create works of art that bring voice, breadth and beauty to the life experiences of those who live in a state of shame, isolation and hopelessness.

Rebecca Rice in *I Might Have Been Queen,* portraits of women on the edge that illuminate the struggles and dreams of Black women: the way it is, the way it never should have been, the way it ought to be. Photo by Sarah Jo Berman.

Calendar of Events

My Life So Far

Rebecca Rice

1970   After fleeing the riot-torn streets of Chicago, I became member of the Living Stage Theater Company, serving the creative needs of children, youth, the disabled, the incarcerated, and other "forgotten people."

1980   First trip to Cuba as guest of the Ministry of Information; toured factories, schools, and theaters.

1981   Worked on prison project to repeal the Thirteenth Amendment to the Constitution, which legalized prison slavery.

1982   Second trip to Cuba for "Taller de Nuevo Teatro" (A Workshop in New Theater).

1983   Worked with Centro de Arte to bring Teatro de Escambray of Cuba to the U.S.

1984   Wrote and performed *Waiting in Vain* (on the suicide of a young Black woman poet) with Living Stage. Left Living Stage after fourteen years. Cofounded the Human Bridge Theater with Janet Stanford. Performed *This is the House* in shelters for battered women. First meetings of Black Artists-White Artists (BAWA) dealing with issues of race in art.

1985   *This is the House* is performed in London. BAWA presented "Black Art/White Art: Conversations in Culture." Began writing *Lifeline—I Might Have Been Queen* (on the dreams and struggles of Black women). Consulted with Latinegro Youth Theater Collective. Conducted workshops on racism with Liz Lerman for Alliance for Cultural Democracy.

1986   Member of Centrifugal Force (women's theater collective). Performed *Lifeline: I Might Have Been Queen.* Artsreach Conference: "Art in Other Places," Los Angeles, CA. Alternate Roots annual meeting in Atlanta, GA. Consultant for incest project with Planned Parenthood of California.

1987   Performed solo works at Life on the Water Theater, San Francisco. CityKids Project on "Abuse and Neglect," New York City. Consultant for Artsreach Theater Project, Los Angeles. Workshops on racism with BAWA members, Boston and Washington, D.C. Joined At the Foot of the Mountain Women's Theater as member of the resident performing company and collaborated in the creation and performance of *Story of a Mother, Part 2.*

1988   Member of Artistic Directorial Team and Artistic Director, At the Foot of the Mountain Theater, Minneapolis. Performed with Penumbra Theater, an all Black professional theater in St. Paul.

Havana, Cuba, 1982

I am sitting in an unlikely looking airport. My plane is three hours late. I have just come from an international working conference called "Taller de Nuevo Teatro." A few weeks ago a hurricane had nearly destroyed the airport and parts of the city. But, in Amerika, since the weather report doesn't extend ninety miles southeast of Miami, we didn't know what damage had been done. Typical Amerikan myopia. Tears are in my eyes as I walk to the plane. The flight renders me in a state of suspended animation. As if it were up to me, I am trying to decide whether the plane should go on to Amerika, or stay in Cuba.

I am thinking intensely of Alan Bolt, the Nicaraguan director who headed one of several collectives of conference participants assigned the task of creating a theaterwork in six days that made a statement, in form and content, about our view of a new theater. "It's not up to me," he would say. "You are the artists. I am here only to ask questions and to focus your attention on your work." The room where we worked was a swirl of people, languages, and activity. Small groups would gather and discuss issues or create a section of the piece and bring it before Alan for criticism. As always he would abdicate to the group saying, "Tell them what you saw." Someone would inevitably begin with a critical statement only to be caught up short by Alan, "Don't trap them and yourselves in your thoughts and opinions, just tell them what you saw. The truth will tell itself." He would then carefully ask questions or call attention to each part of the presentation allowing the performers to critique their own work. His process was sprawling, permissive, and chaotic; but it empowered the performers to take responsibility for their work either out of sheer panic over his "lack of leadership" or because, at last, they felt like more than pawns in the game of hierarchical theater.

I too was empowered. For twelve years I had been in a theatrical ensemble that was headed by a powerful director. Our process was collaborative, but final decisions were his. My Cuba experience made me yearn for more ownership and control over my creative process. As I winged my way home I wondered how realistic that dream could be. I prepared to face anew the reality of being an artist in Amerika, a woman artist in Amerika, a Black woman artist in Amerika. Should this plane land? Should I get off? Should this struggle begin?

Coming Home

It is 1988 and obviously I came back, having set aside any romantic notions I might have possessed about Cuba or the struggle against racist/classist/sexist oppression. The romance had faded largely because I experienced that oppression at tht hands of those who purported to be exponents of that struggle—namely the artists and arts organizations who translate political ideologies into visual and verbal imagery intent on inspiring visions of a just and peaceful world. I stand at this moment in a state of wariness in regard to the ability of many of my white sisters and brothers to stay the course through the difficult dilemmas of cross-cultural collaborations. It takes courage and stamina to absorb the information that will bring about the vital changes in how we see ourselves as artists and how we serve our various communities.

For a long time now artists of conscience have been grappling with the question of whose imagery is being put forth, in whose words, and according to whose vision. In terms of theory, this is all pretty well-worn stuff. It has been worked and reworked during the creative processes of theater companies, in collective meetings, in academic classrooms, and neighborhood arts programs. Of course we know how we have been brainwashed by images from the dominant white culture. And we know the inclusion of imagery from cultures of color is virtually a mandate. We also know that mainstream theater has little, if any, interest in taking up the challenge. And so, it falls to the artists of conscience, who are constantly overworked, underpaid, and under-appreciated, to do a job that should be enthusiastically undertaken by the whole theater community. But this is no excuse for the failure to turn theory into pervasive practice.

We have all witnessed the failures. The explosive meetings where accusations are hurled like tennis balls, the conferences where the question is always asked, "Why aren't there more people of color here?", the dilemmas about why things are not working out according to plan, and the good intentions that didn't produce good results.

I have always held a strong belief in and love for the collaborative process. When all contributions are honored and encouraged each participant experiences the sweet power of their own creative individuality. But, when that process becomes a power struggle, only negative lessons are learned and we lose faith in our ability to work together to fulfill our artistic visions.

Forgotten People

For fourteen years I was a member of the Living Stage Theater Company in Washington, DC. For over twenty years this company has fostered a strong vision of creative empowerment for the disenfranchised populations that comprise its audience of choice.

Since 1970 the company solved the problem of the absence of quality material that focused on issues concerning "forgotten people," by creating works that were original in both content and form. The interracial company collaborated on the creation of over fifty original works dealing with a wide range of social issues from mental illness to the wars in Central America. Workshop processes were also developed to help different audiences understand and express how these issues impacted on their lives. The process for creating these works had at its base the improvisational technique. Under the sensitive tutelage of founder and director Robert Alexander, each actor developed her or his creative individuality, while contributing to the collective identity of the company.

The performance pieces that were developed were the products of a guided collaboration. Alexander provided the directorial eye that shaped the ultimate impact that each piece would have. The advantage of this was having a reliable and dynamic outside eye that would resolve creative confusions in more expedient ways than the mind-racking and time-consuming process of collective deliberation. The disadvantage was having that outside eye be that of a white man (no matter how perceptive and intelligent), limited the degree to which racial and cultural input could be explored and ultimately affect the evolving work.

In an effort to communicate the shame of racism in its harshest light, the tone and character of all of the pieces were excruciatingly intense and deeply truthful in their revelation of hidden emotions. But because most of the pieces were seldom more than a half hour in length, the audiences were left with a picture of unrelenting pain and anguish. This is certainly not an unreal view, especially in light of the rampant drug abuse that is plaguing the Black community today. But it is incomplete. Black culture consists of more than just pain. We are very clever at dealing with white people, we have evolved codes of language and behavior that whites are not even aware of, we have our own methods of passing on our history, customs, and strengths to our children. Because of the director's perspective and lack of knowledge, we spent very little time exploring Black values and how white society can learn from them. The audiences we served reaped enormous benefit from the creative and supportive atmosphere the company established. However, I constantly carried the feeling that we were not sharing some vital information with our audiences, and ran the risk of deepening their wounds.

An especially nagging problem arises when whites become the arbiters in the arena of cultural moods, images, and energies that feed artistic statements aimed at educating audiences who are starving, albeit unknowingly, for the input of people of color in the artwork to which they subscribe. In the pursuit of a multicultural ideal white artists want an atmosphere of equality, but often cast themselves in the role of player/coach, which still gives them room to have the dominant voice. But more importantly, they do not realize that analysis, charisma, processing, rugged individualism, and cause and effect are all aspects of white/Western culture. They don't see that these aspects may block other forms of expression, such as spirituality, sacrifice, love, common sense, and a strong sense of community, modalities that are basic to gatherings of people of color. If these modalities were honored as essential to the creative process they would alter the process and the product.

This unawareness is a very dangerous thing because the dominant culture already possesses a viciously myopic telescope through which they want to see their colored people. Progressive whites, seeing themselves as good people with a righteous multicultural vision, exempt themselves from this reality. But in doing so, they constantly close their eyes and nerve endings to the blunders they inevitably create.

Some Considerations

1. Who Defines Multiculturalism?

The term multiculturalism raises more questions than it answers. For instance, who decides when and how the various cultures will come together? Who pulls the purse strings? Who decides what projects are worthy of support and presentation? And who really benefits from multicultural work? These and many other questions get raised in discussions while collaborative projects are underway, but somehow there never seems to be the proper time given for a deep examination that might radically alter or even dissolve the project if it truly is not meeting its professed goal.

For example: When five women artists arrived to begin their work as the first multiracial resident performing company of At the Foot of the Mountain Women's Theater (AFOM), the conceptual work had already been done by the current (all white) administration. The plays had been chosen, money and contract issues had been decided, and the racial make-up of the company was predetermined. Dates had been set and promises had been made for tours and workshops that were to take place over the next several months. We were installed as a multicolored showpiece, the realization of a multicultural ideal. Alarm bells should have gone off, but the production mentality was in force. The show must go on.

In this atmosphere there was very little room for experimentation, questions, or problems, and certainly no room to question the nature of the project itself. This shortsightedness made it impossible to really look at what was happening between us. We were Asian, Black, Latin, Native American, and White. There are historical problems, as well as current tensions between any combination of these groups. There are also surprising cultural similarities in ceremonial practices, healing arts, and parenting; as well as a common experience of oppression. Any of these issues could have been explored and lead to the production of fascinating theater. This company could have created several performance/workshop presentations that would have benefited the theater enormously while bringing forth sorely needed information and education about the nitty-gritty stuff of cross-cultural communication and collaboration. What the theater got instead was a failed project where only negative lessons were learned. We five eventually were forced to initiate a work stoppage to halt the march of incorrect policies. I know we will all think twice (at least) before reentering the arena of multicultural work.

2. Many Cultural Art Forms Do Not Transfer Successfully to the Stage

Many cultural art forms do not transfer successfully to the spectator setting of theater. Ceremonies, rituals, services, and storytellings are not always meant to be observed, but experienced. For the artists who come from these communities, the theatricalization of their customs can amount to sacrilege.

For example: An Ojibwa woman, who was part of the AFOM company, offered to include the sacred teachings of her people in the material of the play. The director saw the dramatic potential and suggested some blocking that would heighten this. The woman had great difficulty with the direction because, in their natural setting, the teachings would not be offered in a presentational manner. What was necessary to the theater was insulting to the culture. The teachings were withdrawn.

I, too, encountered this problem when trying to stage a gospel service. These services are about calling down the spirit, and when audiences sat passively and watched, the atmosphere became campish, rather than holy. In the rush of production schedules these dilemmas were never adequately explored and the play was weakened because of it.

3. The Problem of the White Male Power Model

Many cultures of color come to power and utilize it in quite different ways than white culture. To the extent that an organizational structure is modeled after the dominant white male power model, the people of color in that organization will reenact their role of oppression.

For example: At AFOM once again (though I must say this has not been the only place where I have seen this occur), because so many decisions were out of our hands, the company began to bicker amongst ourselves, form factions, and play impotent power games which only deepened the misery and weakened our potential collective strength.

The extent to which the directors of the project experienced pain and confusion is the extent to which they were personally invested in the system they had set up.

Some Possibilities

The above examples offer a disparaging view of crosscultural artistic collaboration and give evidence of the increasing racial tensions we all currently live with. But I know there are positive stories that counter my examples. Another story from my own experience offers hope:

The Human Bridge Theater was created by Janet Stanford and myself. Janet, a white woman, came from a completely different background than me. We shared a common theater language and a passion for the work that we were engaged in. We collaborated on the creation of *This Is the House,* a two-woman show on domestic violence. The initial idea came from both of us. The conduct of the project was governed by a strong desire on both of our parts to preserve (and in some instances even play upon and heighten) our cultural and philosophical differences. We did not search for false connections between ourselves or the characters we created. By allowing the natural tensions of race, class, and ideological differences to emerge, we were able to engage in a truly open dialogue and to infuse our characters with electricity. In one scene, two of the characters fuel their racial tensions to a point where a fist fight breaks out. They later come to a temporary alliance built around mutual need. Engaging in this kind of process permeated the performance with the dignity of the experience. Because of this energy and honesty the audiences who witnessed the work participated in discussions on race that were revealing and uplifting.

In another example, Black Artists-White Artists (BAWA), an interracial, multidisciplinary group of Washington, DC, artists, joined together to discuss the effects of racism on the work we produced. This situation was set up as an exploration, not a collaboration. We recognized early on that the lure of creating a product would shortcut the process we had entered into. It would also give us the false security of being able to say we had accomplished something tangible together in our work on racism. With this trap removed, we had to really look at whether or not as a group we had a solid commitment to exploring this difficult and multi-leveled issue. We put meticulous effort into setting up meeting and discussion processes that honored differing senses of time and rhythm. We recognized that *how* an issue is addressed is as important as the complexities of the issue itself. Our efforts payed off in profound learning experiences and a group that maintained fairly consistent membership and attendance for five years.

In each of these projects the focus was on the learning process. *This Is the House* was a powerful product, but never made the mistake of becoming inflexible. BAWA steered clear of group collaboration while having a transformative effect on the work of each member.

These experiences caused me to question the order of priorities in projects where those involved become narrowly focused on a tangible product as the only evidence that something was accomplished. I also question the depth of the commitment to dealing with racism when we allow ourselves to be satisfied with superficial relationships where little is ventured and therefore nothing is gained.

With all this complexity and frustration, and with the high ratio of negative to positive experiences, one might ask why I have continued to work in this form of theater. One reason is the simple racist truth that there is no place in mainstream theater for an intelligent, talented, dynamic woman of color, who is unwilling to play another victimized maid, mama, or prostitute. I realized a long time ago that if there was to be a place for me in theater, I was going to have to make one for myself and others by creating roles that reflected the values, dilemmas, and aspirations of the people who are seldom portrayed in positions of respect.

Theater for social change, even with its problems, still offers the best hope for artistic liberation. Especially if it addresses race issues from a new point of view. The exploration of themes, characters, and art forms that come from cultures of color could bring about a much needed infusion of new blood and energy. Why not feature plays that focus on the issues of Native Americans, the changing relationship between successful Black women and their male counterparts, lesbian women of color, interracial relationships, the human side of the Israeli/Palestinian conflict, or the dilemmas and hilarities of cultural duality. These are but a few of the many possibilities.

By constantly focusing on racism and classism we force ourselves to continually analyze and dissect white society and our relationship to it. And in doing so we continually call up the worst aspect of our dealings with each other and invite destructive energy into what should be a creative process. If greater emphasis was placed on exploring examples from various cultures on the utilization and delegation of power and authority, as well as decision making, this information could influence the way we set up projects and organizations, opportunities for empowerment would increase measurably.

In addition, by creating situations where people of color are in leadership positions and cultural differences and similarities can be positively employed, white directors, playwrights, and actors would have to take a back seat for a while, in order to listen and learn. Control and safety are big issues in the white community and often put major roadblocks in the struggle to create meaningful dialogue and education.

The key to relinquishing control is being willing to take a risk because one is fully confident that there is everything to gain and a lifetime of oppression to lose. Ironically, these are the same energies, together with a sense of courageous exploration, that inspire creativity on the deepest level.

For the Earth . . . For the Universe

Democracy
and Competence
Don Adams and Arlene Goldbard

Some time ago we spent two weeks at an English college, teaching a group of art students how to work collectively. We were free to use any methods we chose, from collaborating on an art-making project to talking theory. We started by getting to know the students—what they cared about and what they might want to accomplish together. This was made more difficult by their prior fifteen years in an educational system which breeds deference and obedience. Our students hadn't had much experience figuring out what they wanted, and asking them to try was like pulling teeth.

Fortunately for us, events intervened. On the second day of our work together, the faculty distributed written evaluations for the previous term's projects. Our students were very unhappy with them. They felt their work had been judged unfairly, using criteria invented after the projects were well underway. They called a meeting to discuss whether anything could be done about the evaluation process.

For us, this was a stroke of luck. We'd already learned that the theme most on our students' minds was "power"—hardly surprising for a group of twenty-year-olds. We'd just begun casting about for a form through which to pursue this theme when the evaluation controversy illuminated the aspect of power closest to home: the power of the college, the faculty, and the students.

Don Adams
Arlene Goldbard

Don Adams and Arlene Goldbard are founders of the Institute for Cultural Democracy and partners in Adams & Goldbard, organizational and cultural development consultants. They are based in Ukiah, California. A sampling of past clients includes the National Asian American Telecommunications Association, The New Museum of Contemporary Art, the National Black Programming Consortium, the Media Alliance, the Kansas Arts Commission, and the Pickle Family Circus. Their essays on cultural policy and politics have been published by many journals including *The Independent, High Performance, In These Times,* and *Art in America.*

Asking Hard Questions

In the balance of our two weeks together, we explored the nature of power and the tools of collective endeavor. The students conferred with faculty and older students, asking hard questions about curriculum and grading systems. They studied the college's plans and policy statements and compared these with their actual experience. They talked about how things could be, and eventually proposed improvements to the evaluation system with a student-faculty committee to monitor them. To their great surprise, the faculty accepted all their proposals.

Through this work, the students learned about their own group dynamics. When we first met, they'd cast themselves as helpless victims of the college. They were convinced that the faculty functioned as a conscious, coordinated power bloc, and that every student complaint was rooted in a faculty conspiracy. They denied having power to change things. Each one knew which of their classmates spoke up for their rights and which were "cabbages."

We were most gratified to see these convictions overturned. Students who'd rarely spoken out found the courage to chair meetings with faculty. Others notorious for grandstanding were taken to task by former cabbages. The whole class realized that faculty members really didn't speak with one voice—that they disagreed, made mistakes and bumbled through like everyone else. From a seemingly clear-cut case of victims and oppressors emerged a more dynamic picture: the students realized that the status quo embodied a tacit agreement on both sides that students would have no power within the institution.

Now, a college isn't a cooperative. The balance of power really is unequal. A teacher can fail a student or, short of that, make the student's life miserable. One might say that in a school the students function as labor and the faculty as management. But from the faculty's point of view, the metaphor stands on its head: the teachers are labor and the administration management. For the administration, the real power rests with those responsible for financing and accreditation. In England, these are ultimately government responsibilities and thus accountable to political power—bringing us back to the students and their families. Interventions anywhere in the network of power can affect the entire system. While simple descriptions of power may have a certain ring to them, they are disabling because they are inadequate.

To Take Democracy Seriously

We loved this teaching experience because it embodied two themes we care about deeply: democracy and competence. Democracy must guarantee each citizen's right to shape political life, to participate in decisions that affect the commonwealth. This right entails crucial responsibilities: to take democracy seriously, to learn all we can so our social interventions will be sound, to mobilize our energies and self-discipline to practice what we preach, to take pride in craft and do a good job.

In our own work we attempt to express these convictions in two ways. We spend as much time as possible trying to spread democratic ideas through writing, speaking and teaching, especially about cultural democracy.* Since we also need to make a living, we consult with organizations, helping them plan, solve problems, raise money, and build community connections. Most of our clients are involved with cultural action: that is, they are producers, such as theater companies and filmmakers; people distributing cultural products; or agencies with some responsibility for community cultural life, such as arts councils. In this work we hear about people's problems and aspirations. We get to know them on the level of deeds as well as words. Our task is to help them navigate the systems and structures through which organizations are sustained and have impact; to help them increase their competence.

We believe a commitment to democracy, to have any real meaning, requires a commitment to build competence in its practice. This starts with recognizing our potential to act. Our British students pictured themselves outside the nexus of power. The educational system had convinced them they were incompetent to do anything but obey the rules and try to meet standards laid down by those in authority. Though intelligent, creative and articulate, the students had internalized this propaganda so thoroughly as to ratify it by behaving as if they actually were incompetent. Their only resistance was to grumble and feel victimized, even in the face of easily solved problems. For instance, many complained from our first day together about being cooped up in a stuffy meeting room, but it took more than a week for anyone to propose moving to another location.

The Culture of Powerlessness

We worry that the culture of powerlessness engulfing our British students seems rampant in the U.S. No authentically democratic society can ever be established and maintained by people who have convinced themselves that democracy cannot be practiced even on the small scale of community cultural life. Yet many people on the cultural left seem to believe precisely this, impoverishing the quality of both their work process and their results.

---

* In this essay we employ the term "cultural democracy" which incorporates four main principles: 1) cultural diversity is a positive value to be protected and encouraged, 2) democratic participation is essential to shaping cultural life (for instance, to determining how cultural industries should be constructed, supported and regulated), 3) authentic democracy requires active participation in cultural life, 4) equity demands a fair distribution of cultural resources and support throughout the society.

Musicians have a stock joke for those moments when tuning up seems interminable. "That's all right," they say, "it's close enough for jazz." The joke is funny because it reverberates with the ironic self-deprecation of a marginalized group. It acknowledges the comparatively low esteem in which the prestige musical world—the opera and symphony orchestras—has held jazz; but it also hints at the stupidity of this bigoted judgment.

Too many artists whose work is situated outside the mainstream might as well take "close enough for community" as their motto, unmitigated by irony. They have so completely internalized their marginalization that they reproduce the contempt in which they are held by the dominant culture. Their work doesn't have to look very good, they don't have to spend much time rehearsing or studying, they don't need to ask for criticism or be open to it when it comes—because whatever their work is like, it's good enough for the marginalized people for whom it's intended. Neither democracy nor competence come into the picture.

Practicing Cultural Democracy

What does it mean to practice democracy in the context of cultural action? For us, the crucial precondition is group involvement in shaping goals and defining principles upon which action will be based.

Take as an example a group of artists striving to change U.S. policy in Central America. Many such groups now operate as adjuncts to solidarity organizations, providing signs and banners, producing posters and sponsoring benefit events. The parent organization typically wants artists to help put its message across, expressing demands or protests in hopes of influencing opinion and policy.

If such a group had deep democratic commitments—to democracy in practice as well as in principle—it could operate in other ways. Different questions could be asked. Instead of "What do we want to say?" people could try to find out "What motivates our opposition? How do people see them? How do they see us?" Assumptions would have to be questioned: "How have people actually changed foreign policy in the past? What is the real impact of demonstrations? Who looks at posters, and how?" Research would be needed: "To whom should we be talking, and what do we know about them? How do they live? What do they care about? To whom do they talk and listen?" Deeper understandings of the problems at hand would enrich strategic thinking about how to address them through arts work.

As another example, a theater company with democratic commitments holds the potential to help create community where strong, self-conscious feelings of community identification are lacking. But this task requires that the theater create new forms of cooperation and communication to replace the buyer-seller relationships that exist with traditional theater audiences. One hears talk about "plugging into the community" as if "community" were a socket and artists held the lamp. This romantic idea has something in common with the Right's romance with "the family," as if *Father Knows Best* were a *cinéma vérité* version of life in the United States. In fact, most of us have to take our "family" and "community" wherever we find them. We create community as we go along, and arts groups have to do the same: start with a handful of people and work out from there.

This approach demands new kinds of democratic competence. As much skill and energy will go into building a theater's relationships as into mounting productions. The theater's organizational apparatus will have to be as tightly rigged and efficient as its production apparatus. Political and cultural goals will be as central as artistic ones. Individuals will contribute to the theater according to their own skills— whether in technical theater, acting, directing or administration and fundraising— but all the theater's members will have to invest time sharing and analyzing what they've learned, setting goals and planning the shape of each year. Ways will be needed to track everyone's participation in implementing plans, to demonstrate respect for each member's contribution, and to hold each accountable for keeping the theater's commitments.

Why has attaining democratic competence been so difficult for cultural groups in the United States? Money is a big part of the answer. Many of those committed to cultural democracy in principle can't put their commitments into practice because of economic exigencies. Sustained, competent democratic cultural practice requires full-time workers, able to focus attention over a long period of time on work which usually doesn't turn a buck. It aims not to generate marketable products, but to build community; not to please wealthy patrons, but to empower through creative expression.

When we look at democratic cultural models in action outside the U.S., we see that they are sustained by funding from the public sector or from quasi-public or international organizations not driven by market forces. Cultural development is intrinsically a public responsibility. It will be a long-term project to attain this kind of public support in the United States, but there are plenty of opportunities for artists and arts groups to take steps toward this goal. New cultural policies will have to be proposed and circulated until they become part of political platforms. Progressive artists will have to form interest groups, as have their counterparts in the red-carpet arts, to demand that programs of support incorporate the values and mechanisms appropriate to democratic cultural work.

The Tyranny of Survival Management

When forced to work part-time, catch-as-catch-can, without adequate support or training, it's hard to attain competence. Lacking support, too many groups deplete themselves in short-term projects. Again, consider arts groups which have been formed around big demonstrations or single-issue campaigns. A disturbing pattern often emerges: coalescing around an event or action, energy builds through an exhausting but exciting gearing-up period; huge efforts are expended in endless meetings called to forge an organization destined to last only a few months; and activity peaks with the event itself, leading to a letdown period when people drift away and the group falls apart. In the course of this cycle, a leadership corps usually develops, frequently giving rise to subplots involving challenges to leaders, accusations of power-mongering, and bitter fights that are often written off as personality conflicts.

Many variations are found, of course. Some organizations stay alive, serving as host organisms for repeated short-term cycles. New cycles of activity begin under the old group name. In either case, the desire to invent authentically democratic practice is clearly outmatched by compelling short-term goals—getting through the campaign, mounting the event—and by internal power struggles.

Other groups aspire to lasting aims and manage to survive much longer, besieged by threats to organizational survival. The pattern of a year revolves around money: mobilizing to meet important grant deadlines; dropping everything to find bigger and better ways to satisfy funders' appetites for novelty and glitz; relaxing a little in between deadlines, but never getting ahead. Members of such groups can seldom conceive of themselves as collaborators in a great democratic enterprise. The past and future hardly exist; there is only a never-ending, crisis-ridden present. These permanent states of emergency dissipate human resources. People with the potential to contribute creative energy never get the chance. They "burn out," dry up, move on to something else.

It isn't only a question of organizations' internal dynamics, of course; they are deeply affected by external conditions too. When your work is critical of established social values and institutions, it is very difficult to escape marginalization. Each day is an episode of struggle: How can you be heard over the boisterous self-promotion of the dominant culture? How can you avoid feeling powerless, inadequate, even invisible? Very often, it is only within small, struggling organizations that activists are able to wield power, to affect events, and to impress their desires on others. In their relations with each other, individuals reproduce the power relations they experience with those in authority. But in the little world of the family or organization, the erstwhile victim can play the aggressor's role. The organization becomes the stage on which to enact the drama of power which apparently cannot be played out in the big world.

No Time for Democracy

People find it difficult to think about the long term in the atmosphere of emergency. The ambiance of the cultural Left eerily echoes the government's excuses for withholding information about its covert activities: no time to be democratic.

When we helped our English students prepare proposals to the faculty, we found that, left to their own devices, they would have exhausted their planning time articulating their desires. Once satisfied with the language they'd devised, they would have felt their proposals were complete. We advised them to challenge their own ideas about each proposal before going on to the next. "What do you think the faculty will say to that?" we asked. "How will it sound to them? How are they likely to respond? How could you reply?"

At first they thought we were asking irrelevant questions. They felt their job was to make proposals, the faculty's to dispose of them. But they began to understand how this notion reinforced the ideas that only teachers were competent decision-makers, and that students' lot was to complain and hope someone in charge would listen. In contrast, democratic competence obliges us to follow our own thinking through to its logical ends in action. If the students failed to prepare for the faculty's response, they were virtually admitting their proposals wouldn't go anywhere. Not only would this have been a strategic failure, it would be a confession of impotence.

What stopped our students from moving toward democracy and competence was obvious. They'd internalized the view that a secure future lies in playing the game by the given rules. They were scared to stand up for themselves and frightened for us.

Like them, most of us have had little authentic democratic experience. We've seen facsimiles of democratic form, wielded incompetently and thus deprived of substance. Most of us were taught that democracy—though a thrilling concept and the inviolable foundation of our whole way of life—really isn't practical in the real world of human affairs. Textbooks teach that political action is the province of those whose skill and knowledge have been validated by their attainment of power. Electoral politics are increasingly dominated by those whose millions pay for television advertising, while most of us cynically accept the fact that access to political power is almost unreachable for those who lack the power of wealth.

Some of us are veterans of the New Left, with its soul-grinding marathon meetings decaying into struggles over trivialities and victories for the loudest and most tenacious. When the smoke of the Sixties cleared, the principal axiom of our political culture remained intact: Democracy is a nice idea, but too much trouble.

Building a Culture of Democracy

We assert that democracy is more than a nice idea; it's actually feasible. We are part of a persistent movement, surfacing in various forms throughout the world, driven by a belief that just and humane society can be constructed of political, economic, and cultural democracy. This kind of democracy is symbolized not by the opinion poll or even the ballot box, but by the town meeting.

To make democracy work will not be easy, especially in a huge, heterogeneous, and intricate society like the United States. Enormous gaps of social ignorance and indifference must be bridged. We need to foster a public dialogue to replace the advertising campaigns that now pass for political discourse. Bringing democracy into being will require the most local and decentralized sharing of authority and responsibility, extending at the same time into national and international arenas.

At bottom, the question is this: are we serious about what we believe? What are we constructing? Even locked into opposition with our government, the raw materials of democratic competence are at our disposal. We are imaginative, inventive, versatile, adroit. But we need to subject our organizations and working relationships to democratic scrutiny, and commit to building lasting, sustaining institutions of cultural democracy.

We should set out to envision the democratic cultural apparatus we desire. We should design the necessary cultural policies and support programs and advance these in the political arena, making them part of every active progressive force's program. It's long past time to launch the long-term project of finding support to enable democratic cultural work to become a real vocation within the United States as well as the off-hours preoccupation of dedicated individuals. We'll need to invent institutions to educate young artists in the skills of democratic cultural practice. To start this effort we'll need to incorporate innovative forms of apprenticeship into our organizations' ongoing programs, then get together to compare and learn from these experiments.

It's true that to put these ideas into practice on a grand scale requires resources not available to us now. It's equally true that unless we move toward democratic competence, step by step, they never will be.

Audience: Exchanges in a Closed Space

Audience:
Exchanges in a Closed Space
Introduction

Several years ago, Big Small Theater invited John O'Neal to work for several weeks as a guest director with our new ensemble company. It was early September when John arrived, and the company was in the midst of rewrites of a play about Guatemala that we had workshopped over the summer and planned to start touring in November. During the first few days of rehearsal, there were recurring arguments over changes in the piece's style and content. Each time someone would turn to John for a neutral "artistic" opinion on how best to proceed, he would ask the same three questions: "Who is the audience that you imagine performing this play for?" "What do you want to tell them?" and "How do you want the experience of seeing this play to change what they think or do afterward?" Only after answering those questions, John insisted, could he, or any of us, figure out which of the options would best accomplish our goals.

The difficulty we had accepting John's approach to resolving our "artistic" differences was not too far removed from the scenario Lucy Lippard envisons when she describes the following paradigm:

> Progressive art, more than any other art, has got to communicate. But progressive artists are caught in (or outside of) an art world that has a certain contempt for its audiences. . . . The mere idea of taking audience into consideration, not to mention taking it seriously, is of course seen as "compromise" in the high art domain, rather than *compromiso* (commitment).

The chapters in this section examine what is involved in a commitment to take one's audiences seriously. To what degree can or do we choose our audiences? What are the implications of how those "to whom" we speak differ from ourselves and the communities "for whom" we speak? How does an understanding of intended and actual audiences expand or limit the artistic languages that we develop and the contexts in which we present our work? And how can this understanding provide the basis for us to change traditional relationships between artist and audience? These are among the questions addressed as contributors explore the depth of communication art can permit to activate more profound response and participation on the part of audiences.

Previous page: Stephanie Skura & Company performing *Travelog*, 1986. Photo by Tom Brazil.

From *Don't Start Me to Talking or I'll Tell Everything I Know: Sayings from the Life and Writings of Junebug Jabbo Jones*

John O'Neal, with Ron Castine and Glenda Lindsay

John O'Neal performing in the character of Junebug Jabbo Jones

My Grandaddy on my mama's side was a jack-leg Baptist preacher. . . . May be some of y'all don't know what a "jack-leg" something is. . . . You ever seen a dog looking for somewhere to go? He run along sniffing first one thing and then the next till after a while he stop and jack up his leg beside a tree or a house or telephone pole or anything—it ain't necessarily no toilet but he make do with it—well, that's what a jack-leg something is—it ain't necessarily what you using it for but it'll do.

So my Grandaddy on my mama's side was a jack-leg Baptist preacher. Big Daddy would tell me lots o things. One time he told me, "Son, there's three things to make up a good speacher: Number one—you got to tell them what you goin to tell them; number two—you got to tell them; number three—you got to back up and tell what you told them."

Now the meaning and the message to be found in the stories I'm going to tell this evening . . . See, right here I'm about to tell you what I'm going to tell you. I am a storyteller. I was called to be a storyteller. I say storyteller 'cause it's a heap of difference 'tween a storyteller and a liar. A liar's somebody trying to cover things over, mainly for his own private benefit. But a storyteller, that somebody trying to uncover things so everybody can get something good out of it. So I'm a storyteller. A storyteller, it's a heap of good meaning to be found in a story if you got a mind for it. So here's the point I'm going to uncover for y'all today: A man with a devilish heart is the one most likely to aim his rump at a seat of power. . . . But then again you can lead a horse to water but you can't make him drink—meaning by that ain't nobody can make you do anything you ain't already got a mind and heart set to do . . . .

Hanging Onto Baby, Heating Up the Bathwater

Lucy R. Lippard

The Left cultural movement—and there is one, fragile but persistent—suffers from a dialectical schizophrenia. It is genuinely nostalgic for its own heroic past, though often fearful of being dragged back onto the premises of the Old Left; it is simultaneously attracted to the flash of the avant-garde and popular culture—and to the larger support and audiences they attract. Left visual culture today, at its best, is a stylistic hybrid, embracing radical folk art on one extreme and sophisticated media criticism on the other. It offers a new menu, or appetite, for forms that are far out in both senses—outreach and *outré*.

Lucy R. Lippard

Lucy Lippard is a writer and activist, author of thirteen books on contemporary art and one novel. She is currently completing *Mixed Blessings: Contemporary Art and the Cross Cultural Process,* to be published by Pantheon in the fall of 1990.

This fairly hopeful mixture of populism, sophistication of form and political content, and openness to unfamiliar responses is often choked off by historical vestiges of early Cold War cultural politics, from overt red-baiting to covert conditioning along the lines of "art and politics don't mix." The dialogue that sprang up in *The Nation* in 1986-87, inspired by two articles by Jesse Lemisch, was typical of the contradictions in which such discussions are embedded. (See *The Nation* of Oct. 18 and Dec. 20, 1986, and letters columns thereafter.) Attacking sacred cows like Pete Seeger in favor of MTV, Lemisch announced that "what we have is a culture descended from a noble tradition of popular struggles—one whose public rehearsal is an important ritual of affirmation for those of us who grew up in it—that leaves us speaking a language that more and more Americans don't understand." Then he adds, "Aren't we all still trapped in the stultifying old Communist notion of art as a weapon and failing to think in large ways about the connections between art and Utopia?"

Lemisch is not alone in avoiding Left culture's lurid past to the verge of throwing the baby out with the bathwater. Sure, the Party has put the damper on plenty of parties, but the idea that art can be part of a critical (or, more fashionably, deconstructive) arsenal was not one of them. Maybe red diaper babies were quicker to abandon "people's art" because they had to rebel against something. I, for one, came to the Left only in my early thirties, from a young adulthood spent in the presumably liberating lofts of the avant garde, and I was exhilarated to find that high art had once reached and might again reach out into the world to move large numbers of people. It also seemed reasonable that this could be achieved only in conjunction with some solid political organization, or collective support.

True, that was the '60s; but during the '70s, thanks partly to feminism, it became clear that there are still plenty of Americans who understand the language, who can hear the dread words Oppression, Exploitation, and Imperialism without flinching, even though they may find it a pain to have to swallow anything harder than prime-time pudding. In fact, I suspect that much left culture is too simpleminded for many Americans, who know very well what's being done to them and by whom, and who would prefer an art that offered more up-to-date weaponry, though not necessarily sheathed in avant-garde or commercial sheep's clothing.

I write this, sadly, at a particularly low moment for the Left cultural movement, at a moment when even liberalism is an unspeakable "L-word." The Reagan years have taken their toll. Now (Spring, 1988) that the end may be in sight, small progressive art organizations are showing the strain and brave façades are crumbling. But I also write in a spirit of experienced optimism. Individuals and very small groups are going strong with all kinds of imaginative projects. Some collective soul-searching is taking place. The results will fuel the next cycle. It may be that the nature and form of the movement are changing. For many artist activists, the last decade has turned up a spread of options within which one's own art can be merged with, or tangentially employed for, social and political ends. These options range (in a random sampling of friends I've worked with on various national projects over the decade) from official and unofficial subway, bus, and billboard projects; street theatre; stencils and graffiti; film, public access TV and video organizing in the community; exhibitions accompanied by town meetings; work with and for the homeless; AIDS protest and education; to those on the front lines teaching in inner city public schools *as* progressive artists.

Ironically, some of the results of this decade's work were celebrated at the Museum of Modern Art (MoMA) early in 1988, and have since been traveling around the continent. Deborah Wye's exhibition "Committed to Print" displays, albeit in small scale and institutional drag, some of the diversity of style and resources in Left visual culture. It is more numerically respectful of women and artists of color than most alternative space shows. And of course it came under outraged fire by that old freeze-dried warrior Hilton Kramer, who delighted participants with the predictability of his attack in the *Observer* (Feb. 22, 1988). Alas, Kramer is almost alone in making Left culture feel its power. He rides to our defense every time, calling our art "garbage," the MoMA show a "meretricious recycling of political clichés" that echoes "the bad taste of the 1920s." (I think he means the 1930s; the '20s in the U.S. were hardly "the heyday of Stalinist social realism.") And he bemoans "the sorry fact that there are now so few people in positions of power—at MoMA or anywhere else—who will really fight to defend the whole notion of high art against the cultural and political campaign now being waged against it." He's been saying this for years, and it gives us strength.

In the meantime, and more problematically, "politics" (understood variously, but consistently perceived as left of center) have entered the visual art "scene" with a plenitude unprecedented since the '60s, though totally unlike the '60s. It's as though the larger progressive art organizations, having collectively nourished the seeds of this previously disdained activity, have become redundant now that some of the plants are flourishing. In one sense, we organizers have become victims of our own successes. In another sense, we have failed miserably, given the fact that what is perceived in the mainstream as "political art" rarely has political insights to offer and frequently fails to specify perpetrators and causes, preferring either over-simplification or the ambiguities of symptomatic vagueness which neither alienate nor instigate.

The political apoliticalism of abstract expressionism that inadvertently lent itself to Cold War propaganda and support of the status quo has been much analyzed. Today we have an apolitical politicalism. The mere presence of images of violence (or of a helicopter, a politician, a Black face, an elegant advertisement demonstrated to be offensive to women) automatically makes a work "political." This is an underestimated residue from both sides of the McCarthy era: the fear of being condemned by the Old Left for being naive or politically incorrect on one hand, and of being condemned by liberals as "Stalinist" on the other hand.

Even during our strongest moments in the last decade, the weakness of the organizational Left's distribution networks predicted a breakdown. One of the most frustrating aspects of being a Left cultural worker is the fact that even as we work our asses off to create, we rarely have the combination of energy, know-how, and discipline to move those creations much further out into the world. Constantly in the shadow of the mainstream, and vulnerable to its economic seductions, we have fewer choices than we would like to think we have. We ourselves see our distribution networks as temporary stopgaps until we can get "better coverage." When we do, we tend to lose control of the venue or the editorial voice and consequently of the means of our communication with the audience, which is often drawn from the middle class rather than from the broader turf we'd prefer.

Since our "business"—the actual maintenance of these small organizations, small magazines, small exhibitions, small events—is inevitably done on a volunteer basis, it gets the least of our flagging energies. It's hard work, but fun, to have ideas and meetings, to study the issues, to organize shows, create spectacles, edit magazines; it's hard work, but not usually fun, to raise money, do mailings, fill subscriptions, fill the houses, and clean up afterwards.

A saving grace—and many are learning such graces—is the double coding, the informed sensitivity to context that progressive artists must develop if they want to have their cake and eat it too. The contextualized alterations that make an artwork really *work*—in a union hall or a demonstration or a political theme show, or in a solo exhibition in the mainstream—are the products of lived experience in each of these contexts; parachuting in does not work as a short cut. Artists are taught from the educational cradle to modify visual ideas for varying scales or mediums; modifications for varying contexts should be the belated next step. I know of no art schools or university programs in this country that consistently ask students to work in public contexts, to study work done in public contexts, or to examine how audiences differ, what they understand and respond to, and why. The result is that the Left cultural movement is always reinventing the populist wheel according to unreal, inexperienced models. It's no surprise when it doesn't roll.

Progressive art, more than any other art, has got to communicate. But progressive artists are caught in (or outside of) an art world that has a certain contempt for its audiences. Respect for, or at least communication with one's audience is best engendered by contact with it. This rarely happens in the isolation of the high art world, where the mere idea of taking audience into consideration, not to mention taking it seriously, is of course seen as "compromise" rather than *compromiso* (commitment). It doesn't happen often enough in progressive circles either. There are still too many engaged artists who truly misunderstand how difficult their art may be to understand for those who don't speak artworldese. It is not a matter of intelligence, but of visual vocabulary—and time to look, think, and get it.

The real possibility for breadth of audience exists in the mass media. But when it turns its toothy smile on art at all, it is on the specialized brands beatified by museums. The neutral pluralism preferred by the art market—based on stylistic obsolescence in which no content is too peculiar or too meaningless—is like TV. It offers the illusion of a variety but the same damn thing is on all the channels/in all the galleries.

So are we talking quantity or quality? The city's large museums and galleries attract a numerically larger (but sociologically narrower) audience than that of many public art projects. They brag about the numbers of people who file past their possessions and claim this as an indication of a growing interest in contemporary art. Is this what we want for *our* audiences? Is this growth or mere curiosity, status seeking and entertainment? All artists need more feedback, but not many have any real concern with audience and most find the lack of exchange easier to take. Progressive artists and organizers expect and need more, so we tend to grasp at straws. We are perhaps inordinately cheered by the presence of any audience, any compliments, any understanding. Sometimes we know a project has worked, we got it right, and we are deservedly ecstatic. It doesn't happen often enough because we don't compare notes often enough, learn from each others' mistakes and achievements.

What we really mean by "a broader audience" is people unlike ourselves. For all the well-meaning "outreach," it has become obvious that this strategy too constitutes a distinct "centrocentrism." The real diversity comes from unexpected jamming, the crashing of parties—like graffiti, rapping, breaking, new rhythms and patterns and color schemes from the African-American and Latino communities, as well as rip-offs, reflections, and respectful loans from cultures and people whose lives have never been reflected in high art. It is an unconsidered and positive aspect of most new art movements that they bring fresh information about the outside world into the incestuous isolation native to high art. The negative part lies in the fact that the art is sometimes respected where its makers are not. For that majority of the visible progressive art movement that is white, listening is now more important than talking. The other part of that non-existent art school program (if it exists, let me know) is being open enough to learn from other cultures, so that relating and interacting become the medium with which to explore new paths—leading in as well as out—replacing the painful paving stones of good intentions with a polyphonic maze. (Mixed metaphors are appropriate here.) Poet James Scully explores this elegantly in his book *Line Break* (Bay Press, Seattle, 1988), when he calls for a "dissident poetry" (or art) that "does not respect boundaries between private and public, self and other," a poetry (or art, or criticism) that "breaks silences; speaking for, or a best *with* the silenced . . . a poetry that talks back, that would act as part of the world, not simply as a mirror of it."

Racism, feminism, ethnocentrism, and cultural/political autonomy are issues for all art being made today, even by artists who are totally unconscious of their omnipresence. The Left has taken the lead in defining these issues, but we need to consider far more thoroughly the broad politics of encounters with unfamiliar cultures and the ways they relate to and affect the dominant culture. This hopefully will be done in ways that are neither the traditionally condescending colonialist rejection nor the traditionally leftist romanticization and unquestioning replacing acceptance of simpler standards—itself a form of ethnocentrism. The lowest common denominator is the lofty "universal" rather than the respectful specific.

There is art coming towards us, from the "margins," which has a great deal to teach us, as Guy Brett argues so persuasively in his book *Through Our Own Eyes* (New Society, Philadelphia, 1987). I am provoked and moved by the tentative emergence of those new cultural models for spiritual and political significance emerging in particular from Latino, Asian, African and Native American communities, as well as from urban and rural artists who are called "folk" or "outsiders," even when they bypass the "standards" of the international art world. This rootedly modest work often stands up very well, thank you, against the immodest but frequently vacuous ambitions of the dominant culture that condescends to it. Cultural authenticity (as I have said before and will say again) can endow a less or differently skilled art with more force than a highly skilled but culturally inauthentic art.

Having used the word modest, I realize that it is for me—at least at this historical moment—a key word. I am deathly sick of the grandiose claims made for those (usually white male) artists selling best at any given moment. To paraphrase a work by Barbara Kruger, "We don't need another [culture] hero." Over a decade ago, Jack Burnham praised feminist art for offering a "vernacular" art to replace a "historical" art. Brett puts the two together, with the important concept that "the individual is abstract and society concrete," replacing the Western assumption of the reverse. What is implied is a different conception of the relationship between artist and audience in which the artist remains a respected artisan or a modestly functioning neo-shaman responsible for communal envisioning, rather than an alienated genius or social dragonfly. As part of this enterprise, Scully calls for "a criticism mature enough to be self-effacing."

Cultural theory—as opposed to art criticism—has a lot to offer the high arts in their alienated isolation, though it won't get into the bloodstream until it is combined with a familiarity with the artworld organism. The weakness of art criticism as a genre has been its inability to see the individual's work as part of the social fabric and not just another blip in the slippery cycles of marketable modernism. In the '80s, art criticism's most interesting contributions have been about *style,* since surfaces seem of the utmost importance in the Reagan error. Activist art (in itself a critique, like postmodernism, of corporate homogeneity) may be unpopular in part because it is confined to no particular style; for much of postmodernism, style is everything, but the theory that is evolving from social practice tends to be ignored.

This is another obstacle. We on the art Left try to keep up with mainstream and academic discourse, but we can't seem to get people to follow in turn the theory gradually developing through trial and error in activist art. Last year I sat through a ten person panel on "Marxism and Art" on which not one participant (though some were activists themselves) so much as *mentioned* any specific practice or artist or artwork. We know it's a mistake to divorce art and politics and we also know it's a mistake to confuse them. But activists for some reason are not given any credit for knowing the latter, and the mainstream doesn't seem to know the former. Even among liberal critics and academics, there is a disturbing level of condescension about activist art from those who criticize but do not directly partake in activist culture. We need a body of "criticism" produced by writers, scholars, artists, and activists who "read" each other. For without models and praxis, the loftiest theory hasn't a chance of effectiveness, and vice versa.

Artists, having been raised in Everyplace like Everyperson, provide a true diversity by bringing with them their own class and geographic and cultural backgrounds. Complete with innumerable contradictions, this diversity bubbles even under the gloss of art-as-usual faking a timid "universality." Once those barriers, those silences, are broken, we can escape from the false dichotomies we present ourselves: choices between selling out and going under(ground), between "establishment" or "alternative," gallery or streets, even "high" or "low" art. There is no reason why some artists can't be at the factory gate trying to invent imaginative new protest forms for labor while others are working inside the unions; why some artists can't be protesting in Saint Patrick's Cathedral while others act up about AIDS in museums; why some can't be at the museum's gates ready to fill up the white walls with meaningful subversion while others are at podiums and typewriters filling in the lost historical backgrounds and putting together new ideas based on actual and current practice. Why can't we respect each other, keep each other informed, criticize each other without paranoia, and then drag each other into unfamiliar contexts for some intellectual or activist stimulation/education?

It's easy to dismiss Old Left or traditional "people's art" for being corny, or out of touch with the commercial sector and the rough edges that still give the avant-garde some bite, especially when it is seen from the viewpoint of years of art viewing or a specialized education. But it serves a different function from experimental and commercial art, fulfilling needs that the avant-garde and mass media rarely fill, even for the specialist or addict. Passion and enthusiasm are in short supply in the mainstream. Is it really so terrible to let one's guard down now and then (even in front of sacred Art), to admit to some unadulterated emotion, some twitch of '30s or '60s nerve ends? Are we doomed to a lobotomized and homogenized emotional life along with an anything-goes-so-long-as-it-doesn't-say-anything aesthetic life?

Sentiment can be the doormat for more profound feelings. It can be a useful gate to empathy. It can hop across class as well as across cultural barriers. It need not lead to fascism. Writing for a daily newspaper does not exclude writing specialized books or making angry leaflets. The different activities inform each other and become more generous in the process. I wouldn't want a steady diet of country music or revolutionary posters, but I'd really miss both if they were banned.

There can be no single strategy for all radical artists. Self limitation amounts to self-censorship (self standing for the Left, or even for the "people" as a body censoring itself). The problem is how to get artists, the Left, and people in general to take culture seriously, not letting themselves be dictated to either by critics or by merchants or by ideologues pandering to the dominant culture's temporary taste buds. Ignoring what is happening on the periphery is just as narrow as ignoring what happens in the so-called centers. People do need art and most people have been deprived of an expression that reflects their own lives and dreams. "Popular art" is not an alternative to an experimental critical art that challenges other "old assumptions" about visual representation in all mediums. It is an alternative view of the world for those with different experiences, which is most of us.

A socialized art seems to be a fearful specter for those in a circle of wagons around the status quo. All good art offers lessons in how to see, and it has to resist the mechanisms of social control which try to keep the undercurrents and peripheries invisible. An art that believes, an art that bears witness, an art that brings people together, an art that envisions a better world should be able to take its place alongside of (or merge with) other kinds of art that are also formally, intellectually, psychically, or psychologically provocative. Making art of any kind, but especially making art for social change, is an act of faith, not to be taken lightly, not to be done as an exercise in subject matter or to get into another show. If we are not honestly moved to make art, and if we are not honestly moved by our own movement's art, we should take a hard look at what we're doing, and why.

This is a much revised version of "Of Babies and Bathwater," first published in my column "Sniper's Nest," *Zeta Magazine,* Summer 1988. It is part of an ongoing series since 1970 in which I grapple with the dilemmas of "oppositional," "activist," "progressive," or "social change" art. For other installments, see "The Dilemma," "Some Propaganda for Propaganda," and "Hot Potatoes" in my book *Get the Message? A Decade of Art for Social Change* (New York: Dutton, 1984), and "Trojan Horses" in *Art After Modernism,* ed. Brian Wallis (New York and Boston: The New York Museum/Godine, 1984).

Moving Target

"Welcome to America's Finest City" is San Diego's immodest slogan, touted along with its tourist-specific "Spanish Heritage." "Welcome to America's Finest Tourist Plantation" was the January 1988 version by artists David Avalos, Louis Hock, and Elizabeth Sisco. So who listens to artists, and especially to so-called political artists whose "effectiveness" is always being questioned within the mainstream? It seemed that everybody in San Diego County listened, at least for a couple of months. Because the artists' line was not confined to a gallery, a small magazine, or even a regular street poster. Superimposed on a striking photomontage, it was affixed to the backs of 100 city buses as a 21" x 72" poster. Advertising experts estimate that such signs are seen by eighty percent of the population. San Diego is the seventh largest city in the U.S. and January was the month of the Super Bowl, when some 80,000 visitors swelled the city's rooms and heads.

The photomontage is black and white, with a series of working hands standing out in brown. The top line of red print is largest, so after it is taken for granted, the replacement of "city" with "tourist plantation" provides the jolt.

The central photo—a pair of hands, handcuffed next to a police gun in holster—is a documentary image from a series by Sisco, and shows an "illegal" being nabbed by a Border Control Agent after being removed from a San Diego Transit bus in 1986. The flanking photos show hands scraping a dirty dish and searching for a doorknob over a "Maid Service Please" tag; these are posed tableaux, representing the restaurant and hotel/motel industries.

Avalos, Hock and Sisco are, respectively, Artist in Residence at the Centro Cultural de la Raza, and teachers at the University of California at San Diego. Following the extraordinary media hoopla—the kind of publicity every public artist dreams of—that welcomed the bus poster to one of America's conservative strongholds, they received an award from the Mexican American Business and Professional Association "in gratitude for the work which raised the San Diego community's consciousness of the plight of the undocumented worker." This was the top layer of the artists' intentions: "If we consider the realistic rather than the mythological landscape of San Diego, then we must acknowledge that the Super Bowl could not be held here if this town did not have a tourist complex of hotels, motels, restaurants, and amusement parks. And without the undocumented worker San Diego could not have a tourist industry."

One irony was the poster's placement; undocumented workers are often "hounded" in and onto buses. Says Sisco, "We're symbolically putting the people who've been taken off back on the bus." And Avalos asks, "Is it negative to yell 'fire' in a burning building? . . . We're pleased and amazed that three artists and a hundred posters have made this kind of impact. We must have struck a nerve center."

They did, and not just in the soft underbelly of San Diego's tourist business-as-usual. The poster raised a number of issues that public and so-called political or critical or social change art is struggling with. Among them is the question of whether the poster is art, advertising, or politics. It doesn't matter, but the distinctions are interesting. According to a pocket dictionary, to advertise is to "make known," and its French root means "to warn." Art is "skill, profession, or craft." Okay. Politics is the "science and art of civil government." Seems we have a hybrid on our hands, which is no surprise, since much or most of the interesting art being made today is hybrid in form, content, cultural background, and—like the bus posters—intent. The artists note that in San Diego (as elsewhere), "private enterprise has papered over the space with commercial advertising," and that if the logical forum for public issues is public space, then "the first task of the public artist would be the creation of such a public space." If art in public spaces becomes "the target of this city's hostility, then public artists will increase their chances of survival by making that target a moving one" . . . .

A progressive artist's job, as Avalos, Hock, and Sisco know well, is not to sell or manipulate or decorate, not merely to compete with commercial ads for jazzy visuals and easy reading, or with high art for beauty and irony, but to produce an image that expands the public's expectations of what they may get from public forms, to provoke thought, and to help people look around them with fresh eyes. It's not easy. It's hard work. And it's an important way to re-imagine what art means when life is not always a Super Bowl of cherries.

—Lucy R. Lippard

This article is a shortened and revised version of an article that appeared in *Zeta* magazine, June 1988. Reprinted by permission.

Bus poster, "Welcome to America's Finest Tourist Plantation," © Sisco, Hock and Avalos, 1988.

To, For, With

Some Observations on Community-Based Theatre

Doug Paterson

I was born just after World War II in Omaha, Nebraska, where my dad had been stationed. A few months later, we moved back to the town where my parents had lived prior to the war, Watertown, South Dakota (population 10,000). I had a "typical" small town, Great Plains youth. I also had the impression, one magnified substantially with the advent of television (finally!) in our town in the mid fifties, that whatever was truly important in the world occurred far away from where I was living. If one viewed life in terms of centers of power, larger-than-life personalities, the evening news, and certainly professional sports, South Dakota was (and remains) on the very periphery.

As a teenager, I developed a great fondness for the theatre, which took me to a small liberal arts college in South Dakota where I soon ran into hundreds of people from those places that seemed

Doug Paterson

Doug Paterson currently chairs the department of Dramatic Arts at the University of Nebraska at Omaha. He co-founded the Dakota Theatre Caravan in South Dakota, an activist rural-based theater, is a co-founder of the Circle Theater in Omaha, which is known for its work in "diner theatre," and has worked on several theatre projects with the Pledge of Resistance and Nebraskans for Peace.

truly important: New York, Chicago, or even Des Moines. The explosion of '68 pulverized my college graduation year as it had the experiences of so many other rebellious youth coming of age, or rage. Graduate school in upstate New York was a horrible and wonderful experience that verged on schizophrenia. I learned theatre by day and politics by night, with days in the library followed by demonstrations and tear gas in the local streets.

When in 1972, degrees in hand, I left graduate school to teach, I knew a fair amount about both theatre and politics, but hadn't the foggiest idea how to combine them. I had very strong emotional connections to the Great Plains but felt I had nothing truly to offer. I knew how to make a lot of different theatre and how to talk about even more, but nothing I did or said had anything to do with the people I grew up with, the people I knew the best, the many blood and geographical relatives I kept leaving behind. My skills were appropriately spent in the real world of urban, middle- and upper-class culture, in those theaters, in those schools. Anything other than that was somehow illegitimate, and remaining in one's home area, especially South Dakota, was tantamount to absolute failure. And these perceptions were the general consensus throughout the worlds of politics, demographics, economics, media, film, literature, and the arts generally. Unless conscious action was taken to resist the stereotyping, the pro-urban, pro-middle- and upper-class, anti rural bias stayed strong. This is one form of oppression, and for all my radicalism I had done that as much as anyone else. I had been appropriated.

So why did I feel I kept abandoning myself? Then came a visit by Robert Benedetti, the acting theorist, who told a workshop, "The really important thing may be for actors to understand where they belong and to stay with their people." I felt terrible. What clarified my confusion shortly thereafter was Mao's observation that to change the art it was necessary first to change *to whom one directed the work*. For me, it was a thunderclap. Suddenly, the region, the audience, and the people that I had considered illegitimate became the most legitimate of all. If the problem was that theatre always tended to play to the same kinds of people, then the radical (root!) action lay in seeking out those who had little to no contact with the U.S. mainstream culture.

To play to the traditional two percent who were the lifeblood of live mainstream theatre meant catering ultimately to their aesthetics, economics, and politics. On the other hand, to start with a rural audience, a truly nontraditional population, was to create a context for really new directions in the theatre. To this end, in 1977 I co-founded the Dakota Theatre Caravan (DTC). We applied Mao's suggestion wholeheartedly: "to whom" was *a* if not *the* primary question. The rural audience became and remains the focus of our theatre, while working with that audience has introduced me to the use of theatre as a tool for community action as described by Augusto Boal and Paulo Freire and as practiced widely in the Third World.[1]

*   *   *

I founded the DTC around a working process whereby all basic material for plays would be taken from interviews with the people of the region. We would ask people what mattered to them most, what they felt mattered to other people in the area, what they would like to see a play about if it was up to them, etc. We wanted to be a megaphone for what people told us. This would be the first step in going to a people, a new audience.

Our choice to change basic audience orientation also implied an indictment. Mainstream theatre, we felt, was trapped by class allegiance and pure market motives. Its economics were capitalist and its primary concern was itself. Its foundation was where the sure dollars were—within the traditional theatre-going audience, which is overwhelmingly white, urban, educated, professional, and at least middle-class. Moreover, mainstream theatre cared about enfranchising a larger audience only insofar as numbers allowed it to compete more effectively for the "entertainment dollar." These lame attempts were lumped under the category of "audience development," capitalism's answer to the impoverishment of vision in its theatre and its audience. New audiences are therefore sought out not because of a need in that audience, but because of a perceived consumer power in these communities that can be exploited. That was the reason the Guthrie Theatre in Minneapolis came to South Dakota: economic benefit. But the Dakota Theatre Caravan gathered for much different reasons.

If commercial theatre is driven by its class foundation and economics, what drives a progressive vision is issues, relationships, struggles, constituencies, and communities. Of course, economics matter, survival matters. After sixteen years of remarkable work, the Provisional Theatre of Los Angeles disbanded in part because the members of the core group were over forty and were economically on the edge. The same is true of the outstanding United Mime Workers from Champaign/ Urbana, Illinois, after a similar period of time. Nevertheless, I think one of the unplanned but truly brilliant collective discoveries of the activist theatre movement in the last twenty years is community and community-based theatre.[2] Obviously this is not the community of mainstream U.S. community theatre, which mirrors the white, male, urban, rich, straight culture from the coasts. Rather it is the community, the many communities, that activists found themselves in after the surge of activism of the Sixties. Because of a political consciousness and analysis, "to whom do we speak?" became a pivotal question for many activist theaters from the Mime Troupe in San Francisco and the Provisional in Los Angeles to Roadside in Kentucky and Pregones in the Bronx.

What are the struggles confronting the people to whom we want to play? What forms, characters, stories, styles, and designs would communicate best? Where should the theatre take place? What should it look like or should there be a specific theater space at all? How are we to be funded and yet not compromise fatally our ability to speak to the chosen audience? And, centrally, what is the concrete relationship of our theatre to the ongoing lives of the people/audience and theirs to us? Having traveled across the U.S. this past year, I can testify that ninety percent of the companies and individuals with whom I spoke—and these were all mainly activist—had already thought through most of these questions. It is an encouraging prospect, for being in concrete relationship with an audience activates a process whereby we avoid generalizing and instead focus in terms of a specific people and context. For a piece to have wide appeal and progressive application, first it needs to be compelling to an immediate and known audience.

*   *   *

But if a company—any company—puts itself forward, intentionally or by implication, as speaking for a given community, how does it gain this authority?

Mainstream theatre is primarily a self-annointed representative for an imagined universal audience. This "official" theatre practice is clearly the most visible, most funded, most extravagantly promoted, and most celebrated. Cultural supremacy results when mainstream cultural *cognoscenti* declare what is best, hire what is best, produce what is best, and can, thereby, best speak for the interests of people in the U.S. In time, the implied authorization of mainstream public performance is assumed by the cultural palaces to be in fact entirely true: they do speak for us all.

What, then, of the rest of us?

Large parts of the population are simply written off as being less legitimate as makers of art and culture. For example, the right-wing Heritage Foundation in 1980 declared that the National Endowment for the Arts was too liberal because it focused on "ethnic and geographic" considerations when distributing money. Determinations under the Reagan administration, they crowed, would be made only on the basis of "excellence and quality." And in fact, funding for "high" culture soared and that for other constituencies has plummeted. High culture is even more officially legitimate than before and entirely capable of speaking for the illegitimate rest of us.

I think our progressive impulses will tell us, first, that excellence and quality are culturally conditioned judgments. What is "excellent" in the white male high culture may be offensive, pointless, or careless to women or people of color. Second, we also understand that nobody can speak for somebody else and that a theatre company speaks for itself. Others speak for themselves. But I am not sure that is sufficient. First of all the power of theater and larger media seems to say that even if an event does not put itself forward as speaking for a point of view, the very public character of the event and the power of the images, story, etc., present to audiences a phenomenon that appears to be authorized by those whom the story represents. In a compelling study of the phenomenology of acting, Bruce Wilshire contends that the very presence of the human being in a theatrical context before other human beings has the effect of authorization.[3] Such a person has a kind of "standing in" function, a function, he says, that needs to be understood and respected to a much greater degree. I suggest this is not an intrinsically positive or negative condition. It is, rather, a property of the cultural form that gives all theatre social value, whether that value is intended or not. It is, in short, what makes all theatre political.

This "authorized" role was one in which we found ourselves over and over with the Dakota Theatre Caravan. We did come to believe that we spoke for various segments of the Dakota populace, and we became increasingly sensitive to the fact that we were distinctly *perceived* as doing just that, especially when we went beyond the region or when our purely rural characters were watched by town and city dwellers. It was a responsibility we realized "came with the ranch," and in time we understood that, valued it, and treated that implicit "authorization" with great respect. We respected the fact that we worked in a political medium, that that medium implied authorization, and that that authorization was political. We wanted to take responsibility for our work on those terms and then acted accordingly.

Yet we then faced new challenging questions, posed this time by the Third World. Paulo Freire has written extensively on the dangers of educators, including radical educators, going to economically and politically marginalized peoples with the intent of "helping" them. I believe this also applies to making theatre "for" people. Freire demonstrates clearly that there must be a dialogical relationship, that those who would help others must in turn be helped by those whom they would help. Without this dynamic as a genuine part of the process, all that is created will be based on the old hierarchy of power. Using Freire's dialogical structure, Third World theatres have emerged that not only appear (in Wilshire's sense of authorization) to be speaking for a community, but who take it on themselves to validate that appearance. They listen to and are involved in the community in such a way that the people represented *can give voice to the theatre.* Thus the theatre not only authentically speaks for, but gives voice to that community.

The Dakota Theatre Caravan moved in this direction. We built DTC with ongoing interviews, discussions, late night talks and lots of play with the people of the Great Plains. This understanding, moreover, went both ways. I believe the more we found out about the people, the more the people found out about us and in a very real sense we participated directly with the widely-scattered rural population that was our focus. But we also encountered the problems of any touring company. Until 1983 and the reconstitution of the Caravan in a different South Dakota town with a new core company, the Caravan was usually on the road and lacked some of what is the heart of the dialogical relationship: daily living encounters with an ongoing community to whom the theatre directs its work.

Other companies in the U.S., however, are having considerable success developing these ongoing community relations. After ten years (Pregones), fifteen years (Roadside), and in some cases twenty-five to thirty years (the Mime Troupe) living in a single community, numerous theatres I interviewed had achieved practical "authorization" through daily interaction with the community as well as Freirian-like processes. Most people in these companies—managers, actors, directors, and designers—knew the local issues, which court cases to watch, what corporate moves were dangerous down the block or in the next county, and how their constituency related to such issues as homelessness, racism, feminism, Reagan, Nicaragua, etc. These interviews convinced me that the key to achieving *legitimate* authorization is some degree of formal, regular dialogue between theatre and community focusing on the theatre's work and assumptions.[4] Combined with the emotional and intellectual growth that usually accompanies working on combustible activist issues, cultivating an understanding of local and wider concerns is a very potent way of achieving the status of being able legitimately to speak for a people. In fact, what I think occurs in obtaining this status is something I would suggest is beyond Mao's "to whom" and is more akin to "speaking with." I would like briefly to describe that dynamic.

*   *   *

Prioritizing the question of "with whom" one does theatre means that the base community will be deeply and actively involved in the entire theatre-making process from conceiving the theatre and choosing a place to work to developing a work or project, performing the piece, and assessing the results. In a sense the difference between audience and theatre can nearly disappear. The concern might be raised that this could restrict the freedom and range of the theatre to do what is deemed best. But a strong, working relationship with an audience does not mean that a theatre cannot do what it wishes or have its own strong identity. What it does mean is that the theatre's community is thoroughly involved in the theater's process, and vice versa, and that if the theatre believes strong steering away from "the word from the field" is needed, that steerage will be taken knowingly, and not in the proverbial dark. In other words, we will be able to make choices (as Freire urges) in terms of a people with whom we are directly engaged, and not make decisions or take action in disregard of the community's legitimate interest in our inevitable appearance as authorized voice of that community.

This discussion would not be complete without a full recognition of the revolutionary role currently played by theorists like Augusto Boal, artist/organizers like Nidia Bustos in Nicaragua and Alan Bolt in Nicaragua, and facilitator/chroniclers like Ross Kidd in Africa. Progressive though some of us in the developed world may claim and/or want to be, working in a revolutionary context can galvanize community and artist to create truly community-based, transformative cultural action. In organizations and towns around the world, those artists whose goal it is to not merely present and represent the world but to change it have generated a theatre for, to, of, and by people struggling for liberation that is itself part of the liberation struggle. It moves the dynamic of theatre from the plane of talking to, for and with a community, to acting with—acting in the most fundamental sense of taking action together.

This approach to theatre is achieving some promising results around the U.S. A group of us in Omaha, combining the efforts of Nebraskans for Peace and several rural crisis organizations, employed this Third World process, as far as we were able to understand it, in the summer of 1987. Non-actors (in the Western sense, fully historical actors in the political sense) gathered to use discussion, scenarios, role-playing, and taking on others' personalities as a way of collectively understanding the rural crisis in Nebraska and generally. The initial goal was not for a "quality" production, but for a "quality" understanding; not for "excellence" of acting, but for "excellence" of relationships. Scenarios were developed that allowed us to understand, to empower ourselves, to sharpen thinking, and to have a good time. Eventually the group chose to take the piece to others to share our perspectives, content, and analysis. Those, too, were exciting exchanges, and drama as a tool for collective discussion came alive for us. But that was not the primary objective. If no one else had seen the piece except those who worked on it, fine. If others saw it, fine. After a while, the group wanted to develop the presentation and make it what for us was "better." That also was fine.

But what we learned was what perhaps is being learned world wide: The goal remains community identity, understanding, and action. As a result, many of the traditional values of theatre in the West can literally be stood on their head. Community first, content first, critical understanding first, clarity first, pleasant social context first—production values and profitability second, or third, or later. It is perhaps legitimate to wonder if Western commercial theatre will ever be able to catch up with developments in the Third World and activist communities, to achieve the human "quality" as well as production quality central to such theatres. Probably not. These theatre practices are on different tracks, are in fact in truly different worlds. And as we move toward a new millenia, the choices of which world to work in, to speak to, to act with, are becoming clearer.

Notes

1. I was first exposed to this kind of theatre on a cultural tour to Nicaragua in 1983, and made most aware of the depth and range of this Third World theatre practice when working with Robin Lewy at the University of Nebraska at Omaha on her master's thesis, *An Approach to Community Action Through Drama in the United States Inspired by Third World Techniques* (1985). I appreciate the eye-opening experiences given to me by the Nicaraguan cultural workers, and am grateful to Robin, who is now living in Nicaragua, for revealing even further to me this remarkable approach.
2. I have heard some reservations recently from progressives whom I respect to the effect that "community" might itself be a word that has too many conventional, ruling elite connotations to be employed effectively in a progressive analysis. I understand the concern and think it valid, but continue to use it because, in addition to the fact that it has some genuine meaning for me, I think it is also still a "popular" word, that is, one that has positive, nurturing meaning for many people.
3. Bruce Wilshire, *Role Playing and Identity: The Limits of Theater as Metaphor* (Bloomington: Indiana University Press, 1982), see especially Ch. V., 38-91.
4. Thus in many mainstream theatres the actors, design and technical staff, and perhaps even directors are barely aware (if at all) of who attends the theatre, and then only through the most limited contact with the audience. Even more obscure for mainstream theatres would be the question of "why this audience." But there is usually someone, tucked away in a back office, who is assembling the marketing strategy, and to that extent those to whom mainstream theatre is addressed are an intentional audience.

Responding
to Cultural Hunger

Elizabeth Catlett

Two incidents early in my career as an artist profoundly affected the form and content that my prints and sculptures would have: In 1941 I was teaching art at Dillard University in New Orleans. Late that fall, when a retrospective exhibition of Picasso's paintings—including the "Guernica" mural—came to New Orleans's Delgado Art Museum, I decided to take the 130 young Black men and women in my art history class to see it. But the museum was closed to us because it was in City Park, where Blacks were not permitted.

Through a friend I arranged a visit for us on a Monday when the museum was closed, and we were bussed in. The students were excited and fascinated by the paintings. They ran from room to room exclaiming, calling to one another, uninhibitedly enjoying these "strange paintings with such glowing color!" No one was bored. No one had ever been in an art museum before.

A few years later, during World War II, I was

Elizabeth Catlett

A figurative sculptor who works in bronze, stone, and wood, Elizabeth Catlett is also a printmaker in lithography, linocuts and silkscreen. Her work is frequently political and social, utilizing the general theme of the Black woman. Formerly a U.S. citizen, she is now a nationalized Mexican who lives and works in Mexico where she was a member of the Taller de Gráfica Popular (Popular Graphics Workshop) for many years.

working at the George Washington Carver People's School in Harlem. Again with all Black students, but these were working people—mostly people who served others—servants, elevator operators, cleaning women and men, etc. One hot summer night, with the windows closed for the blackout, we all sat listening to a recording of Schostokovitch's then-new Seventh Symphony. It was the school's introduction to classical music. Because of the heat and the length of the piece we had planned refreshments after the first movement. But our students were so moved by the music that they insisted on hearing the entire symphony without interruptions.

In both of these incidents, I was moved by the apparent cultural hunger of the students. I realized how often our people are denied art and began to think about the many different ways that this denial is effected; about why it is that Black people, in general, don't visit art museums and symphony halls even when they are permitted entry.

It seems to me that the main method of denial was then and continues to be the fostering of an elitist art which further widens class distinctions. The whole system of museums, galleries, critics, the media, even art schools, is all directed towards middle-class and wealthy white people. The majority of us are not even considered. Money is very important and plays a basic role in buying, promoting, and selling not only art but artists. To appreciate contemporary visual arts, for example, one must have had certain experiences prior to viewing or participating in it. To visit museums presupposes an interest in their exhibitions. If there is nothing in them relating to us, why spend our little leisure time visiting? These thoughts made me question what kind of art I could offer to young Black people (who would later be professionals) and others who live and worked in the ghettos, if I ever exhibited.

"I have special reservations . . ." Elizabeth Catlett, 1947 (Linocut)

In 1945 I applied for a Julius Rosenwald fellowship. My work at the time was figurative with a slight abstract influence, and my proposal was for a series of paintings, sculptures, and prints on "The Black Woman" to be circulated throughout the South; primarily in institutions where Black people gathered: churches, schools, community centers and the like. The theme of the Black woman has continued to be a unifying element in my work to this day. A number of reasons make this true. I am a Black woman, and my sense of what that means is wrapped up in my awareness of the experiences of those women who came before me. My grandmother's stories of her years as a slave greatly impressed me when I was a child. And I recognize that my widowed mother's battles with racism, when we lived in Washington, D.C. while I was growing up, eventually became my own.

Upon receiving the Rosenwald fellowship I continued to work at the Carver School in Harlem. Because of my intense commitment to the students I had little time left to work on my fellowship project. The following year, on receiving a renewal of the grant, I decided to leave the Carver School to get away from this self-imposed pressure. Because the New York art scene offered no opportunities for a Black woman, I knew I really needed to get away entirely.

I chose Mexico as the nearest place without racism and segregation, but also because of the public art movement there, with its mural painting and printmaking—two mediums that reach great numbers of people. Beginning to realize that as a Black woman privileged to have become a sculptor and graphic artist I owed my dues to Black people, I was looking for ways to link my personal expression with broader Black cultural needs.

In Mexico City, I was fortunate to be accepted into the Taller de Gráfica Popular (TGP; the Popular Graphics Workshop), where I met Mexican printmaker Francisco Mora, who later became my husband. In its declaration of principles the TGP states, "Our production must benefit the progressive and democratic interests of the Mexican people." Posters, leaflets, booklets, and illustrations for textbooks and newspapers were produced there in collaboration with progressive organizations or as projects presented by individual members. People came to TGP meetings on Friday nights—working people, students, peasants from rural areas, and others—to tell of their problems and ask for graphic help. Since Mexico has a high rate of illiteracy, the printed picture is of utmost importance.

From the first anti-fascist posters in 1938, project themes have ranged from petroleum expropriation, war and imperialism, and justice for the Rosenbergs and others, to the construction of schools, the high cost of living, and advice to peasants on the sale of crops. In one case we illustrated textbooks in the Indian languages for a literacy program in which adults would learn to read in their own languages.

Working collectively was a completely new experience for me, as an artist who had always created alone. Working collectively provoked new methods of creating, as well as intense discussions on what graphic symbols, what images best expressed the

On Creating Collectively

How did the Taller de Grafica Popular (the Popular Graphics Workshop) in Mexico City make a leaflet or poster collectively? Once a proposal had been accepted by the group, one or more artists would volunteer to work on it, depending on size, importance, and how quickly it was needed. We would briefly discuss the best ways to express the idea needed. Then the artist member responsible would bring a sketch or drawing to the next meeting. This gave him/her time to work out his/her thoughts—be it a day or a week. We would then talk out the strengths and weaknesses of the drawing, at the same time collectively suggesting ways to improve it.

The artist was free to accept or reject the input as it affected his/her idea. S/he could thus draw on the creative thinking and experience of an entire group of artists—from seven to twenty members. This criticism was always positive and always toward creating a superior work. The focus for all of us was consistently on how to project an idea graphically that would be easily understood and creatively well done.

The artist would then complete the project as a direct linocut, lithograph, or silk screen, ready for production. Editions as large as 80,000 copies, as in the case of a poster for building schools; or as small as two or three hundred were printed either in the workshop or by a print shop. Posters were distributed and pasted up throughout the city or the area most affected. Individual linocuts were printed and signed on cheap paper and sold for a few pesos at book fairs and other gatherings, eliminating numbered editions. Of course monied collectors took advantage of this, but thousands of prints went into the homes of ordinary Mexicans in this way.

social or political problems confronting us. We could use easily understood symbolism for leaflets or posters; more complex symbolism for lithographs or linocuts that expressed personal ideas and emotions.

The project that I proposed for collective collaboration was a series of portraits of Black heroes and heroines of the United States. I researched the lives and obtained photographic material on twenty Black Americans from different times and occupations, including W. E. B. DuBois, Paul Robeson, Sojourner Truth, Ida B. Wells and Frederick Douglass. The members accepted the proposal enthusiastically, and after a few months work we presented twenty linocuts to a Harlem newspaper, *The People's Voice,* to be used as portrait insertions with text each week.

Even the individual production of personal work done in the workshop could benefit from the help of other members who might be around when one was working. Lithographs were done on stone in the workshop, so there would always be discussion about works in progress if one so desired. After thirty years this way of working still affects me, even though I left that collective environment. I am constantly asking the opinion of whoever may be around, artist or not, as to how what I am working on affects them. At exhibitions of my work I still want and need real criticism and not flowery admiration.

In the 1960s I resumed my contacts with Blacks in the United States. Up until then, I had exhibited infrequently in group shows. But in 1969, after an individual show in Mexico's Modern Art Museum entitled, "The Black Experience," I was invited to exhibit in the Studio Museum in Harlem. This began a series of exhibitions in the United States. The Studio Museum circulated my exhibition to

"Celie," Elizabeth Catlett, 1986 (lithograph)

Black cultural centers in Boston and Atlanta. I sent works to two very small Black galleries in Los Angeles and Berkeley, California. An article in *Ebony* magazine gave me national exposure and I began to get invitations from many Black colleges, few of which had real galleries at that time. I traveled to seven in Alabama, showing a film on my works and talking about my life as an artist. Exhibitions of my sculpture and prints followed.

Making my work available in non-established art spaces, where it is accessible to Black working people, is very important to me. It is something that I have continued to do even as my work is exhibited more frequently in major museums in the U.S. At the same time, I believe that the struggle to make major cultural institutions recognize the contributions of Blacks and other artists of color is crucial if these are ever to become truly national cultural centers, places where Black men and women will bring their children to appreciate the beauty and power that an art experience can deliver.

I still work figuratively, trying to express emotion through abstract form, color, line, and space. I attempt to reach out to ordinary people, with little or no experience or understanding of art principles, and extend to them what I may feel about a subject— whether anger, indignation, strength, beauty, sacrifice, understanding; whatever but always something. Even in more abstract sculpture I attempt to get a reaction through a strong upward gesture, for example, or a close, tight feeling between two figures.

I have been criticized for being old-fashioned, for not contributing anything new to art, and for exhibiting in places where there are no galleries. To me, such criticism is absurd. I continue to try to bring art to my people and to bring my people to art as I recognize my debt and our need. There has to be something for us outside of the mainstream, and something of our lives that we can offer to others.

"Singing Head," Elizabeth Catlett (stone carving)

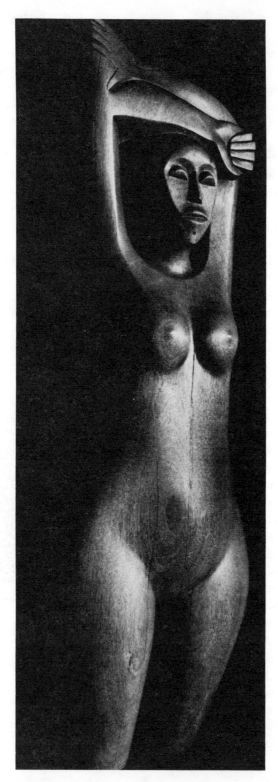

"Black Woman," Elizabeth Catlett (wood carving)

Teatro Pregones
Finding Language in Dialogue
Alvan Colon Lespier

Teatro Pregones (Pregones Theater) is a community-based, professional, Puerto Rican theater collective based in New York City. Founded in 1979 by seven actors, the company grew out of the Puerto Rican community's response to its lack of representation on New York stages. Pregones creates plays for and about Puerto Rican and Latin American people.

By adapting a variety of approaches and theatrical forms to a style consonant with our concept of a theater that is both highly entertaining and critical, Pregones has created a theatrical language that speaks to our audience. This language has evolved in the group's process of collective experimentation. It uses autocthonous musical and theatrical forms that affirm our cultural identity and development. It speaks of current social dynamics, underscoring the need for social change. And, reflecting the lived experiences of Puerto Ricans in this country, it integrates choices of Spanish and/or English dialogue into the theatrical structure of our plays. By continuing to develop this language in dialogue with the primary audience, we are able to present an authentic Puerto Rican voice to our community as well as to the larger Latin American and Anglo audiences of the northeastern United States.

The political and economic relationship imposed by the U.S. government on the island of Puerto Rico has resulted in a tremendous migration of islanders to this country. More than 2.6 million Puerto Ricans live in the U.S., with more than a million and a half in New York City. Theatrical activity in New York's Puerto Rican community began in the early settlements at the turn of the century when readings were staged by workers' clubs and in private homes. Vaudeville, versions of Spanish

Alvan Colon Lespier

Alvan Colon Lespier (actor, director, producer) has been a member of Pregones Theater Group since 1982. He is co-founder of Anamu, one of the leading popular theater groups in Puerto Rico. He is also a member of the Latino Theatre Commission, a group of theater workers from the West and East coasts that came together during the XIV Tenaz Festival.

zarzuelas (comic operettas), and stand-up comedians were the staple during the post-World War II era.

In 1953 Miriam Colon staged the first New York production of a major Puerto Rican play: Rene Marques's *La Carreta (The Oxcart)*. The play tells the story of the migration of a Puerto Rican family, first from the island's countryside to a San Juan shanty town, and then to the barrio of New York City. It presents a swift and piercing questioning both of Puerto Rico's political situation and of what it means to be a Puerto Rican, themes that run through most major Puerto Rican artworks.

The success of *La Carreta* established Colon's company, the Puerto Rican Travelling Theatre. It also spawned a series of groups in the '60s and '70s dedicated to performing works in Spanish. Some of these companies, extremely conservative in style and theme, staged plays exalting the glories of pre-revolutionary Cuba, or in the best of cases, classics from the Siglo de Oro. Still others staged plays by Puerto Rican authors from the island.

Parallel to the development of these more traditional groups, several companies also sprang up that created original works drawing on Puerto Rican and Latino experiences in the U.S. Groups such as Teatro Cuatro, Jurutungo, and the Puerto Rican Ensemble were significantly influenced by popular theater currents in Latin America and the Caribbean; and played an important role in making evident in this country the links between Latino, Latin American, and Caribbean cultural and political expression. Unfortunately, by the late '70s the majority of these alternative groups had folded. The major causes contributing equally to their decline were indifference on the part of funding sources, actively hostile government policies, including FBI harassment, and inadequate organization and vision on the part of the groups themselves.

It was in a context of revitalizing these earlier efforts to promote Puerto Rican drama within our community that Pregones emerged. Under the direction of Victor Fragoso, actors Rosalba Rolon, Luis Melendez, David Crommet, Xiomara Torres, Gilberto Diaz and Eduardo Carrasquillo put together an anthology of key scenes from landmark plays by Puerto Rican authors that covered 100 years of Puerto Rican playwriting. The scenes were connected by *pregones,* a Spanish word for announcements or street vendors' cries. From this the initial touring project and later the company took its name.

La Colección, the group's first original play, further established the company's goal of serving as an artistic voice validating the historical and cultural links between the island of Puerto Rico and New York's Puerto Rican community. It portrayed shared elements of our cultural heritage: the island's history, the manner of speech of its mountain people, internal migration, military occupation, forced industrialization, chronic unemployment, and the struggle of its people to preserve their language in the face of induced migration to the United States.

While *La Colección* addressed the need to find out more about ourselves through our history, *Al Mediodia/High Noon* grappled with some current situations, in particular the bilingual environment in which we live and perform. The play is about hospital workers and their participation in union activities. While the primary audience for the piece is Puerto Rican workers, for the first time the subject matter of the plays made it inevitable that non-Spanish speakers would be present. Realizing that this group—other non-Spanish-speaking workers—would have to be addressed, Pregones began to develop language strategies within our plays.

In a device that mirrors the reality of the hospital where it is set, *High Noon* is peopled with characters that speak only English but understand Spanish, characters that speak only Spanish, bilingual characters, and so on. Working together they have to devise ways of communicating. In one scene, a character delivers a monologue in English while another actor, silhouetted against an upstage screen, sings a song in Spanish with lyrics that convey the essence of the monologue. In this way, both Spanish- and English-speaking audiences understand.

Other circumstances have led us to create new mechanisms to bridge the language differences in our audiences. When we perform for schools—particularly in our South Bronx home—we have found that our mixed Spanish and English audiences include many bilingual children. Given the option of performing in Spanish or in English, we choose to combine them.

In *Caravan,* a troupe of *vejigantes* (traditional carnival characters) travel from town to town telling two stories. The first is a Taino legend about the creation of the world, and we made a deliberate decision to tell it in Spanish because we want to affirm the language as a special and important component of our—and the children's—culture. But at two points during the telling of the legend, the actors stop the action and ask those children who speak both Spanish and English to explain what has been going on to those who understand only English. This is a very valuable and empowering moment for the Latino children. For once, the advantages of knowing Spanish are manifested in a very practical way. The second story of Mr. Saltimbanqui, a cruel magician and his helper, Beatriz, is performed in a bilingual mode and requires the participation of the audience to decide how the play should end.

Another language strategy was needed for a theater project Pregones developed on AIDS education using techniques of forum theater developed by Augusto Boal. The piece is performed for very different audiences and the emphasis we give to either language depends on the composition of the audience. That means the actors have to be ready to perform either in Spanish or in English.

In December 1986, the Pregones Theater opened its doors in a permanent space at St. Ann's. With the generous cooperation of the congregation and the rector, Reverend Roberto Morales, of St. Ann's Episcopal Church who donated the space, and the invaluable help of Hudson Scenic Studios, we converted the old parish hall into a ninety-eight seat theater. Located on St. Ann's Avenue in the Bronx, it is the first professional theater in this community's history. The site not only for Pregones's performances, but also for our theater workshops for community youngsters, special events for Bronx seniors, and performances by visiting artists.

Although Pregones has established residence in a community, we continue to tour. The major issue we confront in touring is the traditional arts presenters (who have the financial resources to provide for an adequate stay in a tour site) are usually not found in the Puerto Rican and Latino places where presenters have established outreach to Latino audiences. As a result, performances at traditional venues remain inaccessible to most members of the community.

Aware of this problem, we attempt to work with local tenant groups, culturally active service agencies, and community organizations active in civil rights, to organize alternative programs during our stay in their city. We may come to the community as a guest of one or more of these groups for a very specific activity (a theatrical presentation) but by establishing links with the community prior to our visit, we are able to function as more than a company of artists that comes to setup, perform, strike, and leave. Our performances become part of an ongoing process—an activist campaign, festival or cultural program—within the community. Moreover, taking advantage of our own and our presenters' resources, we have developed a residency program that includes performances and workshops during our stay. In this way we share both our finished productions and the theatrical skills that a community can continue to develop after we leave.

Recently some producers have unsuccessfully tried to insert Latino theater into the mainstream currents of American theatre. Latino theater cannot be used as bait. When our theater is presented as an exotic cultural product or when it is watered down to make it palatable to Anglo audiences, the result is a deformed or distorted version of our culture.

Pregones is also part of an alternative theater movement comprised of groups, production companies, and individual artists throughout the country. The strategies being articulated by this movement involve linking up with other communities that face similar conditions of exclusion, looking more deeply into the communities that gave us birth, and using theater to unmask the hidden dimensions of our lives.

A Waitress Moment

Jerri Allyn

Dedicated to William Olander, the first to give American Dining a chance

In 1975, Suzanne Lacy, a performance artist and Dean of the California College of Arts and Crafts, and Faith Wilding, a feminist artist, writer, and radio producer, were visiting professors at the San Francisco Art Institute. They introduced us to feminist, conceptual, and performance art. In school previously we had discussed only form and style. Lacy and Wilding introduced the notion of "content" and of targeting a desired audience.

The following year Lacy convinced me to attend the Feminist Studio Workshop, a two-year program for women in the arts at The Woman's Building in Los Angeles. There we came to define feminist art as that which raises questions, invites dialogue, and ultimately transforms culture. [1]

Conceptual and performance art have evolved from artists' desires for more direct communication with audiences, the need to better integrate art and life, and the attempt to address more evocative, emotional, and social issues than standard forms have permitted. While they may include elements of theater, dance, music, visual arts, or poetry, conceptual and performance art transform these for some use we would not otherwise have assumed or expected. Often, this work is critical in stance, innovative in structure, interdisciplinary, and has political connotations. [2]

Performance and conceptual art were free from a history defined by men. These "new forms" were it for me. I was hooked. [3]

Jerri Allyn

Jerri Allyn is a conceptual and performance artist. Her allegiance is not to any particular medium, but to the most appropriate form, depending on the ideas and intention of an artwork. Most of Allyn's work deals with communication theory, and is in a narrative, or storytelling form. She strives to create humorous work that includes political insights and aesthetic integrity. She has been greatly influenced by her schooling with Suzanne Lacy, her multicultural work with the L.A. Women's Video Center, and by working with the public performance art groups The Waitresses and Sisters of Survival. She lives in New York half the year and travels to teach, lecture and do performance/installations the remaining half.

1975: One Year Art/Life Prostitute

San Francisco, CA

LIFE: Cocktail waitressing my way through art school.

ART: Investigation, as a prostitute character, of woman as object, able to obtain money through flirtations and sexual acts. While waitressing, to all come-on's I state, "I'm yours for one hundred bills." Piece ends when I'm unable to accept payment for an evening spent with a liquor salesman, the first man who agreed to pay.

AESTHETIC
ISSUE: Body/experience, declared as art.

AUDIENCE: Myself.

1976: Birth Piece

First public and collaborative art/life performance, with Bonnie Veenschoten. San Francisco, CA.

LIFE: Both of us unwed mothers in high school, before abortion was legal.
We want to create a live performance that lets people know we weren't "sluts." We were caught holding the bag. The fathers went free.

ART: Thirty-minute multimedia presentation using nine-month cycle as a structure. Slides run continuously, starting with one-day-old fetus, finish with birth, then print media image recording abortion referendum defeated in the courts. Bonnie sits audience close, rocking back and forth while reading accounts from a high school diary of her physical body changes. I pace maniacally behind, my voice the inner one that never stops, wondering over and over what to do. A mother's heartbeat is sounding during all.

AESTHETIC
ISSUE: First structuring of live art for an audience through deep understanding of "the personal is political." First use of multilayered sound. This is my life transformed into an art piece, not my whole life as art. In the traditional art world, self-referential means, literally, an artwork referring to itself, having no relation to anything. For feminist artists self-referential refers to oneself in relation to society.

AUDIENCE: My family, friends, art students, teachers. Only the two feminist teachers attend.

FAVORITE
COMMENT: "Gee, you mean I'm an uncle?" from my brother.

1977: Cancer Madness

Seven-day art/life performance exorcising my fear of both cancer and madness. Los Angeles, CA.

LIFE: My mother died young of cancer. My grandmother has been in and out of mental institutions for the last forty years.

ART: Transform my studio into a hospital bedroom, with waiting room and gift card rack. Spend countless hours convincing medical professionals to examine and give me a treatment.

I USED TO HAVE FANTASIES THAT ONE OF MY PARENTS WOULD DIE
AND I WOULD BE A VICTIM OF GRIEF.
IN MY FANTASY I GRIEVED AND IT FELT GOOD.

ON NOVEMBER 8, 1971, MY MOTHER DIED OF CANCER.
I WAS A VICTIM OF GRIEF.
IN MY REALITY IT WAS QUITE PAINFUL.

SOMETIMES I HAVE A FANTASY THAT I WILL BE A VICTIM OF CANCER
AND OTHERS WILL GRIEVE.
IN MY FANTASY I AM MISSED.

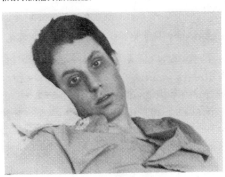

ON APRIL 24-30, 1977, I WILL SPEND 7 DAYS IN A HOSPITAL BED, RE-
WRITING MY MOTHER'S STORY, AND "EXORCISING" MY FEAR OF CAN-
CER AND ALL DEATH WISHES. OTHERS WILL ASSIST IN MY HEALING
PROCESS, EVERY EVENING AT 8:00, 307 EAST QUEEN ST., INGLEWOOD,
CALIFORNIA.

4/24:   PAUL E. KEITH, M.D.: EXAMINATION AND DIAGNOSIS.

4/25:   PAULA MENGER READING FROM DEENA METZGER'S CURRENT
WORK ABOUT BREAST CANCER: "TREE: A FEMINIST MANUAL
ABOUT GUERILLA WARFARE WRITTEN FOR ALL OF US IN THIS
STATE OF SEIGE."

4/26:   SUSAN RENNIE, CURRENTLY RESERACHING A BOOK ON CAN-
CER: DIALOGUES ABOUT THE POLITICS OF CANCER & CANCER
PREVENTITIVE FOODS.

4/27:   DEBORAH KARISH, CHIROPRACTOR: DIALOGUE AND DEMON-
STRATION ABOUT THE HEALING CAPABILITIES AND POLITICS
OF CHIROPRACTICS.

4/28:   ANNA RUBIN & ROBERTA ROTHMAN, PSYCHIC HEALERS: AURA
MASSAGE & COLOR MEDITATION.

4/29:   ANNE GAULDIN, MARY YAKUTIS & ANNE MAVOR: HEALING
RITUAL.

4/30:   JERRI ALLYN: VIDEO, "CANCER MADNESS" & "REFLECTIONS
OF MY HEALING."
KATJA BIESANZ: HEALING DANCE & CELEBRATION OF HEALTH.
FEAST, BARBARA COHEN.

VISITING HOURS: 11:00 A.M.   8:00 P.M.

IN MY REALITY I DO NOT WANT TO DIE. *Jerri Allyn*

women's community inc., 1727 n. spring st., l.a., cal.
photo: carol van duyne
printing: nancy fried

AESTHETIC ISSUE:	Everything within seven-day structure, medical people included, declared "art." The notion of an artwork unfolding over time is absolutely necessary to the piece.
AUDIENCE:	Feminist art community, medical people, healers.
RESULTS:	About twenty to thirty people attend each evening—a marginal art performance. Medical people and healers *do* bring their friends and *no one* doubts the importance of the piece. This has been a life-hanging event for me. There is, however, continued questioning, by myself and others, about why it must be called "art." Why not a healthy "life" all the time?
FAVORITE COMMENT:	"I want to support your art, Jer, so when I got your announcement I hung it on my fridge. Backwards. I couldn't bear looking that death image in the face."

1978: Ready to Order?

Seven-day art/life performance by The Waitresses.[4] Los Angeles, CA.

LIFE:	Between the six of us, we've waitressed a total of fourteen years. We realize the "waitress" is analogous to the position of women, worldwide. Additionally, five of us have been raped. Sexual harassment takes on a new hue. We discover women comprise seventy-eight percent of the food industry, yet men hold the top positions as chefs and waiters in all the best joints; and Hispanic and Black women work mostly kitchens.
ART:	Design seven-day structure for event that includes vignettes performed spontaneously in restaurants during mealtimes, and panel discussions at night offered in English and Spanish to appeal to the forty-nine percent Hispanic population of L.A. Focus on issues of women and work, money, sexual harassment, and stereotypes of women as mother, servant, prostitute, and slave.
AESTHETIC ISSUES:	1. Site-specific performance in public: It is difficult to perform in restaurants with no technical assistance, in an environment we might not find visually satisfying. It remains more important, though, to reach a restaurant public, than to be in a white-walled (and sterile) gallery we have complete control over. 2. Deliberate attempt to use humor, initially for our own salvation. While dealing with sexual harassment, we gravitate toward joking because the issue is too serious. *We* need comic relief. 3. Search for a mode of presentation that does not blame, but rather, elevates "consciousness" of an issue.

AUDIENCE: Restaurant employees, employers, and clientele.

RESULTS: Successful on most counts. We do not attract many members of the Latin community, even though there is Latin representation on the panels. A restaurant in a Black area of town does not get much audience. This might be because the place is newly opened. No doubt it is also because we're an all-white group. I think about continuing to use restaurants in different communities, though, as a way of interacting with a culturally different audience, instead of "hoping" they will come to us.

Due to our popularity, we are asked to present work in many public venues *and* galleries, which I want nothing to do with. My wise mentor, Lacy, advises that while we need not focus on getting gallery representation and producing objects, we'd be foolish to negate the art scene. Better to play all fronts—view the art world as a professional community that provides some financial and peer support.

FAVORITE COMMENT: "When I saw you all come through the door, I thought I was witnessing a spontaneous waitress revolt!"

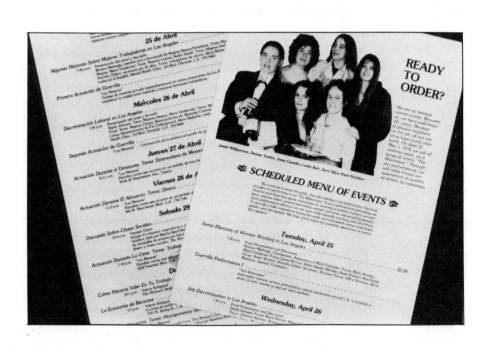

1983: Love Novellas

Eight audio portraits. First installation designed for a gallery. Premieres in Manhattan, travels on West Coast tour, then becomes an artist's book and cassette.

LIFE:
In New York I am living in a *very* small apartment. I have no studio, not even a separate room in which to make art. I am disheartened by a failed collaboration with the Hotel and Restaurant Workers Union over a series of placemats about issues of concern to the union. I feel my work is becoming too didactic. Plus, I am attracted to a *boy,* my best friend. It seems like the last confusing straw. He asks me and five others for a ten-minute audio tape; he will improvise a performance to each.[5]

ART:
I do an audio portrait, "The Bill Portrait," and am so excited I write more about close friends in different circles—my girlfriend, my family, political heroes, a Black dyke—told in a rapid-fire rhythm.

These portraits require only a typewriter, and my voice. I design a gallery environment allowing people to "sink" into another's world, using Walkmans and headphones in various fluorescent plexiglass covers, coupled with chairs that reflect the person represented.

AESTHETIC ISSUE:
Return to completely intuitive art-making, live performance, and layered sound work first seen in the Birth Piece. I have no idea why this urge for rapid-fire speech but I do it, even when people ask I slow down.

AUDIENCE:
Around the country: alternative and performance art scene, university students, public television and radio listeners.

RESULTS:
1. Public response: People tell me they do feel like they're "sinking" into other worlds. Usually they have favorite "portraits," which vary depending upon individual interests.
2. Rapid-fire versus communication: I have such a need to communicate that I produce an artist's cassette and book (edition of 500) in a specially designed box, for those who keep asking I slow down. I design a book so small they can refer to it only, not comfortably read. I want them to listen to those story rhythms.
3. Economics: Every time the stories play over the air, people contact the station to purchase tapes. It's difficult to make an art living, particularly outside of the market. I am heartened to think I can produce "objects in multiple," affordable to a general public.
4. Politics: They surface because politics are part of who I am.

1987: American Dining: A Working Woman's Moment

An art/life installation, including jukeboxes and placemats, in restaurants across the U.S.[6]

LIFE: Desire to work in public again, to return to my art/life roots. And a desire to get art organization sponsorship, for credibility, which provides access to funding. I'm selling "affordable objects" but they don't pay the rent.

ART: Design a site-specific, interactive installation for restaurants that I waitress in. Transform jukeboxes with fluorescent plexiglass "hoods." Wire them to continuous-play Walkmans (with volume control) that tell stories about food, work, and money. Design four placemats in the tradition of fun-and-games placemats. Instead of "Name the Presidents" it becomes "Name That Dame/Who Are These Famous Food Women?"[7] The performance begins when people enter and interact with the elements.

AESTHETIC ISSUES: 1. To maintain my vision of an art/life piece, in close communication with restaurant owners ensuring it happens whether they think it's "art" or not.
2. Design a work available for public interaction if desired. I now want people to have a choice, not to force art on them. Hopefully, humor will once again enable people to deal with difficult issues.

AUDIENCE: In New York, the Hassidic clientele I served for two years in a kosher dairy restaurant. Around the country, the clientele in restaurants chosen by the art sponsors, and artists, many of whom are part of a rapidly growing movement of cultural democracy.

RESULTS: 1. Censorship: Restaurant owners unanimously ask for no four-letter words. This seems fair. I'm not interested in offending children.

The restaurant owner in New York requests I edit things about abortion and lesbians on the placemats, because these ideas run contrary to his religion. He's agreed to this installation right away because of our friendship, though we move in *very* different circles. Many of the restaurant stories are about working for him and this artwork extends the ongoing dialogue we have about our different cultures.[8] Because of *his* gesture of goodwill, I agree to print a censored version of the placemats.

I find there is always a measure of compromise when working in public. When I feel my original intention is not lost, I don't mind much. Finding ways to present "difficult" material that people accept and don't censor, though, is a fascinating artistic challenge.

261

2. Public reaction: In New York, I intersplice Jewish folk music with the stories, and am successful in drawing in the Hassidic clientele.

Overall, about a third of the restaurant clientele doesn't notice the installation, doesn't have time, or doesn't care. The other two-thirds are surprised and thrilled. They enjoy playing the placemat games, though they're tough. People find many of the stories funny yet difficult to hear when there's restaurant noise and, again, because I speak so fast. I finally decide to re-record at a slower pace. Another compromise, but I prefer that people hear.

"American Dining: A Working Woman's Movement," 1987-88. Photo by Ted Rice.

3. Humor: Mine proves to be "twisted." Some people love it, some don't. Men are uneasy with the story about sexual harassment, which includes real-life quotes said to me, because it insinuates that working with men is difficult. Women love it. The "twisted" humor lets them laugh about a wearing situation. They feel men who hear this cannot possibly continue to make sexually harassing comments without thinking twice.

4. "Art/Life": At first I waitress part-time, but the public has many questions and comments. I start waitressing full time.

There is something powerful about "waitressing as an artist." It's a position of strength. These stories say what I've yearned to tell customers, employees, and employers for years.

It's strangely rewarding to be on the spot.

For years, all I wanted to do was art in public, to get out of the art ghetto. In reality, it's the most terrifying. The art world is a safe haven by comparison. I lay my life on the line, and hope people will get *something* from it. My work is dense and demanding of an audience. Still, I want a lesbian and feminist voice in my country's democracy. I have to accept that not everyone wants to listen and debate, but the ones that do are gems.

FAVORITE COMMENT: From a middle-aged woman in Portland, Maine, after looking at the Dame placemat: "I never thought about these women. I teach high school. I teach kids home economics. And I never thought about these women."

Notes

1. This definition was arrived at by Arlene Raven, an art historian who co-founded The Woman's Building with Judy Chicago and Sheila de Bretteville.

2. I find this definition by Laurie Beth Clark, performance artist and professor, University of Wisconsin at Madison, the most expansive.

3. Due to space limitations, I have written about works that relate most to my current art project, *American Dining: A Working Woman's Moment*. I have been involved in many other performance and conceptual art explorations, however, the most notable being the Sisters of Survival (1982-1986), including Nancy Angelo, Cheri Gaulke, Anne Gauldin, and Sue Maberry. These women have shaped and continue to shape my thinking about the issues addressed.

4. The performance group The Waitresses was co-founded by myself, Anne Gauldin, Denise Yarfitz, Jamie Wildman, Patti Nicklaus, and Leslie Belt. During the eight years we continued to design works for restaurants, labor and women's conferences, and galleries, we were joined by over twenty-five others for various pieces. Early on, Chutney Gunderson and Anne Mavor became permanent members.

5. Bill Gordh, performance, "Talking to My Tape Recorder," Just Above Midtown Gallery, New York, NY, April 1982.

6. Sponsored by the New Museum of Contemporary Art, New York; the University Gallery of Fine Art at Ohio State University, Columbus, Ohio; 911 Contemporary Art Center; Seattle and Western Washington University, Bellingham, Washington; the Maine Arts Festival, Portland, Maine; and Art in Action, Rosendale, New York.

7. The four *American Dining* placemats in the set are titled "Name That Dame/Who Are These Famous Food Women?," "Follow the Dots," "Edible Quotes From A to Z," and "Fish and Chicks."

8. He kids me endlessly about doing "conceptual art"; asking customers, "Do you know what she gets paid to do?!" and always offers me a "real job." I kid him about the Hassids who frequent his deli that I'm sure are feminist or homosexual. We share an interest in humorous art and stand-up comics. He actually thinks *American Dining* is funny, and defends it to his more conservative friends!

This Is to Incite You

Gran Fury

Gran Fury is a collective of AIDS activists opposing government and social institutions that make those living with AIDS invisible. Through visual projects, we seek to inform a broad audience and provoke direct action to end the AIDS crisis. Gran Fury was formed in January, 1988, shortly after "Let the Record Show . . ." in 1987, a collaborative window installation at the New Museum of Contemporary Art. Naming ourselves Gran Fury after the Plymouth automobile customarily used as an undercover police car nationwide, the collective has produced numerous public projects including posters, stickers, shirts, fliers, printed ads, billboards and bus signs.

Gran Fury recognizes that "direct action" and "cultural activism" are expressions of different communities' differing needs, and this process can range from poster projects to street demonstrations to free needle exchange to peer education. We consistently attempt to situate our work in the "public realm" in an effort to include a diverse, non-homogenous audience. Through appropriating dominant media's techniques, we hope to make the social and political subtexts of the AIDS epidemic visible and to incite the viewer to take the next step.

THANK GOD
FOR AIDS

Photo by Linda Schaeffer

THIS IS TO SCARE YOU.

SEXISM REARS ITS UNPROTECTED HEAD

MEN:
Use Condoms
Or Beat It.

AIDS KILLS WOMEN

THIS IS TO INFORM YOU.

One million [People with AIDS] isn't a market that's exciting. Sure it's growing, but it's not asthma.

—Patrick Gage
Hoffman-La Roche, Inc

THIS IS TO ENRAGE YOU.

THIS IS TO INCITE YOU.

WHEN A GOVERNMENT TURNS ITS BACK ON ITS PEOPLE, IS IT CIVIL WAR?

The U.S. Government considers the 79,614 dead from AIDS expendable. Aren't the "right" people dying? Is this medical apartheid?

Gran Fury

Telling *Real War Stories*

Lou Ann Merkle
Interview by John Grant

Grant: What makes a high school audience a challenge for someone with a message like yours?

Merkle: This culture has ingrained in people's minds a certain idea about who we are and what our identity is. That identity is often wrapped up with the military in a very positive way. There is nothing else in this culture offering to take young people as they are and mold them into something powerful with a clear purpose. That is what military propoganda offers. Young people want that, they need that. And they are deluged with images of war and the military—whether in movies or advertising or from recruiters—which are usually very glamorous, and usually false.

Also, a lot of these kids have family members—people they love and respect—who were or are in the military. They may feel personally attacked if you are critical of the military, and so how you choose to raise these issues in the classroom is very tricky. When we go into a classroom with a message that is basically the opposite of everything they have ever heard, they want to know why they have never heard it before. To be credible we have to speak in a language they understand.

Grant: So how did you arrive at the idea to make a comic book?

Merkle: I was in Cleveland working with a number of Vietnam veterans. We'd go into high schools, talking with young people about the implications of military service. Military recruiters were in the

Lou Ann Merkle

Lou Ann Merkle is an artist and peace activist committed to the idea of confronting young people with the realities of the military and war so they can make an informed decision whether or not to enlist in the military and register for the draft. She is currently Youth Outreach Director with the Central Committee for Conscientious Objectors (CCCO) in Philadelphia. Besides its work to reach young people, CCCO, founded in 1948, provides counseling and legal help for service members seeking discharge as conscientious objectors or for other reasons.

John Grant

John Grant, a writer and photographer also involved in peace issues, is married to Lou Ann Merkle.

schools encouraging kids to sign up as a way to get jobs, to pay for a college education, or to get out of the neighborhoods. And no one was really sitting down and talking to these kids about where they were going, what they would be doing, and what it really meant to be trained to kill and to use violence overseas.

So we went into classrooms to talk about what weapons and war do to people. The veterans stunned the classes. They talked about their experiences and how it felt to be used to kill people and see their friends die. We talked about what it meant to wear a U.S. uniform and be in the service of the U.S. military. We talked about the problems that lead to war, nonviolent resistance and alternatives.

These are all complicated and controversial issues. But every time we talked, we stirred up a lot of questions and then we were gone. There was no one for them to talk with. The best we could do is leave them our literature.

At the time I was using literature from the peace movement—from groups like Central Committee for Conscientious Objectors (CCCO) or Students Against Registration for the Draft. In every case these flyers were very poorly designed, the wall-to-wall-words type of brochures. They weren't the kinds of things you could expect anyone to *want* to read, and usually they would land in the wastebasket. We also didn't have one piece that covered the big picture. So eventually I put together the best movement literature that I could find. It was really eclectic, combining poetry, photography, drawings, and personal testimonies from veterans with resources for alternatives to going into the military. It also turned out to be a 250-page book. I took this to David Albert at New Society Publishers and he looked at me and said there ain't no way a kid is going to read this. Of course, that is exactly what some of the kids, even those most interested in what we were saying, told me. So David sat me down and said, "Look, you have a great message but you have to understand the average reading level of a kid in high school is like ninth grade. You are better off making a comic book." And I kind of perked up my ears and I said, "Really? You really think that would be the thing to do?" And he said, "Oh yeah, definitely."

Grant: How did you translate this material into the format of a comic book?

Merkle: It went through a couple of transformations. I worked closely with Joyce Brabner, the wife of Harvey Pekar, whose *American Splendor* comic has almost a cult following. I went to Harvey, but as I described the project to him, Joyce jumped in and said: "You don't want Harvey to write this comic book—he writes for an adult audience, and his writing wouldn't reach a youth audience. What you want is the guys who write *Swamp Thing*, *Spider Man*, *GI Joe*." "Yeah right!" I said, "How am I going to do that?" She said, "I'll do it for you." And she was as good as her word, working for two years without pay to get what really are the best comic book artists and writers in the field to translate real stories into comic book format.

The comic book could not have come together without Joyce and I bridging the gap between the peace activist world I live in and the comic book world Joyce was so well connected to. She talked with dozens of artists, writers, and publishers before she found the group that finally did our comic. She explained the comic book industry and their ways of working to me, and she helped the comic book people understand what we were up to.

At CCCO we meet and counsel with many people who are in the military and want to get out, and especially conscientious objectors. We also counsel war resisters and work with Vietnam veterans on the school programs I mentioned. So I knew a lot of people whose experiences would be great for a comic book. I knew I wanted us to deal with Vietnam, El Salvador, nuclear war, racism, and conscientious objection and resistance. Joyce insisted we deal with Women in the military, so this too became part of the book.

She thought that it would be too much to ask any one writer and artist to do the entire comic book. So we divided the book into six stories and had "creative teams," that is, one writer and one artist who would work on one story each. This way they were only responsible for six pages and this seemed manageable, since for many this was a donation.

In most cases, I clearly listed the issues that had to be dealt with. I had interviewed many people, transcribed the interviews and pulled out the main points to be conveyed. In the case of the Vietnam story, Bill Ehrhart wrote a number of books about his experiences in Vietnam and we simply mailed them to Alan Moore who miraculously condensed it into his six pages. Joyce interviewed and wrote Nancy's story. In the case of the Salvadoran story, we were very fortunate that the young man actually wrote it out. And one of the artists was, himself, a CO during the Vietnam war. He wrote and illustrated his own story.

Grant: You spoke of the need for you and Joyce to "bridge the gap" between the two worlds in which you operated. Can you give some examples of how you reconcile the fact that what is acceptable in one context is not in the other?

Merkle: Joyce came to me and said Bill Sienkiewicz had agreed to do the cover for our comic book. Bill is one of the most talented and respected artists in the comic book field. She brought a number of samples of his artwork for me to look at, and right on the top was this *Electra* comic book that he did. On the cover are these military guys in the most sickly camouflage green, and at their feet there is this really sexy woman with breasts exposed, long legs, hair disheveled, her clothes ripped off, and blood dripping from scratches from head to toe. Inside, the book was full of sadomasochistic violence. Now this was the sample I had of Bill Sienkiewicz's work. "Joyce," I said, "we can't have this kind of depiction of the tragic violence in El Salvador. We need something much more sensitive." She was adamant that Bill could do anything. All we had to do, she said, was let him know what we wanted and he would be able and willing to express whatever it was. We ended up getting a book

Real War Stories looks at El Salvador in *A Long Time Ago and Today,* written by Joyce Brabner and Lou Ann Merkle and illustrated by Thomas Yeates and Mark Johnson.

called *Fire From The Sky* that has drawings by Salvadoran children who have seen some pretty terrible things. One child drew a picture of his mother whose head and feet had been chopped off by a soldier with a machete; others showed bombed houses and soldiers shooting peasants in the head. What Bill did is go through the book—and other books—and pick out what really moved him. He reproduced those children's images chillingly and, in the background, he has ghostly paintings of the reactions of ordinary people to such scenes. It is an incredibly sensitive and very powerful cover.

Tim Merrill's story was also controversial. Tim is a young Black man who was a sonar technician on a nuclear submarine. One night, on guard duty, he discovered a sailor who had been violated by a hazing technique called "greasing." Tim told us that this is when a number of larger sailors gang up on a smaller sailor and pump grease into his rectum. And, according to Tim, it is common. He felt a responsibility to expose this kind of activity both because the victims of such greasings are too humiliated to speak out, and because it illustrates the mentality that pervades the military: those with power prey on those who are weaker. Force quickly becomes a part of who you are.

There was a case recently of a man who ordered 700 *Real War Stories* to hand out to young people at a county fair in North Carolina. His peace group had just glanced at the comic and thought, "Oh sure, yeah, we'll hand these out." Well, when the 700 arrived and they began opening them up and reading them, page by page, apparently they were outraged at the comic book in general, and especially by the greasing scene. The man ended up having to send all 700 comic books back, because he didn't have the consensus of the group to use it.

Grant: What about the primary audience, the high school reader? Are you getting through?

Merkle: I was working late at the office one night and I got a call from a young guy in New York City who worked in a comic book store. He had been thinking about going into the airborne rangers ever since he was a kid, and when he saw the cover of *Real War Stories* he felt he would like it. He read it and he was surprised. He thought it was going to be pro-war. When he found it was anti-war he said he wanted to dismiss it. He read the Vietnam story and said, "Ah, that's a Vietnam vet. Vietnam is over, that doesn't apply to me." Then he read the story of the Black guy in the submarine and he said, "Ah, that's a Black guy and he went into the navy. That's not for me; that won't happen to me." He read the woman's story and said, "I'm not a woman, that won't happen to me." But when he got to the story on El Salvador, it began to dawn on him that our military was not defending people as it claimed. It began to dawn on him that, as he put it, our military was a mercenary military out to defend economic interests overseas. That really troubled him. He really wanted to go in. I talked with him for a few hours, wrote him a five-page letter, and eventually he

One panel from *Real War Stories* Comic Book, *The Elite of the Fleet,* the story of Tim Merrill as told to Mike W. Barr, written and illustrated by Brian Bolland and Mark Farmer, artists.

decided not to go into the military. His mother ended up calling us on the phone, writing us a letter and sending us a $100 check. She said all her talking never got through to him but this comic book and our conversation did, and she was grateful for that.

Grant: Since the comic book, you have created the "Interview a Veteran" contest. Describe that project.

Merkle: What compelled me to become an activist in these issues were the personal stories I heard from veterans. The vivid descriptions they have of what they've been through and the genuine feelings they convey when they tell their stories have a unique power to shatter military myths. It dawned on me that instead of continuing to tell young people what *I* had learned, that maybe what we could do is create that listening experience for them, and let the kids tell us how *they* were affected.

The contest asks fifteen- to twenty-three-year-olds to interview a Vietnam veteran, then use whatever form they choose to express what moved them most. They have to find the source of information (the vet) and dig for the message. The contest invites young people to engage in a process where their own creative expression teaches them and becomes transformative.

The first contest was an extraordinary success on a number of counts. We received over 300 contest entries from all over the country. They ranged from Q and A interviews, to poems, to drawings, to a song, "Sad Eyes," by a fifteen-year-old girl about a veteran looking at the wall in Washington. There were two categories, high school and college, and we provided a $500 first prize and ten $100 prizes in each category.

"Interview a Vet" Contest
1988 Winning Entries

In Vietnam

My father was in Vietnam
When I was young I did not know
when I learned, I did not understand.
What was "in Vietnam"?
I burned to know but did not ask
listened intently to every story,
each casual reference made monumental;
"When I was in Vietnam . . ."
sitting in silence as he talked
hands clasped, his eyes wandered but never met my own.

In Vietnam
is a place I cannot go.
I formed my own mind;
words of honor and duty
cannot lead me there.
I can only retrace
the paths my father took
to a tangled jungle far away,
feel his anguish
and mourn for all those
in Vietnam

—Winifred Tate, 17

The First Year
(excerpt)

I have been shaven and stripped;
they lead me like a lamb
away from my former days.
All that was once me
is taken, sent away
clothes, jewelry, books, pictures
even my hair
leaving me naked and exposed
with only a wristwatch to remind me.

Even the names have changed
floor is deck,
ceiling overhead, wall bulkhead, stairs ladders,
left port and right starboard.
I am plebe, midshipman fourth class.

I am not afraid
for I am recreated
in their image;
they will not let me fail.

I swell to complete my uniform
and the serious purposes it implies,
letting loose the edges of my mind
to fill their sharply defined lines.
Duty, honor, love of country
these are real words to me.
I live them with a passion innocent of grey.

—Winifred Tate, 17

For a lot of the vets interviewed, it became an important part of the healing process. There is one case in particular where a vet was interviewed by a young woman. It was a really good interview and they sent it off to a vet center, and the leader of a rap group played it for the vets in the rap group. I got a letter from the man saying it really helped the guys sort out some anger and confusion.

The interview process is significant because the vets are older and are in a place in their lives where they can pass on what they have learned. It is young people who need to hear veterans' stories more than anyone. A lot of kids have heard a lot about Vietnam—whether it's through movies like *Rambo* or *Platoon* or just in the media— but very few have a realistic idea about what that war meant. The contest presents an opportunity for them to explore it.

The thing that surprised me most was how many young people interviewed their fathers. There were an incredible number of young people who used this as a chance to sit down and talk with their fathers about something in their life they knew was very important but didn't really know how to discuss. One of the winners was a seventeen-year-old girl who took three days off school and did twenty hours of interviews with her father. I heard from another source that she and her father had been at odds and this interview brought them back together.

Her empathy amazed me. She wrote seven beautiful poems which recreate a sense of her father's experience that is so real it's uncanny. The poems are sensitive and convey insights that I thought could only be accessible to veterans.

The entries we got for this contest showed how important it is that we stop preaching and find ways to encourage kids to explore and think for themselves; create a dialogue instead of just a monologue. It says to kids: "We trust you. We trust your willingness to listen and to think and to interpret and understand this person's experience, and we want to know how you feel. We want to know what effect this interview experience has on you and how this factors in to the decisions you are making."

It trusts veterans to speak honestly and frankly about their experiences and it trusts the young people to give it back to us. There is something really refreshing about just letting the young generation who needs to know what war really is, tell us how they feel about it. By encouraging them to formulate their own ideas, the contest plants deep seeds.

Grant: Do you have any hopes for these forms of communication in the future?

Merkle: Well, it is a really exciting question. Going into the unknown, you don't have "the answer." You just go in and dance with what comes across your path. The most rewarding way to grapple with painful issues is do it creatively. It's important even if this means taking risks, because creativity is our salvation in the peace movement. The Pentagon spends over one billion dollars a year in advertising to sell a clean image of the military: guaranteed paychecks, training, and respect. When you are the underdog you've got to use what you have. And the point for me is—and the comic book was a real lesson—all kinds of exceedingly talented people are willing to donate their talent (or freelance at a reduced rate) because they believe in the cause; because they see what's going on and they wish they had the opportunity to express themselves. Artists like Bill Sienkiewicz don't necessarily want to just do commercial work. They are grateful for the opportunity to do something meaningful. Denny O'Neil, who used to write *GI Joe* comics, donated his writing for one of the stories because he said he had a lot of bad karma to get rid of. And I think there are a lot of professional creative people who could be tapped if—and this is critical—if we had our ideas clear and if we were willing to work with them, and if we had the guts to ask them.

Right now, my cohorts in New York City at the War Resisters League are coming up with their own ideas and working with people there. They are working with high school students on a fanzine called *Spew*. It is a radical idea for the peace movement. Their first issue was a great success and now they are on their second issue. I see it all snowballing. I see people saying, "Yeah, it's time to break out of our boring little shell, where we always recount facts and statistics and drudge up tragedy in very monotonous intellectual terms. We need to get down to what it feels like, to really allow ourselves be the human beings we are."

In Praise of Melodrama

Joan Holden

Most Americans are not theatergoers. This is reason enough for a politically engaged artist to consider switching to movies or TV. But if you insist on sticking with a preindustrial art form in postindustrial society and still want to make it count politically, you must either content yourself with speaking to a narrow audience, or find a way of popularizing theater.

General Rong Q (Sharon Lockwood) gleefully tells the Dragon Lady (Andrea Snow) of yet another plan—this one includes murder! From the San Francisco Mime Troupe's Obie-winning play *The Dragon Lady's Revenge.*

Melodrama has spent this century in the theatrical gutter. Other popular theater forms are suddenly respectable; physical comedy as New Vaudeville, musical comedy as Music Theatre. Not melodrama: in the modern and postmodern aesthetic, good guys vs. bad guys makes bad theater. Only one thing is sacred—the idea that nobody is right. I believe that this is one big reason the theater audience is shrinking drastically, and that reinventing melodrama would bring lifeblood back to the American stage.

Undeniably, melodrama is a lowbrow art form. It lacks all that is most admired in American theater: subtle revelation of character, intense psychological truth, deep probing of personal relationships, ambivalence, complexity. It overdramatizes the obvious. Serious artists have no use for it—except on the nights they watch *Dallas* or *Magnum, P.I.* Transubstantiated into film and television, melodrama is as big as it ever was.

We are, or we have been, a nation of moralizers; and melodrama: the theater of morality, where the audience joins emotionally in the clash between good and evil, is our national theatrical form. Every American has been steeped in it since childhood. Its rhythms come naturally to our writers; our actors can instinctively reproduce its gestures. Done well, it has the power to make Americans of any class and color—even if some won't admit it—thrill, cheer, and shiver all in the same places.

The mass media have no trouble keeping melodrama up to date, inventing heroes and villains for the '80s, the '90s, and the twenty-first century. But it is not just cigar-chewing capitalists and white-frocked virgins, or noble workers, who have vanished from the "serious" stage; moral conflict has vanished—except, significantly, from Black and other minority theater, theater that still wishes to affirm its audience. For most white theater artists, Left as well as center, the concept of good and evil is outdated, embarrassingly square; the field of "values" can be abandoned to the Right. Meanwhile, the mass audience never seen in theaters lines up for *Fatal Attraction* and *Star Wars III.*

Mainstream theaters are forever holding conferences and panels bemoaning the aging and narrowing of their audience. They look for a remedy in better "marketing"; but the problem is the plays. The fact is that most people have never been much attracted by morally ambiguous plays about unpleasant families who torture each other psychologically. And many who were by now have seen enough of

Joan Holden

Joan Holden is resident playwright for the San Francisco Mime Troupe, a political theater company that despite its name does plays. Their style is based on the three main elements of American popular theater: broad comedy, musical, and melodrama. Her plays and collaborations for the Troupe include: *The Independent Female, or A Man Has His Pride; The Dragon Lady's Revenge; False Promises; The Factperson/Factwino Trilogy; Steeltown; The Mozamgola Caper; Ripped Van Winkle; Spain;* and *Seeing Double.*

them. It's time for serious playwrights to attempt modern, credible heroes and villains. In the avant-garde, while performance art has brought an amazing new richness of imagery to the theater, deconstruction is a similar dead end. The next step would be for progressive, innovative theater artists to find ways of investing that imagery with moral and emotional thrills and chills: postmodern melodrama.

What distinguishes popular from "serious" theater is not that popular theater ducks serious content, but that it frankly offers certain pleasures. Besides music and dance, the main ones are: style—intentional non-realism, the pleasure of seeing a "show"; plots that are wish-fulfilling, larger than life; characters we can respond to wholeheartedly; and above all, clear-cut conflict that the audience can take a side in, usually (though not always) with a happy ending. For all their difference in tone, melodrama and comedy have the same basic plot: an underdog fights an overlord, and wins. In the nineteenth century, the golden age of melodrama, there were plenty of conventional love versus honor plots, but active social questions were routinely brought onstage: slavery, "miscegenation," the ravages wrought by bankers and speculators, class conflict.

Done well, live melodrama makes even the staidest theatergoers vocal: not just formula hisses and boos, but throaty murmurs and primal screams: the audience entering into the conflict. But most of us have never seen stage melodrama done well. Summer stock, dinner, and community theaters spoof it; art theaters don't touch it. The clash of values, the stock characters, the basic wish-fulfillment plot make the form naturally adaptable to political theater. Yet "serious" theater artists who consider themselves political still use "melodrama" as a bad word. They deplore the simplifications, the emotionalism, the seemingly cheap affirmations of good-guy/bad-guy conflict; think heroes and villains and happy endings are too predictable, too easy, fail to surprise artistically or make people think.

These artists' aversion to simple truths, the high value they place on complexity and difficulty, and the emotional flatness of the postmodern aesthetic not only confine the audience to economic and intellectual elites, but also tend to depoliticize our theater.

In the 1950s the New Criticism made "ambiguity" the highest value in art. As a reaction to the sometimes flat-footed social realism of the '30s and '40s, as a reflection of postwar, post-Hiroshima loss of innocence, this was a needed change. But it was also a neat way of de-fanging art in a period of reaction, while the military-industrial complex consolidated its power. Similarly "complexity" is an antidote to what now seems the simple-minded optimism of the '60s and the early '70s. At the same time it inhibits artists from dealing directly with issues that are very pressing and finally, very simple.

We know who the big polluters are; why the country is in debt; what "freedom fighters" are doing in Third World nations and who puts them up to it. We know that the country, plus as much of the world as it can reach, is coming to be ruled by a secret government of spies and right-wing billionaires. These things come down to matters of right and wrong—so for too many artists, they are not the stuff of art. Theater artists who will lend their names to progressive causes, who on their days off will march in demonstrations, in their work stick to the denser terrain of psychology, where they don't have to risk seeming simpleminded by naming the heroes and the villains. Performance art offers safety in obscurity. Even artists who describe their work as political are busy deconstructing character and dramatizing (if that is the word) abstruse social and epistemological theories. I see pieces with fascinating titles which reward the audience with a couple of powerful images for a couple of hours spent squirming in their seats. There is a difference between making people think and leaving them to wonder what you meant.

Granted that there are stringent limits on the power of art to change the world, yet one important power art has is the ability to put items on the social and intellectual agenda. This power is particularly true of performing art because it is experienced in crowds. Conventional American theater, in its obsession with family drama, sanctions private concerns as the only ones worth having. Avant-garde art, in its avoidance of the obvious and its obsession with psychology, does the same. When we as theater artists avoid the big issues, simple to understand but dauntingly difficult to solve, that the mass media oftener obscure rather than clarify, we support the audience's natural tendency to avoid them also.

It is true that forms can become formulas; it is true that in making things clear you run the risk of making them flat. But when that happens, the artist's imagination has failed, not the art form: popular theater no more *has* to be predictable than avant-garde theater *has* to be opaque. The essence of melodrama is not black hats and white hats, it is making the audience really, deeply, take sides. During the Cultural Revolution in China, Madame Mao as boss of culture interpreted the formula: "Extol the people" as requiring only perfect, cardboard heroes, and bored an entire country. In this country you can drag polite applause from a left-wing audience by simply putting a Salvadoran guerrilla onstage. But the deep response, the primal one, is drawn by the heroes that are the most deeply flawed, the ones that have the hardest time finding their way. A disillusioned radical, now a wino; an ex-idealist, now a burnt-out CIA agent; a hippy Rip Van Winkle. Such characters are part ridiculous, part noble; the audience sees its own best and worst selves in them, laughs, but at the same time is on their side, wants them to act on their best impulses, cheers when they finally do right.

Real affirmation does not come cheap. The "older woman" plays of Dario Fo and Franca Rame (*The Open Couple, A Day Like Any Other*, etc.) affirm the human value of the middle-aged female through a detailed account of her doubts, fears, failures, and humiliations. Still we wish her well and wish humiliation on the men who make her miserable; we *engage*. This is what most contemporary plays set out to block us from doing: conventional family dramas by their moral relativism, and avant-garde plays by their blank treatment of character. Most plays I see leave me feeling neutralized; I leave the theater after a Fo/Rame show enlivened, wanting to do like Franca. That enlivening power is what makes a truly political play, as opposed to an apolitical play about a political topic.

What of the objection made by people who still think Brecht is the only model for political theater: that melodrama doesn't challenge the audience intellectually, answers only its own questions, and isn't dialectical? The short answer is that far and away the most effective piece of political theater in the history of the United States was *Uncle Tom's Cabin.* A longer answer would involve analyzing the importance of intellectual versus emotional appeal in the work of—say—Fo, Fugard, and Brecht himself. The purpose of political theater is not only to make people think, but to make them act. For most people this requires emotional engagement. I don't believe, in fact, that people act as often on ideas that are news to them, as on what has been bothering them for a long time.

Popular plays can raise questions; they can be about ideas, including ideas about politics; but their main strength is not intellectual and ideas are not the main thing the audience comes for. A recent history of popular culture reveals that Shakespeare companies did big business in California gold camps, where the miners loved to boo

A Trumpair flight crashes in the San Francisco Mime Troupe's *Seeing Double,* 1989. Left to right: Michael Sullivan, Robin Karfo, Keiko Shimosato, Ed Holmes. Photo by Christina Taccone.

Richard, cheer Henry, and sniffle over Desdemona. Broadway crowds line up for razzle-dazzle but also for laughter and tears. I write for a company that draws thousands to its free shows in public parks. We like to think these people come to hear political analysis, but they can get that from periodicals. They come mainly to vent their anger in laughter: to see false leaders and false ideas satirized, to be part of a crowd, and to get a shot of hope.

These are very old desires, going back to the ritual origins of theater: exorcising evil spirits, welcoming the spring. The same desires drew Athenians to the comic festivals, to see Aristophanes lambast demagogues and generals, then crown his hero with flowers. With all respect to Brecht's theories I believe that what most people seek, beyond entertainment, in the theater is still exorcism and affirmation. I believe it is arrogant and life-denying, a self-defeating kind of artistic Puritanism, to insist on a theater that denies those things.

An art form that is losing its base needs to get closer to its roots. For the American theater, those roots are vaudeville and melodrama. Vaudeville's comeback is being welcomed with great fanfare; an equal excitement awaits the return of melodrama.

A Postscript: "Preaching to the Converted"

No one complains when subscription theaters reaffirm their audiences' bourgeois individualism. But when radical theaters or dance troupes enliven left-wing crowds, we are accused of taking the easy road, not reaching out, being ineffective. To use the evangelical metaphor that is thrust on us: missionary work, spreading the word, is only half the job; we also do revivals, to keep the faith alive. Any ensemble that does original work must have a core audience it is close to, a community of like minds that supports the theater; the people that come to its openings, forgive its failures, and respond to its fundraising appeals. For radical theaters, that community—tribe, really—is the Left.

Everywhere a left-wing performing group goes, the local radicals find it and come to join in the exorcism and the celebration. At times we find ourselves wishing they'd stay away, so we could connect with a new community on its own terms. At other times, we wish we could be free of our faithful audiences' extremely specific expectations. We would like to do a mindless farce for once, or some shock piece, utterly depressing. As individual artists, we should take breaks to do those things; but I have come to accept that through audience support the radical company becomes a kind of community property whose duty is enlightenment and affirmation. People can go to the bourgeois theaters any night of the week to be depressed. To be an activist, full- or part-time or even occasional, in this country these days is to stick to a lonely path, through disappointments and self-doubt. People who persist deserve to celebrate their choice occasionally, and part of the radical artist's work is to help them rejoice.

There is an obvious danger here of sliding into work which follows formulas, avoids unpleasant truths, congratulates the audience while failing to challenge it.

This danger is acute for ensembles, which to keep eating must keep producing new shows, inspired or not. Most radical ensembles I know succumb at times. We know when we are doing it; we also know we don't really get away with it. The audience knows the difference between perfunctory congratulation and hard-won affirmation. In my experience the shows that get the deepest response are the ones in which the artists put their own fears and weaknesses on stage, and have to dig deepest for the sources of their hope. Like the radical artist, the so-called converted audience is full of fears and doubts, and appreciates art which can acknowledge that.

San Francisco Mime Troupe in *Secrets in the Sand*. Poster by Wilma Bonet.

Xenophobia and the Indexical Present
Adrian Piper

My experiences as a third-world woman in mainstream society have been strongly influenced by attempts to marginalize or ostracize me, both socially and professionally, from the mainstream; or, at the very least, to put me in my (subordinate) place. In many ways I regard my marginality as more of a blessing than a curse, since alienation, too, has its uses. In order to survive in a hostile environment, it is necessary to become familiar with its resources, understand the aggressor and anticipate his attacks, and develop adequate strategies for self-defense (yes, combat really does build character). In part my artwork stems from a compulsion to embody, transform, and use these experiences in constructive ways, in order to not feel trapped and powerless.

I want my work to contribute to the creation of a society in which racism and racial stereotyping no longer exist. In such a society, the prevailing attitude to cultural and ethnic others would be one, not of tolerance, but of acceptance. The distinction is important. We *tolerate* bitter pills, castor oil, and the dentist's drill. We put up with these things because we recognize that they are good for us. This is the attitude that prevails among most concerned, thinking people in this society towards interlopers in their community. The alien values, practices, habits, and modes of self-expression of cultural intruders may get on our nerves, but we grit our teeth and endure them anyway, sometimes, for awhile, secure in the conviction of our own virtue. Toleration is consistent with deep-seated and virulent xenophobia.

Adrian Piper

Adrian Piper is a conceptual artist whose work, in a variety of media, has focused on issues of racism, racial stereotyping, and xenophobia for over two decades. She has held a Guggenheim and two NEA Visual Artists' Fellowships. Her twenty-year retrospective, *Reflections 1967-87,* originated at the Alternative Museum in New York in April, 1987, and is currently on tour. She is represented by the John Weber Gallery in New York, and teaches meta-ethics and Kant's metaphysics at the University of California at San Diego, where she is associate professor of philosophy and adjunct professor of art. Her work is direct, immediate, and confrontational, although not indelicate.

285

By contrast, to *accept* something is to be receptive and vulnerable to its effects on us, to discern its value for us, and indeed to rejoice in its intrinsic character and extrinsic ramifications for us. Thus, for example, we accept a person as a friend, a lover with warts and all, or a turn of fate as a blessing in disguise. To accept ethnic and cultural others, rather than merely to tolerate them, is to be disposed to flexible adaptation, i. e. to see them as sources of the personal catalysis and growth that inevitably results from new experiences, and to seek these out rather than barricade oneself against them.

"I Embody," Adrian Piper, 1975 (8" x 10" photo, oil crayon)

In the society I want to live in, for example, there are no subliminal racist hatreds and fears "I Embody." Nor need I delineate a "Self Portrait Exaggerating My Negroid Features" (1981), since my racial heritage is never called into question. In this envisioned society, it is unnecessary to give "Funk Lessons" (1983), because idioms of Black working class culture are not objects of acrimony and contempt. Neither my "Calling (Card) No. 1 nor No. 2" (1986-on) are necessary antidotes to the arrogant presumptions of racism or sexism: No one needs to be warned about my racial affiliation at dinners or cocktail parties because no one is inclined to insult it; no one needs to be asked not to invade my privacy in a public space because no one is inclined to do so. Similarly, in this envisioned society, no one has "Vanilla Nightmares" (1986), so no one needs to confront and exorcise them; questions about one's degree of actual personal contact with Blacks that are too "Close to Home" (1987) do not arise because a fully integrated society makes them otiose.

> Dear Friend,
>
> I am not here to pick anyone up, or to be picked up. I am here alone because I want to be here, ALONE.
>
> This card is not intended as part of an extended flirtation.
>
> Thank you for respecting my privacy.

"My Calling (Card) No. 2," Adrian Piper, 1986– (reactive guerilla performance for bars and discos)

In the society I want to live in, my personal, social, and professional interactions are not crippled by these symptoms of social disease. My social evenings are not ruined by racist or sexist *faux pas*. My personal relationships are not corrupted by deep-seated angers against blacks and women. Members of mainstream society do not presume the intimate access to my person that expresses itself in fantasies of rape and violence, personal remarks about my appearance, behavior, or self-presentation, or morbid speculation about the quality and content of my personal life. These are all invasive forays into my selfhood designed to render my interiority transparent to an eye widened in terror, unable to blink for fear of being blinded by the ineffable. In the society I want to live in, I get to navigate effortlessly through the social world, and take my freedom, value, and sense of belonging as much for granted as do white, middle-class heterosexual males. Like them, in this ideal society I can't even fully comprehend the problems because I've never personally experienced them! This is my idea of heaven, in which ignorance truly is bliss. (What kind of art would I make in such a society? I can't say. Perhaps the kind of art that Frank Stella, whose work I like very much, makes in this one.)

My work tends to target interpersonal manifestations of racism rather than institutional ones. This reflects my methodological individualism. I believe that institutions are comprised of individuals, and that institutional manifestations of racism are comprised of interpersonal ones: the off-color remark, the anxiety at the mere presence of an ethnic and cultural other, the failure of empathy with an other that causes insensitivity, the failure of imagination and self-awareness that elicits the imposition of inappropriate stereotypes and xenophobic behavior in response to them. The atomic, interpersonal level of individual transactions is the most elemental, personal level at which blacks learn from whites that they are unwelcome in mainstream society, so this is the level on which I try to attack racism. Although most of my work is not autobiographical, it is, in this sense, very personal. (I usually use myself in performances and videos because I find myself to be punctual, reliable, courteous, scrupulous in carrying out orders, disinclined to go on strike or give management any lip, and, above all, willing to work *gratis*.)

For this reason I am interested in acceptance of cultural and ethnic others as a social norm of etiquette, not just a moral or political norm. Norms of etiquette govern interpersonal treatment of individuals. Unlike many other kinds of norms, they

II Have you ever had a black person visit your place of residence?

    B. If yes, how did your reaction manifest itself?
       1. averted eyes ____
       2. increased heartrate ____
       3. tightened neck and/or stomach muscles ____
       4. forced allusions to black culture politics or society ____
       5. adoption of black working class vernacular conversational idioms ____
       6. adoption of streetwise mannerisms ____
       7. none of the above ____

Do you feel uncomfortable at the thought of displaying such questions on your living room wall?

"Close to Home," Adrian Piper, 1987 (installation detail)

function (or fail to function) independently of class or economic status. Norms of etiquette that express acceptance of cultural and ethnic others include norms of courtesy (which exclude racist or sexist slurs), of noblesse oblige (which exclude self-serving contempt for and indifference to the less fortunate), of modesty and humility (about who is in fact less fortunate than whom, and in what respects), of tact (which presuppose sensitivity to others' feelings irrespective of cultural or ethnic affiliation), and a sense of honor (which includes extending to others the same respectful treatment one expects for oneself). Judged against these norms, racism and sexism are not only unjust and immoral. They are also boorish and tasteless; and those who practice them overtly in any context betray vulgarity and inferior breeding.

Very often we vehemently deny culpability when called to account on a particular occasion, but nevertheless reform our behavior in the future, for fear of getting caught again. Similarly, were such norms of etiquette commonly recognized, the anticipation of public embarrassment—or shame—at our defects in socialization might conceivably work to discourage future racist and sexist gaffes. Implementing such norms obviously wouldn't solve the problem of racism or sexism right away. Nor would it transform morally or politically corrupt individuals into virtuous ones. But it would effect changes in overt individual transactions, both between and among the races and sexes. That would be preferable to the hypocrisy and self-serving rationalizations by which we now justify the continuation of our personal habits of racism and sexism, while espousing abstract indignation at institutional ones. Like a good methodological individualist, I take very seriously the tautology that if *one* is to start trying to solve these problems, one must start with oneself.

Most of my work targets racism rather than sexism; one difference between them in particular is instructive. Sexism flourishes within traditional norms of intimacy, familiarity, trust, and identification with the oppressor that are so ingrained that even now we are scarcely aware of their degree of influence on us. (This is the content of "Political Self Portrait No. 1 [Sex]" (1979).) Hence liberation from sexism demands independence, self-definition, self-protectiveness and autonomy for men as well as women. By contrast, racism and xenophobia more generally flourish against a background of socially sanctioned habits of mutual segregation, ignorance, fear, and rejection of the other as a human being that are so instinctive that we may never succeed in fully eradicating their influence on us. Therefore, liberation from racism requires cultivating the same kind of intimacy, familiarity, trust, and mutual identification that is such an obstacle to liberation from sexism. Liberation from racism presents the greater challenge to my particular creative abilities and resources.

My interest in the particular, personal, immediate transaction between ethnic or cultural others expresses a long-held fascination with the indexical present—the concrete, immediate here-and-now (see, for example, "Here and Now" (artist's book, 1968)). My work springs from a belief that we are transformed—and occasionally reformed—by immediate experience, independently of our abstract evaluations of it and despite our attempts to resist it. Since my creative commitment is inherently political, I am primarily motivated to do the work I do by a desire to effect concrete, positive, internal political change in the viewer, independently of—or in spite of—the viewer's abstract aesthetic evaluation of my work. I comfort myself with the thought that future generations of viewers, for whom the problems of racism and xenophobia will be less pressing and threatening, will surely provide the positive aesthetic evaluations I would like. Of course I am always delighted when a present-generation viewer joins the ranks of eternity by expressing appreciation for my work *now*.

Thus almost all my work—whether photo-text collage, installation, drawing, artist's book, performance, or video installation—is intended as an act of political communication that catalyzes its viewers into reflecting on their own deep impulses and responses to racism and xenophobia, relative to a target or stance that I depict. Through the work I try to construct a concrete, immediate, and personal relationship between me and the viewer that locates us in an indexical present that is itself embedded in the network of political cause and effect. In this way my work differs from what I call "global" political art that attempts to educate its viewers about issues that bear no direct and obvious relationship to their lives, or that avoids any such relationship in its mode of presentation. My purpose is to transform the viewer psychologically, by presenting him or her with an unavoidable concrete reality that cuts through the defensive rationalizations by which we insulate ourselves against the facts of our political responsibility. I want viewers of my work to come away from it with the understanding that racism is not an abstract, distant problem that affects all those poor, unfortunate other people out there. It begins between you and me, right here and now, in the indexical present.

Work that draws the viewer into the indexical present provides a healthy antidote to xenophobia. Xenophobia expresses fear of the other's singularity through the imposition of inadequate, stereotyped categories of classification. Human beings are inherently conceptualizing creatures; we never have unmediated access to "raw experience." But most of the categories by which we make sense of our experience are poorly drawn rules of thumb that rarely capture the essence of concrete particulars. We get into trouble when the concrete particulars we distort or misidentify are other people. Holding certain kinds of other people at arm's length makes it easier to get into this kind of trouble, because it relieves us of the opportunity to check our theories about them against the particulars of their presence. No amount of abstract analysis, no matter how astute or politically correct, can escape this trap, because xenophobia is merely an extreme tendency of which ordinary failures of vision and sensitivity are the norm. Artwork that draws one into a relationship with the other in the indexical present trades easy classification—and hence xenophobia—for a direct and immediate experience of the complexity of the other, and of one's own responses to her. Experiencing the other in the indexical present teaches one how to see.

I have frequently been misclassified as a "performance artist," although less than one-fifth of my work is in the area of performance. I identify myself, rather, as a conceptual artist, for two reasons. First, I define conceptual art as art that subordinates medium to idea (this follows Sol LeWitt's definition in "Notes on Conceptual Art," *Artforum*, 1968). That is, I choose that medium that best realizes the ideas I am exploring. This results in great flexibility and a wide variety of available media in which to work, depending on the ideas or concepts in question. I have used audio tape, drawing, performance, photo-text collage, video, installation, film, artists' books, and choreography, among other media, in different works. So identifying myself as a conceptual artist is a good way to avoid getting pigeonholed or stereotyped—in the matter of art practice, at least. (Of course it doesn't always work. Misidentifying me as a performance artist depends on disregarding my work in other media, just as imposing racist stereotypes depends on disregarding evidence of the other's complexity.)

Second, the resulting flexibility in available media is strategically important, given the political targets of my work. In order to best achieve my goals, I need to be able to draw on whatever media resources are best suited to achieve those goals, in my judgment. So identifying myself as a conceptual artist emphasizes two salient features of my work: first, the priority of political content over extended formal exploration of a particular medium for its own sake (regardless of the personal pleasure I may take in such an exploration); and second, the priority of strategic over aesthetic considerations in the decision-making process of realizing the work. My main conscious interest is in truth rather than beauty; I rely on my solid artworld acculturation, initiated at an early age, to take care of the aesthetics.

Because I believe we are all implicated in the problem of racism, my work addresses an audience that is diverse in ethnicity and gender. I am particularly interested in grappling with the "Who, me?" syndrome that infects the highly select and sophisticated audience that typically views my work. But the work functions differently depending on the composition of the audience. For a white viewer, it often has a didactic function: It communicates information and experiences that are new, or that challenge preconceptions about oneself and one's relation to blacks. For a black viewer, the work often has an affirmative or cathartic function: It expresses shared emotions—of pride, rage, impatience, defiance, hope—that remind us of the values and experiences we share in common. However, different individuals respond in different and unpredictable ways that cut across racial, ethnic, and gender boundaries: Some people align themselves with the standpoint from which I offer the critique. Others identify themselves as the target of the critique. Yet others feel completely alienated by the whole enterprise. There is no way of telling in advance whether any particular individual is going to feel attacked by my work, or affirmed, or alienated by it. So people sometimes learn something about who they are by viewing my work. For me this is proof of success.

Much of my work incorporates stereotypically defensive reactions to me or my work I have previously witnessed [see, for example, "I/You (Us)" (1975), "Four Intruders Plus Alarm Systems" (1980), "My Calling (Card) No. 1 and No. 2" (1986-on)]. My intention is to generate in the viewer a more sophisticated self-awareness and, eventually, the evolution of more considered and sensitive responses to ethnic and cultural others. Two defensive reactions in particular that express resistance to my work are of special interest to me as possible content for inclusion in future work. The first one asks, Why don't I deal more with sexism? Or other ethnic groups besides blacks? The oddity of these questions may be illuminated by considering an analogous question hypothetically posed of Picasso: Why doesn't "Guernica" deal with the Russian Revolution? Or other ethnic groups besides Spaniards? Clearly no work of art is under even the slightest obligation to be universal in the sense this question demands. Both questions really reduce to the question, Why didn't I do a different work, with a different focus, than the one I did? These questions thus covertly express profound discomfort with the actual work, and the focus of the work, I did do.

"Vanilla Nightmares No. 3," Adrian Piper, 1986 (14" x 22" charcoal drawing on newspaper)

Such discomfort is, I think, to be expected. My work intentionally holds up for scrutiny deep-seated racist attitudes that no individual socialized into a racist society can escape, no matter how politically correct or seasoned such an individual may be. And to have to confront those attitudes in oneself can be particularly painful for those who pride themselves on how politically correct they are. But what these questions most disturbingly reveal is a failure of self-acceptance and self-awareness on the part of those who ask them. They veridically experience the import of the work, and its impact on them, but deflect recognition of the meaning of their response to it into vague complaints that I didn't do a different work that would make them less uncomfortable. I try to promote viewer self-reflection in my work, but I don't always succeed.

A second audience response that deserves more extended treatment is the comment, uttered reprovingly, that my work is actually very angry. This leads me to wonder what emotional stance toward racism would be appropriate, according to this response: Humor? Resignation? Detachment? Cynicism? This audience response implies that art that expresses anger about racism commits a *faux pas*. This, in turn, presupposes that the prevailing racist social practices that elicit such anger are a standard of normalcy or social acceptability, relative to which anger is a social gaffe. One has only to spell out these implications to see the value distortions inherent in the original response. In an ideal society of healthy and nonegoistic values, the prevailing response to racist social conventions would be anger, resentment, and moral outrage on the part of *all* concerned and reflective individuals, not only those directly victimized by them. In a society governed by an etiquette of acceptance of cultural and ethnic others, racism would be the *faux pas*, not anger in response to it. In conceiving particular pieces, I work from the standpoint of a community, however small, governed by such norms of etiquette. Some viewers of my work implicitly identify with this standpoint, regardless of their own ethnic and cultural affiliations. They tend to recognize the intended meaning of my tactics and idioms of expression right away. But I don't expect that everyone will. If they did, doing this kind of work wouldn't feel as urgent and necessary as it does.

Funk Lessons (1983-85)

The performance *Funk Lessons* was subtitled "A Collaborative Experiment in Cross-Cultural Transfusion." It began as a lecture/dance class format and gradually evolved into a Funk/Rhythm and Blues dancing party in the course of the evening. In it I introduced the idioms of Funk, analyzing its musicological structure, origins, themes and influence on other genres of composition; and led the audience in practicing some of the basic dance

movements in synco-
pated polyrhythm. I also
discussed with the audi-
ence some of the socio-
psychological reasons for
its denigration or rejec-
tion by the white main-
stream, and the resistance
of the art audience to acknowledging it as an ap-
propriation from popular
culture having the same
validity as any other.
Sometimes these discus-
sions became quite emo-
tional and personal. The
performance was struc-
tured so as to evolve away
from an audience-
performer dichotomy
and, with increased
familiarity with the
idioms of composition
and movement, toward a
shared experience of self-
transcendence.

"Funk Lessons," 1983 (performance)

Originally I performed it for small groups of six to ten individuals, and then
for larger audiences of fifty to two hundred. The audiences were mixed with
respect to race and gender, and included students, other artists and artworld
inhabitants, street people, and passersby in differing proportions.

One motivation for doing this performance was self-interested: Having
discovered, to my surprise, that appropriation of this particular idiom of
popular culture into my work usually met with incomprehension or hostility
on the part of the art audience, I felt the need to disseminate it didactically so
that I could utilize it as a successful means of communication in future works.
This work was funded by a National Endowment for the Arts (NEA) Visual
Artists' Fellowship.

—Adrian Piper

Dear Friend,
    I am black.
    I am sure you did not realize this when you made/laughed at/agreed with that racist remark. In the past, I have attempted to alert white people to my racial identity in advance. Unfortunately, this invariably causes them to react to me as pushy, manipulative, or socially inappropriate. Therefore, my policy is to assume that white people do not make these remarks, even when they believe there are no black people present, and to distribute this card when they do.
    I regret any discomfort my presence is causing you, just as I am sure you regret the discomfort your racism is causing me.
                                        Sincerely yours,
                                        Adrian Margaret Smith Piper

My Calling (Card) No. 1 (1986– ; reactive guerrilla performance for dinners and cocktail parties).

"Self-Portrait Exaggerating My Negroid Features," Adrian Piper, 1981.

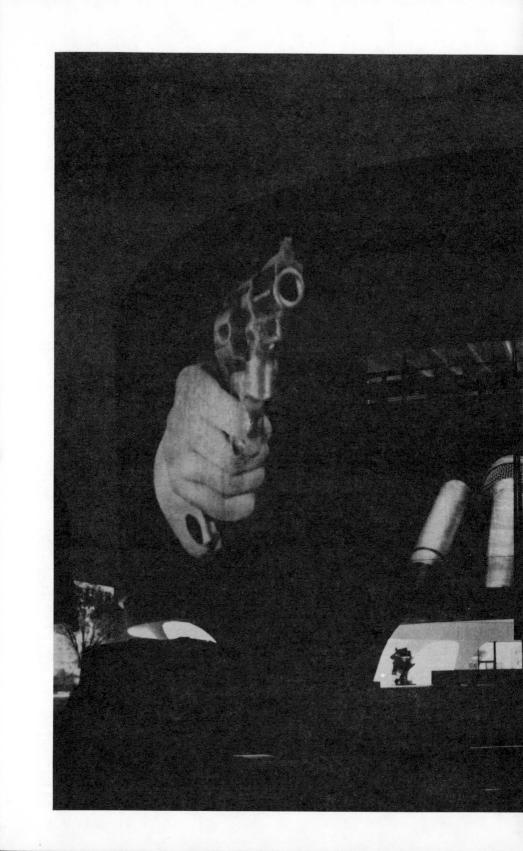

Breaking Boundaries

Breaking Boundaries
Introduction

> There's a force that's always active in national culture, that tends to lock in language—to make fixed meanings, to limit the possibilities of thinking and acting by limiting our relationship to one another, to language and to society. Its basic action is to define, smooth out, and lock in the boundaries of experience. I think the artist should be pushing those boundaries back out again . . . *

The essays and interviews in this section address choices made by artists who are questioning the often self-imposed boundaries and assumptions of activist artmakers.

These boundaries encompass a number of different themes. First is that of representational taboos. The role of transgressor would seem to be one most readily granted to artists in the United States. And for the most part, as recent controversies over censorship and public funding reflect, progressives have come to the defense of artists who challenge accepted social norms. But clearly, there are limits to the tolerance of a progressive or liberal ethos. This may be understandable, even commendable, in the context of condemning a racist, teen-sexploitation slasher flick at the local cineplex. But artistic conflicts with enlightened views about what is or is not an *acceptable* representation of race, sex, gender, and violence are not always so clear-cut. The existence of divergent views is often tolerated more than accepted or embraced, and that tolerance often disappears when the opinion is "flaunted." Violent, angry, self-representation by Black male rap and hip-hop groups upsets this tolerance when it does not conform to our expectations of how Black social protest should be articulated.

These limits do not necessarily carry with them a desire, let alone an ability to censor. However, they do raise serious questions about the viability of long-term relationships between individual artists and political/cultural organizations as a basis for shaping an *alternative* culture. And given that activist artists often depend upon a politically sympathetic core audience for economic viability, it raises very real questions about artists' ability to risk challenging the faith of their core audience.

The work of both Robert Colescott and Lizzie Borden challenge easy normative interpretation. Colescott's paintings are most disturbing when, as in *Saturday Night*

---

* Jill Godmilow, from her interview with Brooke Jacobson, see page 181.

Special or *Knowledge of the Past,* he delves into the nature of black and white sexual identities and fantasies. He pushes the viewer to question gut responses, leaving few clues as to what the *correct* one should be. Likewise, Borden explores topics—middle-class prostitution, the politics of oppressed groups, abortion, sexual domination—that are rarely treated in mainstream films. Her interview focuses on the economic and political obstacles she has encountered in making films that advocate the inviolability of free choice. Her honest, non-judgmental treatments of these *forbidden* topics confront the moral expectations of conservatives and progressives alike.

A second boundary of progressive artmaking is a tendency to lock ourselves into *oppositional* mentalities—limiting the scope of our work, and focusing our efforts on what Mat Schwarzman identifies as "issues of particular interest of the left." This, in effect, cedes control over arenas of experience that comprise what we are calling the public sphere. During the past decade, for example, public celebrations in the United States have been largely privatized through corporate sponsorship of Bicentennials, Liberty celebrations and other historical spectacles. Advocates of free enterprise and other conservative causes have had tremendous success in controlling the spin on collective national commemorations of history. This development underlines the failure of progressive artists and organizers to convincingly articulate any alternative visions for broad-based public celebrations.

A second group of contributors in this section, including Charles Mee, Richard Posner, Krzysztof Wodiczko and Mat Schwarzman, deals with the need for left artists to use public arenas—incorporating often overlapping conceptual realms of history, memory, and national identity, with areas of the architectural space, including both buildings and public monuments—to project critical social visions that can be viewed by the general population.

A final boundary is the sense of ambivalence that many activist artists feel towards mass cultural forms. What Lucy Lippard calls "dialectical schizophrenia" is the fear that in any attempt to exploit mass media and reach new, truly mass, audiences, artists will inevitably become marginalized by their own success. In part, this is a concern that commercial pressures will inhibit the political content of an individual artist's work. A parallel, contextual concern is that mass media distorts how a work is received as much as what is created. Because mass media reinforce the passive role of the audience, one outgrowth of an increasingly politicized mass culture is that consumption becomes a legitimate form of political participation. Merely attending left cultural events, buying products or giving money replace other, more directly activist forms of political behavior.

In spite of these concerns, both Pat Aufderheide and Reebee Garofalo argue for coming to terms with mass cultural forms—both for their potential to reach larger audiences, and because, for many of us, these are the only authentic cultural experiences that we share. It is precisely because mass commodity culture "conditions the terms under which any alternatives can emerge" (Aufderheide) that we cannot afford to ignore or simply demonize it.

Cultivating
a Subversive Palette
Robert Colescott

Paintings are about painters. The way a painter views a given subject, women for instance, tells us about the artist. Some painters have pandered to the male "tastes" of their time, while others have been motivated by a profound admiration of sensuous female form. Personal representations are created by individuals, but it is the culture that creates archetypes. For example, Paleolithic culture created a female archetype that was all breasts, buttocks, and vagina, out of a social focus on reproduction and nourishment. In contrast, the medieval female archetype was slender, breastless, and buttockless, representing a denial of the flesh and its pleasures. Concentrating on heaven and hell will make anybody skinny. In the twentieth century an archetype has developed that is designed to sell products—products that include war. Diabolically effective, she has big breasts, long legs, slender hips, and is usually blonde with big blue eyes. She promises pleasure, active companionship, and racial status. Men spend, buy and perform for her favors.

Robert Colescott

Born in Oakland, California, Robert Colescott currently teaches at the University of Arizona. His work has been exhibited in numerous galleries and museums across the U.S. and Canada. Currently his work is on display at the Phyllis Kind Gallery in New York City.

I suppose artists of each period see the reality and "truth" in their representations if they are integrated into the culture. Today many artists are alienated from the culture at large, and question or deny cultural archetypes. Over the years I've represented women in different ways, depending on what I'm up to. The busty blonde that the men in a society are promised as reward for buying an expensive car or for killing Vietnamese, is an essential representational symbol for me when I speak about the exploitation of sex. My recent "Bathers Pool" series, which depicts the fictional first encounter between two "pure" races, deals with the clash of African and European cultural standards of beauty. In these paintings I have invented a kind of African female archetype. Loosely based on the proportion and exaggeration of African art, she looks a little like a living African sculpture. I hope that it makes a point about the relationship of idealized form in art to standards of physical beauty.

This archetype was useful again for the figures in "The Demoiselles D'Alabama." In "Sunday Afternoon with Joaquin Murietta," based on Manet's "Déjeuner sur l'Herbe," I turn Manet's nude Black, and paint her as a strong, lithe, catlike creature. I'm talking about her power as a female, her physical power, and her political power. There is no hint of the "cutie pie" image.

In all of these instances, I'm painting about ideas, with different representations for different ideas. The art of irony that I employ is based on exaggeration, and art in general is based on distortion. My images are not prurient. Nobody ever got a hard-on looking at the women in my paintings.

*   *   *

"George Washington Carver Crossing the Delaware: Page from an American History Textbook," Robert Colescott, 1975 (84" x 108" acrylic on canvas). Photo by Keith Fitzgerald.

It's interesting that I'm still being questioned about paintings that were done between twelve and eighteen years ago. In addition to "Sunday Afternoon . . . ," they include "George Washington Carver Crossing the Delaware," "Eat Dem Taters," and "Liberty Leading the People." I didn't have a name for the genre then, though I knew that artists had traditionally done their own versions of previous masterworks, usually in homage to that previous artist and artwork. A generic name, *appropriation,* emerged as more artists began subverting other artists' works, playing with or changing the meaning of the work, if not the appearance.

Emanuel Leutze's "Washington Crossing the Delaware" made Washington invulnerable as a mythic hero. Over the years, however, tremendous overexposure of the image, and its role as scenery for the hero's epic performance have robbed it of any artistic significance. The painting itself became vulnerable as it became a prop rather than a work of art. Subversion of this icon, a quasi-religious image that everybody bows to and believes in—but nobody thinks about—seemed like a good idea, a new life for an old shoe.

My idea was to use the Leutze painting to talk about another kind of history: to pair off that token representation the textbooks have allowed us (George Washington Carver and Booker T. Washington) with the overwhelming impact of popular and media stereotypes of Blacks *before* the civil rights movement. What does this whole switch do to the original? It's a serious distraction, for some. If you've seen my painting, you will think of *it* when you look at the original. It also has an impact on the original subject—Washington and his stalwarts. Their status drops because I've taken their painting away.

*   *   *

The irony in many of these paintings is still misread. A large part of the problem stems from the fact that Black people have been neglected throughout Western art history. Some early American paintings represented Blacks, but in subservient roles, reflecting their societal position. One of the only "noble" representations of Blacks in Western art is "St. Maurice," by the Czech Master Theodoric in the fourteenth century. In one of my recent paintings, I used the image of the brave Black warrior saint in a twentieth century context, "A Prayer to St. Maurice" (1987).

Sometimes I have walked a dangerous line in dealing with the subject of white perception of Black. In that regard, some of those appropriated paintings that still prick are more complicated than they seem. At different levels, they carry different meanings simultaneously. They ultimately ridicule the meanness and silliness of the images, which are white invention. They also say, "Look here, I've been left out of (art) history, but if the white man had included me at that time (and what about our portrayal currently?) I probably would have looked like this!" The same prejudice that excluded Black folk from the culture created the stereotyped sambo image.

It's usually okay to laugh with my paintings, at one level, because we aren't laughing at Black people and their condition, but at a silly white invention. We have laughed with Dick Gregory and Clevon Little playing out their broad stereotypical roles for the same reason. Because of the extreme exaggeration in those earlier paintings (to say nothing of the seriously silly humor) reactions are strong and swing from joy to anger. The ultimate effect is to force the viewer to question his or her response. Some white liberals have told me that they understand all that, but that they are still afraid of hurting Black feelings. How patronizing!

*   *   *

Unfortunately, stereotypical images are part of the American heritage. I had to come to terms with it for myself, ultimately controlling the images by making them and making them say some things for me. First I made these paintings and drawings

"Saturday Night Special: (I Seen It on T.V.)," Robert Colescott, 1988 (84" x 72" acrylic on canvas). Photo by Keith Fitzgerald.

as messages from myself to myself, getting in touch with my own fears, frustration, and anger. Others have connected with my statement and empathized with what I was trying to do. Some are intrigued by the puzzle, some reject it. In 1988, some politicians tried to keep my retrospective out of the museum in Akron, but a majority of people (Black and white) refused to let that happen. The museum tripled its attendance—and that extra two-thirds were Black people who were not normally museum-goers. It's what I want to say *about* stereotyping that has given these images new significance. I wonder if it will ever get to a place where this will be noncontroversial?

*   *   *

I don't like to think too much about the alignment of artist's race and subject. Every artist, regardless of color, faces the same creative struggle: the attempt to give form to ideas that have personal and universal meaning, and to do so with integrity. We all need an environment of support and understanding. Each artist, however, brings his or her experience, background, personality, and talent to the task. That's where the difference lies. A Black person who is an artist brings a certain unique background and point of view to the work of art. That artist may even be inclined to see special obligations that must be met because of the role a Black person in this society has been assigned.

The public has a right to reject what is insincere or empty. In art, any representation of Blacks, by anyone, is risky—even the most heroic or idealized image. This is because Black identity is so clouded by white hatred and imposed inferiority. To some extent it is even hard for Black artists' concepts of racial identity to be accepted. If a white artist approaches this area, their motives will be open to question. Freedom of expression is *free,* however. I deal with aspects of white identity at times in my painting, and I think the things I say are perceptive. I've never felt that there were any boundaries or limits to what I might do. Self-censorship is a cop-out. If you think about it, the public outrage that would accompany, say, a play or art piece featuring whites in blackface could be a major objective in itself. In 1989 it might represent the ultimate rejection of cultural good taste. Even if it had meaning (whites playing out their own beliefs about Blacks), it would be despised. The perpetrators would need a lot of self-confidence.

*   *   *

I was brought up to make paintings that were important visually, with an internal structure and rhythm that grabs people, surprises them, and moves them, like Duke Ellington. It is so ingrained that even when I ignore that aspect, it happens. It has a lot to do with my generation of artists. But when I get my work up in a gallery, you see this room full of big, sensuous paintings. It's the first impact that people get. They walk in and say, "Oh wow!" and then, "Oh shit!" when they see what they have to deal with in subject matter. It's an integrated "one-two punch"; it gets them every time.

"Knowledge of the Past is the Key to the Future (St. Sebastian)," Robert Colescott, 1986 (84" x 72" acrylic on canvas). Photo by Keith Fitzgerald.

Putting the Forbidden on Film

Lizzie Borden
Interview by Mark O'Brien

O'Brien: In an interview with Philadelphia radio station WXPN*, you talked about being drawn to dangerous or forbidden areas as subject matters for your films. Could you define some of those areas and describe how you approach them?

Borden: Basically, the reason I wanted to make films at all was that I wanted to explore areas I hadn't seen in films previously. I approach certain subjects almost anthropologically—not as stories but as topics—topics which could be considered dangerous or forbidden simply because they deal either with the politics of oppressed groups, ideas that are not viable within a culture at a certain time, or people who are themselves taboo. In *Born in Flames,* it was women who were marginal because they were gay or Black or punk. In *Working Girls,* it was women who were middle-class prostitutes—seemingly a contradiction in terms—neither poverty-ridden streetwalkers, nor glamorous high-class call girls. By putting them in the center of a film, it becomes apparent that their "marginality" is not a function of their "otherness," but of their ordinariness. They're too disturbingly like us to be acknowledged. Right now I'm interested in exploring areas such as masochism, domination, and the issue of abortion. I'm interested in the issue of who takes power—both societally and sexually.

O'Brien: One thing which struck me about both *Working Girls* and *Born in Flames*

> ### Lizzie Borden
>
> Lizzie Borden is a former painter and art critic, who wrote for *ArtForum* magazine. Now a well-known political filmmaker based in New York City, her two films to date are *Born in Flames* (1983) and *Working Girls* (1987). Her next film, *Love Crimes,* will be about a woman sex crimes prosecutor obsessed with a sex criminal.

---

* Thanks to Julie Drizen and Joan Schuman, whose 1987 interview with Borden that aired during the Voices of Dissent festival served as a jumping-off point for this discussion.

was that while in mainstream films these women are cast as victims, or as background to other peoples' dramas; you show them taking action: making choices—some with good consequences, some bad—rather than only being acted upon.

Borden: Exactly. I tried to present a range of choices available to the women in the films. It's important for me not to present a monolithic political "stance," since I think political choices are messy and emotional, never logical. Often choices aren't clear. I'd rather provide contradictions which encourage debate. Is violent action necessary or irresponsible? Should a woman quit a brothel to see clients privately? Should she quit the "life" altogether to work a regular job? For me, the only absolute "stance" I take is that women should have the right to choose.

One of the major problems I have with any narrow ideological stance—progressive as well as conservative—is how it tends to police attitudes. I am a feminist, but I am dead set against any party-line feminism that is intolerant of alternative choices about prostitution, about how to react to violence or to oppression, or about sexuality. After *Born in Flames,* a lot of feminists told me I was "incorrect" because I showed women carrying guns, women doing so-called "male" activities or having "male" responses. I think this criticism was particularly intense because *Born in Flames* came out during a time when feminism was heavily influenced by the peace movement—Greenham Common and Seneca.

Working Girls provokes the same kind of response. Women Against Pornography came out against the movie not because it's pornographic but because they thought my attitude about prostitution was irresponsible. They thought it was wrong to present some middle-class working girls who had chosen to "work," who weren't forced into it by dire economic need, who chose "working" over other available jobs. While the prostitutes' group COYOTE (Call Off Your Old Tired Ethics) really supported the film, other prostitutes' organizations such as the British Collective of Prostitutes hated it.

O'Brien: As an outsider to the groups you present in your films, how do you deal with the question of authorization—of actually, or of appearing to "speak for" them?

Borden: It's a tough question since I don't speak for anyone but myself. I don't belong to any political groups, nor do I consult with groups before releasing a movie. I do research, however. Several prostitutes read the script for *Working Girls* and corrected some errors before I made the film. *Born in Flames* engaged real women, such as Flo Kennedy, actually presenting their own "real" points of view.

There are a lot of ironies in my relationship with film subjects, particularly since I've been working in the context of independent film. Because my films have been somewhat experimental they've been less accessible to audiences—including the subjects of my films—who are used to Hollywood movies. That's both challenging and disappointing to those audiences. Also, there's a tendency to want the few films that are made about "marginal" groups to be open to everyone's experience. Each film becomes over-significant. *Working Girls* did not address the problems of street hookers, of prostitutes with pimps. And when *Born in Flames* came out, some straight Black women said, "There are too many lesbians in the film. This is not what our lives are about. You should have shown more women with children. You should have shown more women who have boyfriends." I had over-marginalized it for them since they could not identify with Black *gay* women.

While neither film presents the views of groups as such, they do reflect the opinions and ideas of real women. All the characters in *Working Girls* are based on actual women, and most of the characters in *Born in Flames* are expressing their own ideas within a fictional construct.

Particularly with *Born in Flames,* which dealt with the relationship between Black and white women, I didn't want to put words in the mouths of the characters. I couldn't have scripted that film, since I didn't know what the characters would say at first. What had politicized me when I came to New York in the early '70s was finding that feminism was beginning to challenge notions of male dominance and define a language for women's equality. But there was a huge disparity between the language used by white feminists and the language used by Black women, who didn't necessarily define themselves as feminist, even though they shared a lot of the same goals. So when I made *Born in Flames,* I did not want to set an agenda. I drew real women, not actresses, into the film, and I wanted to collaborate with them in creating a film in which there would be *many* languages, not just one.

I wanted to present multiple voices existing simultaneously, nonhierarchically, and ultimately for the same goal. Throughout the film, the different underground radio stations—the punk station and the Black station—coexist. The deejays, Honey and Adele, have different voices. At the end, they work together but don't "mix and match." Their voices remain unique.

In a similar vein, I wanted to present a range of responses to political oppression, from peaceful demonstrations to terrorist action, because I think all of these are relevant to certain groups in certain circumstances. No one response is correct.

O'Brien: This brings up an interesting point. You talk about your *intention* to present all of these actions as equal choices. But I wonder whether in the context of a film—where most people expect a narrative progression to make choices for them— you can expect the audience to see them as equal. Because the terrorist action is the culminating event, the implication seems to be that this is the correct progression, even if you *intend* to present this in non-normative terms. How do you overcome the problem of the narrative form working against you?

Borden: I actually don't mind if an audience feels that's what I'm saying. Especially if they object to it at the end of the film: "No, that's not right, that's too much." I would say that myself. I wouldn't blow up a building in real life. I think movies are a way to play with the possibility of extreme actions—but it doesn't make these actions "correct." By presenting a lot of different possibilities throughout the course of the film, I had hoped I could create enough of a fabric of other choices to give the bombing a context, but which would also allow the audience to go back to the other choices. I was hoping to propose, not to prescribe. I wanted the narrative to *engage* the audience actively in these considerations. Having an explosion at the end was an aggressive question mark: "What can push people far enough to want to do this?" It throws it back on the audience to consider what issue would push them that far.

There seem to be two different kinds of films. The first—primarily commercial— are the ones whose narratives are seamless, which pull you into a world to the degree that you can forget you're watching a film. The second are films which somehow make you think as you're watching; you never quite forget that you're watching a film. As I seem to be evolving toward making more seamless movies, the challenge is to keep presenting characters and frameworks which allow the viewer a more active participation. *Born in Flames* was constructed entirely through montage, which is

Honey, *Born in Flames*. Photo by John Coplans.

very jarring and keeps you from falling into the world of the film unquestioningly. In this respect, it is very Godardian. Godard was a huge influence on me. He invented or at least radicalized the jump cut and later interrupted three-dimensional narrative space with graphics, reasserting the flat plane (the "picture plane," in the language of art). You fall into the narrative for a certain amount of time before you're snapped out of it quickly to read flat images or text. It's totally manipulative.

In *Born in Flames,* I wanted the shots of disc jockeys and TV announcers speaking directly to the camera as if addressing the audience. The film is jarring in texture, since I used material from many sources, including "found objects," especially news items I "borrowed" from TV. Ironically, the most violent action occurs in the news footage I found, not in what I had my performers enact. I wanted to both weave together and contrast actions in the "real" and fictional worlds. I often placed performers in "real" settings—using a real demonstration as a backdrop for a fictional element, or setting up a situation, such as a fictional secretaries' strike on Wall Street, in which real women participated along with the performers. I wanted to blur these distinctions.

O'Brien: *Working Girls* is visually a very different kind of movie. It's much more seamless, narratively smooth. How does your concern for structure apply in this case?

Borden: Each film demands its own style. A more seamless visual structure was necessary, in part, since most of the film was primarily shot in one set and I couldn't use montage as an editing method. I was also trying to do something very different with *Working Girls.* In some ways I think the entirety of *Working Girls* came from a sequence in *Born in Flames* of women's hands doing different kinds of work—including a shot of a woman putting a condom on a guy's penis. When you see *Born in Flames* there is no sense of how the women make a living. How do they make money? And what I wanted to do in *Working Girls* was really analyze the notion of work in this culture—particularly work as value laden as prostitution.

I wanted to deconstruct prostitution by presenting the elemental details of "working": the money, the black book, the towel rooms, the condoms. What does a working girl do with a used condom? How is money exchanged? What are the codes of the bedroom? How is time measured and regulated? I was interested in the passage of time—the stretching out of time as the "working girls" wait for clients to arrive and then swing into action, pulling themselves together, putting on their shoes, sitting up straight, smiling. I wanted to present a "day in the life" so real that the viewer would feel like a fly on the wall. I wanted women to identify with Molly and feel parallels with their own jobs. I also wanted *men* to identify with Molly—not with the johns. Perhaps it was successful because after seeing the film a lot of men told me they'd had bosses like Lucy.

In making work as a prostitute more universal than it's usually presented in films, I was trying to normalize the occupation, since hookers are so often presented as "other," as nonhuman, as cartoons. By allowing the drama of the film to center around a woman forced to work a double shift, I wanted to foil the audience's expectation of the melodrama which usually happens in films about prostitution. This way the viewer can be thinking all the time of his or her own work, the annoyance in any kind of job where you're forced to stay too long, or where you have to work in an intolerable working situation. And since it isn't easy to quit *any* job, there's a big question mark when Molly leaves. Is she really leaving? Is she going to see Elliot, a potential sugar daddy, on the outside? Will she return to the brothel the next week because she needs the money? She doesn't know. We don't know. And to me this is a very real question, because what do you do? This kind of drama has a bearing on the viewer's own life.

On the "molecular" level, I wanted to overturn the expectation of the woman's body as cinematic object. There's a well-known Laura Mulvey essay which asserts that the apparatus, the camera, is inherently male and by its very nature objectifies the female body. The woman is there to be gazed upon by the active subject who is doing the gazing. But I think the apparatus itself is neutral: it is just a question of how one frames shots. Every shot has to be re-analyzed and reconstructed if it is not to do what Mulvey argues. In *Working Girls* I was very careful to construct shots which did not objectify the female body, especially in the sex scenes. One way to do this was to never show any angles on a woman's body she wouldn't see herself. Very often this meant using the woman's gaze, in collusion with herself with the mirror, to show her awareness: she's not being acted *upon*.

O'Brien: Can you be more specific?

Borden: There's one scene with Gina and Molly doing a double on a guy named Jerry. He wants to enter Gina from behind and to go without a rubber, and she keeps saying "Thirty dollars extra," "Thirty dollars extra." He does some things to her that look kind of violent. But Gina and Molly keep exchanging glances, and Gina, through her glances with Molly, lets Molly know she's okay, this is her act. We see her feelings about it and her sense of composure. I was very careful to make the collusion between the women show that they were in fact controlling the situation. Gina wasn't being hurt—she was making money and giving him the *illusion* he was getting what he wanted. Ironically, in *Working Girls,* some men complain that the men's bodies are objectified. In a way, I put men's bodies into the traditional woman's position. Of course, objectification of the body can be erotic, but that was not my intention in this film.

O'Brien: This brings up the distinction between the realms of the erotic and the pornographic. Reactions to *Working Girls* ranged from some who considered it pornographic, to others who saw it as de-eroticizing sex to the point of being "anti-sex" at some level. How do you define the boundaries of pornography and erotica?

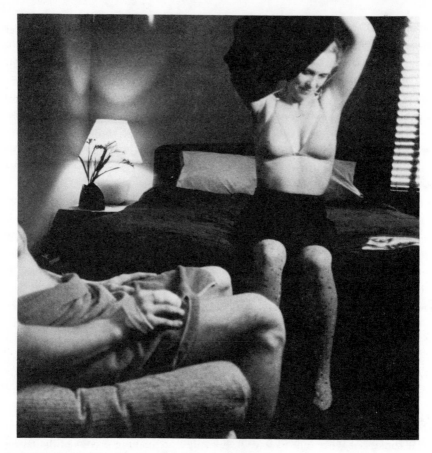

Louise Smith as 'Molly' in *Working Girls*. **Photo by Nan Goldin.**

Borden: I very specifically wanted to make a film which was as far from pornography as it could be. It seems to me that everything or anything about sex that doesn't turn you on is condemned as pornography, because if it does turn you on it's seen as erotic. So, I can see people calling *Working Girls* pornographic because they find it disgusting in some way, because it isn't comfortably erotic, it doesn't somehow make prostitution sexy and fun. It presents it as hard work, even boring. So the film feels like a bucket of cold water to any guy who came in to get turned on. Most sex in hooker movies is presented for a *male* viewer who stands in for the john. But I wanted to demystify paid sex and show a variety of sex acts in such a way that no one could become aroused. The film isn't anti-sex: it's descriptive of the realities of paid sex from the woman's point of view.

I think I was successful in avoiding pornography in *Working Girls*. But I'm not against eroticism. "Erotic" to me has a connotation of something suggested rather than stated. It is less literal than "pornography"—more "atmosphere" and less "act." In fact, I've been wanting to make a purely "erotic" film for a long time. The main problem with pornographic films is they're so badly lit and so literal. They lose the mystery of eroticism. They're like plumbing manuals. There's always been a content/ style problem in pornography. . . . It's not what you show but it's how you show it. My theory is that women aren't as drawn to hard core (penetration) images since we never actually *see* penetration. We don't connect the *image* of entry with sexual experience the way men do. We know what it *feels* like, which is more atmospheric. I will always remember certain images from *Flaming Creatures*—a gloved hand on a breast, for example—or from Kenneth Anger's work. It's interesting that gay male erotic work has been the most compelling. I'd like to tap into female fantasy that way, gay and straight.

I think a true erotic filmmaking has yet to be explored. We live in such a repressed conservative culture that everyone screams "pornography" before the erotic can be discovered or talked about openly. And any attempt to censor so politicizes the term "pornography" that the wrong things are censored. Feminist support of censorship is exploited by conservatives who will use their support and then won't give women a voice in determining how the power of censorship will be exercised.

O'Brien: Are there any barriers for you, any unacceptable areas?

Borden: Yeah, child pornography and "snuff movies" are unacceptable. Anything between consenting adults is fine, I don't care how extreme it is. I do not personally support extreme S & M, because I think that instead of pushing boundaries, it ends up reinforcing a limited kind of response. I do feel that whatever expands your potential for feeling is valid. But anything nonconsensual is wrong.

O'Brien: On a practical level, in film, what's generally considered pornographic is what comes out with an X rating. And the decisionmaking process of the ratings board is not governed by any "meta" discourse on the function of images or the nature of objectification, but by specific shot content. Can you talk about your experiences with the rating of *Working Girls?*

Borden: The politics of X ratings have to do with what is forbidden. Interestingly, the functions of a woman's body are more taboo in this culture than are images of violence. Violence generated by men onto women—rapes, beatings, etc.—are regarded as normal and therefore are not given an X rating. Both *Working Girls* and *Angel Heart* were at the ratings board at the same time. What they objected to in *Angel Heart* and finally ended up cutting was Mickey Rourke's bare ass pumping as he lay on top of Lisa Bonet with blood falling on them. They finally cut twelve frames from the shot. But the board allowed shots insinuating a woman's disembowelment and a woman getting shot with a gun up her crotch . . . shots which seem obscene to me.

With *Working Girls,* the ratings board unofficially told us we needed to make about thirty cuts. Some were from the sex scenes, for example in the scene with "Fantasy Fred" where Fred pushes Molly's head down so it looks as if she's going to give him a blow job. His sexual organs are underneath the film frame but the implication is clear. But many were shots involving hygiene . . . shots of inserting a diaphragm, washing out a diaphragm filled with blood, putting a used condom into kleenex. I was amazed the ratings board considered these to be X-rated! What was obscene to them were the birth control shots—condoms and diaphragms.

O'Brien: . . . and the blow job.

Borden: And the blow job. Exactly. I refused to make the cuts—I wouldn't have had a film left—so we released the film unrated. This was only a problem in Cleveland, where the *Plain Dealer* refused to run our ads. They had run ads for unrated *foreign* films, since these were automatically seen as "art" movies. There was no way to convince them that an American film about prostitution had any art value. Ironically, the film ended up doing well there, because all the radio deejays took up the cause, seeing this as a form of censorship.

O'Brien: You have moved from making a very low budget film, to getting access to the studios for distribution of your films, and now possibly for the financing of new projects. Can you talk about what this change means in terms of the control you are able to maintain over new projects? Do you think it's possible to maintain any political intentions in your work?

Borden: It would be impossible to do an experimental film like *Born in Flames* for more money than it cost. But I do believe political films can be made, on the scale of John Sayles's films, for example. Spike Lee's films are political and he has a built-in audience. So he will keep getting financing for his films, even if they make heavy political statements and scare a lot of white people. It's only economic viability that gives you more economic viability.

With *Working Girls* I had absolute control. I had control over the script, the shooting, the editing, and control over the distribution. What I'm finding is that many industry people were interested in *Working Girls*—in me—simply because they saw a small film make a profit. A lot of studios said they wanted my next film, until they saw the kinds of ideas I was interested in, domination, masochism, abortion. It's like the stories about a studio asking Jim Jarmusch to direct a sequel to Porky's. What could possibly make them think he would want to do that? Same thing with me. I get all of these supposedly feminist vehicles which are really about whether a woman should marry for love or for money.

I feel I'm in a bind. I don't want to be caught in a film ghetto, where grant money has to be scraped together and viewers are limited to the already empathetic. I keep hoping for greater universality. But if you want to go to the other side of the spectrum—making more expensive films for a wider audience—you have to dilute your ideas to such a degree that you're lucky if you can present anything radical or edgy. So "Hollywood"—large studios—seems to be out of the question for me. But there are smaller companies, here and in Europe, that aren't as afraid of tough or political content. But even these companies exercise a lot of control over your work. And they're getting more conservative all the time.

O'Brien: Jutta Bruckner has written that she and other German feminist film-makers learned a valuable lesson from earlier political art movements: art can never be a sufficient substitute for a social movement.* In this culture, can one's politics be contained in a film? Or do they need to be connected to some larger movement in order to provide a context for viewing?

Borden: I think you do have to create a context for your movies. I don't think difficult movies can be put out there with no dialogue about them. The more obscure a movie is, the more you have to explain. People need help in decoding a film if it isn't like anything they have seen before. What I have done with *Born in Flames* and *Working Girls* is travel with the films in order to talk to audiences, writers, and reviewers. And what's interesting is that people tend to write what you say. It gives them a way into the film.

I also agree that film—or art—can only contribute to a general atmosphere of political thinking—it can't bring about social change. It *can* inspire dialogue and introduce possibilities. It can't substitute for direct political work. But being actually tied to a movement can be problematic because you're often forced into a party line. And this feels antithetical to being an artist, for whom ideas are often contradictory.

There are certain issues I will go on the line for. After *Working Girls* I did political work for prostitutes. I went on talk shows to argue for the decriminalization of prostitution. But if people see you as a political filmmaker, all of a sudden they see you as someone who can comment on a variety of issues. Somehow you're liable to be seen as a "public figure," like someone who is running for public office. My issues are very specific. I only feel qualified to comment about issues I've studied carefully, usually as research for making a film.

I have nothing but admiration for real political workers because their work is harder than making movies and more frustrating. At least at the end of making a movie you have an object to show for it. The problem with political work is that it's endless and relentless and always seems to involve compromise. What I try to do in my films is give a voice to people whose voices are not often heard and hope this can color people's thinking . . . just a little bit.

---

* Jutta Bruckner, "Women Behind the Camera," in *Feminist Aesthetics*, ed. by Gisela Ecker, trans. by Harriet Anderson (Boston: Beacon Press, 1985), 120-124.

Of Donatello and Reagan
Charles L. Mee, Jr.

One function of art—though not the only one—is to preserve clarity. Art can do this by keeping those in power from appropriating the symbols, myths, and language of the culture to serve their interests.

I think of the Reagan administration appropriating the statue of liberty as a symbol of the administration. So, even while the administration closed the borders to immigration and the stripped the statue of its meaning, it converted the statue into a symbol of patriotism, empty boosterism, dazzle, bigness, and strength.

It is the job of rulers to rout and confuse potential opponents by converting symbols into their opposite meaning, or into irrelevant references to make it impossible for the opposition to think clearly.

One of the most splendid examples of this phenomenon is Donatello's fifteenth-century sculpture of David. The statue stands for the triumph of little David over the giant Goliath. It was commissioned by the oligarchy of Florence to celebrate the Florentine victory over the Duke of Milan in 1402.

The nice trick in this is that the oligarchy that beat the Duke of Milan had also just put down a revolt of Florentine workers in 1378, the Ciompi Revolt. The workers had thought of themselves as the little guys rising up against the big guys. But after 1402 the oligarchy declared themselves the representatives of the little guys beating an even bigger guy. And the sculpture of David was their symbol—sculpted again and again during the fifteenth century.

So the sculpture of David became the symbol not of the little guy who beat the big guy but of the group of powerful merchants who destroyed the Florentine Republic and kept the workers in their places.

The moral of the story is that it is not enough for artists to create new symbols; they must also keep ownership of the old one and not let them be recast in ways that confuse. In this respect, I guess, art and history serve the same purpose—to preserve honest facts, feelings, and meanings in order to make possible clear thought and understanding.

Charles L. Mee, Jr.

Charles L. Mee, Jr. is a playwright and historian whose books include *Rembrandt's Portrait*, *The Genius of the People*, and *Meeting at Potsdam*. His recent theatre works include a four-play cycle, *The American Century: The Constitutional Convention, The Sequel*; *The Investigation Into the Murder in El Salvador*; *The War to End War*; and *The Imperialists at Club Cave Canem*.

The Homeless Vehicle Project
Krzysztof Wodiczko and David Lurie

Statement

I would like to believe that my work in design or night projections all can be understood as *interventions* in the city, intended to provide critical dimension to the urban experience. Work done in the city, if it's going to be critical and effective, has to question and challenge the way the city operates for most of its inhabitants as an alienating environment in which social and individual concerns and experiences do not correspond to the state and real-estate spatial symbolism. (For a critical discussion on the position of public art in the present urban crisis, see Rosalyn Deutsche, "Uneven Development: Public Art in New York City" *October* 47, Winter 1988.)

Dominant culture in all of its forms and aesthetic practices, in what it says and in what it does not say, remains in gross contradiction to the lived experiences, communicative needs, and rights of most of society, whose labor is its sole base. It projects and imposes its "life-in-fantasy" version of reality not only by means of mass communication media such as TV and press, but also by the Built Environment.

The prime occupation of architectural structures is to appear still and permanently rooted to the ground, abstaining from any visible movement. This static occupation—this annexation of time and territory—creates both a dynamic and a somnambulistic social effect. Circulating around and between buildings and monuments, we are unable to concentrate and critically focus on their bodies. This establishes an absent-minded relation to the "public space"; a dangerously

Krzysztof Wodiczko

Krzysztof Wodiczko has been producing public projections internationally since 1980. His recent projections in New York, Boston, La Jolla, CA, and Tijuana, Mexico, have been concerned with issues of homelessness and immigration. He has also been working on his "Homeless Vehicle Project." His new work, "New York City Tableaux," are interior slide installations addressing the expanding war between the city and the homeless.

Projection on the Soldiers and Sailors Memorial on the Boston Common, Boston, Massachusetts, Krzysztof Wodiczko, New Year's Eve, 1987. Photo courtesy of Hal Bromm Gallery, New York.

unconscious contact, a passive gaze through which we unknowingly absorb its psycho-political agenda.

By imposing our permanent circulation and our absent-minded perception, by ordering our gaze, by structuring our unconscious, by embodying our desire, by masking and mythifying the relations of power, and by operating under the discrete camouflage of a cultural and aesthetic "background," the Built Environment constitutes an effective instrument and ideological medium designed for the benefit of those who want to control and manage the social relations of space.

At the same time, the old urban environment is being fragmented through a process of merciless "redevelopment" which destroys lower-income housing, isolates urban communities, evicts residents, and causes new ghettos. The logic of the new real estate economy creates self-contained environments, citadels for the urban wealthy (such as Battery Park "City"); where they will not have to be inconvenienced by interactions with the others. In the face of these social processes and alienating spatial conditions, the city loses its capability to operate as a communicative environment.

In order to counter this, we must act on the city-state and real-estate space and *use it* as a medium of communication. The artist can bring critical meaning to and encourage social life in gentrifying urban zones by confronting and embarrassing them with facts and issues of which they are a part, but from which they want to insulate themselves.

For example, we in New York City are witnessing a growing restriction of access to public spaces, their transformation into pseudo-public spaces. The homeless (the evicts) are being removed from the public parks that have become their last refuge, and thus removed from the sight of the city's most significant symbolic structures: the statues of Washington, Lafayette, Lincoln, and others. These memorials and monuments, which were built to

Fragments of Interviews with Homeless Consultants

Oscar: . . . See, this doesn't have to be a complicated matter . . . because it can be cheaply made . . . . Traffic won't be a pain in the neck, the police won't hassle you about having such a long vehicle . . . . You can crawl inside, you can sit up, you can lay down, you can keep your personal belongings.

Victor: Make another drawing. Like I told you before, the cart a little higher than this, two feet longer than this, have a top over here that you can open and close, and still have this space for somebody to lay down and stay away from the wind and cold. People lay down here with this closed, ain't nobody going to steal anything or come around bothering anybody.

*   *   *

Alvin: What I'm saying is those snowcone carts use glass on top, and for you, for your safety, for you to sleep . . .

Krzysztof: You're saying it's better if you're visible,

commemorate heroes of liberation, the flight to freedom, civil liberties, and the right of the individual to the pursuit of happiness are, in this process, themselves "evicted" from the realities of contemporary life. The statues can no longer see what is happening in front of them, and we cannot see how astonished *they* must be to see that this is not the society which they envisioned. Prevented from such contemporary critical reflections, the monuments are dying as significant symbols. Historic sites become de-historicized commodities of gentrification, merely sentimental decorations representing "the past."

The meaning of city monuments—whether intentional or unintentional, historic or contemporary—must be secured today through the ability of the inhabitants to project and superimpose their critical thoughts and reflections on the "bodies" of monuments and buildings. Not to speak through these structures is to abandon them and to abandon ourselves, losing both a sense of history and of the present.

This agenda of reopening public spheres of discourse is not only social or political or activist, it is also an aesthetic mission. Just as the contemporary city is dominated by the spatial articulation of the real estate aesthetic, the evicts from this culture-as-environment need their own kind of counter architecture. The Homeless Vehicle Project (HVP) on which David Lurie and I are working, represents the resistance of evicted architecture against evicting architecture. It is designed to literally break through the boundaries between economically segregated urban communities. As it penetrates space, it also establishes a provocative medium of communication between homeless and non-homeless.

The middle classes are well trained as consumers. As good consumers, they know how to quickly and accurately evaluate the "value" of every new

so people know you are there, rather than hidden.

Alvin: Yes. What about if someone gets mad or something? At least they could see that somebody's in there. There's a lot of, you know, crazy motherfuckers on the street, too.

*   *   *

Krzysztof: So this length is a little shorter and narrower than a standard bed, because we don't want this too large.

Oscar: Right, you've got to be able to keep it consumption size. If you have it too bulky, the person operating it will have a lot of problems.

Krzysztof: Meaning weight?

Oscar: Not the weight; but police, traffic, people in general.

*   *   *

Alvin: This is where most of us get it now—from post offices and shopping centers. Most poor people that are traveling do not have money—that's why Safeway stores have been taken from. And that's why a lot of other functional and symbolic form that appears before their commodity-tuned eyes. Every time we see a tool, we look at its shape, its details, its movements, and its position in a particular environment. We guess what it does, who would use it, and what situation creates the need for it. How important is it to have it? If we have not seen such a tool before, we are curiously surprised by its appearance. We examine each movement of its operator in relation to the movement of the tool. We notice how the tool transforms its environment and wonder what this means to the user, and to us.

I realized the importance of this when the vehicle was tested on the streets. Many non-evicts were engaged and approached to ask, "What is this for?" These same people see evicted individuals every day and *never* ask questions. Now they are provoked to ask questions *through* the object.

—Krzysztof Wodiczko

*   *   *

Homeless Vehicle Project

A large portion of New York City's estimated 70,000 homeless people in the winter of 1987-88 was made up of homeless individuals. Unlike families with children, they are not given priority for placement in the city's transitional housing facilities or in welfare hotel rooms. Instead, they are offered space in the growing system of dormitory shelters; dangerous and unfriendly places that impose a dehumanizing, even prison-like regimentation on residents. Their alternative has been to develop a means of survival on the streets.

The fact that people are compelled to live on streets is unacceptable. But failing to recognize the reality of people's situations or holding up the fact of their living on the streets as proof of their universal insanity is a morally and factually untenable position. This recognition of every individual's need and right to permanent housing

people have been losing their shopping carts.

Oscar: A good time to collect is summertime—a very beautiful time—when you have festivals, parades, and so much activity. The weather's nice, there's lots of outdoor drinking—restaurants, clubs, what have you.

*   *   *

Oscar: There is no way in hell you can have an empty cart. Once you start collecting, there's a can laying on every street that you walk down. I can empty the whole cart right now, and as soon as I empty it, there'll be a can right there. So you gonna dump it? Of course, you're gonna take it!

Ian: Where do you take the cans once you fill up the cart? What's the nearest place from here, for instance?

Oscar: Oh, wow, you've got a long way.

Ian: That's why you've got to do 500 cans.

Oscar: Right, then it's worth it. You've got to take a walk, take the stuff out, box it up, then possibly stand in line. Somewhere

Photos by François Alacoque

must also lead to an examination of the immediate needs of homeless people.

Our proposed vehicle is designed to play a role in filling a dangerous gap in the need for shelter. It seeks to be of use to the significant number of individuals who will, for the foreseeable future, continue to be compelled to live a nomadic life in the urban environment, and it addresses the specific limitations and compromises imposed by this existence. Though it cannot appropriately be called a home, the vehicle is a potential means of ameliorating the conditions of life for people surviving under trying circumstances.

Although in our daily encounters with homeless people we are aware of their status as refugees, we generally fail to recognize that they are refugees from the physical transformation of the city itself. The dominant notion of the homeless as mere objects largely explains why we allow people to live and die on our streets without doing much to help them. In a television forum, columnist George Will argued that the presence of ragged masses camped out in front of midtown New York office buildings was an infringement on the legitimate rights of executives working there. In Will's view, dodging the bodies of homeless persons and enduring their incessant demands for small change is an unnecessary addition to the already stressful lives of businessmen. In their familiar position of supplication and helplessness, homeless individuals do not stake a claim to the territory that has been taken from them. They are reduced to mere observers of the remaking of their neighborhoods for others. Their homelessness appears as a natural condition, the cause is disassociated from its consequence, and the status of the homeless as legitimate members of the urban community is not recognized.

Through the use of adapted, appropriated vehicles, some homeless individuals have managed to develop a means of economic sustenance in the along the line, we can talk about an idea I have—I'd like to open up a redemption center. There's a few ideas I have to make life easier for the bottle-can man.

*   *   *

Oscar: Alright, this is the front of the vehicle. This right here is the opening of the front, right? This is where I'd put my bottles; you get more bottles than anything else.

Krzysztof: And plastic bags on top?

Oscar: No, if possible, cans and plastics; but you see, you have beer cans, tall and small, tall cans, little cans, soda cans. So you want to keep your soda cans to the soda cans, tall cans with tall cans, little cans to little cans, glass with glass, beer bottles with beer bottles.

*   *   *

Oscar: The person picking up bottles, cans, whatever, also has a tendency to pick up clothes, books, magazines. I can show you. This is what—November? This is a November magazine. 1987. Magazine—October, city. These people, commonly called scavengers, but who are in fact *evicts,* have become commonplace, especially since the bottle bill went into effect in 1983. Their visibly purposive movement through the city gives them an identity as actors in the urban space. Unlike the immobile figure, whose status is provisional and ambiguous, the scavenger stakes a claim to space in the city and to membership in the urban community.

This shelter vehicle attempts to function usefully in the context of New York City street life. Its point of departure is the strategy of survival that urban nomads presently utilize. Through discussions with them, a proposal for a vehicle to be used both for personal shelter and can and bottle collection and storage was developed. An earlier design was modified according to their criticisms and suggestions. This project is not put forward as a finished product, ready for use on the street, nor is it intended for mass production. Rather, it is conceived as a starting point for further collaboration between skilled designers and potential users, and both parties will have to play roles in the design and production of future versions of the vehicle.

1987. You see, people read these magazines and throw them out, but somebody else might not have read that magazine.

*   *   *

Oscar: You want the simplest way to unload your cart, get everything processed, get your money and get out. As soon as you turn that first corner you come to, there's another can—you can actually work in a circle. I could circle this park three times and come up with shit every time. . . . I only work specific little areas, I don't have to work too far . . . . I can fill up one cart in one block.

The signifying function of the vehicle is as important as its strictly utilitarian purpose. The form of address—the design of the vehicle—articulates the conditions of homeless existence to the non-homeless, even conditions that the non-homeless may not wish to recognize. This allows the homeless to be seen not as objects without human status, but rather as users and operators of equipment whose form articulates the conditions of their existence. It attempts to function as a visual analogue to everyday objects of consumption and merchandising (such as food vendor carts).

The vehicle bears a resemblance to a weapon. In our view, the movements of carts through New York City are acts of resistance, opposing the continuing ruination of an urban community that excludes thousands of people from even the most meager means of life.

*   *   *

The photographs presented here were taken during tests of the homeless vehicle that were conducted in April, 1989 in Tompkins Square Park, on the streets of the

East Village, in Central Park, on Fifth Avenue between the Park Plaza Hotel and Trump Plaza, in Battery Park City, and in the Wall Street area. The tests, conducted with the help of Pierre, a resident of Tompkins Square Park, concentrated on recent modifications to components of the vehicle: larger front wheels; much larger rear wheels placed closer to the point of balance of the vehicle for improved maneuverability; an additional support mechanism and brake for stability and security in "sleeping" and "resting" positions; an enlarged "seat" section (which also functions as a toilet seat) on the collapsible handle; reinforcement of the main structural components; the new shape of the back of the vehicle for easier collecting; the use of semi-translucent reinforced plexiglass (Laxan) for two of the three sections of the "roof" of the vehicle; curtains for privacy; other functional and technical improvements to the "nose" of the vehicle; a new fire escape; and other safety and security features.

Subsequent stages of the project will involve, in collaboration with homeless consultants, who will also have to agree to act as operators, the examination of functioning in the "sleeping" position at night, as well as the building of several vehicles for use in a collective habitat configuration.

During the Tompkins Square presentation of the vehicle, many homeless expressed interest in using the vehicle and in becoming members of the manufacturing workshop to be organized this fall.

Projection on the Art Gallery of New South Wales, Sydney, Australia, Krzysztof Wodiczko, 1982. Photo courtesy of Hal Bromm Gallery, New York.

Twenty-one Gun Salute

Richard Posner

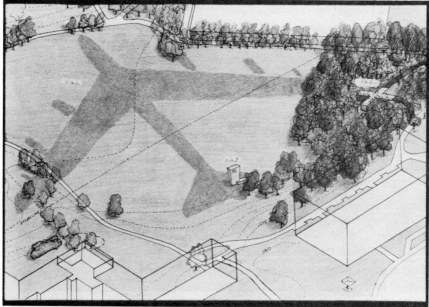

"Kent State University May 4 Memorial." The (proposed) Memorial consists of a living grass shadow, a hillside viewing platform, and markers which locate where the four students fell and nine others were wounded. The May 4 memorial calls for a living grass shadow of a B-52 airplane spread across the Commons area of the University; a spatial and temporal reminder of the shadow of war (American B-52 bombing of Cambodia) which engulfed the campus and the nation on May 4, 1970. As the grass shadow goes through seasonal cycles, the grass shadow will flower during the spring and summer months; and, via submerged heat-tracing elements, become a ghostly outline of the B-52 in the winter snow. Made with the assistance of Landscape Architects Galen Cranz and Barbara Swift; architect Kevin Ryden; and artist Ginny Ruffner.

Memorial Day 1984

1. My ears just popped following the 3,000-mile flight from Washington state to Washington D.C. I've been at the Capitol Mall since dawn. Six ebony horses, a caisson filled with the remains of the unknown soldier from the American war in Southeast Asia, and a riderless mare bearing a saber with a pair of boots reversed in the stirrups are about to come down Constitution Avenue. It isn't even 9 a.m. The temperature is already ninety degrees.

2. The mechanical hiss of the Constitution Gardens sprinkler system reminds me of a sound heard every night on the six o'clock news fifteen years ago—helicopters ferrying troops in and out of the jungle.

3. I mention this to a nearby soda-pop vendor. He nods and fishes out a dog-eared photograph from his shirt pocket. The picture twists in the breeze to reveal "ARVN [Army of the Republic of Vietnam] Ranger 1967" penciled on the back side. It is a studio portrait of him as a young boy in a freshly pressed uniform, with an ear-to-ear grin and a bad case of acne. He studies my reaction; an unlit cigarette bobs from his lower lip.

4. Courtesy of the National Parks Service, "Chariots of Fire" blares from loudspeakers set atop the Vietnam Veterans Memorial. This just makes the military bands play louder as they march past.

Richard Posner

On Halloween, 1970, upon completion of 44 months of alternative service as a conscientious objector, running a four-county literacy program in Hazard, Kentucky, Richard Posner received an honorable discharge from the Selective Service system. A Fulbright scholar and a National Endowment for the Arts fellow, Posner's public artwork focuses on the relationship between the institutions which shape and define American society and the people they serve. An artist's book, *Intervention and Alchemy: A Public Art Primer,* was recently published by the Division of Visual Arts, The First Bank, in Minneapolis. Richard Posner lives in St. Paul.

5. The breeze disappears as I walk down alongside the Memorial. The 57,939 names of the American war dead are cast in deep shadow. They read like cuneiform scars in the black granite skin. The muffled roar of National Airport jets reinforce the feeling of being inside a bunker.

6. " . . . The names are not listed alphabetically," a guide tells tourists, "but in chronological order of death, as the Vietnam Conflict was never an 'official' war."

7. "When the three soldiers are installed next year, will they be reflected in the Wall?" a man with a heavy European accent asks. "Will one of the bronze soldiers be a woman?" his companion inquires. The tour guide does not hear the questions.

8. A few feet away, a sign-language interpreter translates the exchange to her group of deaf visitors. A woman nearby pauses before making a rubbing and presses her palms over a name on the Wall, as if to perform an act of divine healing.

9. A boom box moves through the crowd commanding everyone to "reach out and touch someone."

10. Dozens of plastic Veterans of Foreign Wars (VFW) Buddy Poppies shaped like American flags are beginning to melt in the noonday sun.

11. As the procession approaches, men jockey for better snapshot positions to shoot the unknown.

12. A Black vet in full military dress stands in silent vigil. "PEACE WITH HONOR" is crudely painted in four-inch-high white tempera letters across the front of his uniform. Bystanders stare away at the ground, as if not to notice.

13. Against a nearby tree, Steve Canyon pursues a pair of Asian double agents across a discarded Sunday newspaper comics section.

14. An elderly couple in matching plaid pantsuits, slumped on a park bench, listen to the parade with a shared transistor radio.

15. In the distance, sweethearts in paddle boats glide across the tidal basin past the Jefferson Memorial.

16. "Mr. T," the TV-vet, sprints from a chauffeur-driven limo up the Lincoln Memorial steps. Decked out in chains, feathers, and fatigues, he shakes hands and signs autographs beneath the shadow of the great emancipator.

17. Midway across the Fourteenth Street bridge, a little girl asks, "Daddy, did you notice Lincoln's hands form 'A' and 'L' in sign language?"

18. The funeral procession enters Arlington. The sound of mules' hooves mix with police walkie-talkie static, only to be shattered moments later by the honor guard's fusillade.

19. My ears still ring that evening on the return flight home. At 30,000 feet over the Midwest, passengers watch the in-flight movie, *Trading Places,* while vets in the rear cabin sort rubbings made from the 1,001 Evergreen State names carved on the Wall.

20. I pick up an emergency exit card that has fallen to the floor. It brings to mind a note left at the Wall: "The unknown was my old lady. She was a nurse blown away by friendly fire three days after Thanksgiving, 1967, near Phuoc-Lac in Bien-Hoa Province." The flight attendant calls for tray tables and seat backs to be brought to the upright and locked positions, as I slip the emergency exit card back into place.

21. While the 747 bounces onto the runway, the man next to me removes his luggage from the overhead bin. With briefcase and overcoat in hand, he inquires if I'm here on business or pleasure, but walks down the aisle before I can reply.

Postscript: Veterans Day 1985

"You know where a boy can get any pussy in this town?" asks a young marine on the red-eye Flyer bus from Dulles Airport into the District of Columbia. The wet night traffic reflects off his class ring, which glows in each oncoming pair of headlights.

Bus terminal newspaper headlines announce plans to build a museum at the Vietnam Veterans Memorial to house momentoes left at the Wall. Lest the sacred become profane, the prayers Jerusalem pilgrims leave at the Wailing Wall are burned annually. National Park Service employees, however, dutifully shrink-wrap, catalogue, and tag every nonperishable item left at the Wall. Since 1982, thousands of articles have been warehoused awaiting future enshrinement.

I hail a cab to visit a friend's name. In the past eighteen months, one hundred and ten names have been added to the Wall. While searching the directory, I stumble across Rambo. John Arthur Rambo, from Montana, Panel 16W / Line 126. As I reach toward his name, my arm casts a flickering shadow. For a moment the Wall seems like a hearth.

The "Three Servicemen" statue, installed last Veterans Day, is illuminated by staccato flashes from a dozen tourists' Polaroid cameras. Rumor has it this bronze threesome may soon have company. Additional nurse and K9 Corps memorials are currently under consideration. Another curious, yet unmistakably military salute to man's best friends: the Beauty and the Beast.

There are nearly 300 Vietnam memorials are in the planning stage, under construction, or already built across the United States. These range from classical stadium brass plaques to traffic island bronze nativity creches.

Missing-in-action from much of this commemorative sculpture, however, is the element of prophesy. Not fire and brimstone prophesy. More a simple reminder and a warning: The dead can speak. The *Vietnam* war cannot be abracadabraed into a Noble Cause.

"Twenty-one Gun Salute" is part of a larger work in progress, *The Unpopular Front: An Oral History of Vietnam Era Conscientious Objection*. Thanks to MacDowell Colony, Ragdale Colony, and the Virginia Center for Creative Arts.

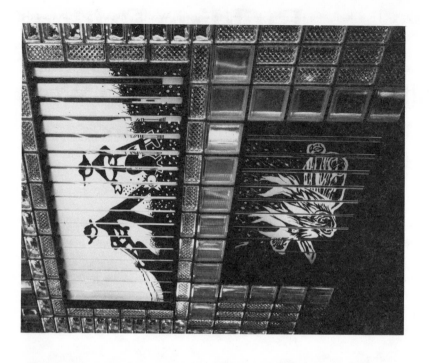

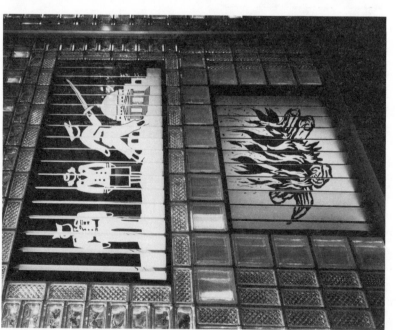

"The Veterans Lobby" is a 900 square-foot glass hearth commissioned by the Veterans Administration Art-in-Architecture Program as the main entry for the new Seattle VA Medical Center; begun March 1982 and completed January 1986. As visitors enter the lobby, they walk past a pair of illuminated three-dimensional murals set into glass block walls (slides No. 1 and No. 2 are 45° angle views of the north wall). Viewer-activated, a glass fire glows inside the fireplace when people pass; while above the mantel, a sword-bearing soldier becomes a farmer behind a plow. The images reverse as visitors exit the hospital. Made in cooperation with the NBBJ Architects.

Building Bridges
Voices of Dissent and the Culture of Cultural Work
Mat Schwarzman

Throughout our country's history, artists have asserted their right to free speech through their art. Their words, images, and music have cried out against injustice, and defined our vision of a better world. Now, as part of the 200th anniversary of the Constitution, the Painted Bride Art Center and Big Small Theater, along with twenty-one other local cultural organizations, have come together to celebrate this tradition and its role in shaping American society. We invite you to join us. . . .

Statement from VOD publicity materials

Introduction

Most of the progressive cultural organizing in this country is done around issues of particular interest to the Left: Central America, peace, civil rights, the environment, etc. Rarely, though, do we organize around July Fourth, Columbus Day, or some other civic holiday (what I call in the context of this article "public celebrations"). These times when agendas ranging from radical to reactionary must acknowledge some level of common identity are, for the most part, consigned to the broom closet of

Mat Schwarzman

Mathew Schwarzman is the director of the Cultural Activism program at the New College of California in San Francisco. He was the project director for the first phase of Voices of Dissent.

progressive organizing work: either we ignore them completely or we exploit them as another occasion to criticize the mainstream and the Right. My argument is that they are also vastly underexploited openings for us to build stronger ties between the Left's disparate "issue communities" and to offer progressive visions to a much broader audience.

The reasons behind this preference for staying within clearly circumscribed

331

boundaries in order to criticize the dominant power structure are understandable. Like most people, Leftists are much more confident on our own turf. But like the kid who punches once and runs home, we're also in danger of ending up with no friends to play with, or, at the very least, being pegged as bullies. Much of our concern is *extremely* valid: my intent is not to make light of the resources and determination of those against us, or to suggest that the Left should stop criticizing the excesses and inadequacies of the system. But from a strategic standpoint, we must utilize all the tools at our command, and one of those is public celebration.

In an effort to encourage more efforts within this sphere, I'd like to share with you some of the questions raised during the organizing process behind the *Voices of Dissent* project. These questions are not unique to organizing public celebrations; it's just that, under these circumstances, they get a little hairier.

*   *   *

As in most cities, the alternative cultural community in Philadelphia is not nearly as organized as it could or should be, and political activists and cultural activists work exclusively of one another. Mark O'Brien and I had been part of a struggling political theater, the Big Small Theater, for several years in this climate; we had become increasingly frustrated and, quite frankly, lonely. We seemed cut off from our community, our history, and ourselves.

It was September, 1985 and the 200th anniversary of the Constitution was fast approaching. Maybe, we thought, we could gather the progressive cultural and political communities together around the idea of a political art festival celebrating 200 years of progressive cultural work.

As we began envisioning what such a project might actually be like, we realized another, equally important reason for doing it: not only to celebrate our history, but to counteract the corporate interpretation of American history that was going to be put forward by the official "We the People 200" group. We knew that under the rubric of "Freedom of Speech" (wave the American flag closest to you, please) we would have a better chance at the eyes and ears of Ms. and Mr. Philadelphia than would come along for a while. It would be one of the few times the notion of "dissent" would be sanctioned in theory; it was our intention to make it evident in practice.

All photos in this chapter are from the Voices of Dissent Festival and Conference, April 1987. Photos by Holly Strahan and others.

First we identified three possible audiences: the arts community; the political activist community; and Ms. and Mr. Philadelphia, in that order of priority. We explored a number of options for serving these very different groups, but soon realized a monolithic approach could not work. Either we would create events that dealt with specific cultural issues to attract the first group, which would bore the second group and alienate the third; or we would focus on connecting art with activism to interest the second group, thereby limiting interest from the first group and still alienating the third; or we'd try and reach a common denominator with the third and end up with a vaguely progressive "We the People 200" clone, which wouldn't mean anything to anybody. After several weeks of deliberation, we hit on the idea of designing *different segments of the project for different audiences.* It may not sound revolutionary, but for us this was a freeing concept that allowed us to think much more creatively and clearly. After more discussions, this overall plan emerged:

> a) a three-day conference targeted specifically for the cultural and political activist community; and
>
> b) a month-long festival with post-performance discussions to interest and inform the general public—these events would be built around activities at the Painted Bride Art Center, our sponsor, but would be spread throughout the city.

Now all we needed was some help and money to make these wonderful ideas happen.

From the beginning, it was evident we needed and wanted a lot of others to be involved. We organized an advisory group of ten scholars, activists, and artists to map out the general outlines of the conference program and to provide lists of prospective speakers and participants. The word was beginning to get out, and it was coming back to us: people seemed genuinely excited. It was nine months before the project would begin, and time for us to organize a town meeting to invite others to participate.

Looking back on that first meeting, it was a very good thing there was a group of us by that time to share the flak. Fifty people came for a two-hour meeting that spread into four. Some people loved us, some hated us, but it was clear we'd touched a nerve. A vocal group of political artists disapproved of the fact that so much was in place already; were they being asked to help as peers, or as drones? A more restrained but equally determined group of arts administrators thought our proposal too vague and wanted to know more before they'd agree to help. Some left, finding us not what

they expected. Most stayed, and they began talking about organizing a Tax Day Parade, a series of Constitutional radio and television spots, a Spring Equinox performance/procession/celebration, and many other possibilities, and they wanted to know how much money we had in our budget for such projects. Suddenly the question loomed: now that we had them here, what to do with all this energy?

The best strategy in these situations is to establish some ground rules right off the bat: state clearly and honestly which areas are complete and which still need input; be willing to admit that the planning has advanced to a certain point and that input are needed to go further; have a solid but expansive organizational structure in place that enables people to take different types and amounts of responsibility. We didn't realize all this right away, of course. But with help from members of what we came to call "The Community Support Group," we did alright. The group split into several committees: fundraising, outreach, conference workshops, documentation, and special projects. Within these they formed subcommittees, charged with everything from organizing a conference workshop on bannermaking, to a Tax Day Parade, to alternative radio and television "Bicentennial Minutes," to raising the $10,000 to pay for all this. We allotted each committee an amount of money from the VOD budget (from $100 to $1,000 each) and asked that they meet about every third week.

It takes more time to generate and maintain a group like this than might be expected, so be sure you know why you're creating one. To be effective, each subgroup must have some sort of coordinator who's willing to arrange meetings and provide a communications link between the subgroup, the whole group, and the staff. Then someone on the staff (in our case, our newly hired Assistant Project Director, Jenney Milner) should have the specific responsibility of providing administrative support for their efforts. There will inevitably be ebbs and flows in the energy of such volunteer groups. These periods must be attended to, and sometimes just weathered. But if a main goal of your project is to build a community, then this is progressive public relations work at its most important; that is, finding out what your audience needs and wants and providing a mechanism for their involvement in making it happen.

On the fundraising front, a new challenge appeared: whom were we willing to get money from? We had already applied to, or were in the process of applying to, several government agencies and private foundations with progressive funding histories. But given the patriotic nature of our project, it wasn't unrealistic to think we could

get money from far more conservative—and wealthier—sources. Several members of the new Community Support Group were urging us to apply to those sources, arguing that as long as we didn't let their agendas affect ours, "Why shouldn't we screw them for as much as we could?"

Under other circumstances, I might well have agreed. Different projects demand a certain amount of pragmatic flexibility. The issues in this case: What is the funder's actual record on the environment, labor relations, etc.? How will your concern for their support affect the project? Will their support of your project bolster a deservedly bad public image? They have to be looked at as carefully and honestly as possible. Fortunately, watchdog groups (such as the Council on Economic Priorities in New York City) exist that can help in these matters.

Left cultural organizers quickly become accustomed to going through the foundation directory and automatically eliminating the corporations; the vast majority support only operas, ballet, and major theatre companies. They have no interest whatsoever in "political art." Why should they? But with the impending Constitutional celebration, it was suddenly acceptable to dissent. Through someone in our group, we found an executive who was willing to anonymously donate the use of a flatbed truck for our Tax Day Parade. The fact that his company was also a major defense contractor would have, under normal circumstances, prohibited his helping us, but as I said, who could turn down the Constitution? I described what the event was going to be, carefully leaving out specifics that might only serve to upset him. The event went well and we were covered by the local media. The next day I got a hysterical phone call from him: "You tricked me!" When I calmly asked him how I had done that, he told me to look at the newspaper photo showing a man dressed as Uncle Sam wearing a hat made of ICBMs standing on the flatbed. I did, and suddenly noticed that Uncle Sam was pointing to the corporate logo proudly emblazoned on the door of the truck. "Someone in my company found out that I authorized this, and I'm about to lose my job!" It was the first time I experienced the feeling of my heart dropping into my bowel. He told me about how hard and long he'd worked to get where he'd gotten in his company, and about his family, mentioning each soon-to-be indigent member by name. In the end I learned he didn't lose his job; I, however, learned a potent lesson about playing hardball in this world of shared public celebration, and the danger of getting what you wish for.

For organizers working on public celebrations, the questions of funding are particularly thorny. The terrain we're trying to traverse, namely, the very nature of

shared public identity, is hotly contested; and we're in constant danger of being transformed by the mainstream instead of the other way around. We decided that, in this case, getting money from public agencies was dangerous enough.

We debated at long length on the relationship between the VOD festival and the constituent arts institutions. We could: 1) give grants to in effect "hire" each institution to produce events with our approval; 2) negotiate a shared co-sponsor relationship with each of them; or 3) convince the institutions to produce works on their own that reflected our theme of "Free Speech in the Arts."

While in some ways the third choice seemed the most limited politically, economically it was the only possibility; we had barely enough money to hire our assistant project director, let alone start producing major arts events. We sent out letters and made appointments with thirty-five local arts institutions, ranging from a mainstream opera company to community arts centers, in an attempt to persuade them to either schedule VOD-type programming, or, if they'd already planned appropriate events, to simply let us list them on our calendar. As a result, the festival for the most part was an eclectic collection of programs brought together under the title of Voices of Dissent.

I'd hoped that we could organize a more thematically unified set of events, but once April came I realized that there were distinct benefits to structuring the festival in this way. As sole producer of the festival events, VOD would have been perceived as a monied outsider simply foisting its liberal agenda on arts organizations too needy to turn us down. As it turned out, with the institutions producing themselves, the VOD umbrella helped to transform the context in which they themselves and their audiences perceived the events taking place: for the first time, twenty-one arts organizations across Philadelphia were working together, presenting events linked by a common thematic thread. Local (and some national) media covered us extensively, and a major reason for their interest was the concept that this diverse group of institutions was able to work together. In effect, the structure of Voices of Dissent became as much a political statement as its thematic content.

The Painted Bride Art Center, fortunately, remained a place where we had a greater opportunity to apply our personal vision of Voices of Dissent. The "Bride" (as it's affectionately known) is a twenty-year-old organization with an impressive, if rugged, past. It began as a visual art gallery in a bridal shop on South Street, Philadelphia's answer to Greenwich Village during the 1970s. It moved several times, and acquired a broad, multidisciplinary scope, but was able to hold onto its

original vision as a place where the uninitiated and the inexperienced can still get a break. The programming for the month of April, 1987 was handed over to Voices of Dissent and, along with the Bride's programming consultants, we went to town.

It had always been our intention, as the Philadelphia Inquirer quoted us, to "invite dissent rather than attempt to define it," and hopefully the excerpted VOD calendar on these pages shows the incredible diversity of approach that typified even the Bride events. All the artists who performed or exhibited there shared an explicit commitment to social change, but that was about it. New Age musicians butted up against agit-prop comedians, kitchen-sink realism clashed with post-modern nightmare, and radical anarchists tried to relate to liberal reformists. Looking back on it, I can't truly say this diversity illustrated a specified agenda. Rather, I think it came out of our largely personal desire simply to see what was out there.

Several months after our events, another political art festival called "Only in America" was held in the city. This festival was organized completely by professional consultants hired by We the People 200. Several nationally known political theater groups took part, and it was great to see our kind of cultural work legitimized. But it was also an instructive case study in the politics of content and context. Many of the "Only in America" events were better attended than ours, but without our kind of grassroots organizing behind them, one thing was clear: however radical some of the performers' pieces might have been, it was still business as usual. None of those events had the kind of energy or ideas it took to spawn subsequent organizing projects. Voices of Dissent wasn't simply a month-long festival and a three-day conference, a book or even a combination of these things. It was and is an ongoing process—a response to a deep-seated need for us to make coherent sense of why we do our work. Because of this it has continued to bring together artists and arts organizations on a local, regional and national level for almost five years.

American activists have a tendency to think that only the Message is the message, and that people can't be as affected by irrational communications as powerfully as by rational ones. Sometimes this backfires; recent presidential campaigns are a very good example of this. But once you accept the fact that culture and art have a deep and lasting effect on social values, you must also accept that the *culture* of your own organizing work has meaning as well; not only the content of the things you say, but the language you use, your appearance, the make-up of your audience, the nature of the space in which you're speaking, all have great symbolic significance. It's a vague, ephemeral dynamic that's very hard to gauge, but it's also very real.

Despite our insistence on the importance of cultural work to social change, cultural activists are ultimately hard-pressed to measure or prove how it makes a difference. The link between the organizing of a mural project and the political consciousness raising of a community may be clear; certain concerts and films have been major catalysts in the anti-nuclear and environmental movements. But for the most part audiences don't usually experience a piece of art and become instantly radicalized. Only when we look back on the histories of social movements does the pattern of cultural and political transformations really begin to take shape. On a day-to-day basis, the commitment to cultural activism is taken mostly on faith; we have to believe that the Rock is changed by water as well as by pickaxes.

This is why the "mission statement" becomes so crucial for cultural organizers. In the midst of all these opportunities for doubt and confusion, the mission statement is the glue that hold your work together. It's the foundation of agreement between the often diverse individuals involved, the guide by which you judge the thousands of major and minor decisions you need to make in order to have anything happen. It's also the central and overriding theme that should be evident in all of your public expressions and all your private machinations, from the logo on the brochures to the ticket prices and locations you choose for events. It may never be asserted as such, but the mission statement is ultimately the reason why you're doing what you're doing. In this light it's important to note that it was never our primary intention to convert the masses. Instead we sought to explore our own history as progressive artists; the more people that wanted to join us, the better. Voices of Dissent thus became an example of an alternative vision rather than an argument for one.

Outroduction

We are entering a new century, and with it new demands will be placed on progressive cultural organizers. Demographic and technological changes are already suggesting a more important role for artists as minorities become majorities, and our atomizing, mass culture moves further and further away from the community-building functions it once fulfilled. Cultural activists must develop new strategies for utilizing their work to build bridges between oppressed communities, between struggles in the past and struggles in the present, and between the actions of the individual and the actions of their society. We must work to literally reimage America into a society that can believe in its ability to change.

The realm of public celebrations can thus be, especially in our particular historical moment, a very potent tool. So far, the Powers that Be have used them to exert their hegemonic vision of the past, present, and future. The progressive movement has, for the most part, avoided broad-based public celebrations out of a fear of nationalist cultural politics ("patriotism") and co optation. We must move past these fears. Cultural organizers, and the Left as a whole, must be willing to navigate these waters if we are ever going to offer progressive visions that the general population will embrace. If not, we're in danger of remaining merely the Opposition forever.

For up-to-date information, call the
VOICES OF DISSENT HOTLINE
627-4433

VOICES oF DISSENT

Festival Locations
Balch Institute for Ethnic Studies
18 S. 7th St.   925-8090
Cinematheque
1619 Walnut St.   787-1529
Chester Senior Center ("YEARS")
3111 West 9th St.   497-3551
Community Education Center
3500 Lancaster Ave.   383-1911
Gershman YM & YWHA ("YEARS")
401 S. Broad St.   545-4400
International Visitors Center
Philadelphia Civic Center
34th and Civic Center Blvd   823-7264
Momenta Gallery
309 N. 3rd St.
Muse Gallery
1915 Walnut St.   963-0959
Neighborhood Film Project
3701 Chestnut St.   387-5125
Nexus Gallery
2017 Chancellor St.   567-3481
Old First Reformed Church
4th and Race Sts.   922-4566
Painted Bride Art Center ("YEARS")
230 Vine St.   925-9914
Pennsylvania Academy of the Fine Arts
13th and Cherry Sts.   972-7600
Pennsylvania Opera Theater
Performing at Walnut Street Theatre
1345 Chestnut Street   972-0904
Philadelphia Company
Performing at 1714 Delancey St.
21 S. 5th St.   #735 923-3491
Philadelphia Drama Guild
Performing at 3700 Walnut St.
112 S. 16th St.   563-7530
Please Touch Museum
210 N. 21st St.   963-0667
Revival
22 S. 3rd St.   627-4825
Swarthmore College ("YEARS")
Swarthmore, PA 328-8227
Swords Into Plowshares
Performing at 3400 Spruce St.
327 E. Walnut Ln.   842-3242
Taller Puertorriqueno
2721 N. 5th St.   426-3311
WXPN-FM
3905 Spruce St.   386-0423   88.9 FM
Walnut Street Theatre
9th and Walnut Sts.   574-3550

Nelson Mandela, the Concert

Mass Culture as Contested Terrain

Reebee Garofalo

"We Shall Overcome" evolved from a religious hymn to a labor song to the theme of the civil rights movement. It has been exported to dozens of countries around the world and has become familiar to millions of people. This process has taken well over one hundred years. One performance of "We Are the World" at LiveAid, on the other hand, reached 1.5 billion people in single instant of historical time. Some will shudder at the very thought of comparing the two songs. "We Shall Overcome," after all, is a time-honored anthem of liberation, that has spread through grassroots political struggle. It evokes images of courage, righteousness, and ultimate victory. "We Are the World," according to many, is a self-serving pop ditty that sounds more like a Pepsi commercial than a political song. Its message is, at best, paternalistic and it has been accused of trivializing one of the most important issues of our time. But beneath a discomfort with such a sacrilegious comparison, do we not also find a reaction of distrust for anything that smacks of mass culture? The purpose of this paper is to challenge that distrust.

As activists committed to building a better world, we are, in one way or another, engaged in organizing a mass movement. This means that, by definition, we are trying to reach masses of people. In this regard, mass cultural forms and technologies hold out hitherto unimagined possibilities. Their effectiveness is the subject of much debate. There are those who believe that mass culture is the debasement of culture. Others celebrate its democratic potential. In the final analysis, its tendency to level

Reebee Garofalo

Reebee Garofalo teaches at the University of Massachusetts in Boston and is the coauthor of *Rock 'n' Roll is Here To Pay: The History and Politics of the Music Industry.* He has written numerous articles on music and politics, and has produced benefit concerts and music-related videos. To preserve his sanity, he enjoys drumming and singing with the Blue Suede Boppers, a '50s rock 'n' roll band.

all it touches must be weighed alongside its power to influence greater numbers. It is not entirely clear that an in-depth analysis that reaches hundreds of people is somehow more effective than a more superficial one that reaches millions. I am not arguing that small can't be beautiful. I am simply hypothesizing that big isn't necessarily ugly. Moreover, the choice here isn't simply either/or. Political activists must operate on all levels. The task is to insure that our efforts compliment one another.

For better or for worse, we inhabit the society of the spectacle. Mega-events such as LiveAid will continue to happen because they can. Given this reality, it is important to critically evaluate and use the potential of these events for social change at a local level, rather than to reject such happenings out of hand. In this spirit, I have chosen to analyze a huge rock festival produced on the occasion of Nelson Mandela's seventieth birthday, not because it was an unqualified success, but rather because it embodies all the contradictions that enable us to see the possibilities and the pitfalls of mass culture.

On June 11, 1988, the Nelson Mandela Seventieth Birthday Tribute was staged at Wembley Stadium in London. The eleven-hour extravaganza featured artists as diverse as Whitney Houston, Sting, Dire Straits, Tracy Chapman, Peter Gabriel, the Fat Boys, Jackson Browne, Natalie Cole, Little Steven, Eurythmics, Freddie Jackson, Phil Collins, UB40, Al Green, Midge Ure, Miriam Makeba, Hugh Masakela, Simple Minds, Aswad, the Bee Gees, Youssou N'Dour, Salt-n-Pepa, and more, with a surprise appearance by Stevie Wonder. The Tribute was broadcast whole or in part to an estimated 600 million people in more than sixty countries.

Historically, the Mandela Tribute takes its place as one extension of the "charity rock" phenomenon which began in the early eighties with projects like USA for Africa, BandAid, and LiveAid. As politically innocuous as these projects were, they focused international attention on Africa to an unprecedented degree and created a climate in which musicians from other countries felt compelled to follow suit. Consider the following partial list of African famine relief spin-offs compiled by Dutch music journalist Stan Rijven:

- Great Britain—BandAid—"Do They Know It's Christmas?" (37 artists)
- USA—USA for Africa—"We are the World" (37 artists)
- Canada—Northern Lights, "Tears Are Not Enough" (53 artists)
- West Germany—Band fur Ethiopia—"Nackt im Wind" (Naked in the Wind)
- France—Chanteurs Sans Frontieres, (Singers without Frontiers) "Ethiopie" (36 artists)
- Belgium—"Leven Zonder Honger" (To Live without Hunger)
- The Netherlands—"Samen" (Together)
- Australia—E.A.T. (East African Tragedy)
- Africa—"Tam Tam Pour L'Ethiopie" (50 African artists including Youssou N'Dour, Hugh Masakela, Manu Dibangu, and King Sunny Ade)

Even the most cautious humanitarian efforts can generate a momentum which goes beyond the intentions of their producers. In so doing, they can create the cultural space for bolder undertakings. Just as LiveAid begat FarmAid, the whole "charity rock" phenomenon inspired other, more politicized ventures like Amnesty International's Conspiracy of Hope and Human Rights Now tours. The Nelson Mandela Tribute would have been unthinkable without LiveAid. Many of the artists who headline mega-events have also donated their time and talent to local communities and political organizations. Witness Little Steven's work with the Native American community or Jackson Browne's series of dates for the Christic Institute. Bruce Springsteen rallied when 3M proposed closing its plant in Freehold, New Jersey. And a number of rap artists including Public Enemy, Boogie Down Productions, and Stetsasonic have initiated the Stop the Violence Movement to protest the explosive conditions which exist in communities of color.

An artist's involvement with political issues and events can also be the occasion for the emergence of a more politicized popular music. There is a clear connection, for example, between John Cougar Mellencamp's involvement in FarmAid and his "Rain on the Scarecrow," a song about the despair of modern rural life. Jackson Browne's interest in Central America led to his involvement with the Christic Institute and to "Lives in the Balance," a moving criticism of U.S. intervention in Central America. The video of the song won a first place award at the Cuban Film Festival.

The focus on Africa which began with the relatively safe issue of hunger, quickly targeted the more compelling issue of apartheid. Using "We Are the World" as a model, Little Steven assembled more than fifty rock, rap, rhythm and blues, jazz, and salsa artists to create "Sun City," a politically charged anthem in support of the cultural boycott of South Africa. U2's Bono wrote "Silver and Gold" for the Sun City LP. The album also includes "No More Apartheid" by Peter Gabriel and Gil Scott-Heron's "Let Me See Your I. D." Gabriel's "Biko" and Scott-Heron's "Johannesburg," of course, preceded this more organized focus on apartheid. Following the release of "Sun City," Stevie Wonder jumped into the fray with his recording of "It's Wrong (Apartheid)," as did Kashif with "Botha Botha." Jim Kerr wrote "Mandela Day" especially for the Seventieth Birthday Tribute. As more and more songs born of political experiences enter the popular market, the development of a political culture gets validated. Criticism and debate regarding the connection between music and politics becomes more acceptable. This connection was intended to define the Mandela concert.

The Mandela Tribute was originally the brainchild of Jerry Dammers of Special AKA, who wrote "Free Nelson Mandela." Dammers was one of the founders of Artists Against Apartheid in London. He is passionate about his politics, to a fault in the eyes of many. A few years before the Mandela Tribute, he had been involved in producing an anti-apartheid concert at Clapham Common which attracted an audience of 200,000 and featured Peter Gabriel, Sting, Sade, Boy George, Gil Scott-Heron, Style Council, and Billy Bragg, among others. "The concert was a strong political event," according to Peter Jenner, Billy Bragg's manager and long-time political activist, "but it lost money." Jenner described Dammers as "great on the creative side, not so good on the organizational side." As to the Mandela concert, Jenner said that Dammers "wanted to do a big event again, but he couldn't afford to lose money."

For the Mandela Tribute, Dammers started talking to Tony Hollingsworth from Elephant House Productions, a company that handles both television and live events. "Jerry Dammers had been talking to me for the last three years about a big event," said Hollingsworth. "And I said to him, I'll put you on a big event as soon as you have one major act interested in doing something for you." Hollingsworth understood and acknowledged that the concert "had to make money." But after Dammers convinced Simple Minds to come forward with a conditional offer, he absented himself from the process. Hollingsworth ran with the ball alone for the next nine months. It was Hollingsworth who was credited as the producer of the live event. While there is no question that the concert benefited from Hollingsworth's organizational abilities, it may have suffered from the lack of a more politicized vision that could have been supplied by someone like Dammers.

According to Hollingsworth, the concert "had two points. It had to raise the consciousness of the situation of apartheid in South Africa and the way to do that was to use Nelson Mandela as the symbol of fighting against apartheid. It had to make some very simple statements: it had to say the apartheid regime is wrong, it should be stopped, Nelson Mandela should be released unconditionally. And, furthermore, it had to show the sort of people that were prepared to make that statement were the favored stars of the public." A discussion of the degree to which the concert reached its stated goals—indeed, the question of the appropriateness of the goals themselves—is necessarily complex.

Perhaps the most incredible thing about the Nelson Mandela Seventieth Birthday Tribute was that it happened at all in a country where the government itself is one of South Africa's staunchest allies. British royalty who were conspicuously present at the less controversial LiveAid concert in London in 1985, were nowhere to be found at the Mandela Tribute. "We didn't have people dying of starvation," explained Hollingsworth. "We had a ninety-year-old political problem where there was an enormous amount of entrenched interests." In England, the concert was broadcast live by the BBC, which in and of itself caused no small controversy. Within hours of the announcement of the BBC's decision to carry the show, the Thatcher government was besieged by protests from the South African regime acting through certain industrialists and members of the British Parliament. Ironically, according to Hollingsworth, "their objection was a wonderful publicity machine for the event," which served to politicize the issue even more.

In the United States, the negative tendencies of the mass media were more apparent. Here the celebration was carried in its entirety by a number of radio stations in different regions, and televised nationally by Rupert Murdoch's Fox Television Network as Freedomfest, a five-hour edited broadcast. The telecast was saturated with advertising, often by firms doing business in South Africa. With some of the more outspoken artists like Little Steven ("Sun City"), Jackson Browne ("Lives in the Balance"), and Peter Gabriel ("Biko"), the political raps they used to introduce their performances were simply edited out. Most of the African performers were excluded from the broadcast altogether. Fox's president, Jamie Kellner, defended the company's editorial choices in *Rolling Stone* by saying, "Certainly, musically, you had 'Biko,' you had 'Sun City,' you had 'Mandela Day,' you had all of the important songs, which were the message." Kellner's limited defense did little to stem the critical tide; the Fox broadcast was widely criticized for having depoliticized the event. Little Steven went so far as to write an editorial in the *New York Times* charging that "the show was neutered, the issue downplayed, and the message muzzled. . . . If people didn't know who Mr. Mandela was before tuning in, they weren't any better informed after five hours of programming." Steven's sentiments were echoed in most 'reviews of the U.S. broadcast.

Given the purpose of the concert, one might logically wonder what would possess the promoters to go with a broadcasting company owned by the ultra-conservative Rupert Murdoch. For Hollingsworth, there were relatively few options. "The three main networks, ABC, CBS, and NBC, were obviously only prepared to talk to us about a couple of hours of network time. . . so, the pitch became between the Fox network and MTV," he said. "They were both offering about the same money. We went with Fox because their demographic figures gave a much, much higher viewership." Hollingsworth made some attempt to preserve the politics of the event by having legal language built into the contract which "specified in general terms that they would honor the spirit of the day and reflect that spirit." Accordingly, and in contrast to Little Steven's comments, the Fox broadcast was introduced by actor/ director Robert Townsend ("Hollywood Shuffle") with the words:

> It's more than just a concert. Just as with LiveAid, Amnesty, and some other mega-events, pop and rock stars from all over the world have gathered again to call attention to something they believe in—in this case the anti-apartheid movement and its most visual and spiritual leader, Mr. Nelson Mandela. Imprisoned for over twenty-five years in a South African prison, Mandela and others have come to represent the struggle for freedom and equality in South Africa, an issue of worldwide attention. Welcome to Freedomfest.

As to the rest of the U.S. broadcast, however, even Hollingsworth admitted that he was "very disappointed. But, you can't cut out a picture," he added optimistically. "You can't cut out the backdrop of Nelson Mandela." Still, there was some sentiment among activists in the music industry that Hollingsworth could have negotiated a stronger wording in the Fox contract and that by dropping the ball, the politics of the concert may have been needlessly compromised.

Clearly, the Fox broadcast emphasized the entertainment function of the concert to the detriment of its consciousness-raising function. But, even in the U.S. telecast, a few memorable passages managed to slip through. Jim Kerr of Simple Minds, one of the first bands to get on the Mandela wagon, introduced "Mandela Day" by calling for "an end to the murder and the torture and the terror that's going on in South Africa." Surprise guest Stevie Wonder told a non-attendant Nelson Mandela, "We're here celebrating your birthday, but I and we are all very conscious of the fact that this day you are not free. We are all very conscious of the fact that until you are free, no man, woman, or child, whatever color or culture they may come from, are really free. . . oppression of anyone is oppression of everyone." While statements such as these were admittedly among the few informative moments amidst hours of what Little Steven referred to as "celebrity gossip" and "inane chatter," they do suggest that the mass media are not invariably antagonistic to such pronouncements.

The second goal articulated by Hollingsworth, that of linking the issues with "the favored stars of the public," was evident even in the U.S. telecast. Aside from the impressive lineup itself, the stars allowed themselves to be queried as to their feelings about the event. "I think that apartheid is a moral issue," said Annie Lennox of Eurythmics in her off-stage interview. "I'm obviously very much against it." Even the reportedly nonpolitical Whitney Houston managed to tell her audience, "I think it's important that they know that we are aware and that we do care." While this goal was realized, it is important to recognize that in this instance the goal itself was controversial. The question naturally arises: are big stars appropriate spokespeople for a movement that they are not a part of?

It was Whitney Houston who most often served as the lightning rod for criticism along these lines. "The real mistake was Whitney Houston," Peter Jenner told me. "The story around was that she would not do the show unless it was nonpolitical. The moment they agreed to those terms, they lost the battle." Such a criticism must be considered in terms of the degree to which the concert was already politicized simply by its choice of theme. "What we were doing in this event was very different from the LiveAid situation," argued Hollingsworth. "We had a political issue. We were saying [to the artists], 'This is mainstream politics. Don't come on board if you think that it is not politics.' " Hollingsworth told me that "Whitney agreed to pay tribute to Nelson Mandela as a symbol of fighting against apartheid." At the same time, he acknowledged that the Houston camp made a "sharp division" between "what is humanitarian grounds and what is politics." Such distinctions often obscure the reality that issues such as apartheid are fundamentally political.

Houston, for her part, delivered easily the most animated performance of the day. She appeared in front of a backdrop containing the slogans "Isolate apartheid" and "The struggle is my life," which could be seen, albeit with some difficulty, even in the Fox telecast. While she is vulnerable to the charge of playing it safe (both musically and politically), it is also the case that she was one of the first artists to commit to the festival. Her overwhelming popularity contributed significantly to making a controversial event that much more attractive to broadcasters all over the world. And, interestingly, she was the "favored star" of imprisoned African National Congress (ANC) leaders in South Africa.[1]

As with most large events, there were trade-offs evident in the Mandela Tribute. While the concert traded depth of analysis for breadth of viewership, some 600 million people around the world ended up with a greater awareness of the importance of Nelson Mandela and the issue of apartheid than they had previously. In the final analysis, a critical evaluation of the impact of an event like the Mandela concert cannot be limited to the merits and shortcomings of the production itself. Because the worldwide simultaneity of the festival created a shared experience of such staggering proportions, this is usually the focus for analysis. But it must also be noted that the Mandela concert was a very different event depending on where you saw it. Its impact was determined in large part by how it got used. In areas where local political movements were able to use the Mandela Tribute to advantage, it served as an important buttress to local organizing and education.

England, of course, was the site of the live event. At Wembley, a capacity crowd of 72,000 fans thrilled to half a day's worth of live performances complete with political commentary on the part of some of their favorite artists. There the concert dovetailed nicely with the needs of the local Anti-Apartheid Movement, which used the interest it generated to mobilize the troops for their "Nelson Mandela: Freedom at Seventy" campaign. Commenting on the level of politicization of the concert, Chitra Karve, a spokeswoman for the Anti-Apartheid Movement, told *Rolling Stone* that in the context of their campaign, "Every second of it was political." According to Hollingsworth, the momentum produced by the concert even forced a change in the nature of media coverage of Mandela and the ANC. "When we first started this, Nelson Mandela was referred to by the BBC News Service as the leader of a terrorist organization, the ANC," he said. "What this event did was both to mobilize the existing support and create a much greater bedrock of sympathy within the general public, so it can no longer be reported in such stark terms."

Italy offers another such example. In Rome the festival was sponsored by *Il Manifesto,* an independent left-wing newspaper; and it was broadcast on public television channel 3, the communist channel. In the Piazza Farnese, an historic outdoor plaza, the concert was projected on a ten-by-fifteen-foot television screen to an audience of thousands for free. Here the mega-festival was consciously used to create a local political event. The character of this outdoor gathering was described by Italian journalist Paolo Prato as "somewhere between Woodstock and a political rally" complete with "people on the ground smoking dope." A small stage served as a platform for anti-apartheid speeches by Italian and African political leaders. Again, the entertainment function of the event was consciously used in the service of political education at the local level.

While the anti-apartheid movement in the United States did not make direct use of the Mandela Tribute, a progressive side effect of mega-events like LiveAid and the Mandela concert, and the all-star performances of "We Are the World" and "Sun City" has been the breaking down of the apartheid of our own music industry. In the United States, audiences and radio formats are quite fragmented, ostensibly along lines of music taste but, conveniently, these tastes correlate highly with divisions of class, age, race, and ethnicity. The artists who appeared on "We Are the World" and to an even greater extent on "Sun City" encompassed a broad range of audience demographics and radio formats. "Whoever buys [the 'Sun City' LP]," remarked co-producer Arthur Baker, "is going to be turned onto a new form of music, just as whoever sees the video is going to be turned onto an artist they've never seen before." Similarly, any radio station which carried the Mandela Tribute in its entirety played artists who had never appeared on that station before. In Boston, for example, progressive rocker WBCN broadcast artists such as Salt-n-Pepa, the Fat Boys, and Freddy Jackson, not to mention Youssou N'Dour, probably for the first time.

On the other hand, mega-events are tough acts to follow. As awesome and inspiring as they may be, it is also possible for them to have a negative impact on other efforts. The Mandela concert was "so big," complained Peter Jenner, "that no one wanted to do any other benefits at that time. It was a catastrophe for other events." Jenner claimed that an AIDS benefit which featured George Michael the previous year had to be cancelled, and that an Amnesty International concert at Milton Keynes at around the same time lost £100,000 because it was so overshadowed. To the extent that mega-events are designed as fundraisers—as was clearly the case with LiveAid and FarmAid—they pose the further problem of suggesting that simply raising money can solve political problems. Mandela was supposed to be different. "We weren't working on 800 numbers," Hollingsworth pointed out. "This is a political concert," Jim Kerr insisted to *Rolling Stone*. "It's not a little namby-pamby money raiser." The fact remains, however, that the concert could have been more political in its conception. At the Nelson Mandela Seventieth Birthday Tribute there was no firsthand testimony, no in-depth analysis, and no documentary footage to make the point. Furthermore, the Mandela concert was conceived as a one-time event. It did not provide for any follow-through of its own. These are all unnecessary shortcomings since there are a number of models which hold out possibilities for greater impact.

At the most obvious level, a live LP or a commercial video can enable the event to live beyond itself. An edited video has certain advantages over a live broadcast. As was the case with the Fox telecast of the Mandela tribute, a live broadcast can place editorial control of the event in the hands of companies whose priorities may be different from those of the organizers of the event. To the extent that profit is their motivation for carrying a given broadcast, the demands of the marketplace will encourage certain patterns of censorship. Distributing an edited video sacrifices the simultaneity of a live broadcast, but it enables the organizers of the event to retain control over content and presentation. Field interviews and documentary footage can be spliced in to produce a package that is both educational and entertaining. As controversial as Paul Simon's "Graceland" LP was, the video of the concert in Zimbabwe—with appearances by Miriam Makeba and Hugh Masekela and documentary footage of Black Africans portrayed as normal human beings— succeeded admirably in putting a human face on Black South Africa.

A number of mega-projects have also attempted more creative ways of linking mass culture to local efforts. Album packaging can be filled with a level of analysis not possible in the live concert setting. The "Sun City" album jacket, for example, was crammed with facts and figures about apartheid. Furthermore, the song itself was prescriptive. In addition to providing a creative indictment of the policies of the United States government toward the apartheid regime, the lyrics were intended, in the words of composer Little Steven, to deliver a message to "the musical community to please not play Sun City."[2] The "Sun City" project also issued a "Teacher's Guide" which showed how to use the record and the videotape as educational tools in the classroom. Here the attempt was made to build on the familiarity of the mass cultural product to create exercises which could be tailored to local use. The Amnesty International Conspiracy of Hope tour identified and publicized the plight of six political prisoners as part of the event. One of the goals of the tour was to recruit 25,000 new members who would become "freedom writers" joining in the letter writing campaigns Amnesty uses to call attention to the political abuse of these individuals. In this way, the mass cultural event was used to enlist people directly into local activity of the organization.

Mass culture is not without its contradictions. But it must be recognized that mass culture is also a site of contested terrain. Turning our political backs on this fertile arena will simply render the Left anachronistic in a world of high technology. Like rock 'n' roll, mega-events are here to stay. We must determine how their production can be influenced in progressive ways and how the current state of the art can be used to advance the struggle.

Related Reading

Reebee Garofalo. "How Autonomous is Relative: *Popular Music,* the Social Formation, and Cultural Struggle." *Popular Music:* Vol. 6, No. 1, pp. 77-92 (January, 1987).

—. "Applying Popular Music to Social Problems." *Radical Teacher,* pp. 5-10 (May, 1985).

Michael Omi. "A Positive Noise: The Charity-Rock Phenomenon." *Socialist Review,* Vol. 16, No. 89, pp. 107-114 (1986).

Stan Rijven, Greil Marcus, Will Straw. "Rock for Ethopia." *Working Paper No. 7,* pp. 1-36 (International Association for the Study of Popular Music). Presented at the Third International Conference on Popular Music Studies, Montreal, Canada, July, 1985.

Neal Ullestad. "Rock and Rebellion: Subversive Effects of LiveAid and 'Sun City.'" *Popular Music:* Vol. 6, No. 1, pp. 67-76 (January, 1987).

Related Organizations

International Association for the Study of Popular Music. For information on the U.S. chapter, contact: Reebee Garofalo, Downtown Center, University of Massachussetts/Boston, Boston, MA 02125.

S.O.S. Racism, 19, rue Martel, 75010 Paris, France.

Notes

1. Ahmed Kathrada, one of the ANC rebels who received a life sentence along with Mandela, sent a message which was distributed by the London-based Anti-Apartheid Movement and quoted in *Rolling Stone.* "You lucky guys," wrote Kathrada from his cell. "What I wouldn't give just to listen to Whitney Houston! I must have told you that she has long been mine and Walter's [Sisulu] top favorite. . . . In our love and admiration for Whitney we are prepared to be second to none!"

2. It is interesting to note that the original version of "Sun City" named the names of performers who had appeared at the South African entertainment complex. Ultimately, the organizers of the project felt that it would be divisive to name names. The version of the recording that was released to the public contained no reference to these performers.

Independent Publishing and the Politics of Social Change

Opportunities, Obstacles, and Outlooks for the Future

John F. Crawford

Much has been made during the last decade of the role of the small independent presses in the United States in providing alternative points of view, especially with regard to radical politics and social change. Some attention has been focused on the relationship between these presses and funding sources in the federal government; on the capacity of small presses to withstand market pressures affecting the media industry as a whole; and on questions of organization, that is, how are small presses most likely to endure in a capitalist system? I would like to discuss these issues as best I can from an insider's perspective.

My small press, West End Press, began its existence lacking the kind of capitalization thought necessary to support the editing, typesetting, printing, promotion and circulation of a book. I started in 1976 by investing my personal savings account of $5,000. I currently produce four to five books a year off a gross income of between $20,000 and $25,000. While the Press has never been in serious debt, except to myself, about one-fourth of its income regularly comes from grants or royalties, making the Press effectively dependent on non-

John F. Crawford

John F. Crawford edited and published *West End Magazine* (1971-76) and is publisher of West End Press (1976-present). He is also the publisher of *Peoples Culture* newsletter. Still a political activist as time permits, he has lived in the past two decades in New York, Cambridge, MA, Kansas City, Minneapolis, and his native Los Angeles before settling in Albuquerque in 1985. He has recently co-edited a collection of interviews with southwestern authors, *This Is About Vision,* for the University of New Mexico Press, and is writing a book of Quincentennial essays, *Here Come the Anglos.*

sales income. As a result, it is condemned to a vicious circle. Without access to capitalization above the amount necessary to meet production expenses, it is doomed to continue to produce low-run, inadequately promoted materials which will not sell much in excess of earlier materials similarly produced. Opportunities for entrepreneurial growth scarcely exist.

Grants such as those administered by the National Endowment for the Arts Literature Program and related state agencies tend to foster such a vicious circle. In the first place, there are no NEA start-up grants. Fledgling publishers must produce a certain number of books of a certain quality before they can be considered for grant assistance (currently pegged at $2,000 to $12,000 a year). Then, in order to be considered for a *higher* level of assistance (beyond $12,000 a year, at the current levels), they must produce a *much larger* number of books within a given period. Thus rich publishers become richer, modest publishing efforts such as mine remain modest, and poor ones never see any grant money at all.

This situation is even more self-reproducing than it used to be, because the Literature Program now expects the undercapitalized small publishers to compete in the publishing marketplace and uses their marketing viability as one determinant of future funding. Grant guidelines therefore encourage ambitious promotion campaigns, setting up the need for capital from sources outside the grant itself. Meanwhile, while the NEA pushes for bigger promotion budgets, the Small Business Administration, another federal agency, will not offer loans to publishers that could support such efforts, and most banks and lending institutions follow suit. This is a Catch-22 situation.

Some matching grants are available. But it is often more difficult for a small press to find support from the state arts councils or the private sector than it is from the federal government, because the rules accompanying these grants may be even more capricious or restrictive than NEA rules. Often the smaller state agencies just don't "have it together" to fund literature, and foundations can be openly motivated by restrictive political ideologies.

There are horror stories about the politics of federal grants. It is commonly speculated that the two National Endowments have killed politically questionable projects by a variety of means, including choosing conservative panels to judge submissions, selectively vetoing grants already passed by the panels, and defining whole grant categories out of existence. Some of these speculations are correct. But federal grants more subtly restrict the freedom of the independent presses by positioning the effort of the publisher within, but marginal to, the capitalist economy. An application ties the publisher to a mission statement, a specific goal for the book, a plan for sales and promotion, and a schedule of payments. (In the case of a small for-profit publisher, it also necessitates the involvement of a fiscal agent.) Thus as the grant establishes fiscal accountability, it also confines the publisher within the more abstract framework of a capitalist definition of purpose and intended audience. This renders *other* matters that ought to be of concern to the alternative publisher—the political goal of the work, its hope of reaching an audience that *cannot* be assumed or projected beforehand—practically invisible. So static conceptions of producer and consumer prevail over any dialectical account of the relationship between the two.

I do not mean to suggest that the rules of the Literature Program of the NEA are responsible for most of the woes of the small publisher today. Indeed, with the steady rise in postal rates, the change in the law concerning taxable inventories of books, and the increasing monopoly control of distribution to bookstores, the "grants game" could no longer dictate the rules for so-called independent publishing even if it tried, because there are too many other things to worry about: Even the best of grants cannot protect the publisher any longer from the play of market forces.

Let me give an example of "the play of market forces." One way for a small publisher to raise capital is windfall profits off the sale of rights—giving permission to reprint, translate, or otherwise reproduce a work, with the proceeds divided between the author and publisher. This lucrative possibility forces one to think in terms of producing books that are the most marketable for resale; as a result, one may publish according to formulas. The relative independence that the sale of rights buys thus has its hidden cost of increased dependence on market trends or fads.

Any book is produced in order to be sold. Generally speaking, books are marketed in groups; a publisher produces a "line" of books, with certain recognizable themes and subject matter, physical production features, and so on. The cost of getting the word out that the books are available is very high; to a beginning publisher, it seems prohibitive. One therefore joins publishers' associations, co-op marketing schemes and so on, and finds there are many other small entrepreneurs also trying somehow to catch the attention of the reading public. One seeks out small press distributors, who, themselves overwhelmed by the increasing number of small publishers, consequently demand glitzier, more marketable small press titles and ask for higher discounts. Finally, one discovers that the chain bookstores don't want small press books at all. A recent publicly announced decision by B. Dalton to drop any customer presses whose accounts with the company do not gross over $100,000 a year is only another step in a long-running campaign to get the "little guy" out of chain store distribution.

Whatever type of promotion the small publisher chooses, marketing questions prevail. Seen from this perspective, it is inevitable that the book as *product* tends to replace the book as *vehicle of communication*. The style of work one consequently falls into raises questions about the politics one is pursuing. Are there not more desirable marketing forms for the politically oriented small press publisher to utilize?

The oldest remaining political presses from the traditional Left represent political parties, such as International Publishers (Communist Party) and Pathfinder Books (Socialist Workers Party). Those from the independent Left include Monthly Review

Press and Lawrence Hill Publishers. The newer progressive publishers begin with Feminist Press, started in the '70s by Florence Howe and Paul Lauter, run collectively but attached to an academic institution, and South End Press, started in the '70s from loans and gifts raised in the Boston and Cambridge area and also run collectively. New Society Publishers represents a religiously oriented social change collective in operation before publication started. Smaller, more recent presses include Kitchen Table, a woman-of-color press started on a shoestring in the early '80s and run collectively; Thunder's Mouth Press, the result of a collaboration between a New York and a Chicago publisher in the late '70s; and a variety of other presses headed either by a single person or a team working together, including Curbstone Press, Africa World Press, Firebrand Press, and Cleis Press. These presses may benefit from loose working agreements with one another, by sharing space at book events or promotional information when convenient.

A recent development is the growth of progressive imprints within university publishing houses, especially around topics such as women's studies and labor history. I have already mentioned Feminist Press, currently under the wing of the City University of New York, where Florence Howe teaches. Presses such as the Industrial Labor Relations Press, a branch of Cornell University Press, work with institutional publishers yet still enjoy a degree of autonomy.

By and large, all the progressive publishers listed above enjoy *some* kind of financial help 'besides proceeds from sales—the support of a political party, subscription support, donors who are regularly solicited, institutional backing, or grants in the case of some of the newer presses. The most stable of these presses, one might note, are dependent on a closely identified group of supporters with funds available to meet emergencies and underwrite expansion. The newer presses are the least well provided for, often surviving on loans, mortgages, and the sweat of the brows of their producers.

West End Press has followed a broad, loosely defined program of publishing the literary work of writers *not* acceptable to the corporate publishers, particularly along lines of class, race, gender, and political background. When West End started in 1976, few publishers had a program for publishing such writers under one roof. The older Left houses showed little interest in literary writers as revenues turned down and the need to keep up with more obviously political material intensified. Feminist Press was just beginning to move beyond a single category—feminist writers—to address matters of gender and class. South End Press was leery of publishing literary writers, no matter how political they were. Other presses devoted to minority or feminist writers were usually single-topic presses. The small press movement as a whole was anarchic and petty-bourgeois in character, lacking a political agenda outside the broadest and most liberal definition of "free speech."

West End started with the encouragement of Leonard Randolph, director of the literature program of the National Endowment for the Arts, in 1976. At Randolph's suggestion, I travelled from Cambridge, Mass. to the Midwest to meet Old Left writers Jack Conroy, Meridel Le Sueur, and Thomas McGrath. I decided to publish neglected works of Le Sueur and received NEA support for it. At the same time, I published three books by younger writers. Our first three poetry chapbooks featured the daughter of a Mafioso gangster living in Boston, a young Slovakian glassworker from Pittsburgh, and an African American communist activist in New York City. The glassworker's poems went into a second edition (he sold over a thousand copies himself, going door to door in his neighborhood). The activist's poems sold out after several years, just as he was purged from his political party, which then demanded (too late for it to matter) that I suppress the book. I still have unsold copies of the poems of the Mafioso's daughter.

Over the years, as West End sought out writers and elaborated its program, definite publishing categories began to take shape: working class writings from the Appalachian South; labor and minority drama; poems by Native American, Hispanic, Asian American, African American and white writers—predominantly women; and books from Latin America. At the same time, five volumes by Meridel Le Sueur accounted for over 50,000 sales, half our total.

We have sought support from a number of areas over the years. We made no formal affiliations with Old Left political parties, both because we were reluctant to narrow our work and because little practical help was forthcoming from them when we needed it. The New Left foundations across the country have never been any help to us, because the funders don't perceive the production of literature as an active ingredient in the formation of Left culture. (There is still, sadly, a dead-last, "And Beetlebomb" ranking of culture as a form of political struggle in America.) As our grants from the NEA and state arts councils have dried up over the years, as the political climate in Washington has degenerated and our politics have stayed the same, we have been caught in a double bind: the Left does not see our work as political enough to deserve funding, while the federal and state agencies regard us as *too* political to receive it.

We have received payments from foreign publishing houses for editions of our books—from Great Britain, the Federal Republic of Germany, the German Democratic Republic, and the Soviet Union. For four years, Meridel Le Sueur's novel *The Girl* has been under a movie option with Roland Joffe and Warner Brothers, for which Le Sueur receives royalties and West End receives an agent's fee. These windfall profits have rearranged our publishing schedule from time to time (a European edition of half a million copies of Mike Henson's *Ransack* allowed us to reprint the original book in a modest U.S. edition of 2,000), but has never affected the political content of what we publish.

Promotion has long been our weak spot. As independent stores continue to decline, the chains shut out the small publishers, and the distributors consolidate under monopoly pressure, the prospects of improving promotion are not good. For several years I have had my orders filled by a professional service—they mail books to purchasers and handle the accounts—but they do no promotion of their own. I attend book events and fairs, though those have shrunk over the years. We displayed in Nicaragua at the first International Managua Book Fair, where sales were negligible but contacts with publishers and writers in this highly politicized field were gratifying.

The tendency of books to function as commodities is dreaded by the progressive publisher. The fluctuating interest in radical topics from year to year (Nicaragua one year, racism the next, gays the next) is skillfully manipulated by the major publishers, who get in and out of markets as fashions change. But working class literature, for example, has not sold well since the McCarthy period. The situation is Orwellian: When a definition for what we want to market scarcely exists, it is up to us both to define and market the product, or else to consent to its oblivion.

Beyond this, some of our titles don't locate an intended audience even when one *expects* a well-defined market. Cherrie Moraga's *Giving Up the Ghost,* a play about a working class Chicana lesbian which is written partly in Spanish, has not tapped a solid audience of either lesbians or Hispanics. Sharon Doubiago's *Hard Country,* which explores sexual oppression, has never attracted a feminist audience, perhaps because it is too male-identified. Books about Appalachians sell badly, partly because the intended audience is so poor it can't afford books.

But we have discovered that good definition of a market isn't everything. Moraga's book has been selling well to *some* audiences, however defined, and has been produced as a play, providing us royalties. *Hard Country* has sold out two print runs, showing a remarkable ability to cut across lines of readership. The collected poems of Appalachian radical preacher and organizer Don West have sold 5,000 copies because Don has sold them *on his own,* half of them after becoming incapacitated by triple heart bypass surgery and prostate cancer!

One of the deadliest things a progressive publisher can do is to assume a "correct" theoretical stance and try to win the audience to a position that has been thought out in the head and not tested by experience. This is a province best left, I think, to fanatics. One of the *best* things a publisher can do is put out political material that appeals to the personal judgment of the reader. The Viet Nam experience can be dealt with in terms that take into account the enormous pain suffered by our own soldiers, without sacrificing politics in the process. Topics such as political torture, family incest, and alcohol dependence have won massive audiences in recent years without sacrificing their "message." Reports of visits to Central America, which put the reader in the position of discoverer, often overcome ideological barriers. This is another decade where the slogan "the personal is political" is being tested for its value; more aptly, the trick is to make the political personal.

Several factors point to the coming decade as the beginning of a new era in small press publishing, with special meaning for the progressive publisher. They are as follows.

1. New developments in technology. Within a few years, desktop equipment will eliminate the need for a typesetter. Printing costs are already quite low for short-run jobs, making a book of a hundred pages or less a manageable project.

2. Ways to get around the problems of promotion and distribution. Distribution co-ops, using computerized record-keeping, can warehouse, package, and sell the books of a number of like-minded small publishers at the same time. Once politics are defined, sales marketing ventures can be worked out in common.

3. Nonprofit umbrellas for fundraising when a number of publishers are involved in a common project. In such a project the style of work will be very important. Instead of the loosely collective style common to the counterculture of the Sixties, the new organizational model might resemble the industrial worker cooperatives that have been attempted in Europe and Canada in recent years.

4. Most of all, a new understanding of our cultural/political situation, growing out of contemporary theoretical writing. This writing is coming from diverse places: the field of Cultural Studies, from Britain; other academic writings on feminism and colonialism; periodicals and magazines dealing with culture and the arts from an activist perspective; and works such as this book, which try to bring divergent viewpoints together under a single cover.

West End Press may not survive to see the new period. Who can say? We have already outlived a number of shocks, and it is not easy to adjust to structural changes within an existing environment. But presses such as ours, defining both their programs and politics as they go along, have something to offer the future. We publish working-class writers, marginalized women, and people of color when there are class and color bars in the major corporate houses. We publish some radical literature when it is not even granted the dignity of a name. While our books sell in the thousands, for the most part, rather than the tens or hundreds of thousands, we have never been content with the bourgeois idea of the book as product. We seek instead to teach our readership, through newsletters and other means, that radical publishing is a *process* for storing knowledge for later use. Nothing, as Meridel Le Sueur says, is ever lost, so long as there are still more battles to come, and the only battle that really matters is the last.

Charting Cultural Change

The Role of the Critic

Pat Aufderheide

When I was hired as cultural editor of *In These Times** in 1978, I asked the editors what they expected of the cultural section of a Left weekly. "That's what we expect you to show us," one said. "All we know is that politics isn't the same thing as culture."

The approach of *In These Times* to political coverage neatly demystifies political action—separating it from attitude and personal gesture, for instance—but it leaves cultural questions a *tabula*

Pat Aufderheide
Pat Aufderheide is a senior editor of *In These Times* and an assistant professor in the School of Communication at American University in Washington, D.C.

rasa. In defining the cultural sections, I have had to confront basic questions about art, culture, and criticism, as well as confusion over them among readers, who are a cross section of the American Left. My approach begins with the mandate of the Left: social change toward greater equity. Within that, the Left cultural critic's mandate then seems clear: to chart how culture is shaped, so that we can understand how it changes, and seize opportunities to alter it in ways that create possibilities for greater social justice. Culture, in this sense, doesn't just mean the arts, but the assumptions, attitudes, and actions that make up our lives as we experience them. The arts create cultural texts in which the tissues of the social fabric are woven finely.

A Left critic's job is never simply to offer a consumer guide, to judge what is good or bad, but to explore how the concepts "good" and "bad" are constituted. It is all too easy to substitute for the "good art"/"bad art" judgment one based on "good politics"/ "bad politics" or "good intentions"/"bad intentions." At the same time, the Left

---

* *In These Times* was founded in 1976 with a commitment to nonsectarian approaches toward democratic socialism, i.e. approaches that avoid self-marginalization and political fundamentalism. It is read largely by leftists who do organizing or other practical political work, through labor unions, universities, schools, churches, nonprofit organizations, and local and regional government.

critic's work makes explicit the moral judgment inherent in all criticism, but usually unspoken in cultural criticism that operates at the center of cultural hegemony. That is, for a Left critic good art has to do with what best illuminates the dynamics, the contradictions if you will, of our culture and empowers people to understand how they do participate and can participate in shaping it. Cultural criticism within the mainstream typically assumes the values of the elites, however they may differ among themselves about how best to validate those values. That moral judgment, inherent in any critical endeavor, obviously does not free a Left critic from exploring how a cultural expression achieves its goals (or doesn't). But in deconstructing and reconstructing the meaning of cultural expression, a critic can create ways for people to think about both mainstream and marginalized cultural expressions in social terms—as processes and results of social relationships, and with implications for them.

It is, however, much easier to set that broad critical agenda than to exercise it. The reasons are several, stemming from the fact that there is no single Left aesthetic today. This is because there is no single or preeminent leftist *political* movement in the U.S., no milieu in which such expression could be fostered. Cultural balkanization follows on political balkanization and reinforces it in turn, and this impairs the debate that is the critic's field of play. Of course, this political reality for the Left is of a piece with the larger social configuration. Explicitly political activity is not a popular cultural expression in the U.S. today. In fact, a fascinating feature of this society is the way in which political decisions and results are imbedded in social, cultural, and economic structures and processes.

To say the left is balkanized does not mean there is a lack of leftist activity. There are a number of third party movements; coalitions of Left-leaning union members, populists, and other coalitions within the Democratic party; "Rainbow" movements; policy work; and cause movements (nuclear freeze, Sanctuary, gay and lesbian rights, "monkeywrenching" or direct environmental action, or the homeless). The different initiatives share common problems in facing mainstream media, corporate power, and institutional bias. But a feeling of kinship across issue lines is rare. Today, many people work for leftist goals without participating in an explicitly leftist culture; this creates clusters of habits and tastes of remarkable diversity.

This is not an era like that of, say, Communist Party-led culture of the '30s and '40s, or the New Left counterculture of the '60s and '70s. Both those Left cultures were set in motion by political movements—resistance to the Depression; and the civil rights movement, women's movement, and opposition to the Vietnam war— and both were strongly marked by the historical juncture and the nature of the political movement. The former collapsed of a kind of involution, following the same fate as the Party's sectarian politics. The counterculture, which was both resistance to and expression of a postwar youth culture, eventually became engulfed by commodity culture, which can use as many revolutions per minute as are fed into the marketing machinery. In both cases, for better and for worse, a common culture both marked off the group and also gave it an identity within which people could see unities across particular causes, issues and projects. Both cases were exceptional moments in American Left history.

Although there is widespread consensus on the Left that cultural expression is empowering, the notion that art offers a way to envision other ways of being is less common than the notion that art is something pleasant and extra at the end of a hard day. *In These Times* advisors, for instance, have often seen the cultural section quite simply as a "lure" to readers in order to get them to pick up the newspaper and read the "real" news. And there is little consensus about who are the important, interesting, relevant artists outside the mainstream. Coverage of out-of-mainstream artists often has to overcome hurdles of disinterest tinged with mild guilt ("I ought to care about Holly Near or Dario Fo or the Labor Heritage festival, but I don't"). More revealingly, it must overcome suspicion on the part of many readers who spy cultural Stalinism or in-group cheerleading in positive coverage of Left-oriented cultural expression that is not already familiar to them. Founded as a vehicle to communicate across these communities and help develop a less fragmented movement, *In These Times* has thus had great difficulties even in making clear that the paper itself is not the preserve of any one group. At its most basic level, this lack of a shared culture is evident in the absence of two frequently suggested features: a recipe column and a gossip column. The brown rice casserole one reader wants to see would be of little use to the reader who only has fifteen minutes to cook and wants a cans-in a-pan special. One reader's hot gossip tip would draw a blank with another and offend a third. And almost every attempt at humor or satire has plunged *In These Times* into a swamp of misunderstanding. Indignant letters pour in. The problem isn't that "the Left can't take a joke," but that there's no single entity, "the Left," to take it.

*   *   *

Ironically, whether they desire it or not, the culture in common for leftists is mainstream culture. This is evident not only in a shared suspicion of high-gloss marketing and hard-sell attitudes, but also in a taste for some products of commodity culture. By commodity culture I mean the production of meaning through commodities, tangible and intangible, where the profit objective is overriding— network news and the suburban ranch home with its lifestyle as much as He-Man toys and *E.T.* This production is a process that has become increasingly standardized and centralized since the end of World War II. Leftists may like John Sayles and not John Boorman, *Hill Street Blues* rather than *Three's Company,* Tony Hillerman and not Robert Ludlum; but they're still going to the movies, watching TV, and buying cheap paperbacks.

Balkanization of the Left may be seen, in fact, as a consequence of the dynamic of a consumer society (which in itself is predicated, although obliquely, on the fact of American economic as well as political empire). The erosion of political culture, whether mainstream or partisan, goes hand in hand with the dominance of commodity culture. It is precisely commodity culture's hegemonic and universal role that make constructive criticism of it and its expression in the arts the greatest challenge for a Left critic.

Commodity culture is the normal, accepted, ever-present part of our daily lives. Criticism should strip it of its apparent naturalness, to reveal its social construction. But cultural criticism on the Left is affected, just as the cultural experience of the Left generally is, by the hegemony of commodity culture. Commoditized criticism is the norm, be it in the form of opinion-nuggets mixed with image-nuggets that TV reviewers provide or the slick opinions and pictures retailed in *Vanity Fair*. So even if *In These Times* readers haven't read or seen or heard the phenomenon—a Spielberg movie, a Michael Jackson commercial, a new TV show—they know about it, have opinions, and want to read our "take." The focus is on products, not processes, and on what's hot and what's not. So a Left critic is bucking both market forces and reader expectations in the effort to describe the *process* of cultural creation and consumption.

But with the increasing speed of commodification in our culture, the division between the world of business and art is breaking down, and with it the traditional distance between arts critics and reporting about business. One goal of a Left critic is to understand and make understandable the "business side" of cultural issues in order to capture the process of creation. Areas of particular interest include the rapidly conglomerating cable and network TV businesses and the film industry, as well as governmental bodies such as Congress, the Federal Communications Commission, the U.S. Information Agency, the National Endowment for the Arts, and the National Endowment for the Humanities. What implications do funding guidelines at the Endowments have for works that express American cultural diversity? If the movie studios own theaters, will we see any significant changes at the box office? If cable companies achieve first amendment claims against municipalities, what is the fate of public access cable? Does the privatization trend in European TV threaten U.S. independent filmmakers, who have long depended on sales to public TV there? These are questions, not foregone conclusions, and require both textual analysis and hard reporting. They must be informed by a critic's understanding of the cultural expression affected by structural change.

During the Reagan years public interest regulation of broadcasting was gutted, including the lifting of the rule requiring TV and radio stations to be held for a minimum of three years (and thus forced to engage with the local community rather than be used as trading chips). Within three years, half the stations in the U.S. had been traded. The consequences were far reaching in terms of programming. With stations used as trading chips, prices soared, and so did debt loads. As debt loads soared, news budgets were slashed, local news reporters were dropped, affirmative action departments disappeared, and "shock jocks" and scandal-mongering "reality" shows emerged. The link between economic practices and programming is a crucial link to make, especially outside the trade publications where it is regularly reported as a business item.

The long-range success of broadcaster Paul Harvey and the splashy success of Morton Downey, Jr., to pick two examples, are both important for leftists to consider and are not explained by simply dismissing the former's platitudinous vulgarity or the latter's rowdy crudeness. Paul Harvey's success, in fact, is a fascinating personal trajectory across a changing landscape of commodity culture. A media star who virtually invented himself, he peddles the image of authenticity. With his aggrieved tone, his characterization of consumption as social action, his creation of an imaginary past, and his isolationism, he is the lost soul of the domesticated American incarnate.

A historical perspective does a lot to avoid the teleological curse in leftist analysis inherited from the Frankfurt School, in which reified abstractions such as capitalism inevitably grind out *Rambos*. Commodity culture does not stay fixed. Indeed, its constant permutations are not purely a result of innovations, opportunities, and challenges only from within the terms of commodity culture. It draws from and is altered by noncommercial art, by political acts, and by social movements. Television's look, for instance, has been greatly altered by the work of video artists experimenting with new technologies. It is hard to imagine a *Cosby Show,* with all its limitations, occurring before civil rights changed the racial landscape. The primetime TV series *China Beach* and *Tour of Duty* provide peculiar resolutions to the conflicts still alive in the U.S. about the Vietnam War. But their existence alone testifies to the importance of those conflicts, put into motion by activity outside the center of commodity culture.

In spite of bottom-line conditioning, products do appear that assist in the discovery of self-as-an-actor that is central to social change. I think of my choices in movie criticism, for instance. John Sayles's movies, such as *Matewan,* operate within the expectations of the mall cineplex, but center on social tensions and conflicts. Jonathan Kaplan's too-little-seen *Heart Like a Wheel* has as its driving narrative the struggle of a woman to become her own person (it's the true story of stock-car racing champion Shirley Muldowney).

Conversely, a film such as Errol Morris's *The Thin Blue Line* reveals the social constructions that limit purely individual endeavors. Films like the Brazilian Suzana Amaral's *Hour of the Star* and the Indian Mira Nair's *Salaam Bombay,* in styles that owe much to neo-realism but also to the conventions of international feature film, put names and faces and psychological intensity to social issues of poverty in the Third World. How and why these succeed, both artistically *and* economically, should be of interest to critics assessing the viability of alternative cultural forms.

A Left critic's proper terrain also includes analyzing change in cultural institutions that offers hope for greater diversity, new perspectives, and a greater understanding of the way that social relationships determine social reality. The battle over the "canon" in universities and liberal arts colleges redraws the map of knowledge for the next generation, and challenges traditional assumptions in terms that come out of a Left critical tradition. Museums have increasingly programmed social history exhibits. These exhibits, such as the Smithsonian's "Field to Factory" (about Black northward migration) and "A More Perfect Union" (about Japanese-American internment during World War II), revivify American history and empower their subjects. This trend reflects the influx of Left-leaning and minority social historians into the museum field since the 1960s. The critic's question is how their revision challenges people's understanding of past and present.

*   *   *

Commodity culture conditions the terms under which any alternatives can emerge—cultural activities that construct meaning with a primary objective that is not profit, and that address the potential audience primarily as something other than a consumer.

When dealing with these emerging forms, reporting and criticism from the Left often suffers from a style that is either public relations hype or soft-hearted goodwill. The enormous difficulties of fostering responsible criticism, at a national level, about "alternative" cultural work are a reflection of the lack of a nationwide, media-wide cultural movement, one that can withstand—or even have a serious stake in—an argument. The fact that most serious Left criticism is national, and that there are so few local or regional venues for serious Left criticism, is another reflection of that lack, as well as a reflection of the conglomerate grip on publishing, especially at the local level. The lack of a set of common references at the national level bedevils the attempt to assess and discuss the multiplicity of local cultural projects operating outside the mainstream. Consider the national critic's challenge faced with a video project done with a tenants group in New Jersey or with Black schoolchildren in Chicago, or the creation of dramas drawn from rural tradition in Kentucky, or a photographic display in the Museo del Barrio in New York. Each may have an empowering role with their communities but may be unavailable to a national audience; or may require local research to situate their importance for a national audience.

In these circumstances, a Left critic needs to acknowledge the diversity of the audience as well as the importance of the subject. The critic must therefore set the scene as well as evaluate the work, making clear what the obstacles were faced, what techniques used to overcome them, and whether and why they work.

One therefore hunts for cultural expressions that do more than merely service a small demographic segment of consumers, but work toward expanding the field of expression. Regional media arts workshop Appalshop, the Deep Dish TV enterprise, New York union 1199's Bread and Roses program for labor art, and projects by the Labor Institute for Public Affairs including a play that featured service workers' stories are all examples of cultural work that has as its primary mission that of empowerment. Such work needs to be not only celebrated for its intentions but analyzed for its effectiveness and for the obstacles presented to its success by the cultural context.

Inevitably, there is a sobriety about this kind of criticism. It cannot depend on ironic references, comparisons with similar but more familiar work, and perhaps most importantly on the assurance that the readers share something in common in their approach to the work. A critic must curb the impulse to make an acerbic remark that will seem funny to some but offensive to others, or a metaphor that only some will understand. Still, misplaced kindness is a patronizing attitude that fails to take seriously the undertaking. The real job is the same one as faced in criticism of commodity culture: to locate work within the appropriate context, and to create reader interest in the challenge that faced the creators.

*   *   *

This is an era of crisis in social action generally. Left audiences may be predisposed to cast a critical eye on the status quo, but underneath the shimmering surface of consensus brought to you on nightly broadcasts, the general population increasingly suffers the experience of social balkanization that is so boldly evident on the Left. I think there are many people who would ask questions about the way the world is organized; or would take a step out of their private daily routine to participate in a social action, group, or movement; or would simply stand up in a work situation to say that they think something is wrong; if they didn't think they were all alone. The many different projects on the Left have as one of their objectives to provide examples and options for such people.

The naming involved in cultural expression is a powerful counter to the rootless anxiety that seems to mark our era and cripple action. The cut-up quality of modern life can easily lead to a dulling of the conviction that what we do and who we become matters. Challenging criticism and sound cultural reporting can let people know that having principles, integrity, critical voices, and projects that resist the impetus toward greed, self-indulgence, ignorance, and cruelty are important.

Resources

Alliance for Cultural Democracy
(ACD)
P.O. Box 7591
Minneapolis, MN 55407
  (612) 781-9462

Alternate Roots (Regional
Organization of Theatres South)
Little Five Points Community Center
1083 Austin Avenue
Atlanta, GA 30307
  (404) 577-1079

Appalshop
P.O. Box 743
Whitesburg, KY 41858
  (606) 633-0108

Highlander Research
and Education Center
RFD 3, Box 370
New Market, TN 37820
  (615) 933-3444

Labor Heritage Foundation
815 16th Street, NW, No. 301
Washington, DC 20006
  (202) 842-7880

National Association of Artists'
Organizations (NAAO)
918 F Street NW
Washington, DC 20004
  (202) 347-6350

Social and Public Art
Resource Center (SPARC)
685 Venice Boulevard
Venice, CA 90291
  (213) 822-9560

Syracuse Cultural Workers
Box 6367
Syracuse, NY 13217
  (315) 474-1132

Teatros Nacionales de Aztlan
(TENAZ)
c/o Guadalupe Cultural Arts Center
1300 Guadalupe
San Antonio, TX 78207-5519
  (512) 271-3151

The Association of American
Cultures (TAAC)
Stables Art Center
410 8th Street NW
Suite 605
Washington, DC 20004
  (202) 727-4083

Union for Democratic
Communications (UDC)
P.O. Box 1220
Berkeley, CA 94701

Voices of Dissent
183 Berkeley Place
Brooklyn, NY 11217
  (718) 789-4407

Index

On page i, you saw a photograph of the Western blot test, a standard test to determine HIV antibody seropositivity.

If it took you 2 hours to get from that photograph to this page, at least 10 people with AIDS have died.

If it took you 48 hours, that is how long a person with AIDS would wait in a New York City emergency room to get a bed.

If it took you 2 weeks, this is the time you would have in Colorado to prepare a list of all sexual contacts from the last 10 years, after positive test results.

If it took you 7 years, it took Reagan that long to publicly utter the word "AIDS."

If it took you 8 years, the Food and Drug Administration, using the standard approval process, may have released one of the more than 100 promising AIDS therapies.

If you never got to this page, that is how long it takes the government to provide adequate health care to most women, people of color, IV drug users and the uninsured.